PIMLICO

216

LANDMARKS

David Craig was born in Aberdeen in 1932. He
now lives in Cumbria with the writer Anne Spillard
and teaches creative writing at Lancaster University.
He is the author of several volumes of poetry and
fiction, as well as a book about rock-climbing,
Native Stones (also available from Pimlico), which
was runner-up for the Boardman Tasker Award. His
most recent book, *On the Crofter's Trail*, is about the
Highland Clearances.

LANDMARKS

An Exploration of Great Rocks

DAVID CRAIG

PIMLICO

PIMLICO

An imprint of Random House
20 Vauxhall Bridge Road, London SW1V 2SA

Random House Australia (Pty) Ltd
20 Alfred Street, Milsons Point, Sydney
New South Wales 2061, Australia

Random House New Zealand Ltd
18 Poland Road, Glenfield
Auckland 10, New Zealand

Random House South Africa (Pty) Ltd
PO Box 337, Bergvlei, South Africa

Random House UK Ltd Reg. No. 954009

First published by Jonathan Cape 1995
Pimlico edition 1996

1 3 5 7 9 10 8 6 4 2

Paper used by Random House UK Limited are natural,
recyclable products made from wood grown in sustainable
forests. The manufacturing processes conform to the
environmental regulation of the country or origin

Printed and bound in Great Britain by
Butler and Tanner Ltd
Frome, Somerset

ISBN 0-7126-7320-2

For Bill Brooker
and in memory
of Kenny Grassick
with thanks for
The Talisman

CONTENTS

Contents

ILLUSTRATIONS

Gibraltar, North Face
Urçhizar, Cappodokia, Turkey
Sybil's Rock, Delphi, Greece
Conglomerate toers, Kalambaka, Thessaly
The Sacred Stone and Huaynappicchu at Machu
    Picchu, Peru
Puma Rock, Saqsahuayman, Peru

All the colour photographs are by David Craig with the exception of El Morro by Davidson Photo and Gibraltar by Adrian Cabedo.

Black and white photos   *between pages 272 and 273*

Longships Promontory, Land's End, Cornwall
Two Climbers, Portland Sculpture Park, Dorset
Brimham Rocks, Yorkshire
Adel Crag, Yorkshire
Napes Needle, Cumbria
Macartney's Cave, Northumberland
Old Man of Mow, Staffordshire
Bowden Doors, Northumberland
Warkworth Hermitage, Northumberland
The Woman Stone, Ben Avon, Aberdeenshire
The Old Man of Hoy, Orkney
Hole o' Row, Orkney Mainland
Ern Stack, Yell, Shetland
Dore Holm, Shetland Mainland

(All the black and white photographs are by Andrew Rafferty)

Before the wig and the dress coat
there were rivers, arterial rivers:
there were cordilleras, jagged waves where
the condor and the snow seemed
    immutable:
there was dampness and dense growth, the
    thunder
as yet unnamed, the planetary pampas.

> Pablo Neruda, 'Amor America (1400)'
> from *Canto General*, trans. Jack Schmitt

New hope convinced him that he would
interpret the needs of all men, the souls of
rocks, even. In that more tender light the
bare flesh of rocks was promisingly gentle.

> Patrick White, *Voss*, chapter 8

PREFACE

From the day I climbed up the rock of Sigiriya, in the heart of Ceylon, I was bound to write this book. I went there with my infant family in the dry season of 1961. Leaving the two little children sleeping under mosquito nets in the government resthouse, we went up the north face by the rickety staircase. Beside us, on silken cement, a heavenly frieze of women had been painted in blues and russets a thousand years ago. From stylised clouds pairs of them bent forward graciously under the overhang of the rock, the foremost light-skinned, the hindmost duskier. Their hair was coiffed in curls and ringlets. They were full-breasted, naked to the waist. Their expressions were professionally bland, rather like the Mona Lisa's. They were at least life-size. To be level with them up there was ethereal, as though cloudland had taken us in.

A little higher up clumps of wild honeycomb clung to the rock. On a platform hewn level at two-thirds height (say, a hundred and fifty metres) the paws of a lion carved in stone jutted out, as high as a person: the remains of a huge feudal power-totem, once painted red, that had glared eastward over the semi-jungle. On top we strolled between basins carved out in the rock. Here the grandees had enjoyed their hanging gardens, their spiceries and baths.

Or so I remember it. It is the one place in this book which I have neither researched nor revisited recently. It is the single most beautiful use I have seen made of a great natural rock and I am content that those thirty-five-year-old images should stay as they are. They showed supremely what rock can do, or we can do with it.

Wild rocks had occupied a deep space in my mind since my memory began — the cliffs south of Aberdeen harbour, the blocky summit of Bennachie, the Three Kings at the Western end of Cullen beach. Born in a granite house on a coast of granite, I had always thought of rock as the most real stuff of the Earth. From the ancient upstanding ruggedness of those Scottish crags at one end of the gamut to the gorgeous sophistication of Sigiriya at the other, rock came to be for me the chief thing in nature. A single rock as it rears out of the flux enters into me with the gravity of time solidified. So I set out to visit as many as I could all over the world, to touch them, climb them and walk round them, and find out what they meant.

One of the rocks on the horizon was imaginary. When Mary of Unnimore, whose surname was probably Cameron, was evicted from her village in Argyll in 1824 by an absentee landowner who had never seen the place, she crossed the mountains with her husband, who was carrying his mother in a basket on his back, and their three children, one of them 'an infant at my breast'. They were not allowed to milk their goats, which were 'bleating on the lip of the rock'. High up at Knock-nan-carn — the Hill of Cairns — they stopped for a 'last look at the place where we had been brought up. The houses were being stripped . . . The whistle of the Lowland shepherd and the bark of his dog were on the brae.' So rock was everywhere in her experience, and when she came to express her pious sense of it all in her old age in Glasgow, she put it like this: 'The higher the tempest strikes, the closer may they flee to the shadow of the Great Rock in the weary land.'

Few sentences have sunk deeper into my imagination. They re-focussed places I had already seen. Bare summits looming out of cloud or blizzard — Liathach in Wester Ross, the Old Man of Coniston in Cumbria — where I had been anxious for evidence of where exactly I was. The highland of Sinai louring in a coppery haze at dusk as we sailed north through the Red Sea coming home from Sri Lanka, with no prospect of a job back home. They foreshadowed places still to come, seen through thunderstorms in Arizona or across the waves of red desert in the centre of Australia.

Mary Cameron's words are close to many verses in the Bible. For Samuel, 'The Lord is my rock, and my fortress, and my deliverer.' For David, in his Psalms, 'The Lord is my rock, and my fortress, and my deliverer . . . my buckler and the horn of my salvation, and my high tower.' For Isaiah, 'the Lord JEHOVAH is everlasting strength' — the last phrase, in the Hebrew, actually means 'the rock of ages'. In the Middle East two thousand years ago, a natural citadel such as Masada was as integral to the terrain and to people's imaginations as the rocks of Argyll to the cleared crofters. For me Mary's version of the meta-phor is supreme, because of that word 'weary'. The Hebrew bards are overwrought by comparison. Samuel craves a harbour from 'the waves of death' and 'the floods of ungodly men'. By calling the land weary

Mary puts us in touch with the hardship of people living near the margin of survival.

At all events those words of hers have been a prime motive in sending me round the world to touch great rocks, to go round and up them, penetrate them, pore over them. Some are famous — these days the image of Uluru [Ayers Rock] is almost as familiar as St Paul's Cathedral. Some have been noticed by few people from outside their own place, such as the 400-metre North Wall of the Blouberg in the Transvaal, which looks across the Limpopo to Zimbabwe.

Some are colossal, like Gibraltar, or Mulanje on the border of Malawi and Mozambique. Some are lowly but pregnant, like the outcrop of Dunadd in Kintyre with its 'footprint' where the kings of Dalriada stood to be crowned. Some are unclimbable, by me, like Spider Rock in Canyon de Chellay, Arizona. On others, like Pillar Rock in Cumbria, I have spent entire days clinging happily to their cracks and inching along their ledges.

In the end I was even more struck than when I started by the versatility of the record which the rocks create. We say that 'such-and-such a poet wrote lines' on a subject — Wordsworth's 'Lines on revisiting the banks of the Wye', for example. Long before us and our language, lines were inscribed on rock by ice. On the south-west shore of Hudson Bay I saw turtlebacks of the rock called greywacke scored with grooves aligned north-north-east/south-south-west. Their meaning is, The glacier advanced this way. We could call such markings 'geoglyphs' or 'geoscript' ('write' is derived from the Old English word for 'scratch'). Sometimes the geoglyphs are illuminated, like the beautiful coloured drools on Castle Crag in Borrowdale, which Gordon Stainforth has photographed. Their meaning is, This place is usually wet.

Presently people wrote on rock, with colours made from earth, or by pecking out glyphs with a pointed stone. At Ewaninga, near a waterhole south of Alice Springs, I saw an emu footprint chipped out on a slab of red rock — advice, perhaps, to other hunters that here was a good place to get emus, for their flesh and feathers. This is the start of writing, only one remove from prints left spontaneously in the ancient mud — the dinosaur footprints we saw west of Tuba City in Arizona, or the tracks left by Palaeolithic people in the estuary of the Usk.

In all these cases rock is a fine medium for the lives of animals and plants alike, because it rises clear of the flux and resists obliteration.

PART ONE
North America, The Desert States

I Black Mountain to Earth Fire Country

From where we stood, the edge of the Mohave Desert in southern California was a rim of low hills that looked as though they had been charred. Below us, in the gulch where the city of Barstow had begun its life, plugs of volcanic rhyolite stuck up from a bed of yellow gravel like spoil-heaps from a mine. I was talking to John Harper, who heads a highway crew for Caltrak, the California road maintenance system. He struck me as pure pioneer American, hefty and grizzled, and he revelled in the physical extremity of his beloved desert.

As we stood outside his house in Cinnebar Road, I felt the exhaust of his Jeep Cherokee playing on my legs. The engine wasn't running. These hot breaths were the gale, air at a temperature of 38°C driven at fifty miles an hour by furious convection winds. When I asked John what had happened to the river, he laughed heartily.

'*Sure* they's a river! It's upside down and back to front. It's eighty foot down and it flows EAST!' — to its final sink in Soda Lake. The water has been hijacked by the town of Victorville forty miles south, where John's wife Pat works for the American Automobile Association. From now on we would be navigating by means of the A.A.A.'s classic map called *Indian Country*.

In the glaring haze to the north the most noticeable landmark was the beautiful peaked breast of Pilot Rock. Standing here 120 years ago, before this region was mapped, we would have had to take a bearing on it. Now, with John as guide, we were attuning ourselves to this new world of sunburnt, dusty plateaux, and canyons that opened sudden gateways into the earth's crust, and towering rocks red as though still hot from a fiery epoch.

There were four of us at first, then three. Anne, my wife, has been my companion on uncounted miles of journeying through Europe, the Middle East, Africa, and North America as we have tacked from great rock to great rock like mariners on an ocean of stones and sands. Our landfalls have been located wherever the planet juts up sharply enough to have offered a citadel or a haven, a begetter of life-saving waterholes, or a god who had tired of this world, left his body here as a butte, and set off into the cosmos in spirit form.

Now we were travelling with the Weslings from San Diego: Donald, a dedicated scholar from the campus at La Jolla, and Judith, equally dedicated, who organises the junior football leagues of southern California from a garden shed knee-deep in files and letters. As the temperature rose above 40°C north of the Bernardino Mountains, she turned up the air conditioning in the car, then swaddled her neck in scarves against the draught and entertained us with epic anecdotes about their struggles to get rid of a manager who had been interfering with the boys in his team.

Beside her Donald was formidably silent. He had a disconcerting habit of putting on a pair of dark glasses with leather blinkers that entirely screened his eyes. Inside this personal cocoon he would fall asleep, sometimes in mid-sentence, then wake up enough, when I was driving, to remark, 'I see — for you a vehicle on the road ahead is there to be overtaken.' A fair comment on my driving style, which to me at least felt safe enough on these sweeps of highway with little else on them except an occasional pick-up crammed with a Navajo family or an even rarer easy rider, tanned and lean, with no crash helmet, his bleached hair flying wildly.

On two successive days John Harper put a handgun and a rifle behind the seat of his jeep and drove us thirty kilometres north into the Mohave to look for petroglyphs. These signs or symbolic images were pecked out by 440 generations of Indians, using pointed stones to make pale marks on the desert varnish of the rocks — a dark umber coating formed from metal oxides enamelled on to the stone by sunglare and wind-blast. Barstow showed what it was made of in a stark monument set on a concrete plinth at an intersection — one old-time shunting loco, one Sherman tank, and one boulder, standing for the railroad, the army, the mines. Beside the river-bed, in the marshalling yards of the Santa Fe railroad, box-cars were being coupled up into crocodiles a hundred metres long for the crawl westward to the coast. The original railway families' cottages, made in the 1880s, had been mined into the rock of the hillside above the yards and fronted with irregular chunks of rhyolite. It was a world of metals, stones, and dust.

'Yeah,' John had said, above the musical frenzy of the chimes hanging under their porch, which were being tossed straight upward on their strings, '*it's* desert alright, out there beyond Black Mountain. There is no living thing there *at* all!'

As I walked out on to the parched surface beside the dirt track, the reflected heat tightened the skin and rasped the eyeballs in a way I had felt just once before when I looked into the open door of a blast furnace in a Tees-side steelworks. Half a mile from the jeep I felt absurdly committed, as though this torrid place could breathe me in, then cough me out as a husk. In the 1850s a party of pioneers, following the Mohave River Trail from Salt Lake to the western goldfields, only avoided starvation near what is now Barstow by eating the entrails of a wolf. At the mouth of a gulch where we had parked, a two-by-two had been driven into the ground — a claim stake, looking so weathered and solitary it seemed to be saying that the prospector would not be back.

Plants were growing here but there was no humus. Seeds and pollens cannot form after May and the stems are too sapless to make a compost when they fall. Fleet doves were darting from seedhead to seedhead of the parched milkweed and trumpet-weed, desert primrose and Russian thistle — not yet blown loose and balled into tumbleweed. John was prowling, eyes on the ground, somehow never missing a turkey buzzard cruising high above or a flitting gamebird. He had a passion for collecting and seized on the semi-opaque beige of agate, the bruise colour of common opal, white fibrous asbestos, jasper fragments like stranded sea anemones. He picked out exquisite flakes and argued that they couldn't be artefacts because their edges were not rippled.

The Mohave was created by the warming and drying after 9,000 B.C. which turned wetlands into savannah, savannah into the arid plain of today. Its surface is a loose mosaic. Light blond scintillae have sifted over beaches of heavier, brick-red motes, washed down by the most recent flash flood from one of the blue-black rainstorms that hover above the high plains like swarms of locusts. For centuries the Indians pictured them on the rocks as down-curved glyphs like weeping willows. Between the ghostly dried-out flowers and the greasewood bushes with their tarry stink and their roots thirty feet deep in the water-table, the surface was engraved all over by snaking tracks, whole systems of tributaries and mainstreams, as though we were looking down from a jet-plane at the big rivers themselves — the Colorado to the north, the Rio Grande to the east.

The flanking hills were heaps of sooty lava chunks, belched out by eruptions 15,000 years ago. In a hollow I saw my first petroglyph, marked with a neat sign by the Ranger Service. I'd rather have come upon it by chance, or missed it for that matter and gone on looking. On a small brown rockface framed by golden seedheads, patterns had been chipped out. A rectangle full of parallel zigzags was flanked by a sort of hourglass. To its right, an oblong with limbs at its corners looked like a stretched hide. To the right again, an inverted heart split by a line looked somehow genital and female. All this was baffling. On the other side of the track a similar rock displayed two Big Horned Sheep, schematic, finely observed, the pairs of horns curving back to mid-spine, the legs of the hindmost sheep coping elegantly with a high step up, forelegs bunched, hindlegs at full stretch. Vandals had been here too. Having had the ancient writing pointed out to them by the notice, Phil and Speedy and Wayne had scratched their names on the rocks.

John was taking us especially to see an earlier item from the white man's visitors' book. He had found it here as a youth when he was out shooting. The local hunters build guzzlers — waterholes lined with cement and walled round. When the doves and partridges come to drink, they shoot them. One of these was our landmark, a scabby concrete structure. As Donald and Judith walked over to it, they saw a snake flick over and down. A quick swirl in the water, then stillness again. By the time Anne and I arrived, the black surface three metres down showed nothing but a dead branch and the bleached corpses of three gophers.

On the slope at the other side of the track was the rock John had found years ago as he waited for his quarry to fly in — a boulder inscribed in pale letters on wholemeal brown speckled rusty with lichen:

> J. & A. Tilman
> Sep 30 1874
> San Francisco
> Cala.

Two brothers, perhaps, heading east to prospect for the silver which was struck rich near Barstow a few years later. The lettering was craftsmanly, the 'J' formed in half-imitation of classical chiselling.

The gale had died and the lustrous gold apparitions of the seared rice-grass were barely trembling. This silent calm felt like pure desert — a moon-like *mare tranquillis*, as though nothing was happening that had not happened for century after century since the eruption or the drying-out. When we left the territory of the doves, we saw no animals for miles, except one on a side track leading to an abortive mine. A little creature crouched motionless on a stone, like a stone itself, its head and belly pale jade, its back panelled in gamboge and withered-oak-leaf brown. Its cranium and nape were armoured in arrowhead scales that formed a deadly defensive frill across its shoulders. As Anne held it in the palm of her hand and stroked it, John told us that it was a horned toad. When predators threatened, it shot blood from its eyes. Maybe it trusted us. When Anne put it back on the ground, its camouflage instantly disappeared it. Later I came across a precise and humorous Navajo story about how the appearance of the People (meaning animals as well as humans) became fixed at sunrise during the creation time:

All night they played, and the eagles and all flying creatures and the water animals were there; when dawn came, they all dressed themselves and appeared as they would be in the future . . . Horned-toad decorated himself with arrow-points and lichen. After they had all gone, someone woke up Bear and Crow. In his haste Bear put on the wrong shoes, so that his feet turned in, and when he went up the mountain he was overtaken by the Sun and burned brown on top; meanwhile the Crow covered himself with charcoal.

On our left, as we veered east, the Mohave stretched for 120 kilometres to the southern mouth of Death Valley. On the horizon low blue bergs of mountains showed like islands hull-down. To our right, among the lava hills, John spotted a brown-faced rock every so often and a petroglyph came into focus, like an insect that had just alighted. Sometimes they were recognisable (stick people, a Horned Sheep linked to the lamb beneath by an umbilical line), sometimes they were symbols from an 'alphabet' with no obvious meaning — the split 'heart' again, a row of 'eggs', parallel curves or zigzags, sometimes in a frame.

Scholars have worried away at the codes and unearthed many meanings, especially a man from Utah who was brought up among Paiute people. What we have to understand is that most of the rock images are not pictures but signs in an alphabet. A circle can mean 'holding' or 'possession' and concentric circles therefore mean 'many possessions', for example the big flocks owned by the Navajo before they were decimated by Kit Carson's soldiers early in the 1860s. A schematic 'sheep' means 'travel' or 'direction'. The 'split heart' is a spear held in its atlatl or throwing-sling. The 'hourglass' made of two triangles joined at the apex can be a human torso, or it can mean 'war' (and if it is tilted, it means 'war ended'). Zigzags can be a numbering system, each angle representing a unit or a ten. They are also very like tribal emblems on war-shields (from Africa and Australia as well as America), in which case the sign would be saying, 'The Paiute [or Shoshone or Hopi] from Fifth-Bend-of-the-River have been here,' a statement which could be bellicose, or possessive (related to land claims), or plain factual. The position of each sign on the rock and in relation to the signs next it is equally part of the meaning, as are its size and the sharpness of its cutting. It is a nuanced language, created by people without paper, to carry out a whole gamut of jobs, from keeping records to telling stories, from demonstrating patterns for rugs or blankets to signalling the purpose of a ceremony.

We had reached a haven where the low cliff drew back to let a wash run through from the hill behind. It was dry now and the rock under our feet was polished like the bowl of a *meerschaum* pipe. The sides were covered with images. This had been a caravanserai for the Mohave tribe, who carried red ochre and textiles west to trade with the Coast Indians for abalone shells and ropes, then carried these back to trade for pottery and pigments with the Hopi and Yavapai from points east on the Colorado plateau. We had arrived at a major junction in the western-American trailways. Long before Highway 66 was driven through, the Atlantic and Pacific Railroad linked with the California Southern at Barstow. Before that again, the Grape Vine Ranch was staked out where Barstow now is. In the seventeenth century a Jesuit called Francisco Garces, the first white man to describe the area, came baptising his way up the Colorado from Yuma and named the dry bed of the Mohave the Arroyo de los Martires. When the original colonists of America had the land to themselves, this was the junction where the north/south route from Paiute country down into Cahuilla country at Joshua Tree crossed the east/west route from Zuni country across the Sierra Nevada to the coast.

Now this ancient watering place and bazaar was silent, or was until a big black Chevrolet came wallowing through the hills from the south and two Japanese got out for a short, intensive photo-session. They said nothing to us and we said nothing to them. Presently we were joined by an off-road vehicle driven by Ranger Moore. He appraised us shrewdly and courteously.

'You-all jus' lookin' aroun'? Well, you're very welcome to do that.'

In his khaki shirt and broad-brimmed hat he looked like a Boy Scout six feet three inches tall. He had a revolver at his hip and a Ph.D. in anthropology. He was on the alert for vandals who come to let off shots at the petroglyphs or prise them off and cart them away to sell.

'Y'know what we can *fine* them for that offence? One — hundred — dollars.' He said this incredulously and sadly.

Nearby we could see the raw grey of a bullet scar above the rump of a horned animal. A yellow wound showed where a decorated face had been levered off above a 'spear'. A line of chisel dints along the top of a flake had been made by some scoundrel trying to force off a complete panel bearing a glyph like a six-spot ladybird with four beansprouts growing out of its head.

Left to itself, rock is the most durable of the world's records — coloured by the prehistoric firing, polished and engraved by ice, inscribed by people with alphabets and pictures. Each of these left the rock whole, not yet uprooted from its own place, tamed in rockeries, or crushed down for cement or artificial stone. In the 1860s the Mohave tribe were finally forced to knuckle under to the whites. Now the last of their archives are being looted.

Some days later Donald, Anne and I flew to Flagstaff in north-central Arizona, 300 miles east of Barstow, and drove north on Highway 89. When we turned off on to a narrow side road, we were folded at once into the eerie purity of nature as it is being conserved by the National Parks and Monuments. No advertisements for Baskin Robbins ice-cream, no houses or fast-food outlets, no barbed wire, no wrecks or litter or derelict cabins, no gas stations and few other cars. Nothing but the narrow channel of black-top winding out of sight ahead between bristling forests whose pines and hemlocks were of all ages from seedling through bush to tall veteran. It was like looking into a Russian fairy-tale, or a dream of America before invasion — the 'fresh, green breast of the new world' imagined at the end of *The Great Gatsby*.

In this fairy-tale a sinister transformation had occurred. The ground had been torn up and scorched. We were driving through a welter of massive, blackish cinders that looked as fresh as yesterday's clinker. Only a few pines had managed to find a footing among these rocks like petrified sponges or giant gingerbreads. Now the source of it all was rising up behind some denser forest — a symmetrical cone 300 metres high, dark brown with a burnt-sienna glow at its hollowed summit. This was Sunset Crater, a heap of hardened magma thrown up during eruptions that started in the winter of A.D. 1064 and fulminated for two centuries.

The blazings and upheavings were turned at some point into an epic story and a version of it was copied down a few years ago from the reciting of a Hopi who had served in the Second World War. The eruption became a metaphor for revenge. The earth was set on fire to punish some young villains who had seduced a married woman. Her beautiful young husband was actually a *kachina*, or being from the other world. When he fired the brushwood to terrorise his tormentors, the whole range went up in flames:

> The elders, who had suggested the idea of the fire in the first place and who were there with the youth, now exclaimed, 'How terrible! It looks as though you dug the hole too deep, and now the fire is moving in the wrong direction. It's burning downward . . .' Right inside one of the hills there was a mass of what looked like boiling coals pushed upward. As this was going on, the fire rose sky-high. Some time later, as it reached its peak, it spewed out molten embers . . . Finally [they] reached up so high that they poured over the rim of the fire pit . . . Eventually the hill sprung leaks at several places around its base. Spewing forth in every direction, the molten embers started running everywhere . . .

The aftermath is a drought and a famine, all the animals shrink away from the blighted place, and the people migrate eastward to the Rio Grande. So the chief geological event of the area is nicely fused with the chief demographic one. The parching aftermath of the fire that consumed the ground prefigures the time, two centuries later, when the forerunners of the Hopi and the Navajo — now called collectively the Anasazi — were forced out of these lands by a drying and cooling of the climate.

The people before the Hopi have been named the Sinagua — the waterless. The remains of their villages and great houses perch on outcrops like stone boats stranded forever when the 'big ol' flood' went down. As we travelled further away from Flagstaff, we left behind the last of the volcanic hills, with Hopi names like Hovi'itstuyga and Lohavutsotsmo — Buttocks and Testicles. We were embarking on an ocean of land which to my eyes, accustomed to a little island off western Europe, looked like the whole world made visible at last. It was as though we were *seeing distance* — the dimension itself made visible. Not tangible, because when you got 'there', a yet further distance planed off beyond the earth's curve. At our feet a pale peach-coloured desert scrubby with blue-green sage and salt-bush and sap-green greasewood expanded towards a white edge beyond a dip, lifted a little, then stretched away again towards a far cinnamon expanse with still further levels beyond.

The map told me I was looking across the Little Colorado to the terrace where the Painted Desert steps up on to the Moenkopi Plateau and the whole breadth of the Hopi Reservation. Rim after rim just showed itself, almost as though the tectonic plates themselves were laid bare edge on.

On this crust the few reefs of Moenkopi sandstone that were still upstanding had attracted villages as skerries attract barnacles. At Wupatki a ruined pueblo held up its stumps of vermilion wall. Centuries of pitiless wind had focussed a blow-lamp on it, smelting the stones back into rock. The terra cotta stone had split easily into 'bricks'. The back wall of one room was a six-metre rockface. The walls and corners ran straight up from the natural crag to make three storeys of housing. The red heart of the complex was a huge angular rock from which passages radiated like arteries. It had been embodied into the dwellings because it stored the day's heat and gave it out again at night — life-saving at 1,700 metres above sea level — as well as to economise on the building of walls. The sandstone had formed from dunes and silt layers in the Cambrian Sea. One rounded hulk of rock near the core of the buildings wore an embedded girdle of white shells, so unchanged it was like walking along a beach and coming upon a strand of cockles left by the tide.

East of the pueblo or citadel, the innards of the rock reached out to us in the most unexpected way. This place had been the home of religious and political leaders. A dance plaza or amphitheatre and an oval ball court have survived, each surrounded by low stone walling. The ball game may have had a religious function, not unlike the ancient form of football in which the ball signified the green god's head. The Anasazi often sited the ball court near a natural blowhole. At Wupatki the mouth in the rock has been built round with a flagstone parapet and topped with a steel grille. Its character lives on. Donald and I knelt down beside it and leant our faces into the draught. A cool current was streaming upwards because of the greater pressure underground. When we stood up, our faces instantly poured with sweat.

Down under, the cavern system in the Permian limestone is 1,100 kilometres in overall length. In the story this was the home of the wind god Yaapontsa, who was called up by the wronged *kachina* husband to help in the retribution. He came out of his cave 'rocking back and forth, stirring up everything in his path', blowing on the fire of revenge as it died down and roaring it up again into one 'huge blaze'.

Maybe housing the wind god was function enough for this fine hole but as we travelled north and east and south again, and came across hole after hole in rock, often natural, sometimes carved out, I began to think of them all as linked with the *si'pa'pu*, the Hole of Emergence in Navajo belief — the opening in the dome of the universe that led through from one creation stage to another. We came upon them in the cliff villages and towns of the canyon country towards New Mexico and in isolated natural arches that were seen as sacred. In the meantime we journeyed out of Sinagua country via a last pueblo at Wukoki. It looked like a small medieval castle, its built sandstone walls planing down straight on to the terra cotta rockface, then to the desert floor. It felt unutterably lonely, marooned on the sunburnt plain, just out of sight of its cultural centre at Wupatki, with no sign of a surrounding web of walls and fields and tracks in which life might have been lived.

These single buildings were often famed as landmarks, like the Red House of Chichilticalli, in the valley of the Gila River 200 kilometres south of our furthest point. Coronado's expedition saw it in 1540. Now it is lost. Some believe that these isolated rock-sites were chosen so that 'the enemy' could be seen coming for miles. They were not occupied only in warlike times, and in any case these vast vacancies are of the present and not of the ninth to the thirteenth centuries. In those days the Sinagua worked in the clan fields, storing their tools in stone huts, irrigating their beans and corn by means of ditches and check-dams.

The image of a great spread of virgin land with a single squaw or a single brave nobly contemplating the distance from the top of a picturesque butte is part fiction, spun from our own need for a primal paradise. This is still fed by postcards and the dust-jackets of books, and it was given a seeming authenticity by the photographs of such pioneers as Walter McClintock. His charismatic shots of the Blackfeet in Montana early this century tend to show single people or very small numbers isolated on seas of grass. They look beleaguered, and though the land was vast and the native population was small, McClintock's vision feels to have been shaped by his knowledge that in the generation before him the Indian lands had been laid waste, the people decimated.

In the Navajo creation stories the first world was red. So it seemed week after week as Anne, Donald and I followed a huge circle north-east from Flagstaff, Arizona, through the portals of Monument Valley, then south past Mesa Verde to Albuquerque, and west again by the mesas of El Morro and Acoma, the oldest inhabited settlement in North America, and Towaya'lane, the Corn Mountain, where the Zuni took refuge from the 'big ol' Flood' and the Spaniards. By Canyon de Chellay, last stronghold of the Navajo, we closed our circle at Walnut Canyon, a little east of Flagstaff. Here the gods had run out of red and fallen back on the drab greys of limestone.

By then we had passed through every hue of red, from the bleached flowerpot vermilion of the reefs and houses between the San Francisco Mountains and the Painted Desert, through the ox-tongue colours of Monument's buttes, the raw beef and salmon and the delicate rose and peach of the canyon walls, to the Zuni mountains whose great pillars were striped white and red as the fat and lean of ham. The 'redness' of the Indians, it turned out, was the colour not of their skins but of the rocks and earths on which they lived.

2   The Canyon of Broken Shards

The journey north to the crossing of the Little Colorado at Cameron Trading Post, then west to the Kaibab Forest and the Grand Canyon, was a reversal of the Hopi Way from the Earth Centre, where they emerged, to their homeland in what is now northern Arizona. We were also on the old trade route which had plied as far south as tropical Mexico. Parrot bones and a copper bell have been unearthed hereabouts. My own goal was Keet Seel at the head of the Tsegi Canyons 250 kilometres to the north-east. This Anasazi cliff village had attracted me because it was hard to reach. The twelve-kilometre walk in followed a river-bed prone to flash floods, especially in mid-summer. It was now July. Only twenty people could go in there each day and Donald had had to book our places two months in advance. Altogether there seemed to be a fair chance that the place had remained itself. The Grand Canyon is perhaps too huge to spoil. It swallows up the incessant light aircraft and helicopters that fly the tourists in and out as a dragon would swallow midges. It remains a sublime prodigy, the planet's most extraordinary entrance. Peering down from South Rim, I saw it as a graveyard of gigantic battleships, their shattered superstructures towering into the heat haze, or as the stretched out krangs of inconceivable beasts. It was the aorta of America west of the Continental Divide, pumping, pumping, blue with the strain of keeping California alive.

While Anne took an inflatable down river from Bitter Springs, we turned east towards Tuba City and Black Mesa, driving through classic bad-lands — miles and miles of gamboge clay moraine, like spoil from the biggest open-cast mine in the world. Layers of mudstone were printed with the tracks of a dinosaur which had run on two legs like a giant emu. We were shown the petrified three-toed marks by a young Navajo. He was thinly dressed in spite of a gale that whined and tattered in the most friendless way on earth through the stall nearby where his mother sold turquoise jewellery.

The Navajo still live scattered across the land in the way described in their oldest epic stories. At the ends of dirt roads strung out along the highways, low one-storey huts have replaced the tepees and hogans. They drive their government issue pick-ups to the supermarkets, where day after day we were the only whites among fifty or sixty shoppers, or to the craft stalls along the highways with flags on long wands straining in the wind. On the road from South Rim to Cameron, a series of well-printed signs had advertised a tribal jewellery business. Successive boards promised 'BEST — PRICES', then added 'ALL — GOOD — INDIANS' — a nice satirical glance at the bad old image of the treacherous and bloodthirsty warrior. For weeks we saw Indians mostly — whites only at Reception in the motels or at viewpoints, camera in hand — and we relished their laconic self-sufficiency. Instead of the commercial bubbliness of white waitresses — 'Have a good day!' and 'I'm sorry, we're all out of French mustard, but the blue-cheese dressing is just *great* today!' — a Navajo serving in a restaurant would say at most 'No', a short guttural monosyllable, or occasionally 'Yes'. If real communication is not possible, then why pretend?

On the plains to the north a great dark rain connected cloud to earth as though with weight-bearing trunks, wiping out the blunt tower of an isolated rock, Square Butte, another place fated to remain on the horizon. At night we camped among big juniper and piñon pine. Crows and bluejays perched on the branches, waiting for scraps. In the dark we picked our way down Sandal Trail by hairpins of gravel and naked rock and peered from the overlook into the soot-black gulf of Lower Tsegi Canyon. Down there, we knew, was the cliff village of

Betatakin, lived in by Anasazi for just one generation from 1250 to 1300 A.D. The arch of its cave was flanked by leaning jambs of sandstone 120 metres high. They glimmered faintly where the light of a half-moon barely reached them.

After a silent quarter of an hour on the brink, we turned back up the hill and followed a drumbeat to the campfire. A Navajo dancer was showing a ritual to a small audience. It was a sturdy, stamping dance, legs spread and knees bent — a display of strength, not of grace or seduction. His garments were decorated with bright shreds stitched on and big eagle feathers so lightly attached by their shafts that they bobbed as he stamped. When the drummers stopped, he stood still, not breathless, arms and shoulders shiny with sweat, and explained how he had inherited the costume from a veteran and added his own sacred emblems. Then we were ushered into a ring and conducted in a simple dance, stepping sideways, feet apart, together, apart again, until we had gone full circle: fifteen or twenty Caucasoid visitors, doing our best, making amends perhaps, wanting the older culture of the place not to die out entirely.

In the morning we set off at 8 o'clock, under packs bulging with tent and sleeping-bags, two days' food and four litres of water apiece, and walked northwards through sands and river-beds for half a day. The 300 metres of descent to the canyon floor led down a stairway hewn from the rock of Tsegi Point. Near the top the axe work was elaborate. Nonslip grooves had been etched on the steps, criss-cross decorations cut into the kerb of the rain-gutter at the side. These faded out until the last cuts seemed to be little more than axe-blade sharpenings on the rock-wall. To our right a tan profile jutted massively, chin and forehead salient against blue sky. In England it would be a wonder; here it was one of thousands. Along the wrinkles in its brow cliff-swallows flew in and out of their holes. Sometimes these creases secreted salt, little white weeps of it smeared down the sandstone, and I wondered if the birds had first clung there to sip, then found that the soft stone could be mined to make shallow nesting burrows.

Up above on the forest trail a Navajo wrangler with two horses had been tightening their girths in readiness for the go-down. He greeted us with a gloved hand as we filed past. He overtook us on a terrace among dwarf pines, where we kept passing neat piles of dung, each scoop of it bright green and fibrous. Then we were ski-ing down a hundred metres of dune, formed in a hot age 6,000 years ago, with much foreboding of how toilsome it was going to be plodding back up. At the first branch of Laguna Creek, three more riders came past, a wrangler silently attending a pair of ladies with well-tailored trousers and widebrimmed felt Stetsons, like figures from photos of the artistic crowd at Taos in the thirties. They ignored us; the Navajo man gave us his courteous, wordless salute. We were all dwarf people between the towering walls.

The air-space in the canyon was like a broad mass of crystal, diminishing us, forming a tough medium in which we made headway as gradually as the shadow on a sundial. We became part draught-animal, part stoical nomad. The waymarks weren't obvious. At the Visitor Centre the ranger had added words to a simple pencil map, 'Don't go left', where you first meet the river-bed. This was fairly important.

'Last summer,' she said, 'a guy turned down Long Canyon and finished off somewheres in Shonto country. They had to fetch him out with a helicopter.'

We turned downstream, which felt peculiar, since we were homing on the head of the canyon. At the confluence where Keet Seel Canyon met the Tsegi, we headed upstream at last, feeling more oriented but still alert. Our only man-made landmarks were a few mapped posts. These bleached old items, it turned out, were easy to miss and couldn't always be seen one from another. The first waterfalls were unmistakable. To pass them we trudged up the point of the terminal moraine where Keet Seel Canyon proper forked north-west. In a meadow of tall purple flowers like wild beans, horses were grazing, brown, grey, and dapple. They startled and streamed off, long manes and tails flowing. The black leader waited until they were well away up the north-east branch before he followed them.

Our last company was a brief reunion with the wrangler we had met before as he came up from the river after watering his horses. I had heard that there was a great rock in the canyon called Kachina Mother, the god of the place. 'Which is she?' I asked the man. Silently he waved his hand upstream towards a bend, then trotted off out of sight.

Much of the time we were walking in the creek itself, never more than two inches deep. The water was like pale blood with its burden of sandstone silt. Continuously the buttresses, towers, walls, spires reared ahead of us, came abreast of us, fell behind us in a stately file, the tall red elders. When Kachina Mother appeared high up on the true-right bank, she was unmistakable, a pyramid on a plinth above the canyon, tapering fiercely to a spear-head, hard brown Navajo sandstone looking indestructible above terraces of the more friable Kayenta series. As we drew north of her she grew less shapely. She hunched her back, and her back was double, or cleft. From well up the canyon she became single again, blunt-headed, no longer wondrously beautiful. The Anasazi who settled here around 950 A.D., driven from their farms in the plains when the ground gullied out and the good soil washed away, would have seen her first from downstream and her sheer beauty would have made her a totem.

The river entered a gully with crumbling, sandy sides, never more than ten metres high. It must have been cut in historic times. At the rim of the dune-like profile the perilously shallow layer of humus was like a threadbare brown carpet lightly embroidered with flowers and grasses. So that was all the biome that the Anasazi had to live on, to gather from and till. It could still sustain a herd, apparently. Dried-out cow-pats were dotted along the path and once we smelt pure cow, that mix of blood and milk and leather. A trail of bucket steps led up an earthy red bluff to a broader pasture where the invisible animals must have been. Soon after we were walking through a gap in an ancient stump fence, weathered bones of piñon pine laid length-wise to keep herds and flocks from straying downstream where the banks were steep enough to kill them.

On the upper terrace, we found ourselves waist-deep in meadows of flowers growing on sand, with tender leaves and spires of purple petals — bee-weed, I was told — which the Anasazi ate after boiling it to make it less bitter. A crushed blossom of it smelt intensely savoury, like a curried nut-roast. On the slope ahead, a green mist resolved itself into a stand of broad-leafed trees. They looked luxurious and unreal to me, after days among bristling conifers — stage scenery representing Arcadia. They were Gambel oaks, from which the Anasazi gathered food acorns. In a niche of the rock beside the path a long-haired young man was sitting beside a big pack and a guitar in a waterproof cover. When we left him with some light remark about getting there before him, he said earnestly, 'I am walking *as slowly as possible.*'

After the idyllic wood we laboured up and down hillocks of tormentingly fine sand before shade trees gathered thickly again. We hauled up a steep bluff out of the river-bed. An ironical notice on a tree said 'RECREATION AREA AHEAD', and we saw in dappled light a tall white horse tethered to a tree, flicking its tail slowly and munching fresh green alfalfa from a swathe at its feet. We drained our last water bottles and lay down with our heads on our packs. Between tree-trunks we could see the great cliff making a wall above an elbow in the canyon, brown stripes of iron oxide 'painted' right down the overhang.

Below, as weirdly miniature and perfect as a child's playtown, the buildings of Keet Seel perched in shadow.

The clarity and intricate detail of these cliff settlements prints their reality deeply into the mind — far more so, for me, than the best preserved of European medieval castles. Dwarfed beneath 200-metre cliffs, at first they look miniature and only slowly become full-size and human-scale. This trick of perception gives them time to grow on you, whereas the massive strongholds of Carcassonne or Conway look instantly like sets for a Cecil B. De Mille film and never quite get over it. In contrast, the fine domesticity of the cliff settlements allowed us to feel we could move in there now, ourselves.

We strolled the last mile and met the Parks ranger who lived nearby in a sort of luxury hogan, an octagonal bungalow-cum-office made of laminated pine. She showed us a beautiful loose mosaic of pottery fragments laid out at the base of the glacis. Many were black on white, in classical Anasazi style, found also at Mesa Verde and the metropolis of Chaco Canyon; some were bluish white like the insides of mussel shells; a few were sea-anemone red. 'Keet Seel' is Navajo for 'broken potsherds' and these shards were from pots, or *ollas*, in which the staple maize used to be stored. When we climbed the fifty-five steps of a rough pine ladder up the glacis and stooped below a colossal transverse tree-trunk to enter the settlement, its true scale became apparent. These were medieval rooms a little under two metres high. You had to stoop below their lintels to get through the keyhole doors but you could live in them all right. Their floors were dry and solid, shaded from that naked Arizona sun. They looked out on the long cradle of the canyon with its arable floor, its spring in the bank of the tributary gully immediately below, its monumental beauty, its safety with just the one possible approach.

Keet Seel has a hundred and fifty rooms and six kivas, the biggest of its kind. Although this is a village by our standards, its clustered intricacy of roofs, canopies, steps, walls, terraces, lean-to's made me exclaim: 'It's a little town!' The Ranger repeated this with pleased agreement. She was white, she taught Navajo art to Navajo children, as she ruefully admitted, and she was engaged to a Navajo, which is most unusual.

This settlement grew up over many generations and the first houses have gone, their timber and stone re-used in the final building around 1250 A.D. The broad cove it occupies formed when water seeping down through the sandstone met an impermeable layer of rock and eroded sideways. Lesser coves, like shallow mouths with arched upper lips, stared out at us from the cliffs. The floor had been levelled with stone waste. The front walls of the outermost buildings clung to the glacis like wild bees' nests and towards the left corner of the mouth (facing out) another little wall, and another, crept down the smooth rock apron as though the builders had been playing chicken. The innermost rooms had sloping back walls consisting of the mother-rock. Stones were set in mud mortar, smooth sides out, to make masonry outer walls. Logs made joists for flat roofs on which people sat to spin or chat or chip petroglyphs — we could see a zigzag snake and a Big Horned Sheep. The protruding ends of the logs were thatched with split branches and twisted yucca fibre to make a canopy. A further wall was built supporting this to enclose the front of a room. The cells in the hive were built forward, sometimes three deep.

It looked as though the people had only just left. Corn cobs littered the slightly hollowed earthen floors. A loom-bar (a smoothed branch with cuts round it at regular intervals to take the threads of the weft) leant against a wall. Slim tree-trunks, the stubs of their lower branches still sticking out, stood up here and there along the street — possibly perches for captive birds used in ceremonies. These poles and the joists protruding from adobe houses made it look like a tidy building site with home-made scaffolding. Any moment now the builders would come back after their siesta.

The corn cobs were so small, like the baby ones we eat in salad today, that I assumed they had shrunk through drying out. Later I found that they were normal for that time. Examples from Mexico plot a growth from 1.75 to 8–10cms between about 6000 B.C. and the centuries when people were growing and eating Indian corn in these canyons. When the climate cooled and dried in the thirteenth century, the families started to leave. Those who stayed turned houses into granaries, and when they too left, they sealed the doors in readiness for their return. They never came back. The Navajo who later colonised these parts rarely re-occupied such buildings, for all their convenience, because people had died there. In their belief a home of the dead was a *hovee'hooghan*, a death-dwelling to be shunned forever. Maybe this was sensible. The few human bones found at Keet Seel had swollen joints, suggesting arthritis, and we now know that this can be endemic and infectious.

Today the place felt wholesome. There is no standing water, or marshland even, between the brown walls of the gorge. The medieval timbers are still sound, above all the great tree-trunk that stabilises the front retaining wall, re-bar style. It is white pine, and this puzzled the Ranger and a pair of archaeologists who were here on a working holiday. The wife was lean and taciturn, her husband was a Falstaff in plaid shirt and Stetson, bursting with curly hair from chest and head and chin, and unable to hold back the information that purled from his lips.

'There is no white pine growing anywhere near here *at* all,' he announced. 'And it must have taken *real* good organisation to haul that tree so far, and hoist it and install it. And look at that end — it's blunt, there was nobody *cut* that end. Those stone axes could not cut *dead* wood. This tree was green when they got it, sure enough. No, they couldn't *cut* too well with those — they virtually battered that tree to death.'

The timbers for the roofs, he told us, would have been split by hurling logs from the canyon rim to its floor.

It would have been sweet to stay here. The mere hour allowed in the settlement, the single day in the canyon, was upsetting evidence of our fevered life-style. We're forced to worry about visitor throughput, about vandalism, about equal access opportunities for each one of the millions who may want to visit, about the logistics and for that matter the insurance position if anyone with health 'problems' starts dying in the wilderness. 'If you have heart or respiratory problems, don't attempt the hike,' warns the leaflet issued by the National Park Service. 'EARTHQUAKE PREPAREDNESS CLINIC SATS. 10 A.M.' proclaims a hoarding on the highway north of Beverly Hills. Worry seemed to have unnerved a Keet Seel visitor today. The wrangler with the two horses had been ordered on short-wave radio from the Ranger hogan by a man who did the walk in, then felt he had overdone it and paid $50 to be shipped back out.

At night we brewed and cooked in the open air while the moon was riddled into silver pieces by the shivering of the oak branches above our heads. Beside us were drifts of the wild currant bushes whose fruit the Anasazi ate — like orange redcurrants with a flavour of pleasant, insipid apple. Nearby the white horse was still munching and the women who hired it ($25) to carry their packs, four hiking members of the Sierra Club, were reclining against a fallen tree and swigging wine from paper cups. Keet Seel under its cliff had withdrawn into blackest shadow. Nearby, the jambs of a tributary canyon stood up out of the talus like seventy-metre timbers; where the lintel would have been we could see Orion. If ever there was a place that asked to be lived in . . .

When the people of the Tsegi decided to move on, they sent out scouts to pick a new place from the plenitude of sites available. That was more or less what we must do tomorrow. The curly archaeologist pointed out that the Anasazi had no draught animals and could take only what they could carry (or haul on sledges?). At least we were doing it their way. Up at 5 a.m., with the moon still casting shadows, we were away by 7, so as to finish walking before the sun was at the zenith. We were weighed down with eight litres of fresh water drawn from the pipe inserted into the crumbling strata of the hill below Keet Seel. The cliff village was folded again in its past. We met nobody and no animals, only a dark-brown coyote turd beside the track near camp, and in the fine sand beside the stump fence a hollow made by a pad and the blunt prints of digits — perhaps a cougar? From a side canyon a crash resounded and echoed — rockfall? or a wild sheep dropping to its death? Our senses were stretching to touch the life of the place. It was withdrawing from us. The time here seemed to have lasted days, not a mere sunlit and moonlit eighteen hours.

Already the head of the canyon — I almost wrote 'glen' or 'dale' — is curling round my mind like a homeland known from some hybrid of dream and childhood and forebears' childhoods, retold at so many removes that it has composted into legend. I would dearly love to go back there — of course I won't. In any case, my nostalgia for it, already irreversible, was probably inherent. Keet Seel was found by migrants, built up, farmed, and worshipped-in for a handful of generations, left in favour of lands that brought no security, that were invaded, wasted, overrun. It was daunting to think that we were now going out into the lands where the Indian cultures met their Culloden and their Clearances at the hands of the new Americans. Already Keet Seel was becoming another epitome of all those places which historic tides have sluiced through, scoured, and left lying, their old life fixed as a stark exhibit in the world's museum.

The sandstone bounds of this place, its sun-trap hemmed by glowing uprights, its ever-pulsing river, both wellspring and cascade, its groves of oak that mutter in the convection breezes — these are not tragic. They are a perfect piece of nature, and it is confirming simply to know that they are there.

3   Disenchanted Mesas

Our goal was now the mesa of El Morro in Zuni country west of Albuquerque, with Inscription Rock at its base — a stone logbook incised by every sort of visitor from the Conquistadores of the sixteenth century to the soldiers and road- and rail-builders of the nineteenth. Zuni, the fabled Cibola of Spanish times, had engendered every kind of greedy and romantic fantasy in the friars, free-booters and commanders who arrived with the white invasions. The Spaniards had come in from the south by forking eastward from the Camino Real, near what is now the Mexican border south of Tombstone. We were approaching it by a big curve through northern Arizona. Our landmarks were the red buttes and pillars of Monument Valley, the lonely Anasazi outpost at Hovenweep, a little north of Four Corners, Sleeping Ute Mountain, and the long drag south where the map runs out of names between Farmington and Grants.

In Monument Valley the single giant rocks, whether they were tall upstanders or long carcasses, had so much presence that they effortlessly came into their own, displacing all those images from the Marlboro adverts and the John Wayne films. Wayne had taken a fall already in the concourse at Phoenix Airport. As we walked past the door of the Wild West Best Boutique, a life-size cut-out of the 'King' keeled slowly over and clattered to the ground. A black man in a beige linen suit, himself both taller and more beautiful than the movie star, had knocked him over and was trying to stand him up again, looking round with a sheepish grin to see if anyone had noticed.

The names given to the great red rocks of the west by the white pioneers are on the whole unimaginative and unsuitable — Courthouse Rock, Coffee Pot Rock, Hen and Chicken, Monument itself. The Navajo names embody stories or show how sharply a people without maps had to focus their landmarks among these undulating plains: White Ash-streak Mountain, for example, or the butte called 'White-lines-inside-rock', describing its sunlit inner faces; Rock of Wool 'where Black-god threw a buckskin over the rock to scrape off the hair' and tanned his elk and buffalo skins; and the simple Standing-rock, in the branch of Monument Valley called Valley of the Gods, which Talking-god left behind like a pupa case when he tired of the world and took off in spirit form 'so that now he can be everywhere at the same time'.

This fifty-metre spire, like all the others, stands there saying — the world is millennially old. It is their stature above the scrubby plain; their sedimentary layering, the equivalent of the rings in a tree-trunk; their distant likeness to historical monuments, Greek temple pillars or the colossal carved stone kings of ninth-century Ceylon; or any other upholder of the world. Hours later, 90 kilometres east-north-east near

Montezuma Creek, we looked back west for one last time and caught sight of the Monument Valley buttes, towering silhouettes at the end of a vista roofed with blue-black clouds. What a visionary portal for the pioneers! They were caught between terror at what lay beyond and avidity for its fruits. Would there be still more sweltering heat? or less fitful rivers? or richer lodes of gold? What a sign for the tribes! Among the Dakota Sioux, for example, you could become a heyoka, a wizard or sacred fool, only if you had had a sight of 'the thunderbeings of the west'.

After these revelations it was a matter of putting our heads down and many, many miles behind us. Beyond low hills orange plumes flared — burn-off from the natural gas fields. On their slopes the drill-arms of little oil wells nodded and rose again, nodded and rose — exactly the 'melancholy mad elephants' of Dickens's phrase for the power-looms, only these ones had their trunks deep in the oil-rich strata, sucking at America. All over this terrain the fruitless and leafless land at least bore minerals. Both here and in Nevada it was eye-opening to see how the legendary drive to strike gold or silver lives on so long after the glory days. Down hundreds of dirt roads single caravans and pick-ups roosted beside a small rig, a derrick or the head-gear of a drill. Claims are still staked, the law still makes it easy for a single prospector to burrow into the rock and extract what he will. In Barstow John Harper's eyes still glistened as he talked about the biggest nugget he'd ever found and pointed out the dusty wooden skeletons of the dry-shakers which hopeful miners had used to winnow out the pay-dirt.

Meanwhile the older powers lay dormant. Sleeping Ute Mountain was a recumbent giant, blue limbs loosely dressed in shreds of cottony cloud, known in one Navajo story as Sisnaajiní, the peak raised by the First Man and the First Woman 'where the water flowing from the fourth world gathered' to mark the cardinal east point.

The Ute Mountain Reservation, the Jicarilla Apache Reservation over towards Los Alamos, the Navajo reservation down whose eastern flank we drove between Farmington and Crownpoint looked like the drabbest terrain in the world. If there could be a place with no land-marks, this was it. For 95 kilometres the road is called the Vietnam Veterans' Memorial Way. Perhaps it was twinned with a tract of the jungle which the U.S. Air Force wiped out with their defoliants.

Across the greys and buffs of these barrens, dirt roads led off to mission after mission. Who worships there — prospectors maddened by failure to strike lucky? neighbourless farmers? hungover Indians sick with alcohol? In Crownpoint we parked at a mall called T'iists'oozi, among Chevrolet pick-ups plastered from windscreen to grille with pale ochre mud. We bought lunch at Basha's Bakery and Deli. Everyone in there was Navajo, walking slowly about in T-shirts, jeans, and trainers, vastly overweight from early teenage onwards. The bakery counter was laden with iced cakes and buns in every chemical hue of poison-green and carmine. There were even bright blue buns, which seemed grotesque until I found out that the traditional piki-bread was coloured blue by the wood-ash in which it was baked. Donald was chuffed because he'd found some cholesterol-free New York flatbread, onion flavour. They seemed like what would happen if you poured thin soup on to the beige desert anywhere between here and Farmington, let it harden, and split it off in flakes.

Munching steadily, we moved on south to the less forlorn and more arterial country where every thoroughfare passes along the 35th Parallel — the old 66 (now nostalgically celebrated in restaurants and window displays), the Santa Fe railroad, and the ancient trailway by which groups of Sinagua, for example, migrated east to settle near the Zuni Mountains when the great drought, and possibly the raids of the Shoshone, drove them out of the Colorado basin.

Cortes, Guzman, Coronado and the other Spanish adventurers made for Cibola/Zuni from the south. In a sense their people had been questing towards it for 400 years, ever since 'seven bishops' escaped from the Moors in Merida (Spain) in 1150 A.D., fled across the 'western ocean', and landed on 'the blessed isles' where the Seven Golden Cities of Cibola glittered with allure. In 1539 a Franciscan priest called Fray Marcos de Niza set out to look for Cibola, guided by a black slave called Estevan who had escaped from the Mariames Indians. He was killed by some Zuni people while he was scouting and lives on in their oral history as 'a large man with chilli lips'. He seems to have pleased his employers by talking up the Seven Cities, which he said were 'decorated with turquoise' with 'houses of stone and lime'. Back in Mexico Fray Marcos wound his people in still deeper by claiming to have seen Cibola, 'the best and largest of all those that have been discovered . . . larger than the city of Mexico'.

So the great *entrada* was set in motion. As the Zuni remember it, 'they came back, these Black Mexicans, and with them many men of Sonora. They wore coats of iron, and war bonnets of metal, and carried for weapons short canes that spat fire and made thunder, so said our ancients, but they were guns, you know. They frightened our bad-tempered fathers so badly that their hands hung down by their sides like the hands of women. And this time these black, curly-bearded people drove our ancients about like slave creatures.'

Coronado came to Zuni with 800 soldiers, 500 war horses and 1,000 baggage animals. The 'meagre reality' he found consisted of some 'small mud towns, without gold and with very little turquoise, none of which encrusted the buildings'. Having found 'nothing', they destroyed the pueblo of Hawikuh (just south of the present Zuni) and emptied the pueblo of Tiquex (near the present Albuquerque) of its corn, salt, meat, and finally people. He ravaged on eastward, lured by stories of places where people ate off gold plates and the chief slept in the afternoon under a great tree hung with golden bells. He found 'nothing' again (that is, no gold) among the nomads called the Querechos and the Tejas (origin of Texas) and straggled finally back down the Rio Grande into Mexico, starving and disgraced. So horses, cattle, guns, and the Bible entered the lives of the Navajo and the Zuni.

Acoma, touristically named Sky City, may be the oldest continuously inhabited settlement in North America. People have lived on this cliff-sided mesa for more than six hundred, perhaps for a thousand years. We drove towards it through desert scrub — too fast. I had reached 63 m.p.h., forgetting the Reservation speed limit of 50. A young Indian policeman of the Acoma Pueblo flagged me down and fined me $30.

'I hate to do this to you,' he kept saying. 'I've only been back in this job for a week.'

'It's okay,' I assured him, 'I don't mind at all. It's no more than I deserve.'

Great stubs of a greyish stone began to rear from the plain and we saw Acoma, with a dirt track climbing steeply to its flat top between knuckles and buttresses of heavily faulted rock. We had to park here and be driven up in a minibus. To our left the Old Trail with its steps hewn from the mother-rock twisted upward through the entrails of the cliff. Up above, the life of the village was on display. Our guide was an Acoma called Randy, a non-stop comedian with a lean expressionless face. He led us like the Pied Piper through a maze of streets, floored with hard clay and naked rock, puddled by the last two days' heavy showers. Pick-ups and cars of all sizes were wedged higgledy-piggledy between flat-roofed, shabby houses with insect screens at doors and windows. At one house he rounded up a dozen of us and talked us into buying tamales and spicy unleavened fry-bread for a dollar apiece, handed out from the kitchen door by a workworn woman of middle age. Household after household offered pottery or jewellery, often from the hands of the craftspeople themselves — finely finished work in the angular shapes and desert colours (terra cotta, evening-sky blue, sandstone brown) which are the uncorrupted style all over Navajo and Zuni land.

Everyone was good-humoured and embarrassed. No photography is allowed, and rightly so, though we may be glad that a few images survive from early this century. Randy's own family were sitting on chairs outside their door, with set brilliant smiles, all ready to be shaken by the hand. Gaggles of teenage lads went past 'ignoring' us, heads down, nudging and grinning at each other. Randy explained that a rooster-pulling festival was happening today — Santiago Day.

'They hang up a rooster,' he explained, 'and pull it apart. The Christians sacrificed the Lamb, we pull the rooster. The Spaniards introduced us to that. It was either that, or bull-fighting, or chicken-juggling.'

A crowd of two hundred, mostly young, were seething from street to street while people on the roofs threw down items from crates of groceries — Jello candy bars, packs of biscuits — and shouted out names. When they called 'Peter', all the Peters in the crowd below were entitled to grab for a prize. Later I found a forerunner of this in Bandelier's novel *The Delight Makers*, set among the Queres of Tyuonyi Canyon west of Santa Fe, where the sacred fools, with corn-husk topknots and white body make-up, frolic through the streets of the pueblo and 'The people on the terraced roofs exhibit their joy by showering down corn-cakes from their perches.'

Randy's compulsive joking kept us at arm's length. Holding up a two-necked pot, he said, 'This is the wedding vase. The husband and wife drink out of a spout each. Not at the same time . . . Then when they divorce, they tear it in two . . . I'm just kidding. If only it were that easy . . . '

The unease of being a 'native' on show was sharpened when he said in answer to a question, 'No, I can't speak Acoma. I'm one of the lost generation.'

He was alluding to Indians of the sixties and seventies who were settled in the cities under an assimilation policy which came to grief and was replaced by the new policy of maintaining Indian life-styles. Randy's sense of Acoma's history was forthright and unflinching. 'In the Pueblo revolt,' he told us, 'the children were taken to Mexico as slaves. The men had one leg cut off, then they went into lifelong servitude.' This piercing item telescoped the whole bloodstained

The Old Acoma Trail (c. 1909)

history of the Acomans, who were leaders in defying Spanish rule from their seemingly impregnable stronghold on the rock.

The decisive Pueblo revolt took place in the summer of 1680. A knotted cord was passed from settlement to settlement, through the lands of the Navajo, Apache, Zuni, and the pueblos proper, signalling that the time had come at last to rise against the *castillos* who had been enslaving Indian women and children, commandeering food, whipping people to Mass and executing them for 'devil worship' in their kivas. Now they turned against the Roman Catholic Church, repudiated baptism and reclaimed their own names, buried the bells and crucifixes, and washed themselves in soapweed baths to cleanse the 'stains' of baptism.

Resistance was splintered by inter-tribal wars. Then, at a conference near Acoma, an anti-Spanish alliance was forged. The Spanish armies were relentless and by the middle 1690s the Zuni were besieged on their sacred mesa, Towayalane, the Corn Mountain. In 1696 five men were captured and executed at Acoma, which had become the head-quarters of the Navajo–Pueblo alliance. This was the culmination of a century's resistance there. They had fought with a Spanish expedition travelling with slaves from Zuni to the Rio Grande in 1583. In 1598 their revolt against merciless plundering brought down on them the retribution Randy had touched on. A Spanish patrol was surrounded in the village: eleven were killed, four escaped by jumping off the cliffs. In retaliation a force of seventy marched to the mesa and called on it to surrender. The Acoma replied with 'wild and insulting derision, all the Acomans and hundreds of Navajo allies dancing and shrieking defiance from the top of their impregnable cliffs'.

After two days of fighting the Spaniards reached the mesa top and slaughtered the people with 200 shots fired from a pair of cannon. In all 800 were killed; prisoners were cut to pieces and their limbs thrown down the rockface. Both the inherited oral evidence and a blank-verse poem written by a Spaniard soon after the siege record that women clutching children jumped over the cliff (150 metres at its highest) or into the flames of its houses.

The Acoma, along with the other pueblo peoples, were feeling the force of a drive to transform their culture to the root. In the madness of the massacre people who had been driven to Mass on pain of torture believed that they saw St Paul fighting for the Spaniards. The following month, having been tried and found guilty of 'failure to submit peace-fully', all males over 25 years of age were condemned to have one foot cut off and to be enslaved for 25 years. Girls under 12 were to be 'distributed in this kingdom or elsewhere'. Two Hopi were sent home with their right hands chopped off as a warning to their tribe. Sixty girls were sent to the Viceroy of Mexico for placing in convents.

Still, Acoma lives, its unquenchable character expressed now in the vigour and practicality of its crafts and its tourist industry, in Randy's flow of satire, in the supple pride which allowed us to walk its streets and view its people but not to take their photographs. Even that punitive religion has been partially accepted and lives in the bleak yet handsome adobe church with its curtain wall and its two blunt towers — although, as Randy pointed out, 'The padre lives down below, with his colour TV and his fax machine.' Inside there are no saints, no Stations of the Cross. On the walls are painted — awkwardly, with none of the Indians' usual mastery — the basic native emblems, a stalk of maize growing under a rainbow, a sun, a moon both crescent and full, a single star. Outside is a terrace where 'we put the dead people in blankets, four feet down'.

From this bumpy graveyard, without stones or any other memorials, we looked across the plain to the yellow buttresses and sheer faces of Kadzima — Enchanted Mesa. It seemed inaccessible and uninhabitable. It houses a story which epitomises the Acoman sense that these great rocks of theirs were both trap and refuge. Kadzima was inhabited by ancestral Acomas. One day the people were cultivating the fields in the valley when a violent rainstorm broke out. It washed away the access to the mesa, leaving a young girl and her grandmother stranded on top. Rather than die of starvation, the two leaped off its cliffs.

4 Inscription Rock to Corn Mountain

We travelled westward to El Morro and Zuni not by Interstate 40 but by a much older route that curled round the eastern end of the Zuni Mountains, through glades of pine and juniper. This was the way a detachment of Coronado's headed east for Acoma and the Rio Grande; the way the Espeje expedition of 1583 — first contact between Spaniards and Navajo — made for Mount Taylor, the sacred mountain of the Navajo; the way the emigrant trains along the 35th Parallel struggled west towards California in the 1850s; the way the Union Pacific planned to drive a railroad until it was beaten to the draw by the Atcheson Topeka and Santa Fe 40 kilometres to the north. 'The explorers followed main trails beaten by many generations of Indian travel . . . as direct as the terrain, the need of food and drink en route, and reasonable security permitted . . . The Spanish and American explorers reconnoitred an Indian country, with Indian guides, between Indian settlements . . . Footpaths and pack trails rarely differ.' It was nice to think, as our tarmac path unwound between the shady clumps of conifers, that this still held good.

At first El Morro (the Nose) showed as a low, bright reef. Slowly it stood up to its full height, a stockade of towering metallic uprights, pale gold and tarnished silver. A beautiful waterhole on the south side makes the marrow of the place. This sunlit face has been water-sculpted into crannies, clefts, funnel-mouthed holes — I wanted to stretch out my eyes on stalks and reach them into the sinuses and canals of this bony head. Its sockets wept continuously. From some supply, sixty or seventy metres above us, enough moisture was oozing down the rockface to make a stripe black as a raven's wing which glistened in the noon-time glare. It stretched down from a curved notch up on the rim — the spout, presumably, of a rain-fed pool. It broadened between sheer faces of palest pink and roseate bronze till it was five metres wide, disappeared behind a crotch formed by white converging limbs and issued in an oval of opaque Nile-green water ten metres long and five across. I might have scooped up a handful and drunk it — dogged, it's true, by worries about amoebic dysentery, Bilharzia, liver fluke — had not the inevitable metal fencing held me back.

It was not the original waterhole exactly. (Why does one so often arrive just too late?) In 1942 a rockfall destroyed it and it had to be banked up again and lined with cement. The fluid surface, its mingling greens, the depth suggested by the reflected shadow of the overhang behind it — all these lave the mind, assuring you that there is relief available from deathly parching in this land of shrunken streams, seasonally vanishing lakes, major rivers that run out in salt sumps.

El Morro would have been wonderfully visible and glamorous, intrinsically satisfying to arrive at after gruelling journeys. Practically, its importance was in its water. In these deserts, and even more acutely in Australia later on, I came to see that what the great rocks in the weary land afforded above all was the water they concentrated, in natural ponds on their tops, sometimes improved by dwellers there, and in the run-off which streams from them, drilling and then filling hollows in the soil around their feet.

The pale gold rockface that stretched away to our right, so plane that it attracted the scratching and chiselling of travellers, is Zuni sandstone, made from the grains deposited by rivers 140 million years ago and heaped into dunes by hot winds. Above it is layered the darker Dakota sandstone made 60 million years ago from the beaches of an ocean. During the last few million years, while the Zuni mountains were buckling up to their present height, urged by the earth's plates, more than 3,000 metres of sedimentary rock were worn away by floodwater, leaving the strongpoints of El Morro and the neighbouring mesas to stand up as isolated reefs. The erosion is still going on even in our calmer epoch. The petroglyphs here (hands, zigzags, 'rainbows') tend to be higher than the autographs of Spanish and American incomers because the ground has been worn away by the boots and hooves of those who came to drink. It has shrunk a good two metres down the rockface since the early Indians built the village on top, which the Zuni call A'ts'inna (Writing-on-rock).

The later writings made history rise into visibility under our eyes with the magical effect of images developing on photographic paper. Here was Ramon Garcia Jurado, like ourselves *'paso por aquy para Suni'*, passed by here on the way to Zuni on 21 June 1709; he was the Alcalde Mayor of Keres south of Santa Fe. Here were 'Williamson', 'Holland', and 'John Udell', 1858; they were members of the first emigrant train to try this new route to California. Further west they survived an attack by Mohave, retreated starving to Albuquerque, and made it through to Sacramento the following year in the company of Lieutenant Edward Beal, who was testing a team of 25 camels for use in expeditions against the Navajo. A gentleman called Long from Baltimore cut his autograph in immaculate copperplate. Ramon Jurado added random curlicues and a logo like a wine-press. One Lujan carved hastily in a jagged shorthand: *'Se pazz[aron] d[e] m[arzo] de 1632 A[nos] a la Bengsa* [i.e. *venganza*] *del P[adr]e Letrado'* — 'They passed on the 23rd of March 1632 to avenge the death of Father Letrado', flanked by a crucifix like a child's drawing of a pylon. The priest was transferred from Salinas (Albuquerque) to Zuni in the February and killed a week later.

Now the implications of these messages were making my back shiver. The oldest, on a natural plaque sheltered by a shallow slanting overhang plastered with derelict wasps' nests, read: *'paso por aqui el edentalado don ju[an] onate del descubrimiento de la mar del 16 abril de 1605'*, in a homely scrawl interrupted by a kind of geometrical doodle: 'Governor Don Juan de Oñate passed by here from the discovery of the Sea of the South [the Gulf of California] on 16 April 1605.' Don Juan, direct descendant of Cortes and Moctezuma, son of the discoverer of the great Zacatecas silver mines, had come this way before, in the summer of 1598, on his expedition to claim New Mexico for Spain and Christ. The day he blessed the region in the name of San Juan Bautista, heavy rain fell, ending a disastrous drought. He persuaded the pueblo Indians that this was a sign. In December the Acoma rose in revolt while Oñate's favourite nephew was requisitioning supplies, and killed him. Two months later the dead man's brother organised the massacre I have described above.

On the top of El Morro the sort of peace reigned that suffuses settlements so ancient that their troubles, and for that matter their glory days, have been lost to sight. We reached it by a stony way up the north face, past a huge half-separated buttress whose angular snout seemed to be pecking at the mother-rock like a Cubist dinosaur. The summit was another world, all on the same contour but faulted into hummocks and gullies by the pressure of the younger sandstone that buried it 60 million years ago. On the most level tract, between 1100 and 1300 A.D., more than a thousand Anasazi lived in more than eight hundred close-built rooms. A few that have been excavated show their walls of trim blocks and flagstone floors, some with circular fireplaces rimmed with neatly-dressed stone. At 2,300 metres above sea level, the short growing season must have made survival hard. As the climate cooled and dried in the middle of the thirteenth century, the people moved forty kilometres west, by the route we would be taking, to the lower and more fertile land where Zuni is now.

If we had not met Virgil Babilu there, we might have been as disappointed as Coronado was by the 'small mud towns' of fabled Cibola. Today the settlement has back streets floored with mud, although a good many of the houses are built of quarried stone. More people were hanging about in the yards and alleys than you would expect in the middle of a working day. It had the slack water feel of the reservations (creepy bureaucratic word) where the economy is dependent, not thriving or self-sufficient. We were introduced to Virgil (now a councillor for alcoholics) by Wally Davidson, photographer from Albuquerque. Virgil welcomed us to his brother's house, which was the picture of a neat working-class home with its shiny furniture, displays of sports trophies and souvenirs on every surface. The conversation faltered at first, sticky with a sense of 'white man meets friendly Indian' and Wally's palpable anxiety that it should work out.

As we stood at the door drinking Budweiser from cans, I said to Virgil, 'What do you call that mountain?' — a resplendent red-and-white massif towering out of the plain a few miles south.

46

'Towaya'lane,' he said.

'Has that got a meaning?' He made no reply to this foolish question. Thinking of the Valley of the Gods and Standing-rock, I tried again: 'Have the rocks got a life of their own?'

'No-o-o,' he said, then told me at once about the twin pillars, storeyed in red and white, which stood up on the brow of Towaya'lane. 'When the big ol' flood came,' he said, 'it drove the Zuni people up to the top of that mountain. They sought their refuges there. So then they chose a boy and a girl, and they dressed them in their ceremonial clothes, and gave them prayer sticks, and they walked into the waters. And when the waters subsided, the pillars were there.'

Like a stone rolled away from a cave-mouth, a path had opened through to the imagination of this place and its people. The twin pillars are perpetual beacons, bound by their salience and their beauty to be as potent for the Zuni as the white cliffs of Dover for the English or Gibraltar for the Phoenicians and later the Spaniards. I asked Virgil if we could get nearer them, perhaps climb up to them. His brother's pick-up was available. We put in $5 worth of petrol and drove off south down a tarmac road before turning off on to dirt tracks. At last we were stopped by a channel cut deeply into the pink sand by the summer's heavy rains.

The mesa from the west was a colossal front of sandstone, marbled white and rufous like the finest beef. The girl and the boy were the southerly high-point of a crenellated castle jutting from its north-west corner. We climbed towards them between dusty moraines and masses of rock the colour of ox-tongue, through a wild garden of sword-leafed yucca, cushions and clumps of cactus, and aromatic maquis.

As the girl and the boy speared up into the glaring blue above us, I asked Virgil, 'Do you know which is the boy and which is the girl?'

'She is the girl,' he answered at once, pointing to the southerly figure. 'That is her *ma'ta'ta* — her woollen skirt.' The glacis of the pillar was a spreading apron, angled at perhaps 80°, scored vertically with barely-divergent grooves and striated horizontally to make a tartan of rose-red and white.

The four of us were rising more steeply now, rounding the base of the figures, climbing the slabs behind them. On our right the massif hollowed in a broad bay, far bigger than any British corrie or combe. The rampart at its foot was silvery Zuni sandstone, its vertical curtain-wall was red layered thinly with white, its rim a shallow stratum of pale-brown humus fledged with scrub.

47

'As you can see,' said Virgil, pointing at this 'tide-mark', 'the big ol' flood reached nearly to the top. They took all their animals up there and they had to live there for a while, atop the mesa. There are still a few deer there.'

He was forging unhesitatingly up the slabs, sure of the route and of the friction under his trainers. I would have had no idea of his age — he had four children — from his shock of dense black hair, his firm brown skin and muscular games-player's calves. Donald and Wally were growing more dubious by the minute, staring around in wonderment at the magnificent building of the cliffs, silently appalled at their situation as dreaded gravity sucked at them from behind and below. High above, on our left, the back of the boy was an almost sheer red face broken by one massive flake. Bird-lime whitened its tip, and from it an arrowy chicken-hawk took off and arched above us with quick, troubled wing-beats. Swifts or cliff-swallows fled across with the frictionless speed of stones on ice. To our right the twin shadows of the girl and the boy on the silvery glacis showed topknots like the heads of harlequins.

The slabs levelled out at a white threshold between the pillars and the rest of the 'castle'. It shone like chased metal, as though the entire westerly windstream came rifling through here. Far below us, formations which looked from the approach track like five round-topped grey pillars had become the thighs and knees of Buddhas. The airiness of it all was getting to me, sending my mind soaring straight up out of my skull. I stepped up on to a bulge — the boy's right hipbone — and tested the rufous sandstone for climbing. Almost anywhere it was easy to lift bits out or break bits off. Down on the threshold Virgil waited patiently, knowing the way. I followed him sideways along rippled white bulges, contouring eastward, while Wally and Donald decided it was crazy going on without ropes or gear above a thousand-foot rockslide on to scree and lacerating brush, and settled down to wait for us.

Where were we heading? Virgil said nothing, assuming, obviously, that if you set off up a mountain, what you're making for is the top. We crept crab-wise, feet splayed on a white cornice, palms on a terra cotta face, until we were stopped by a little ravine that cut upwards to the sunlight at an average angle of perhaps 70°. Prickly bushes half blocked it. We clambered round and past them and stared up at the red vee of the cleft as it steepened. I wouldn't have dreamed of going up this without a rope. Virgil didn't pause. He set his feet to the rock on either side and started to bridge upwards on little but friction. The redness glistened. It was a watercourse, still damp. I followed him, perhaps too closely — I was feeling lonely! — until he stopped, just poised, his trainers gripping less firmly than my ripple-soles. Now that the angle was almost prohibitive, man-made holds had appeared on the left, pockets with sides and floors still chisel-sharp though worn by centuries of water-fall. (The first white explorers of Mesa Verde found just the same.) The purchase on them was delicious, nothing could stop us now. We made it out of the shadow of the 'castle' on to a hanging boulder field and left this by what seemed the only way up to the summit plain — a natural rock stair.

Here, as I later discovered, the Zuni retreated to live for the best part of a decade during the last spasms of the Pueblo Revolt. Were the Spaniards the 'big ol' flood' which drove them up into this waterless harbour? Or were the whites only the last of the epic dangers that had beset the tribe? If we believe that a prehistoric flood gave rise to the Noah story in the Middle East, then a similar thing could have happened in America, after humans arrived. The first *entrada*, across the Bering Land Bridge, is now being pushed back more than 120,000 years as older and older artefacts are found round the pluvial lakes of the south-west. We also know that a lake 300 metres deep covered much of western Utah, for example, after the glacial melt of some 10,000 years ago. In any case, the story of the girl and the boy and the big ol' flood need not be so literal. A gender pair with the role of saviours figure in the creation story both in *The Book of the Navajo* and in *Dine'bahane*:

> They tore the robe from Coyote's shoulders and two strange little objects that resembled buffalo calves, but were spotted all over in various colours, dropped out. These were the children of Tie-holtsodi [Chief of the East]. At once the people threw them into the hole through which the waters were pouring and in an instant the waters subsided and rushed back into the lower world with a deafening noise.

The meaning of this might be that the representatives of humanity have pitted themselves against chaos — been sacrificed to it — and so it has been overcome for a time. The dual spirit-sticks are also significant. In a Hopi ritual the initiates are set to make pairs of sticks, beautiful blue-green for the female and black for the male.

So Virgil's story mixed prehistory and history in one vision that glimpsed the range of ordeals inflicted on his people. As we took a twisting route across what looked like a never-inhabited scrubland, crusty sand embedded with big gravel and clumped over by maquis, low juniper, and dwarf pine, he stopped and picked up a shard five millimetres thick, the size of a postage stamp, curved enough to be part of a good-sized pot. Its inside was pure burnt-sienna, its outside grazed and slightly blackened.

'Zuni pottery,' he said as he gave it to me. Did the besieged people carry corn in it, or water, for their long camp up here? After a quarter of an hour's trudge through the scrub, which would have disoriented me had the sun been covered, we reached the eastern rim and looked down at a less sheer, still difficult maze of slopes and bluffs, then south along the face to a family of lesser girls and boys, like chess pieces, standing out from the cliff.

'There was a way up there for the people,' said Virgil. 'I used to run cross-country right round the mesa,' and he gestured to the web of pathways through the scrub 500 metres below. 'I haven't been up here for a few years now.'

He was in no hurry to leave and palpably relished coming back to this historic fastness which was also the playground of his youth. I could have stayed here indefinitely. We were at the hub. The rim of the horizon, oil-blue under a few shoals of fair-weather cumulus, wheeled round us in a slowed motion that spun the mind out, out from the present to the future and the past simultaneously. No wonder this mountain was their sacred centre and figured prominently in their solar observations, particularly the sun's movement along the horizon and the moon's appearance at the winter solstice, when the sun 'turned around', the New Year began, and their ceremonial cycle started again. Once more I was *seeing distance*, and it brought tears to my eyes, tears of realisation, not of sadness. We were seeing, as you cannot among the dales and hills of western Europe, the extent of the planet itself.

The pioneers felt this. Jesse Applegate, leader of a wagon train from Minnesota to Oregon in 1843, was still full of it thirty years later. 'Though everything is dwarfed by distance,' he wrote, 'it is seen distinctly . . . It is with the hunters we shall briskly canter toward the bold but smooth and grassy bluffs that bound the broad valley . . . [How to convey] the vast extent and grandeur of the picture and the rare beauty and distinctness of the detail?' These great levels, with the slightly younger but still ancient levels present in the table-tops of the mesas, say to you, Here is what there is for you to live on. Make your ways over it. Your own time and your own space are fractions. You may get a lodgement somewhere beyond that skyline or you may not. It is Lawrence's vision through Tom Brangwen's eyes at his step-daughter's marriage in *The Rainbow*:

> He felt himself tiny, a little, upright figure on a plain circled round with the immense, roaring sky: he and his wife, two little, upright figures walking across this plain, whilst the heavens shimmered and roared about them. When did this come to an end? In which direction was it finished? There was no end, no finish, only this roaring vast space. Did one never get old, never die? That was the clue. He exulted strangely, with torture. He would go on with his wife, he and she like two children camping in the plains. What was sure but the endless sky? But that was so sure, so boundless.

The way down was difficult. Frankly, we lost it, and that was good too because I was in no hurry to lose sight of that mind-expanding distance. When we got back to the western rim, we took a different way down to the boulder field and then to the level of the serious rock. We padded uneasily down gullies that led to impasses, we contoured then crept downward a little further. I was still assuming that Virgil was my infallible guide. He seemed to feel that nothing could stop us. It nearly did.

We were above a drop of unknown depth. The narrow terraces on either side ran out in impassable ravines. Virgil crept down a foot or two, leant forward, peered over and announced, 'We must jump here,' and went for it. A thump from below, then his voice from out of sight, 'It is alright.'

He had proved that it was, but I now felt as hatefully abandoned as I do when my partner on a difficult rock-climb has disappeared round a corner or beyond an overhang. There was nothing else for it. I eased downward on my backside. My rucksack was forcing me horribly out and therefore down. Virgil's face came into sight, unsmiling. At least he had waited. The drop looked like four metres on to a narrow white balcony with a rounded outer lip and the stony scrubland far below. I knew that waiting, sometimes called 'plucking up your courage', actually drains away your nerve. So I jumped. The rock came up and banged against my feet, and I trotted forward a pace or two in case a sudden stop should tip me forward uncontrollably. Virgil's hands were ready to hold on to me if need be — who would have held him? Thank god that's over.

Then we had to contour some more and do it all over again. At last we could sidle down an area of white slab and walk along to rejoin

Donald and Wally with tingling feet, lightheaded with the joy of the heights, which would last for days.

5   Holes of Emergence

Tapping into Wally the photographer's local knowledge had worked so well for Zuni that I now let him guide us north via Santa Fe to a range of rocks I had never heard of, the Bandelier National Monument. Along with a later episode at the rim of Canyon de Chellay, this gave us the wherewithal to imagine these places in their heyday. It showed they had lived. The present sun-dried and wind-scoured vacancy was only an eerie aftermath.

The way up the Rio Grande to the 'medieval' town of Tyuonyi in Frijoles Canyon [Canyon of the Beans] wound through an America of the present, even of the future. There below us as we drove by on the overpass was Santa Fe, expensive centre of Western style, designer fusions of ranch and pueblo, houses handsomely combining timbered patios with concrete curved and reddened to simulate adobe. Wally from Albuquerque was bristling at the thought of all this prestige, and Los Alamos of the scientists, hidden among forested hills, irked him still more.

'These people,' he kept saying, 'they have a different language. You can't speak to them.'

All we saw of the famous Faustian place, nerve centre of the nuclear culture, where the deadly bomb had been first conjured up, was a broad saucer made of whitish alloy in a glade among pines near the road west to Bandelier. It was watching the sun. As we drove past at noon it was facing south. By the end of the afternoon it had turned to look westward.

The road was of a beautifully graded smoothness we found nowhere else in the desert states — clearly nuclear physics, or call it the weapons industry, attracts money. Down in the canyon we walked among the remains of a much earlier affluence, created by Anasazi who had migrated south and east from the Four Corners in the middle of the twelfth century. In Chaucer's time they were rising towards a peak, building pueblos near each other with more than a thousand rooms. By Shakespeare's time, when the Spaniards arrived, Frijoles Canyon was deserted.

By as weird a coincidence as I ever met, the start of the trail passed a rock-wall on which erosion of the surface has left in bas relief a mushroom with a khaki cap and an oatmeal stem, almost exactly the shape of the atomic cloud. Once past this spook we were strolling along a wooded vale whose goodness was palpable. The Rito de los Frijoles which waters it never fails. Stands of broad-leaf trees rose high between walls of yellowish tufa, so soft it must have been easy to dig out and shape with axes of harder stone. A million years ago a volcano 20 kilometres to the north-west erupted twice, each time with six hundred times more force than Mount St Helens. The ash built to a depth of 300 metres and then compacted into a stonelike custard petrified.

The rock-walls were a fantasy of holes as riddled as the tufa spires in Turkish Cappadokia. Round mouths in inaccessible places showed where bubbles of trapped gas burst. Square holes lower down were the doorways of dwellings and storerooms. Rows of neat holes at a little above head height, running along the cliff of the left bank for 250 metres, were the sockets of log joists for a street of houses, a condominium. It is an architecture which makes our way of building up all four walls from masoned stones or bricks seem inconvenient and thriftless.

The supremely fascinating holes are in the floors of the kivas — the sacred buildings used by males only for ceremonial weaving, the instructing of initiates, and so on. I first saw one of these at Keet Seel — a sunken circular area with a smoke vent in the wall and a stone deflector slab in front of it. Near the middle of the floor was a cake of adobe on a base of sandstone, rounded at edges and corners, with a black hole perhaps 15cms in diameter at its centre. Here was another in the big kiva at Tyuonyi, next to a village of some four hundred rooms round a circular plaza. In the ceremonial cave fifty metres up the cliff and two kilometres up the valley we found another in a deep pit kiva which we had to climb into by means of a wooden ladder.

These *si'pa'pu's* were modern reconstructions in terra cotta adobe, smoothed with the inside of the hand. Nothing could detract from their symbolic potency. They absolutely drew my eyes to them, these dense black nothings, which had no prior meaning for me. No cultural meaning, that is. I had delighted in them in sculptures of Henry Moore's: Moore said, 'A hole can have as much meaning as a solid mass — there is a mystery in a hole in a cliff or hillside, in its depth and shape.' Andy Goldsworthy has taken the experience further by making holes not through figures but in the surface of the land — in orange earth, in peat, between the roots of a sycamore, in art gallery floors, and (most like the *si'pa'pu's*) in a tilted flag of rufous sandstone. All these can be seen, like a sequence of poems with a mesh of meanings, in *Hand to Earth*, where he says, 'The black of a hole is like the flame of a fire . . . I am drawn to them with the same urge I have to look over a cliff edge.'

What these artists are drawing on is our impulse to imagine through from our present state to another one, from here to there and by implication from present to past or future. Looking into that black focus, we know there is 'nothing' down there — a foot or two of inert air, smelling of earth, mildew, cement, then packed subsoil with, again, 'nothing' in it, quite possibly no bones, nor fossils, nor dormant seeds. It remains magnetic for what it represents — unknown otherness, a space to which we can only just relate because there are no bearings for us through there, no sense of points to be steered by or touched. Still it draws us; we feel our being draining into that sump. I remember reaching such a place at the end of a pitch called Millipede Crawl, in the cave-system called Southerscales Pot below Ingleborough. The tunnel ended in a circular well whose depth I didn't know. The perfectly still black roundness of the water-surface was wonderfully final and devoid of qualities — nothingness become actual. Or it is the pupil of the eye, opening into the thinking brain. Or it is the polar opposite of the sun, lightless and hollow instead of the dense fire that keeps us alive. It is certainly the opposite of rock, penetrable not resistant, impalpable not hard.

In Tolstoy's story *The Death of Ivan Illich*, the dying civil servant sees what is coming as a 'black hole' or 'narrow, deep black sack into which he is being forced, extinguishing him'. Years before I read this marvellously true tale I had come to see death as my self poised in black space, space yawning all around and myself without wings or supports or powers of any kind — a moment's terror — then nothing. This too is in the black focus. In the Indians' conception it is by no means the end, it is the source. It is called the Hole of Emergence. In the Navajo creation story the third phase of genesis goes like this:

> [The people] circled upward until they reached the smooth, hard shell of the sky overhead. When they could go no higher they looked down and saw that water now covered everything . . .
>
> Suddenly someone with a blue head appeared and called to them:
>
> 'Here,' he called to them.
>
> 'Come this way.'
>
> 'Here to the east there is a hole.'

They found that hole and entered. One by one they filed through to the other side of the sky. And that is how they reached the surface of the second world.

. . . While the first world had been red, this world was blue . . . Each blue house was cone-shaped; each tapered toward the top where there was a blue entry hole.

As the tellers of stories sat in their hogans, their bowies or humpies made of bent-wood and earth, they could see the fire-smoke wafting towards the smoke-hole and the sky beyond. After a death the body was carried out through a hole broken in the wall. In ceremonial rooms in the pueblos a hole in the roof let the sun through on to the floor. At the solstice the people 'pulled down the sun'. The chief pointed upwards with a stone knife and threw pollen towards the roof hole. 'Now the sun drops down on the spot of sunlight on the floor. It is a round object white as cotton, which opens and closes. To this the chief ties the prayer feathers, as all sing. All stand and throw pollen towards the sun object . . . All breathe on their clasped hands. As the chief waves the sun around his head the sun goes back through the roof hole.'

At Hovenweep, during the spring equinox, you can look through a tunnel-mouth in the old cracked adobe wall and see the intense gold spot made by the sun on the opposite wall.

Such apertures were real ways through to another state and provided a richly actual ground for the stories in which Indian peoples imagined their world. Each culture designated a 'specific Emergence Place — usually a small natural spring edged with mossy sandstone and full of cattails and wild watercress'. There was no agreement on 'any single location or natural spring as the one and only true Emergence Place' — there was no Mecca or Jerusalem or Rome. If there had been that kind of unity (or spiritual tyranny), the native Americans might have been a little less incapable of resisting the European invasions. One Navajo medicine man, called Curly Toaxedlini, told a priest how deer came into being as 'people from the Emergence-place who, at the time, had come up with the rest'. Another called Claus Chee Sonny told how the deer emerged at Fish Point south-west of Chinle (our next goal): 'An entrance hole is there. It is the door to the ancients. Just as we have doors to our houses, so this door is draped shut. Through it the deer entered a long cavern which leads to the place — the inside of the Black-god's house — from which they had been released. So their sojourn on the surface makes a complete circle.' So it was with the Cherokee and the Iroquois, the Shoshone and the Beaver. Such were the beliefs which the Franciscan friars wanted to root out as 'devil worship'.

Everything original is in the image and the reality of the hole — the pelvic arch, the openings of the vagina and the penis, the belly-button, the womb, the wellspring or waterhole, the split in the seed from which radical and plumule feel outwards. The Emergence Hole is able to be a metaphor for all essentials, including the source of the race or species. 'Indians generally deny that their forebears crossed a land bridge from Asia. "Our ancestors came out of this very ground," they will say, and discourse on this theme with eloquence.' Navajo who bathe in the sweat house (a hogan with no smoke-hole) assure themselves of belonging in the world by singing a verse which goes,

> He put it down. He put it down.
> First Man put down the sweat house.
> On the edge of the hole where they came up,
> He put down the Son of the She Dark.
> He built it of valuable soft materials.
> Everlasting and peaceful he put it there.
>> He put it there.

If such assurance were lacking, if a group were demoralised, then 'the return passage through the emergence hole [was] known only to specialists of the rituals [and] many Navajo survivors in successive generations have found it advisable to turn their own homes over to the dead and build new ones for themselves from the materials they can find locally'. A few weeks later I came across the same practice at Uluru in the bush beside Ayers Rock.

After walking for half an hour beside the clear current of the Rito de los Frijoles, in a dapple of light filtered through the leafage of Gambel oaks, between vanilla-smelling trunks of ponderosa pine, the canyon culminated for us in a climb by stone steps and wooden ladders up the porous yellow flanks of the tufa to the ceremonial cave. At the outer lip of its sandy mouth a reconstructed kiva showed its circular rim of stones with log joists jutting through. Ladder-poles emerged through a hatch in its roof, which was the floor of the cave. Under the ground it was perfectly still and a little humid. High above we could see a pine, sunlit, and shreds of cirrocumulus on the blue. The eye of the *si'pa'pu* looked up from the floor, its black making the deepest shadows seem well-lit and transparent. Once the way back up and out would have been a ladder of three poles, symbolising (as Randy had told us at

Acoma) 'the way to the next life'. When he admitted that only males could take part in the kiva ceremonies, he made one of his wisecracks out of it.

'We-e-ll,' he drawled in a mock aggrieved tone, 'the women have taken over everything *else* — the *house* . . . '

On either side of the cave-mouth, chambers carved out of the rock, with round-topped entrances two metres high made inscrutable dark eyes. Above a pair of them was a row of joist-holes in the rock — perhaps a canopy had been built to make the chambers into twin shrines? I was peering into the past now, trying to make sense of alien things, to see every hole as meaningful — which it must be if it was made at all, or was found and fixed on as some kind of inspiration.

They are still inspiring. The mere name of Window Rock drew us as a place that must be explored, and so we took the short detour north from Highway 40. The Rock had been a special place for the Navajo for its excellent waterhole, and perhaps for the symbol of the shape itself — free-standing arches are called 'rainbows-in-stone'. Now it is the centre of the Navajo nation, which was reconstituted sixty-five years ago at the urging of a white man.

Buttressed cliffs and small buttes of buff sandstone stood up from the semi-desert. Neat prefabricated huts were labelled with names like 'Pensions' and 'Farm Bureau' and 'Speaker's Office'. Was ever a seat of government less like the Palace of Westminster or the Reichstag? Behind, among scrub, trees half-screened a rocky crest and a twisting sandy path headed for the Rock. The window under the bow was perhaps twenty metres in diameter and slightly skewed, so that from one angle it looked circular, from another almost egg-shaped. The glacis below its threshold was salmon, glowing in sunshine. The bow, which was gnarled where gravity, stress, and weather are plucking flakes from it over the millennia, was brown-vermilion like blood dried and bleached. The skyline rose in little peaks like wave-crests turned to stone. That next-world blue shone at us through the window. As we watched and wished we could pass through it, but knew it to be sacrosanct, the eye clouded as though with a cataract. Before we left it was sheer blue again.

6 Hoskee Begay and the Long Walk

As we approached the South Rim of Canyon de Chellay, 250 kilometres east-north-east of Flagstaff, Arizona, we heard the last sound you would expect in this eerily purified world of the preserved 'wilderness'. At Junction Overlook the air was throbbing with engine noise from an invisible source. A helicopter? A generator? The former seemed more likely, on this high plateau where people might get lost among the tracts of scrub and conifer or in the labyrinth of the canyons. The nearer we approached the rim the more the sound seemed to be pumping out of the ground itself, or even from the great cleft whose floor, 300 metres below, snaked off downstream like a long narrow map unfolding towards Chinle.

The floor looked neither wild nor barren. It was chequered with those unmistakable traces of civilisation, straight lines. They looked like old field borders. And maybe not so old — inside each oblong area were broken stripes of green. Even from this eagle-height they looked like crops, struggling with drought perhaps but still alive. As the throb grew louder my eyes homed on its source. A tractor was passing up and down a striped green allotment and behind it the surface rose and fell in short-lived waves. A farmer was tedding hay, still in the sun although the shadow cast by the South Rim, at four in the afternoon, was growing fast towards him. So Navajo people still farmed here, 130 years after their expulsion and the Long Walk 650 kilometres to the concentration camp at Fort Sumner in New Mexico, and 126 years after they were allowed home again.

Further up the North Branch, at Massacre Cave Overlook, is the point where a woman wrestled with a Spanish soldier from Narbona's punitive expedition in 1805 until they both fell down the cliff to their deaths. Bullet marks on the cave walls (invisible from here) show where marksmen tracked down the women, children, and old people hiding there and began the massacre. Agony so scars and stains the history of this place that even the shadow of Spider Rock looked sinister — a pier of darkness stretching across the floor of the eastern branch from a slim sandstone pillar, ending in a double claw. The Navajos' meaning for it is not sinister at all. Although Spider Woman, Tse'itsi'nako, was sometimes used to frighten naughty children, she was in essence a being of inexhaustible wily knowledge, an earth mother, both intimidating and supportive. At the Creation-time she 'thought about it, and everything

58

she thought came into being. First she thought of three sisters for herself, and they helped her to think of the rest of the Universe . . . ' One of her specific powers was fundamental. She taught the Hopi and the Navajo to spin. For them that 'double claw' at the end of the shadow would be the mouth from which the life-preserving filaments first came into the world.

If the Navajo with their heritage of skills and stories had not made it back to their own land and re-established themselves (they are now a 'nation' of 130,000 people, with a community college and a fair income from tourism and mineral royalties), we could not have met Hoskee Begay, who drove us up the canyon from Chinle in a jeep–bus and regaled us with his ideas. He was a massive man, more than six feet tall, with a meaty aquiline nose above a dense black bush of moustache, half walrus half bandido. We never saw his eyes, behind broad shades, or his hair, under a Stetson with a curly brim. He was stylish and his laundered shirt with pink candy-stripes swelled over a noble paunch.

At first he reeled out his commentary in the guide's cadence that hits a top note four syllables into the spiel, then tapers off into a monotone for the rest of the sentence he has uttered a thousand times. As we drove deeper into the great red–walled trench, jokes began to surface with no change of tone.

'As you can see,' he said reassuringly, 'we drive in the river. Sometimes we lose the vehicle inside the canyon.' Pause. 'We save the people. When I go for this job, they say, "You bring back all nineteen, you got the job." I brought 'em back. If the vehicle hit the hole, it may jump high. If you don' like you' friend, push 'im out . . .'

Before he engaged the clutch he had introduced himself. 'My name is — Hoskee Begay. It mean — Strong Talk-too-much.' Now his banter was bristling, testing our capacity for outrage, showing he could do just what he liked; he was in control here. 'One time I spit out, and the wind blow it back in mah friend face. He said it taste good . . . This is the Canyon Muerto — they call it the Canyon Death. I hope you all come back . . . We call the river the Canyon Wash. Not got no name because it ain't always there.' His view of life, and really of us, came into focus as soon as incomers were the topic. A woman fanning herself with a Navajo National Monument leaflet made him say, 'Yeh, *it's* hot. They go out white man, they come back red man. So how we know they come from *California* or not?' — 'California' being stressed to treat it as the Big Apple, or possibly the Gomorrah, of these parts.

He was full of history and of his explanation for it. He wanted to feed it to us in his own good time. As we drove past some cottonwoods whose leaves were shivering in the heated breeze, he said, 'Trees planted this century. Take five thousand gallon of water a day. The Navajo cut them — that's one problem. Three hundred people used to come here, sixty, seventy year ago. Now, four.'

When somebody wondered if anyone had recorded stories of the old time, Hoskee said, 'No. The old guys don' like it; they *live* behind the story, that's why. The rangers ask them what the Navajo think about how the Anasazi disappeared — the Navajo say, Don' know. They don' pay them, that's why. They don' say anything unless they ask.'

This is a mind-set of the invaded and colonised. In the centre of Australia, it turned out, the Aboriginal people feel so pillaged of their stories that some believe we shouldn't even read the books in which anthropologists have set them down, and in California the Cahuilla tribe in the Joshua Tree area use their word for 'coyote' to mean 'anthropologist'.

When Hoskee's questioner stuck to her guns and asked him, 'Is there a danger that the stories will be lost?', he answered 'Yes', in the briefest Navajo monosyllable. He wouldn't elaborate, or not just yet. It turned out that he wanted to give his view of the past at his favoured stopping place and not before. Parking in deep shadow below the North Rim, he switched the engine off, stood up, and turned to face us.

'You wan' to ask how this canyon was made? Why the Anasazi disappear?' Long pause with his shades pointing straight at us. 'The Anasazi, they start to fool around with the Spirit, the sun exploded, they were burnt to death. That's why they disappear.' Pause. 'They take the subway out — half of California disappeared, that's why the earthquake. Too much foolin' aroun' with the Spirit. The Anasazi, they raise up too many houses, that's why. The temperature went to between six and seven hundred degrees . . . Those dark cliffs,' he says, not looking at them, 'they come from sunburn. Found skins dried up to the bone, they suffocate to death . . . They had three names. First one, they didn' tell me. Then Anasazi. Then the Hopi . . . We got four times. This is the last chance. If it happen, the waters will come back. This will disappear. The coyote will have this place.'

Nobody asked any more questions for a while. How much did he believe this? or which bits did he believe out of this extraordinary yet fairly recognisable mixture of drought and global warming, the hydrogen bomb and the San Andreas Fault? Behind all that facial equipment, moustache and shades and hat-brim, even the wads of pockmarked beige flesh between smoked lens and jowl, he was virtually incognito, professionally masked. If his mind had been visible, we'd have seen arcs flashing between its poles as the phrases and notions sparked across and across. He wasn't raving with the rabid flow of the crank — more the certainty of the seer. He was speaking from a sober awareness of history. When we came abreast of a flat-topped hefty pillar, he told us that this was Fortress Rock, where the Navajo made themselves impregnable by climbing up a log stair which they took up after them. This had sometimes worked against tribal enemies. When the American Army surrounded them — having first destroyed their live-stock, their fields, five thousand peach trees, two million pounds of grain — they were helpless and had to surrender. To have holed up in so impossible a place smacks of a collective suicide pact which (unlike the Zealots' in Masada eighteen centuries before) aborted.

'This was a bad thing,' Hoskee said. 'And that was worse.' He nodded up Canyon del Muerto towards Massacre Cave. 'Too many die, Spanish soldiers, Navajo people. Too many were killed, and I do not want to talk about it. But if you got any questions . . . '

Nobody had. They were getting down from the jeep now, shaking Hoskee's hand as he stood there like a *padrone*, and going off to the motel. I knew the problem, having often felt like a ghoul as I travelled through the Highlands of Scotland and eastern Canada and questioned people about the travail of their forebears who had been evicted, sometimes by fire and club, from their crofts in the nineteenth century. I recalled what Alasdair MacDonald of Kilmoluaig on Tiree had said to me.

'Maybe we should not be remembering such things.'

'Because they're bad?'

'Because they are bad.'

Then he told me a fierce tale of resistance to the clearance, involving strangling.

Such episodes, such epic pains in the life of a people, will surface. If they are kept down, as in Stalin's Soviet Union before Solzhenitsyn, they only fester. At all events, as I shook Hoskee's hand, I thought to ask him if his own family had been on the Long Walk to Fort Sumner.

'My grandfather's grandfather was there,' he said, it seemed quite readily. 'The soldiers, they cut into the head of an Indian and' — here he mimed pulling a skull apart with the fingers of both hands — 'they took his brain out, and they made it into a soup, and they gave it to the people to eat. That is what my grandfather's father's father told to his son, and he told his son and *he* told it to my mother, and that is what she told to me.'

The Long Walk was an atrocity, both casual and deliberate. On the 650-kilometre march of 8,000 people across New Mexico, the death-roll was horrific: for example, 197 out of 2,400 who set off on 4 March 1863 and 110 out of 946 who set off on 20 March. These were people who had been starved out of their fastness, who had lived for a winter on game and piñon nuts and had been unable to visit their salt flats for salt because armed soldiers surrounded them. Many were nearly naked. If they fell down, weak with dysentery, they were shot. Children were kidnapped on the way to be sold as slaves. Of course the extraordinary cruelty recounted by Hoskee may have happened. Sixty years later, when the Spanish had colonies in North Africa, an aristocratic lady who organised volunteer nurses in Morocco was inspecting a detachment of the Tercio Extranjero. She was presented with a basket of roses with two severed heads in the middle of the flowers. When General Primo de Rivera inspected them a few years later, a battalion paraded with Moors' heads stuck on their bayonets. More recently, soldiers coming home by troopship from the war in the Pacific trailed Japanese skulls behind the boat to turn them into clean white souvenirs, and G.I's in Vietnam went head-hunting and carried the ears of Vietnamese strung on their belts.

The mutilation of the dead in Canyon de Chellay is pictured in a large complex petroglyph in Largo Canyon. It shows bodies lacking an arm or a leg, bodies hanging upside down, dismembered. If Hoskee's story were not true but fabulous, then it would stand as a metaphor for what was about to happen to the Native American people. This 'secret history' — that is, the history known perfectly well to the victims and their descendants but not to the wider world — is now being filmed by the new Indian film-makers, among them Phil Lucas, a Choctaw from Arizona. One of their chief concerns is the cultural injuries inflicted in the boarding schools to which the children were forcibly sent for 'assimilation' all over America and Canada from the 1880s onwards.

'The schools,' says Fidel Moreno, 'were stage two of what should be known as the American holocaust.'

On arrival, children were stripped of their traditional clothes, shorn, and put into uniforms. More than three-quarters of them were sexually abused. A girl who tried to escape three times was tied to a table by the nuns, sterilised, and left bleeding for three days. They were kept in these places (until 1958 in America, 1964 in Canada) up to the age of eighteen. Or they were taken away from home 'to be vaccinated', never to return. In such a context the story of the plundered Navajo brain figures the experience of those who suffered the most drastic denaturing that one people can inflict on another.

Nevertheless the Navajo came back. This afternoon it had even been possible to see them lit by the sun as they busied themselves between the colossal glowing walls. It was as though crofters still reaped oats and lifted potatoes beside the moor at Culloden. Near the Junction the farmer and his family were at the hay again, like families I had seen working the alps of the Dolomites. Nearby, a white-haired woman had taken a chair outside and was sitting in the speckled shadow of a cottonwood, between the old hogan and the new shack — exact equivalents of the thatched black-house and the kit bungalow in any Scottish Highland crofting township.

Such canyons are not desert and have not been wilderness for many centuries. Corn and beans and squashes can be grown on the floor, as well as up on the rim, because the water-table is often only a few feet down. As if to demonstrate this, two pick-ups laden with young famil-ies had bogged down to the axle on the red quag of the river-bed. As we passed them on our way upstream to the Keet-Seel-like White House ruin, with its finely preserved white-plastered walls, the young men were delving away with shovels in the almost liquid sand. When we came back down, the trucks looked if anything sunk deeper. Children were starting to paddle and dart about, shrieking. When Hoskee stopped for one of his talks, a girl with her two small brothers appeared and offered necklaces for sale, prettily threaded with juniper berries and bought-in beads. She firmly refused to keep the change from a $5 note.

The few left living here looked like the usual drift from remote places where there is too little year-round work for the new gener-ation. It reminded me of meeting a crofter on Skye, far out on Mingin-ish peninsula, who suddenly pushed his cap back from his forehead and said wearily, 'I do not know how I am to go on living in this place which the Lord created last, I am thinking, in the ends of time.'

Physically the canyon was supremely handsome. Our four hours in it had given us at least a flavour of what it is to have your bounds and your thoroughfare so forcibly chosen for you by the sheer fall and adamant closure of the ground. In the jeep people craned and leaned back to take in the height of the place. They reached out their hands to finger its barrier hardness as the jeep rounded the aretes of buttresses with only three inches to spare. The cleft had started inno-cently enough with just a lumpy stack or two half-blocking sandy entries into the hills. Then it reared to its 250-metre stature and never let up again.

The rock is sandstone, formed as dunes 200 million years ago in the Late Permian. It cleaves straight down. Arcs of wide diameter score the rosy and khaki walls, as though a compass-engraver with a diamond tip had swung from the zenith upstream and back again. One section of wall was raked by slanting grooves which all ended along the horizontal of a bedding plane, showing the prevailing wind that had heaped them up from the north (the Hopi/Navajo Ghostland or ancestral home of the dead). Especially on the loftier facets of the towers, scooped shallows changed the colour of the rock as though a giant plane, skiffed upwards, had shaved too deep and gouged into the fibre before surfacing again. Surfaces gleamed as though cast in a smooth mould, then finished by the hot blowing of the sun. And all this was furnace-red and rust-brown, iron and manganese and copper smelted in the mix, leaving the colour of heat indelible on the

> high red stones the wild
> thousand-handed air
> built up into structures:
> the blind scarlet rose from the abyss,
> becoming in them copper, fire and strength.

These rock-forms have mattered to people for so long that their creation has its own story in the Navajo epic. A terrific storm blew up, threatening the lodge where Naayee'neizghani the Monster Slayer lived with Asdzaa'nadleehe the Changing Woman. For protection he covered their place with a blanket of cloud and fastened it to the ground with shafts of rainbow, a blanket of fog fastened with sunbeams, another cloud-layer fastened with sheet-lightning, and a final fog-layer fastened with chain-lightning. For four days 'Hail such as no one had ever seen lashed the countryside. The air was full of sharp stones driven by the wind, which carried everything before it . . . ' When it was over, Naayee'neizghani went outside and took off the coverings. The lightning, rainbows, and sunbeams soared back into the sky. Amazing beauties were revealed, bands of shimmering light and the sun 'making its way across the turquoise sky':

Near their house a deep canyon had been formed by the force of the wind blowing away loose soil that once filled an area between two giant walls of rock. The bluffs overlooking the slopes around the dwelling were now stark in rocky nakedness. The mountain grass and the soil in which that grass had rooted itself was gone, having been torn away by the wind and washed far downstream, in swollen, rapid rivers.

Solitary pillars of rock now towered above the high desert plain, although they had once been fertile mountains of sandy loam. And the canyon walls, once slopes green with grass and aspen, were now sheer, vertical cliffs of red and yellow rock. A new terrain had been hewn, giving the land the shape and character it bears to this very day.

On leaving such a place, you find your image of your own scale has changed, become dwarfed, though not discomfitingly so because your eyes are still full of soaring. It is a wrench to turn your back on that magnificently displayed earth-stuff and creep across lands where the materials are back in their usual unremarkable forms, where minerals are dirt and dust, no longer the makings of a giant structure. And yet these great hard heights were once so many drifting grains in their time. When the Equator angled across what is now Texas, the immense highlands called by geologists the Uncompahgre Uplift were decomposing slowly, wearing down to rolling hills, covering what is now New Mexico and Arizona with the thick beds of red sediment that compacted to make the sandstones known as Navajo, Zuni, Wingate, de Chelly. Wonderful are the visionary reconstructions by geologists — as stupendous as anything John Martin painted — of primordial landscapes that were never seen at all, not even by dinosaurs!

To the Uncompahgre Uplift we owe the reds of the canyon country, the iron in the 'cement' that binds together the silicaceous grit of the ancient sand. This red is so potent that it figures as the colour of the Navajo First World and surfaces again and again in their genesis stories as the blood of the land. When the two heroic brothers Child-of-water and Slayer-of-alien-gods beheaded the drought-monster Yeitso,

The blood from the body now flowed in a great stream down the valley, so great that it broke down the rocky wall that bounded the old lake and flowed on . . . so the elder brother took his great knife and drew a line across the valley. When the blood reached the line it stopped flowing and piled itself up in a high wall . . . The blood of the monster Yeitso fills all the valley today, and the high cliffs of black rock are the places where Slayer-of-alien-gods stopped the flow with his knife.

7 Voices Singing Out of Empty Cisterns

To leave those reds behind, as we returned west towards Flagstaff, seemed against nature, especially since for me red is the colour of the west — in the sun setting over the Atlantic near my home, in the Torridonian sandstone and Lewisian gneiss of Wester Ross that form my most beloved mountains and shores, in the climax of Cumbria at St Bee's Head. Our last landfall on Arizona rock, in Walnut Canyon, was a return to the limestone of home, or at least of north-west Yorkshire — Littondale, say, with its slabby sides blotted darkly with yew trees, its slopes jutting into scars as they steepen towards unseen watercourses down there in the deepest penetralium of the dale. Only here in Walnut Canyon the darknesses are piñon pine and Douglas fir and the rock has been worked intricately into villages along the tiers of the limestone.

The upper reaches of the Canyon sides lie back at too easy an angle to make the back walls of dwellings, the lower are too steep. On the middling contours, Sinagua from south-east Arizona perched for a time, if 'perched' is not too transitory a word for a people who cut so much rock to hollow out and build up street after street of cliff-house. No native word survives for 'Walnut Canyon' (whereas Yuvupku, for example, meaning 'Cave-in' or 'Sink', survives for Sunset Crater). Perhaps this shows a comparatively short-lived society here. The Sinagua were hereabouts from 700 A.D. and presently found this deep fastness where stone tool-points and animal figurines made of split twigs showed that hunter-gatherers had sheltered here some thousands of years before.

We followed a made path down to the inhabited contour, threading a wild garden, both rock-garden and orchard. Limestone backs and haunches bulked up everywhere like walruses on some Antarctic reef, all tusked and fanged with pinnacles that made the rock as spiny as the bristling flora, the thorn and yucca and cactus. It was textured as densely as the west coast of Ithaca, or the north end of Majorca where the ridge of the Sierra del Caval Bernat fortifies the island against the Mediterranean and the rock is liable to draw blood from your fingers as you climb.

The joints in the crags of Walnut Canyon provided the trailways or stone staircases between the villages. The Sinagua hunted deer and bear on the rim for their meat and skins. They must have inhabited rock as intimately as the people of the Hebridean outpost of St Kilda, only here the sun is so high in the sky that a wealth of usable plants flourish in the crevices of the rocks. Yucca springs up in explosions of green darts — it yielded meal and vegetables, needles and thread. Its fibres curl off the leaf edges in rows of elegant hooks. You can test their strength by trying to snap them — it can't be done. Salt-bush supplied blue to dye the piki-bread. A quinine substitute grows here. The black walnut that gives the place its name yielded a staple dye. Dice made from mahogany have been found here, and tobacco-smokers made from cane. The Indian poetry of smoking suggests something more than a casual drag. Tobacco was smoked in the kivas during prayers and smoke was blown through a pipe in the Hopi ritual called *oomawlawu*, 'cloud-making'. The Navajo medicine-men smoked and chanted with a family to relieve one of them from illness —

> From the top of Blue Mountain
> now you may smoke, now you may smoke.
> Small son of Female Wind,
> Now you may smoke, now you may smoke.
> With a jet pipe
> now you may smoke, now you may smoke.
> With leaf tobacco
> now you may smoke.

The Pima smoked in rituals against their enemies —

> In the centre of our council ground the fire burned and,
> lighting a cigarette, I puffed smoke towards the east.
> Slowly a vision arose before me . . .
> On the mountain tops was a yellow spider-magician,
> upon whom I called for help. He went to the enemy,
> darkened their hearts, tied their hands and their bows . . .

Under the overhangs front walls of houses were built up from a jigsaw of blocks cut in all manner of rhomboidal shapes, like parapets in Spain to this day. Doorway after doorway opened companionably on to the terraces, many of them in the keyhole style with the upper half maybe half a metre broader than the lower. If you blocked the upper half, it focussed the draught and cleared the fire-smoke. If you blocked the lower half, it saved younger children from rolling down the slope.

The Sinagua left this close-built and growthy haven after its heyday from 1125 to 1250 A.D., abandoning it almost abruptly as did the Anasazi at Keet Seel. The final traces of the Sinagua, before they left for lower ground to the north-east, have been found at Anderson Mesa (originally Nuvakwewtaqa, 'One-wearing-a-snow-belt') a little south of here. We could see its summit, like the tabular top of a Maya temple-pyramid in Yucatan, showing just above the south rim of the canyon as if it were slowly diminishing into the earth. Why did the Anasazi or the Sinagua disappear? Of course they didn't 'disappear'; as some dinosaurs became birds, they became Hopi, Anasazi, pueblo Indians, Zuni, Acoma and the rest. The peoples swarmed

> Over endless plains, stumbling in cracked earth
> Ringed by the flat horizon only,

steering for the great rock landmarks that meant water and shelter. As the water-table sank with over-use, the arroyos trenched still deeper, or droughts simply happened,

> the dead tree gives no shelter, the cricket no relief,
> And the dry stone no sound of water. Only
> There is shadow under this red rock
> (Come in under the shadow of this red rock) . . .

T.S. Eliot came from the well-watered flood-plains on the other side of America, yet it is as though he was looking out over these western lands when he had his vision of people as forever peregrine.

8   Great White Volumes

My last main landfall in America, and a Mecca of many years' standing, was the granite massif east of Yosemite, at Tuolumne Meadows. 'Tuolumne', with the accent on the 'o', had always felt so caressing a name that saying it was like letting larch tassels run through your hair. We had come north via Death Valley, a dreadful mineral cleft where the very water and air seemed sick; north again across the vacant uplands of south-west Nevada; and west around the tail of the White Mountains to Big Pine and Mammoth Lakes, to visit the Devil's Post-pile, a stack of vertical 'timbers' twenty metres high which are actually columns of crystallised basalt identical with the organ-pipe formation near the Giant's Causeway. Here the tops of the hexagonal cross-sections have been worn glassy by the feet of countless visitors and Anne just managed to save a little boy, without alarming his parents, as he pranced happily backward towards the brink of the drop.

Tuolumne turned out to be less luxurious than its name. It had a Canadian asperity, due to its height (2,000 metres above sea level) and also to the treading of many thousand mountain pilgrims' feet. The grassland is trodden permanently close so that it looks like the upper valleys of the granite Highlands in Aberdeenshire when the snows have not long melted, leaving the sward flattened. In the 1870s, when John Muir, the pioneering genius of the Yosemite, first came this way, nobody had been here except the Tuolumne tribe themselves. They are now extinct.

From these open green lands and their flocks and herds of pine-trees, the domes arise. They are silvery white, like crystalline re-frozen snow. Moon after moon of them rises out of the upland, voluptuous as swathes of silver fox fur. Your eyes stroke them, as they curve up in the distance. Close up they are formidable, sheer as snowdrifts, with scarcely a weakness to let in the fingers or the toes. I was climbing with Michael Cohen, after writing to him on the strength of his deep-reaching interpretation of Muir's wilderness ideas in a book called *The Pathless Way*. He turned out to be a seasoned climber from western California, now based in Utah, still in love with Yosemite. He and his wife, a Parks guide, had had their wedding ceremony on one of the domes and lived in a log cabin originally built by Lembert, a pioneer who had reached here not long after Muir.

We went for a route whose line followed a huge exfoliation — a swan's wing of white granite fifty or sixty metres high that opened slowly out from the shoulder of Stately Pleasure Dome. How could they call it that! What has this broad head of enduring rock to do with Coleridge's abortive little fantasy, his tawdry special effects, his incense-bearing trees and demon lovers? Michael too winced at it. The valley of Yosemite and the domes of Tuolumne are absolutely places that you want to remain unviolated by signposts or handrails or marketing gimmicks. I had asked for the route, from several Michael suggested, purely on the fine simplicity of its name, Great White Book. It was as beautiful as its name, foam-pale and smooth as a magnolia petal parting from the sleek candle of its bud. Magnolia may sound too tender for such a place yet the tree was wild at this latitude 40 million years ago, in the epoch of the global jungle, until it was replaced by Joshua trees and cacti as the climate dried.

We padded unroped up a smooth glacis, getting used to its leaning. It was the merest doorstep of the dome yet we were already fifty metres above the road and the glittering lake beside it. Above our heads, astride the cleavage between wing and mother-rock, a young man was climbing rapidly downwards, alone and unprotected — jogging, you might say, as though the surface under his feet were at 0°, not 60°. In his dusty black jeans he looked like a cross between a hippy and a raven, with his hair permed in a kind of Afro-shock. Courteously he perched on the crest of the wing to let us pass and conversed briefly.

'Some days,' he said with the playful self-absorption of the West Coast youth culture, 'I think I'll come up here and kill myself.'

'We-e-ll . . .' said Michael with a shrug that implied 'A man's gotta do . . .'

'Well *what?*' the raven broke in, pretending to be hurt that anyone should write him off like this. 'Naw — I wouldn't *do* that,' and he danced on downwards. It must have been wonderful to inhabit the dome with your gaze turned outwards like that, scanning across the entire range. We resumed our canny balancing upwards, facing inwards.

On our left was the naked, shallow-dimpled shoulder, or breast, of the dome, on the right the wing, with a cool morning shadow under it that made it possible to see the slender lodgements that were all we had for our toes. Further up, in the full glare, the surface was all blind white and it was as well that Michael led the final, unprotectable thirty metres — his sun-glasses filtered the light and made the dimples visible. Choosing these minimal holds was fascinating, a very thinking type of climbing — playing chess with your body, as Al Alvarez calls it. The two lower pitches, between the wing and the breast, were by contrast gymnastic, strenuous, demanding leverage I had never used before. Steady the right haunch against the wing, wedge the right foot in the cleft, perch the left foot on any minimal fulcrum — a felspar crystal, the lower rim of a scar where a flake has spalled off — and palm downwards with the left hand, trusting the friction . . . If you bit off too much with a move, the delicate mechanics of it all would burst outwards from the centre of your gravity and cast you off.

It had all been security itself compared with the final pitches on the nakedness of the slope above the wing. Entering on that was a space-walk, or at least a moon-walk (for me; a good climber would have found the angle child's-play). As I turned my back on Michael's progress above me, to avoid being dazzled by the sunlight reflecting from the granite mirror, I concentrated my mind by focussing on the slack of the rope lying on the slab below me. It slowly shrank upwards with the contraction of a snake — no limbs, no visible eyes, only this slim continuous muscle inching towards me, leaving no trace, until it had all crawled past me and it was time for me to climb.

The saunter back down the back and flank of the dome was as beautiful as the climb up its steepness. The place is pure. It is an environment made up of only a few things and all are visible: rock, whose colour varies only from ice-white to pale grey, with no veins of intrusion; hard-leafed dwarf shrubs sprouting from the crevices, like fruitless berry bushes; a small population of pines, squat and twisted by cold and lack of water. Here is an alternative planet, dry and stark, managing not to be bleak because the sparse flora are kin to the growthier world of the tree-line below, and because the arcing planes of it steal into the mind-and-body so naturally, with so springy a rhythm. We were gliding down, the weight of our ropes and metal gear unnoticeable, and Michael was talking me into this terrain, naming the great crowd of peaks and domes surrounding us as though they were members of his family. He told me that Muir was disturbed by the pines that had been stunted and riven by drought or avalanche because this showed that nature was fraught with conflict, was not all benign.

These western-American domes, so far-flung from my own beginnings, were coming to feel like a place I had always known. In the afternoon we walked round and then up the dome called Fairview. At the northern foot of this 500-metre rock the forest had been blasted. The boles of the pines and hemlocks, two or three metres back from the point where the rock sprouts out of the ground, were scarred to a height of at least seven metres. Their bark had been wounded off in big scabs, still unhealed. The previous winter's ice had prised off hundreds of tons of rock from an overhang above us and sent it down to hit these trees and wallow on down the slope, tearing a pathway through the forest.

Or had it been an earth-tremor? This area does quake. Seventy kilometres east, on the far side of the Sierra Nevada near the Devil's Postpile, we had made a detour into the forest and gone down into a split in the ground caused by earthquake. It was a sheer tear in the hide of the planet, still so jagged (after many thousands of years) that it stays with me as daunting evidence of how infirm our *terra* is. In his book *The Yosemite*, Muir describes a quake he lived through early one morning in March. Indians and birds fled before a 'roaring rock-storm' which went on shaking with a 'blunt thunder in the depth of the mountains' for two months. He argues that the talus of big boulders is so consistent in its vegetation that it must have been formed by one 'grand ancient earthquake'.

Stepping through the more recent wreckage, we followed round the pale-gold west face of the dome (whose apparently blank scarp had been climbed solo quite recently) and made our way up the huge apron at the back. Here all was permanent and stable, much as it was left by the Tuolumne Glacier which 'swept over it as if it were only a mere boulder in the bottom of its channel'. The silvery incline reached and reached towards the sky, a tranquil dream-mountain. We used our hands just once, to surmount a five-metre overlap. As the dome levelled out near its summit, the wings of our seeing began to spread and carried us far off sideways along the contours of the air. Towards the south, Cathedral Mountain raised its exquisitely steepening horn. An entire tribe of senior peaks and scions, all named by Michael, filled the circle of which Fairview was the apparent centre. Down in the Valley you look up continually, following the colossal verticals of El Capitan, the pulsing white currents of Bridal Veil. Up here you revolve, eyes in head, head on neck, whole body, as you pass yourself out into the rockscape graved by the glaciers through the granite crust.

At first it wasn't credible that all these surfaces were integral rock, not gravel or heath or turf. It was as weirdly homogeneous as the Black Cuillin of Skye and made an angelic counterpart to that louring, jagged country. Here the brows and backs and shoulders of the domes showed all the tones of a cloudscape seen from a jet-plane. Here were the whites and greys and blues of silver-fox fur or the roots of the hairs when you blow into that fur or into musquash. Here were the layered pallors of frozen water, the lightenings at the edges of snow-fallings in a winter sky, and the satiny whites of birch-bark (though not its pinks and bronzes). In most lands you would be looking at slopes and summits mantled with vegetation. Here was a world purely of rock, which would probably remain its naked self for what we call 'ever'.

Looking out and across and down was like tobogganing from an elephant-grey boss towards the dark green conifers, swinging up the next curve on impetus, mounting to a fine-drawn peak. The miles-long rising and coasting and dipping of the terrain were so consistent, so close grained and hard bonded, that it was all one work, Beethoven transposed into rock, unfaltering in its cadences. The summit of Fairview was an austere garden where two long beds of gentian held up bright purple trumpets. A few deep-orange butterflies danced almost helplessly in the updraught at the brink of the north rim where a whitebar fir, very old, not three metres high, made a densely bristling eyebrow. As we stood there, content to look and look, two climbers surfaced like divers, ropes already coiled. Still glittery-eyed from the day's elations, they asked us to take their photograph. It was four o'clock in the afternoon — they had started up Regular Route at seven in the morning.

We trotted back down, letting the speed of the descent drive our toes into the points of our trainers. As we rounded the base again we looked up and saw a rope of two climbers not that much higher than they had been three hours before. They were following the mounting sinuous valleys of a route called Lucky Streaks, as fine a natural line as I have ever seen. No doubt it will still be taunting me, unclimbed, as I grow old.

Petroglyph of Kit Carson's campaign, Largo Canyon, New Mexico

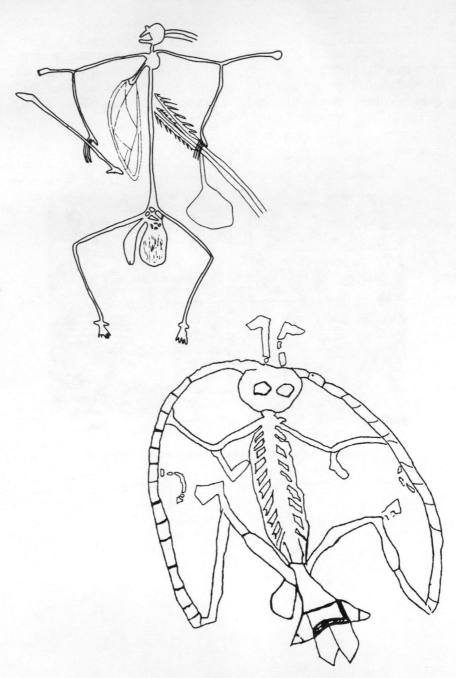

Rock figures from Ubirr and Nourlangie, Northern Territory, Australia

PART TWO
Australia

***

9   Painted Rocks in Eden

For 7,000 kilometres south-east from Los Angeles, the Pacific Ocean might as well not have been there. From the window of the Boeing the night deep below was perfectly dark. Then, at 4 a.m. on Sunday, 16 August — by sunrise it would be Monday, 17 August — a short arc of whitish lights was visible 12,000 metres below. We were four hours, therefore 4,000 kilometres, from New Zealand, so it was probably Tahiti. Then nothing more was visible until the sun rose.

America for me had been sandstone canyons, the hot reds of the ferrous sands, the ice-whites and silvers of Yosemite's granite. These three are integral too in the skeleton and flesh of Australia. Through the seabed of the Pacific the same forms and materials prevail. The one-mile depth of the Grand Canyon is mirrored, and exceeded three-fold, in the canyons of the ocean floor. As the bed of the Pacific is pulled apart by the movement of the tectonic plates, heavy material from the earth's mantle is dragged down into the trenches, heated and re-melted, smelted into lighter rock that surfaces as lava and granite. The continents of America and Australia are granite slabs thirty-five kilometres thick that float on the denser mantle.

Huge parallel faults — the Clarion Fracture Zone west of Mexico, the Clipperton west of Guatemala — seam the rocky plain that under-lies the eastern Pacific. Along the 140° meridian it suddenly spikes up in the petrified forest of spires and ranges whose tips we see as islands, the Marquesas, Tuamotu, Tahiti. So the rock of the earth's mantle stretches continuously beneath the Pacific. For a time it had looked as though my journey would not. I had seen Anne off to stay with friends

75

near Seattle and watched her jet-plane tilting steeply upward into a golden sky west of Los Angeles before it veered north, leaving me feeling like the last man on earth. Until the sun set I stared into that sky through the glass wall of the airport lounge, as though willing Australia to levitate above the horizon.

Shortly before midnight I went to check in at the New Zealand Air desk. The woman scrutinised my tickets and passport and said at once, 'You have no visa for Australia.' Her tone was firmly reproachful. I suppose I gaped. Having been brought up on atlases well plastered with red bits signifying 'British Empire', it hadn't crossed my mind that you needed permission to go anywhere in the Commonwealth.

'Wait here,' she said, and disappeared through a door, which she shut behind her. For fifteen minutes I miserably imagined thirty-six hours in the limbo of some L.A. motel, waiting for the Australian consulate to open its doors on Monday morning. Then she reappeared and said, 'We are sending you as far as New Zealand.' Transportation indeed — but a bearable sentence. Since this was Saturday, we would be crossing the International Dateline and arriving in Auckland on Monday not long before offices and consulates re-opened.

We also crossed *the* Line, the Equator itself, without rituals. The passage from American late summer to Antipodean late winter was like being conjured back into my own world. In the blowy, gull-grey atmosphere of the harbour front in Auckland the bollards and cranes and concrete kerbs looked as familiar as Aberdeen or Lerwick or Penzance. For several hours just one thing showed me that I had entered a land where people of my own race had been invaders two hundred years before. A sign low down on a building across the road from the docks recorded the site of a Maori settlement, a *pa* called Ngahuwera. Above it towered the skyscrapers of Coopers Lybrand and Price Waterhouse.

Seen from England, my first Australian goal had been the Red Centre — Alice Springs, Uluru (Ayers Rock), the Chambers Pillar in the western tracts of the Simpson Desert. This was transformed by browsing through the library of the Information Office at the Australian Consulate in Auckland. Colin Samson's *Adam in Ochre* held me like a revelation. Published forty years ago, it was the first full window opened for outsiders on to Aboriginal rock painting. Along with Robert Edwards's more recent *Australian Aboriginal Art* it oriented me irresistibly on the far north, on Kakadu and Arnhem Land. Up there, it seemed, overhang after overhang in the biscuity cliffs had been made into glowing bestiaries. For years I had known about these sites in a general way and had collected some materials about them. They seemed impossibly farflung and I had lost any sense that I could home in on significant places in the immensities of the outback. Now Samson and Edwards's fervour about the painted rocks and their citing of such names as Oenpelli, Nourlangi, Ubiri brought them spiralling down out of the general dazzle and into my hand.

Oenpelli in particular sounded difficult to reach. At first this seemed likely to prove true. When I arrived in Darwin, in the Northern Territory, and went to the Northern Lands Council to get a permit for Arnhem Land, the white woman at Reception simply repeated several times, 'At least ten days will be necessary to obtain the documentation.' She was as comfortable among her regulations as a goose on its nest. I stood there for some minutes, insisting, apologising, but not grovelling. Mother Goose refused to budge.

As I turned away, a brown woman, part Aboriginal, came forward from the back, listened to me all over again, looked at the form I had filled in, and said 'Leave it with me — I will see what I can do.' This formula is so tantalising, meaning anything from 'Why not give up now?' to 'There is just an outside chance but . . . ' At least she hadn't closed me out. The contrast between the two women turned out to say much about the mixture of attitudes that now hovers uneasily over Aboriginal land and culture.

For four hours the negative atmosphere of the office seemed to extend itself infinitely eastward in the drive along the coastal plain. It was a road without bends or forks, through a forest — I would have to learn to call it bush — without peaks or watercourses. The winter trees, not wholly leafless, wove their tapestry of faded browns on either side, English-looking like some race-memory of Sherwood Forest until the naked grey-satin trunks of eucalypts shone out, or dwarf palms skulked in the shade of the broad-leafed trees, or a guinea-flower tree stood out in a glade, a leafless wand decorated with one yellow blossom like a star cut out of lemon peel. Then it was more alien again as flames ate hungrily through the mulch of fallen leafage, or termite pillars rose from the baked red soil to twice the height of a man, groined and pinnacled like towers in the Dolomites.

Such were my fragile efforts to link this remote and utterly foreign place to things I knew. The road ahead was as purposeful and as empty as an autobahn I had taken through East Germany towards Poland thirty years before. What strategic master plan did this one serve? The Ranger Uranium Mine, I presently discovered, with a tourist spin-off to placate and reimburse the Aboriginal people for this invasion of their sacred homelands. To the wearied eye, nothing much was happening here. At the occasional caravanserai, Corroboree Park or Humpty Doo near Fred's Pass, where I bought stamps and a can of fruit drink at the Hard Croc Caff, one lean and stubbled old-timer would be drinking Castlemaine or Foster's in a twilit bar, or a land-train (a truck or cattle-float pulling two or even three trailers) would be standing clarted all over with brown mud among the crisp leaves fallen from a shade-tree.

The miles spooled off the reel. Once in an hour a big off-road vehicle came out of the east, dusted with red, stout roo bars defending its radiators against kangaroos and wallabies, its roof stacked high with jerry-cans of water. Sometimes I overtook a clean one, similarly equipped. Nothing but the fires moved between the tree-trunks. Once a black bird, large as a buzzard, took off from the upper branches on my left and flew parallel with the road, wings wafting lissomely in slow-motion, caressing the air — so silent and dark an emanation from the unknown fauna of an unknown country that I felt myself in abeyance, as though I had passed through to the other side of an enchanted glass.

Were beauties of gorge or billabong lurking behind that tapestry?' There was no telling. Just once a low rock hill appeared — relief in both its senses. It was breaking slowly outwards in boulders ten metres high. They stood with their swarthy heads together like Indian elephants wondering which way to move. The only stone for a hundred kilometres previously had been a few chunks littered along the gravel shoulder, sunset pink and toasted brown, garbage of some conglomerate reef blown up by the roadmakers.

I was looking for the bone of the land, not yet seeing through to it. As the day began to die and I approached Cooinda in the Kakadu National Park, a square-headed cliff reared up out of the bush like a sperm whale rising to blow. It was terra cotta — baked earth precisely — and desert-sand-yellow and earth-brown, colours of hot embers cooling, as though its processes were recent or still happening. It was eaten deeply away between its layers as the age-old mass of it aged still more. The very colours of it had the look of time passing. At each sunset in the week that followed, the stratified clouds in the west imitated Nourlangie as their greys were browned and reddened by the filtered rays. I had found my focus, or hearthstone — one landmark which jutted up from the world's surface, proud not prone, after all that slur of silt and humus and melding-down:

They hae dwyneit intil a thick nonentitie:
The reid clay drank the white identitie,

as Douglas Young wrote, turning Valerie's *Cimetière Marin* into his own Scots. Here is what I was seeking out landmarks for — entity not yet merged back into the flux.

Day after day, frequenting the bush and forest round Nourlangie, I felt a peace sink into me that was like the restfulness of being ignored. The animals remained secret. Nothing spectacular demanded attention. Many of the rock paintings could easily be missed. Few birds were flying. They were roosting and feeding at the waterholes, waiting for the warm rains to come in October. The sun was not fiercely exhausting and the wind was at most a breeze. It scarcely soughed in the forest canopy and yet, as I listen back to that time, it's as though I catch a music, stringed instruments almost beyond earshot, tensing their chords across the spaces between the boles . . .

Of course this is a cast from my own civilisation, an effort to find metaphors for a slow-growing quietude that stretches forwards and backwards in time. I was immersed in the Australia classically described by its wisest historian, Mary Barnard: 'The continent was old and delicate, it had reached the end, or nearly the end, of an evolutionary cycle. Its vegetation, animals, and birds had become so perfectly adjusted that there was no need for change. It was immobile. It was sufficient unto itself.'

To enter upon all this I simply needed to walk into the trees beyond the Anbangbang rock-painting site in a cluster of overhangs that had been shelters for nomadic people; head north via broad tiers of rock, contouring beneath them, stepping up them at their more gradual points; then cross the plateau, before losing height through cliffy and bouldery valleys and turning off anti-clockwise round the whole berg by forest paths that brought me back full circle to my car. Twelve kilometres. A gentle day. The *Kakadu by Foot* guide warns you that you must be fit, must carry at least four litres of water per head, must not go alone. Such worries slough off painlessly as you let yourself into the bush and the bush into yourself.

As I gained height, the character of Nourlangie began to look out at me. It was much more than a mass with a square forehead. This south-west flank was layered into galleries amd hanging copses. Orange faces glowed, as though heated an hour before dawn, when the sky was still stretched grey silk.

The sun, when it rose, would be shining from the north. On a high ledge a squarish boulder balanced. At this place, in the Creation-time, Namandjolg and his sister broke the taboo on incest. The boulder is a feather she took from his headdress and planted to make her mark.

Down below in the Anbangbang 'gallery', Namandjolg is painted as a human figure with splayed legs and outstretched, all-embracing arms. He has a brown scrotum and a split-ended prick, a full ochre rib-cage, and cross-hatched legs. (Later he became Ginah, the great salt-water crocodile. This species did in fact reach up the East Alligator River as far as Kakadu, when the ocean rose.) His lover's posture, below him on the rockface, is like his. She's a quarter his size, her vagina is a slot. Below them again are groups of people with wheel-like aureoles round their heads. Two of the women have flecked breasts, signifying that they are suckling.

That tribe of images on the walls, jigging and gesturing on the warmly coloured background, peopled the place and stayed with me as I climbed. The path was waymarked by occasional red tin arrowheads nailed to trees. Slowly the terrain was expanding inside a huge circle of horizon. The weave of the forest was marled in blue and green and looked continuous. Down the left side of my vista stretched a Barra-blue scarp, the western edge of the Arnhem Plateau, from which lighter pillars stood out — the home of Namarrgon, Lightning-man, and his wife Barrginj, parents of Aljurr [Leichardt's grasshopper], who appears when a storm breaks. In the rockface gallery Namarrgon is a scrawny figure with goggling eyes. His power is a white circuit painted from foot to outheld hand to ear through head and round to the other foot. Stone axes to make thunder or split things on Earth hang from his knees and elbows. As usual I was feeling more at home among symbols of the elemental and organic than I do in a cathedral, say, where a Jesus seems to embrace his suffering and the powers of the air are rendered as po-faced angels.

After this, for some hours, branches and leaves and rocks took over and our species seemed to have passed without trace. The way climbed the stair of a dry stream-bed, hairpinning round slabby cliffs where I could take short-cuts by climbing on to little ledges where surface sheets had split off, then pulling on to the upper rim by horns of the strong, rough-crystalled sandstone. The expanse to the west and south filled up in me one last time as I looked out from a natural belvedere in the rock. The unbroken blue tract far off down there said 'South' as clearly as a low hill called Kincorth that marked my boundary as a child in Aberdeen, beyond which lay everything alien and possible. Here most of it would remain alien; beyond lay ultimately the Tasman Sea, the Antarctic. It looked perfectly pacific. It was without event. It bred contentment from the centre of the brain to the soles of the feet. Its low-lying breadth was the shape of time, its jade-green fabric shirred with subtle changes of hue and density was the texture of nature, the final sky-blue rim was the colour of distance. It seemed insane to move from here, where I wasn't in the least 'at home', geographically or as a citizen — wholly unalienated as a bodily person, mild sunshine on my skin, warm air ruffling my scalp, evaporating my sweat.

The forest closed off that cosmos, brought my focus tight down to things near at hand. It was an easy jungle — you could see between the trunks of it at all times to more, and more, and more of the same, the next thousand white-satin or dull-olive boles, charred stumps, and (up on the Burrunguy plateau) towers which are the remnants of strata long since pulverised and washed down into the forest floor. These towers were gnomes' hats, drunken dancers, botched and abandoned statues or heads from an Eastern Island culture, or they were joined to make cockscombs, or stockades barring the way. Through the trees they bulked up like ogres, shrank a little and lost their broken noses or Cyclopean eyes as I approached.

To make myself at home I climbed one, pulling straight up over an orange cave, then clambering more easily from one weathered lip to another until I was perched ten metres up, near the canopy. I waited, all ears for the promised 'loud wing-beats of chestnut-quilled rock-pigeons, and the piercing calls of white-lined honey-eaters'. The only voices were the multiple rustling of leafage, like rainfall starting, and the hollow impacts of huge leaves curled up into bags that parted abruptly from their twigs and fell straight down like shot birds. Unidentifiable clickings and tickings sounded as desiccated particles dropped and touched in an infinite rearrangement of tissue. Again it was hard to leave this perfect vantage-place; it is still with me; and I made it my own when I described it on a postcard to one of my sons and named it in climbing-guidebook style — 'Termite Job. 11 metres. Severe.'

The way dropped down steps that would be cascades in the heavy rains of the next few months. I jumped into pits of leaves and toiled up long reefs where it was easy to lose any sense of line and miss the right exit. Predominantly it was downward and then I was walking for hours through unadulterated forest — the experience familiar from old explorers' epics, *Green Hell* by Julian Duguid, or the colonial tales of Rider Haggard and R.M. Ballantyne, only here it was all benign, too dry to harbour insects (in winter at least), too canopied to allow prickly or strangling growth on the floor.

Fear bristled only once, when the tin arrows ran out on me. For a while I was steering by nothing except the shadow presence of Burrunguy looming through trees to my left. The sparse bush thickened — no way through. I dropped into a dry gulch and crept along its tunnel of branches for a time. It twisted back on itself, disorienting me. With difficulty I retraced and found my own footprints in a patch of dusty sand. A few more false casts and retracings and I was on course again, following a faintly trodden line, happy to dispense with waymarks and trust to the circumvention of the mountain as the best way back to base.

Wonders stood out from the staple browns and olives — a pale-pink leaf from a eucalypt, half-buried edge-on in the sand, sticking up like a shark's fin. Injured tree-trunks bled clotted raspberries which were tasteless and odourless. Two fruits were lying on rocks, as though placed there, the one like a tapering cricket ball clad in tortoiseshell, its husk made of umber hexagons with dark centres, the other a raceme of some kind, as long as a millet head, covered with wriggling yellow filaments ending in potent orange anthers, with a comb of olive seed-cases hidden at their bases. I guessed them to be a pandamus palm nut and a hakea or grevillea. Most wonderful of all, as I approached Nanguluwur, was a stripe of yellow bordered with black that stretched for thirty metres, crossing the path. It led to a structure like a grey clay oven — a termite nest, built by the insects that ate up the wood of the tree until it collapsed, or else it was burnt where it stood. The yellow was the denatured wood, now brittle as popcorn, and the black was the bark turned to charcoal.

The rock paintings came into focus unexpectedly out of the forest's texture. A leaning mass of rock, bounced down from Burrunguy millennia ago, stopped me and drew me off the path by the beauty of its intense pawpaw oranges and watermelon magentas, which were its natural colours.

On the overhung north-east face was a greyish trail. At first I took it for one of the little roofed thoroughfares that termites sometimes make, or a bleached root exposed by flaking of the rock. It was one of the eaves of silicone that the archaeologists apply above a painting to lead off the rainwater and stop it from effacing the pigments. These paintings are in nature as much as they are of nature. When buffalo were here, they rubbed against them. Ants crawl over them. Blisters erupt and spall off whole images. Sheets of stone peel away, woodwasps secrete their cells on them, varicose veins of semi-soluble salts leach out from a weakness and build their disfigurements across the painting. Red soil dusts up from the ground, and rising damp plagues them with boils. This painting had been destroyed up to three feet from the earth. I could make out one yellow-ochre figure, in the oldest style — a silhouette with none of the latticing or 'x-ray' definition of internal organs that came much later. It was almost a pin figure with rudimentary female breasts. Next to her, nearly touching but looking unrelated, were two slender red fish, one above the other, nose to tail. The pigment was still brilliant, a luminous fox-brown. Perhaps the eave would now save the ochre from seeping back into the ground it had come from in the first place.

This was the first human trace for three hours, the first animal one apart from six little turds two centimetres in diameter, black on the outside, dried green of chewed grass on the inside — dropped, I supposed, by the black wallaroo or barkk which gives the trail its name. I came on a signboard where a track leading from a motorable dirt road to the concentration of paintings at the big shelter-overhangs of Nanguluwur joined the path. It was getting more madly human by the minute. On the path a bulky woman in a big hat, very red in the face after walking one level kilometre from her car, paused abreast of me and said, 'I hope it's worth it!' She sounded game, not aggrieved. Soon her husband appeared, also bulky, with a big belly, glum jowls, and a face creased with problems, a character from *EastEnders*.

'Good, is it?' he asked. I told him I thought that the best single pictures were at Anbangbang but the range here made a marvellous sequence of images down the ages. 'Lot of *art*, is there?' he still wanted to know, worried in case his Kakadu holiday failed to deliver the goods.

The murals were strung along a lengthy crag, unlike the mazy chambers and neuks at Anbangbang. The scarp itself was beautiful, a badger-pelt of soot-black drip stripes bordered white with lichen exactly like the dark ochre outlined in lime white which was common in the paintings. These made a gamut of the ways in which people living, or sheltering, here perceived the stuff of their lives over 40,000 years. The oldest was a crowd of hands stencilled in blown colour, more often seen singly in the caves of southern and northern Spain. Some of these showed the two middle fingers touching. These usually appeared next to the younger dynamic or 'warrior' figures, who leapt and danced in clear black silhouette against a yellow sky. Sea animals swarmed, mostly painted in the 'x-ray' style of c. 8000 B.C. which stylised the organs and skeleton of fish, reptiles, and mammals as lattices patterned inside the animal's outline.

Night after night at the Cooinda motel I had been enjoying the fish called barramundi, which has rich white flakey flesh. Here I was looking at a row of them with ample bellies, noses upwards. On a shallow face immediately above the eave of the lowest overhang a fish one metre long swam southward, its backbone rendered in vivid burnt-sienna blots. Behind its splayed white tail a skiff with three sails steered in the opposite direction — a realistic image complete with masts and halyards. This was the 'contact art' of any time in the last 2,000 years until the death of rock painting a generation ago. It had no more style or fine detail than any average picture by a child. The boat would be classed as a *prau,* or Macassar boat, one of the thousands that represented the chief contact between Australians and alien cultures before the Europeans arrived. The Macassarmen came to live for a season. They caught the trepang or sea-slug in the shallows off the north coast and took them back to the Celebes to dry and smoke, then sold them on to Canton as an aphrodisiac. What more curious reason could there be for a mingling of cultures which was so fruitful that it also influenced Australian ways of canoe-building and hair-cutting, their vocabulary, and their funeral songs?

The animal panels among these murals seem accessible enough in their meanings. They figure abundance or the wish for it, the will to make it happen. Plekhanov argues in his writing on early art that this type of work is integral to the hunter-gatherer cultures, not only in being totemistic (staple foods took on cult status) but also in calling out the same powers from the artist as from the hunter. If you knew the animal well enough, were quick and handy enough to catch it, by the same token your hand-arm-eye-brain were probably co-ordinated enough to draw or paint it ('capture' it in the other sense). This is perfectly embodied in the most celebrated (and last) Aboriginal artist to work at Kakadu, Nayumbolmi, who painted Lightning-man at Anbangbang. It is unclear how much he originated and how much he touched up, and this is as it should be, since this work was not done for individual gain or kudos. His nickname was Barramundi Charlie, in recognition of his other great skill — spearing fish.

Plekhanov was rather dogmatic in calling all this work figurative, or lifelike in its rendering of the species. A little further along the main wall at Nanguluwur, the bulging jamb of a bay was occupied by figures of the kind called *mimi,* who are ubiquitous at these sites. They were ambiguous humanoid spirits, feared and admired. When they wanted to return to the rock, they blew on it to soften it, then merged into it. This particular group were beautifully elongated up a pier of sandstone and lithely fitted into each other's curves. The left-hand figure was a simple white ghost with very long legs streaming up like smoke towards its little head. The other was ferociously elegant, like a very slim female, clad from shoulder to foot in a tigerish body-stocking rendered in umber and pale-yellow stripes.

These two could almost have been dancing the Charleston together. At Anbangbang the panel that impressed me most for sheer imaginative mastery showed a horde of dancers, rather like Picasso's frenzied figures of 1925 but more numerous, some bent forward at the hips and cycling with their hands, some striding as though going away, then comically returning, one with a low-slung lope like Groucho Marx. There is dance in it, palpably. Does it figure a ritual that included dance but signified more than a good time — initiation, for example, or shamanistic frenzy fuelled by a drug — or is it a fantasy, a delirium of pure movement, though possibly to illustrate a story being told to an audience rather than a wholly personal fancy or whim?

The more one looks at images on rock, in Australia and Africa, Spain and Scandinavia, the more they turn out to be bound up with rites to tap into the powers of nature and 'enter the spirit world'. In African Bushman culture, for example, a quarter of all the men and women can be shamans. The shamans dance themselves into a trance (often not using hallucinogens). In it they pass through into a state where they symbolically harness the powers of animals, or rain, or illness. The women sing and clap, the shamans dance until their potency begins to rise up their spines like steam, 'explodes' in their heads, and they 'enter the spiritual dimension'. They feel hairy as animals, they catch the male and female rains as though they were eland, they go 'through the rock face, bring back visions of the spirit world, and then paint them on the rock for all to see'.

Although styles vary round the world, many of the images are almost interchangeable. The same suns look out from rockfaces in Malawi and the Kalahari, the same snake or river wriggles in Dakota and Arnhem Land, and (most striking for my purpose) the same dancers shake and shimmy on a rock near the Vaal River in southern Africa as on the rockface at Nanguluwur, kicking their legs up behind them, swaying from the hips. The two beautiful slim ghosts may well express the tranced feeling of attenuation — 'A Bushman once pointed to a tree and said that he was that tall when he was in trance' — and the fish at Nanguluwur whose spine stands out as a row of rich brown blots is akin to the leopard at Main Caves in the Drakensberg. Its spine is far more spotted than its body in order to express the 'boiling' sensation that shamans feel as the trance comes on.

This is certainly not the abstract art that Plekhanov was bent on disbelieving. It is wonderfully bodily. The point is that its link with the means of material survival is much less simple than Plekhanov envisaged. Fire was such a means and the rock artists did not paint flames, they painted Algahigo, Fire-woman, one of the Nayuhyunggi or First People, who made the world. She planted the yellow banksias and used their smouldering flowerheads to carry fire from place to place. With her own pack of dingoes she hunted possum. She was feared and people avoided her *djang*, her rock-home, on the Arnhem Plateau. At Nanguluwur she is rendered with four arms and banksias growing out of her head.

Such images painted on natural roofs and walls by the Murumburr and the Djok, using colour mixed in the holes that pepper the floors of all these shelters, are the mingled traces of a complete way of life. They fished, trapped birds, speared crocodiles. They were uneasy about lightning because its fires were less controllable than those they set themselves (as the Park rangers do today) to burn off old bush and give new growth a chance. They worried about sex inside one family and about the bringing-in of brides from other tribes — the potent, errant penis is shown as a snake with a split head, a tentacle which the male can carry draped over one arm. They danced to get out of themselves and to enhance morale about the weather, about disease and their relations with their neighbours. 'After a dance, people who had been quarrelling with each other can be seen chatting amicably.' They worried about the darkness in unplumbed caves — First People called Namarude might live there, invisible, nocturnal, carrying their dilly-bags not for yams but for the liver, lungs, heart, and kidneys of their prey. At the lower right-hand end of Nanguluwur three of them are shown with six fingers and elongated nipples, 'lying down' in the seam of a stratum, making one think of the dead, as in Dylan Thomas's noble line 'Robed in the long friends'.

None of this work gathers to a great formal statement or composition. Maybe my glum-jowled 'EastEnder' concluded that it was not 'art'. The willingness to touch up and overpaint, to let damp and roots and insects have their way with them, the placing of the images on whatever rockface came to hand (which amazed me when I came upon deer and hands and bison on all sorts of crannies in the limestone caves of Cantabria) — all this means, not that the painting was casual, but that it was socially necessary, not a prestigious commodity. It is never slapdash. It could hardly be when you had to mix the colours for yourself, from ingredients you had searched for, and then transfer them to surfaces which were often hard to reach — Michelangelo was not the first artist to paint above his head while lying on his back.

Our art of rough surfaces — graffiti — is always slapdash and can't help being so because it is hasty and furtive. It is beyond the pale. It is going to be obliterated, if the Council can afford it, or get at it. 'JUSTICE FOR VIRAJ MENDES' is still to be seen in black aerosol on a bridge over the M6 motorway. Our graffiti are daubed in defiance, and usually in haste, by teenagers who are doing nothing, defacing the walls of buildings they can't afford to enter belonging to institutions that won't give them a job, scribbling on advertisements for flash products they cannot afford. It is all as useless as running the edge of a coin along a parked BMW. They can be witty and militant — in Uruguay, 'ASSIST THE POLICE: TORTURE YOURSELF'. The lettering is sometimes inventive, as in the chunky Flintstone style that came in during the 'seventies. It is hit-and-run art, whereas the Australian hunter-gatherers were working inside a settled pattern, for the eyes of people they knew, harried often by drought and shortage, accustomed to facing these together. They knew they would be coming back to this sheltering rock, that billabong. They sensed that their remote forerunners had depended on the same game and vegetables, the same sequence of rains and heat: 'nomadic societies in Australia were characterised by an intimate sense of the future and by seasonal planning that was almost rigid'.

What none foresaw, until it was upon them, was that the 40,000-year habit of painting their totems and demons and their own hands on the rocks would sink away abruptly into the red sand in the middle of the twentieth century. Where have the people and their painters gone? In the 1986 Census 206,000 identified themselves as 'Aboriginal' (1.3 per cent of the Australian population). This was a 42 per cent increase over the number in 1981, possibly because of a change in self-perception, a rise in ethnic morale. Seven of every hundred Aboriginals live in the Northern Territory and three-quarters of these are rural. There were an estimated 300,000 Aboriginals in 1788, when the British invasion began. So where have the *painters* gone?

A good many of them, it turned out, were working at Oenpelli. One evening, after returning to Cooinda, I found a message from my ally at the Northern Lands Council pinned to my door. My permit to go into Arnhem Land had arrived and could be picked up at Jabiru.

This unearthly new town a few miles to the west had been built on parched savannah to service the Ranger uranium mines. Oenpelli is fifty kilometres to the north on the road to the long dead-end of the Coburg Peninsula. The road was unsealed, a corrugated vermilion track that shook the teeth out of my head, until lo! it turned briefly into immaculate tarmac, coinciding with the Jabiluka uranium ore-body which has been earmarked for exploitation. The annual rake-off for the Aboriginal owners of the land is displayed on huge placards near Jabiru. It comes to 6,500 Australian dollars per head per year, the price-tag put on the destruction of more than 300 hectares of land where a thousand Aborigines still live in their own way, the introduction to the area of sulphur dioxide and radioactive water, to say nothing of alcohol, and the likelihood of disturbing the Rainbow Snake who lives nearby in Mount Brockman.

At the Ubirr fork with its washrooms, gift shop, one-way signs, and neat Park notices, things changed abruptly. For twenty-five idyllic kilometres the road was the only imposition on the land. To the east crags stood up, hot orange and hoar grey, layered and beaked and split. To the west huge grasslands expanded, watered by the invisible East Alligator. From the reed-beds white egrets sprang up, then planed off deeper into the verdure or alighted again and stalked intently through the shallows. Sixty or seventy horses browsed and swished their tails on the margin of the waterland. The bone-shaking track ceased to matter. Impatience and self-pity died away as this garden of the world, this seeming Eden, broadened around me, folding me in.

Oenpelli has been lived in beside its billabong for 22,000 years. In its present form it is a cluster of shacks and bungalows, mesh fences, a hangar or two, small tanks for petrol, propane, or whatever, squatting on the rufous dust. I was looking for Donald Gumurdul, owner of the hill called Injalak where the painted shelters were. I had been told to look for him 'at the craft shop' which was shut from one o'clock until two. The single-storey breeze-block building was painted blue with an artistic arrangement of boulders in front, drifted up with beer cans, plastic bags, and greaseproof take-away wrappers.

I went for a kind of siesta to the one place that looked open, a refreshment stall where I could get a can of Sprite and a Chikroll, both lukewarm. I ate and drank sitting on the world's most popular article of furniture, the white plastic patio chair. Beside me a brown baby rested in her bouncer among withered weeds. The view was of the supermarket, a windowless hulk like one in the most desolate parts of the Scottish Highlands. Some lines with washing fluttered in the wind near four large parked cars with no wheels — car-cases, as it were, their bulbous bodies sandblasted dull bronze. Cars and pick-ups tend to lie around derelict because if somebody gets one, everyone regards it as their own and uses it freely, so nobody feels responsible for repairs.

Above me, under the flawless blue, white galahs with roseate under-wings cawed and flustered among the dangling, rustling foliage of the eucalypts and kites quartered the streets as they did in Shakespeare's London. Now and again a dirt-reddened pick-up cruised past, as laden with people as a bus in Sri Lanka or a taxi on an outlying Greek island.

An hour later the shop was still locked shut. As the afternoon threatened to become eternal, a white policeman arrived in immaculate shirt and shorts and dirty scuffed old trainers and suggested I might try to find Mr Gumurdul at the supermarket. Its metal shutter was just sliding up. When I asked on the verandah, a dwarf woman with weird slit-eyes like those of the banjo virtuoso in John Boorman's film *Deliverance* pointed across the yard to a pick-up which was about to drive away. I asked the crowd for Mr Gumurdul and the man himself, grizzled, fiftyish, in a trilby hat, spoke up. He was dour and suspicious.

'Who signed that?' he asked when I proffered my permit. He scrutinised it for a full minute and finally accepted my handshake without once looking me in the eye. 'Go to the shop,' he said at last. 'They will maybe fix you up with something.'

Happily Injalak Arts & Crafts had come to life. Round the back six or seven tipsy men were sitting on dusty concrete, painting. Lizards, crocodiles, barramundi were taking shape, mostly in white on russet card, spread out between the artists' legs among cans, little pots of colour, scrap wood and bundles of spear shafts. When I said my piece about visiting the painted rocks, a tall slim man in dirty cotton shorts and a ragged purple T-shirt got to his feet and said, 'Alright, can go there. How long? One hour? You got some water?'

As we drove off, first south, then east round the tail of the billabong towards low hills, he introduced himself as Gabriel Maralngurra. He was smoking and a deafening odour of booze came from him. He badly wanted to know whether I had a wife and children and where they lived, and about the situation in Europe, because 'I like to add to my knowledge'. I told him that jobs were hard to find but you could live quite comfortably if you had a job. As we turned off the red road on to a yellow one with jutting stones, the quest felt to be fading in the breathless heat. The suspension grated on rock and we nearly stuck as we turned off yet again on to dusty stony ground almost unmarked by wheels. I reversed, charged the drift, and made it to the foot of a boulder slope. Gabriel led off athletically uphill, his bare footsoles at ease on the jagged stones. Abruptly he stopped under a sparse tree and stretched out full length to burp, cough, smoke, and finally doze.

A hundred metres above, huge rock masses loomed, split off from the mother-hill, canted to the brink of the slope. Through alleys between them still bigger masses showed darkly, deeply undercut, resting on pedestals. When we got in amongst them, under the roofs of their open mouths, bestiaries swarmed — a great many x-ray paintings of frilled lizards, portly barramundi, rock pythons, wallabies. A lizard's backbone was beautifully articulated in alternate patches of custard yellow and dull magenta. The water species, I later found, had appeared thickly once the sea level rose 6,000 years ago and the estuary penetrated much further inland. The animals, many of them edible, overlaid and often nearly effaced the 'dynamic' figures, lissome black silhouettes dashing sideways, swaying at the hip like acrobats. Where the stratum was shallow, a python stretched out. Where it was deeper the snake coiled and the artist had wholly enjoyed the deep-dyed umber herring-boning with which he had rendered its skeleton or its skin pattern, or both.

Here there were no silicone eaves, no wooden walkways, no noticeboards, no wire fences to keep us from touching. The place was still intact, a maze of shelters in which more than 70,000 generations had had unlimited scope to make their marks.

'Why did they make these paintings?' I asked Gabriel.

'To keep the culture alive,' he said at once. 'Because these things, they would die with the old people. But because they are here, we know them.'

It was a completely satisfying affirmation, and perfectly true. Years before, Big Bill Neidjie of Kakadu had told a biologist, 'My people all dead. We only got few left . . . that's all, not many. We getting too old. Young people . . . I don't know if they can hold on to this story. But now you know this story, and you'll be coming to earth. You'll be part of earth when you die. You responsible now. You got to go with us to earth. Might be you can hang on . . . hang on to this story . . . this earth.'

When Colin Samson was asking questions here in 1950, the tribe that is still here, the Gunwinggus, had no idea who painted the rocks. (It may have been the extinct Mangaridji.) When I asked Gabriel who did the paintings, he seemed to say 'Mimi.' He may have thought I was asking about their subjects. It has even been suggested that the mimi were invented to account for the most ancient Aboriginal paintings by peoples who came later and used quite different styles.

Gabriel was showing me everything now, leading me through to one rock cluster after another, indicating single images round backs of boulders the size of elephants. Some were hard to reach. I had to bridge up between a face and a separated slab, stride over on to the slab with camera dangling dangerously near the rock, then back-and-foot down a cleft on the far side to get down again. In the meantime Gabriel stretched out on a bed of rock and snoozed before waking up and smoking another cigarette, eyes pursed against the fumes. He commented on my antics to reach the furthest images.

'Lofty, he my father-in-law, he told me the painters got high up there by leaning forked trees up against the crag, then they lay a timber between the forks and stand on the timber.'

Down at the shop, at the end of the afternoon, when the manager was haggling and pleading with men who wanted more than the going rate for their table-mats and decorated didgeridoos, Lofty turned out to be a gnarled man less than five feet tall, with big green eyes, who had done the most exquisite work I saw there — pictures in fine brown and white lines illustrating stories about lizards, grasshoppers, croco-diles, and anthropomorphic demons with complicated genitals.

The hilltop of Injalak seemed inexhaustible in its wonders. High up on one wall four birds filed along, stout-breasted, in darkest ochre. Gabriel identified them as magpie geese. Later I saw them feeding in the shallows of the Mamukala wetland, silhouetted in a frieze against the glitter, the image of their likeness at Injalak. A kangaroo had been drawn in sienna outline, unfaltering curves of back, belly, and tail, the far ear nicely distinguished by angle from the near one. The painters were also seeing other things. Jeruober, the largest kangaroo, was one of 82 totem animals still known to the Gunwinggus in the 1950s, and traditionally the red ochre stood for his blood, the yellow for his liver. According to a story told by a man called Gadjibunba at Oenpelli in 1950, the barramundi in a previous incarnation was 'trying to put himself somewhere, to find a Dreaming site for himself'. He crossed creeks, made holes in the rock and slept, put sand in rivers to create beaches. In the end 'he became a rock. So then, when the salt-water tide comes in, he is submerged. When the tide goes back, he comes out again, Namangul, Barramundi, he stands there.'

So every being was also something else, and had been transformed before. The red-ochre snake I had seen bending along a roof will have been Rainbow Serpent, called Numereji at Oenpelli. He appeared in the Creation-time travelling south, head held high. He arched to get across the South Alligator and went to ground at Mungayerungyera, which is where rainbows tend to disappear after a storm. The abundance here makes it look like the source of all animals — on this hill, after the Flood, they issued from the Ark.

In front of Thunder Man's Cave I lay down, sated, and looked out west towards Oenpelli settlement on the other side of its whale-shaped billabong, the reason for its existence. This is the western verge of Arnhem Land. Way beyond the green wetlands the Coastal Plains stretch out along the shore of Van Diemen Gulf towards Darwin. Greens of foliage blur off into the blue created by the evaporating oils of a continent of plants. Levels beyond levels, the world's surface manifest, supine under the sun. Its mind-expanding beauty has been felt for generations. A song from the neighbourhood says,

> Come with me to the point and we'll look at the country,
> We'll look across at the rocks,
> Look, rain is coming!
> It falls on my sweetheart.

Why do people hanker for heaven when there is all this? Not that it's 'good'; it is wildly mixed. Famine and drought, rot and poison, all there among the seeds and the honeys and the flesh. The scope is inexhaustible, across these plains we can see it, here is our gamut.

10   Pillar of Fire by Day

The routes in northern and central Australia looked simple, at least in concept. They swung in great shallow arcs across land with few contours, or settlements. Across wide blanks on the map roads ran with few intersections, linking places with poignant, immigrant names such as Tobermorey, Maryvale, Newcastle Waters, each of them no doubt utterly unlike its faraway Scottish or English original. The first ways across the Tanami and Simpson Deserts or the Barkly Tableland would have tacked from waterhole to great rock to waterhole, sidling round the ranges we have named 'Petermann' or 'Stuart Bluff' or 'Macdonnell', picking steps through the rare gaps in their crumbling teeth.

I now had to go south, 200 kilometres beyond the geographical centre of Australia, to Alice Springs and on to Chambers Pillar. That is one way of putting it. Another way shows in the words of a tradition-bearer called Mowarljarlai:

> The whole of Australia is *Bandaiyan*. The front we call *wadi*, the belly section, because the continent is lying down flat on its back. It is just sticking out from the surface of the ocean. Deep down underneath are the buttocks, *wambalma* — from where the leg joints run into the pelvis and right across to the other side.
>
> Inside the body is *Wanggud*, the snake. She grows all of nature on the outside of her body. The sides are *unggnu djullu*, rib section. This rib section goes right across the country, above the navel. *Uluru* [Ayers Rock] is the navel, the centre — *wangigit*.
>
> The part below the navel is *wambut*, the pubic section. There is a woman's section — *njambut*, and a man's section — *ambut*.
>
> Right up top is the head part, *ulangun* — Cape York, Arnhem Land . . .

For me Injalak Hill near Oenpelli, with its lustrous images, had been the eye in the head. And of course Uluru was the naked, raw-red *omphalos*. My own sidling approach, via Chambers Pillar 300 kilometres to the east, gave me space in which to conceive of Uluru as integral — as in truth the *wangigit* in the *wadi* of *Bandaiyan*, and not some outlandish freak or tourist attraction or mere confirmation of its likeness in a thousand calendars and photos.

The way south from Alice Springs looked as uncompromisingly bare as a beach after the ebb. You could make your mark there, you could plod for hours with little sense of headway. Your traces would be wiped out behind your back as sand and sea came into their own again. Alice is where it is, just north of a major cleft in the Macdonnell Ranges, because this gap made it possible for camel-trains, telegraph line, and railway to squeeze through on the route north a little over a century ago. The sight of this passage must have acted like a draught of pure oxygen on the exhausted pioneers. Now, heading south, you had to take a breath and brace yourself as you do when you swim out between headlands, and see the salt water slope up ahead of you, and feel its surge contend against you, belittling you.

Not that there was anything so terribly daunting about my 190-kilometre journey. I'd hired a newish Suzuki jeep, black and trig inside its skeleton of roll-bar, and fortunately I didn't know that *Which?* magazine was about to advise against it under the curt headline 'STABILITY PROBLEMS: DON'T BUY' because of 'their vulnerability to rolling over if cornered sharply even at low speeds'. When I pressed the car-hire man for information about petrol supplies, he reassured me. 'There's usually fuel at the outstations,' he said. My map showed two of these, Deep Well, a little way off the road, and Maryvale. It's pathetic how much mental energy I wasted during the next hundred kilometres on complex calculations.

'That's getting on for half of the upper half of the petrol gone, according to the gauge, and I've done seventy of the four hundred total, so *if* I'm getting fifty-five kilometres to the gallon then I *could* just make it even if I draw a blank at Maryvale . . . '

Once the disused railway line and the slim fingers of the telegraph poles had wandered off, unnoticed, to the west and disappeared, there was nothing but the billowing desert and the road. The Old South Road is a channel of red marl. Many wheels had worn it into grooves which can't be avoided. They made the jeep slew as though on partly-frozen snow. After a while it was not alarming, for there was nothing to collide with and no wall or fence to hit. In two hours two vehicles came the other way, big travel-dirtied 4-wheel-drives stacked up with water and petrol and men wearing khaki bush hats. They didn't wave back.

Ewaninga, to which I had been looking forward, was like an oasis — a dry oasis. A vermilion path snaked over to it between tussocks of spinifex. Beside a clay pan, which becomes a shallow tarn during the rains, a hillock of broken sandstone tablets rose ten metres from the plain. The rock had weathered from its inner warm peach to damson purple and on this surface nomads had pecked out three-fingered emu prints, as clear and lifelike as though the bird had trodden the stone when it was mud. Like the dinosaur prints between Cameron and Tuba City in Arizona, it was a beautiful reminder of the likelihood that the track or spoor was the prototype of writing: 'The trail leads the wolf to the deer. The latter by its hoofprints intimates to the former where it has passed and in which direction. What the animals wrote with their hoofs was of the greatest importance in the life of the primitive hunter.' So the Brazilian Indians drew fish on the river sand, so the Australians pecked a glyph that said 'Emu' on the tablets at Ewaninga.

It had been the most unassuming of memorials to lives lived in the grain of the land. Now and again the next civilisation to try for a foothold here displayed its signs — a galvanised water-tank on a low hill, a tyre hanging discarded in the crotch of a bleached dead tree. Twice a herd of nine or ten lean cattle could be seen nosing at blue-green weeds. It seemed no place to make a living, a margin to which people were forced by congestion in the cities, famines in Scotland and Ireland, and the dreams of free farming to which those gave rise.

The expanse of the land was so great that I felt as though I was sinking, barely keeping my nose and eyes above the surface. The first white travellers constantly felt this. Many of them were hardened to the sea, like the New South Wales gold prospector Thomas Hargraves who first came to Australia to fish for *bêches-de-mer* and tortoiseshell in the Torres Strait. Hovell, a sea captain from Yarmouth, first crossed Queensland between the points where Geelong and Canberra are now and noticed that the men looked better once they had won through to the meadows: ' . . . we had so frequently to turn back to take another road, or an unfavourable looking mountain to ascend or descend, that I have seen them with faces similar to those I have seen of sailors when on a seashore in a gale of wind, feeling great doubts whether it is possible the ship can get off or not, but as soon as it is known that the ship is out of danger a change is perceived immediately in the countenance of every person aboard'.

The waves around me were dunes the colour of tomatoes, the currents were lateral veins of red soil that flared among the scrub like cracks re-opening in a scab. Two of the early travellers, Gregory and Sturt, both felt 'baffled . . . by countless ridges of red sand' which they likened to 'waves of the sea'. Occasionally a reef of brown sandstone lifted out of the parched herbage — the backbone of a hill that shortened the horizon like a heavy swell at sea and imposed a patience because there was nothing visible to make for any longer. After the night's downpour vibrating on the tin roof in Alice, a sheer turquoise sky had opened out in the east, encouraging me to believe that there would be no flash floods to make a quag of the track.

This blue now stretched its unflawed membrane infinitely southward, pale and undazzling because the sun was behind me. It felt as though all change had stopped. Nothing here would either develop or revert, only wear away. A day would last a thousand years and nothing as seasonal as cloud or sunset would happen in my lifetime. Not just me on my little craft but the whole austral continent was adrift on a slow motion tide of geo-time.

Gates appeared, double ones, loosely chained, and I had to get out to open them and then again to shut them behind me, five, six, seven times. On one a metal notice warned of the need to control TB and brucellosis. Perhaps the lack of cattle would help with that . . . After 106 kilometres from Alice, trees clustered ahead. Shapes among them looked too geometrical for nature. Cattlesheds? Houses even? At the next gate a sign announced 'MARYVALE STORE FUEL COCACOLA'. It all looked empty as old pods. Two sandblasted petrol pumps flanked the road. Nearby were nondescript buildings with shuttered or open unglazed windows. The tin and wooden walls were green or grey, dulled matt by the sandstorms which had twice made me shut the windows of the jeep.

Ah, a good sign — white plastic chairs! They were lurking under shade-trees beside a bungalow with an open door. A man came out and hung some dripping jeans on a wire between the trees. He didn't notice me until I went over and asked him if he could let me have some petrol. Somehow I couldn't assume that his pumps were working. He padded across in the dust, one big toe showing through a hole in his sock, and filled up my tank, complaining that they couldn't get the bowser to come this far with Unleaded.

'How far to Chambers Pillar now?' I asked him — knowing perfectly well, but wanting something to say.

'Forty-three k's,' he said at once, and that was that. He was neither dour nor in need of conversation, just compacted deeply into himself by all that distance and the invisible grinding of time.

Two more forks set me on course. At each a leaning post with a battered tin sign pointed me to 'Chambers Pillar'. After Maryvale I could have headed south into a loop of track on the verge of the Simpson Desert. Instead I bent westward towards the line of the Stuart Highway, the trail blazed by MacDouall Stuart, first European to cross the continent and namer of the Pillar after a richly undeserving politician. Now the Highway links the south coast at Port Augusta near Adelaide with the north coast at Darwin. Out here, eighty kilometres east of the Highway, there might as well have been no road at all. I was driving on the surface of the gibber desert, an ocean of shingle barely colonised by drought-proof clearer bushes.

Now and again a rib of hard white rock shook me briefly up and down. A low range rose on my left. I thought nothing of it until the track headed slap for it. Surely it was impassable in a vehicle? I got out and locked the offside front wheel into 4-wheel drive, as the man had shown me, engaged the gear called 4-LO, and went for it. The jeep clambered up scarred reefs, using its wheels like hands. From the crest, the Pillar was visible in the south-south-east, its sore red head glowing like an ingot cooling — the ultimate landmark, utterly distinctive, vertical among the dead levels all around. It alone has survived from an epoch when all this surface lay at least seventy metres higher above sea level than it does now. In Utah or Arizona a family of buttes would be

The cliff settlement of Keet Seel, Arizona

Left,
Kachina Mother,
Tsegi Canyon,
Arizona

Below (facing page),
El Morro,
(Inscription Rock),
New Mexico and (*right*)
Window Rock, New Mexico

Right,
Kata Tjuta
(The Olgas),
Northern Territory,
Australia

Below,
Chambers Pillar,
Northern Territory,
Australia

Uluru (Ayers Rock),
Australia

Below,
Wave Rock,
Hyden,
Western Australia

Above,
Blouberg
North Wall,
Transvaal,
South Africa

Right,
Tufa/basalt towers,
Göreme, Turkey

Gibraltar, North Face

Urçhizar, Cappadokia, Turkey

Right,
Sybil's Rock,
Delphi, Greece

Below,
Conglomerate towers,
Kalambaka, Thessaly,
Greece

The Sacred Stone, Machu Picchu

Below left, Huaynapicchu, Machu Picchu, Peru

Below right, Puma Rock, Saqsahuayman, Peru

standing up on all sides. The Chambers Pillar stands by itself, as though for a sign. When Stuart first saw it on 6 April 1860, he likened it to a 'locomotive engine with its funnel', which exactly catches its incongruity. Another of his party saw it as 'so pillar-like that I for a moment thought we had found some old ruin the work of man'.

Downhill the track was even worse and I drove off it on to naked gibber where a few other wheels had shown a way. The Pillar had sunk again into the dunes. How the explorers must have hated such a moment, as though the map had been wiped blank again. Under a casuarina a little way off the track a couple had stopped in the frail shadow for a bite of lunch. Ahead of me a dune lifted its vermilion breaker. I charged it, lost momentum, and was quenched quietly and completely by the heaped sand. I reversed, charged again, lost way, and revved impatiently. The rear wheels spun without gripping and gave off hot blue smoke.

The feeling of being thwarted by this infinity of little grains was like asphyxia. When I got out to inspect the problem, a snake with a pipestem neck and amber markings appeared on the sand at my feet — dead, still eerie. I began to be glad that there were two other humans near at hand. When I had spooned away masses of warm red sand from the wheels with my hands and reversed back out, the man with a luxuriant beard strolled over in his bush hat and spoke — clearly an expert.

'I'm surprised your Suzuki can't make it. Tough little vehicle.'

'Should I try the detour to the left of the dune?' I wondered aloud.

The Beard genially agreed. I revved, charged, slewed, and did exactly as badly as before. What now? Would the Beard be able to tow me out? At this moment a big 4-wheel-drive lurched into sight from the Pillar side of the dune, its roof laden with safari equipment. Luckily it was on the main track, not on my loop. It stopped at once and a lean man with a pointed beard came over to see what was stopping me.

'You stuck? Got a shovel?'

I sheepishly admitted to being shovel-less. He took out a lightweight plastic shovel from among his neat and extensive equipment and with a few strong sweeps shifted enough sand to free me. Once he had gone, the Beard, still fascinated by my plight, strolled over again with his fine air of having a recipe for all predicaments.

'My brother's Suzuki once got bogged down like this,' he recalled thoughtfully, in contrast with his previous good write-up for the vehicle.

Having less mechanical sense than a wombat, I hadn't realised that the hire-car man had meant I must perform the locking operation on *both* front wheels. Obviously! Every other driver in the entire world knows that. I adjusted the nearside front wheel, started up, and went for the obstacle again. I nearly reached the crest. After I had backed down for another shot, the Beard gave me his final advice.

'Is it easier after this?' I asked him.

'We-e-ll,' said his wife, who had joined us, 'it's still *soft*.'

'This is the worst, though,' said the buoyant Beard.

'There was that other steep one,' she insisted, 'and it was on a *bend*.'

'You'll be right,' said the Beard confidently. 'And if you do stick, there's a whole heap of parties at the camp. As long as you don't meet one of them coming out! No — you'll make it — you might need a parachute to get away again but' — his beard parted in a Falstaffian grin — 'you take a good run at it. Fast as you can now.'

I backed off a good fifty metres and drove as fast as she would go in first. The orange meal hugged the wheels — hugged closer — and still churning forward, we broke through the crest and were over, trundling briskly towards the Pillar through lateral furrows filled with sand that bounced me up to the roof and almost stopped me dead by turns but never dowsed momentum entirely. After ten minutes I pulled off the track under sparse shade-trees, among a little *lager* of camping outfits, Land Rovers, igloo and frame tents.

A hundred metres to the south the Pillar had risen to its height, enough to make you tilt your head as you eyed its summit. It was a classic monolith forty metres high, dazzling white shaft and burning red head where the whole ferrous content of the sandstone has been sucked upwards by intense droughts and heat, metallising and therefore hardening it, making this beacon whose glow can never be extinguished until it all falls down.

From the hill of yellow stones which makes the plinth of the Pillar, the far south from which Stuart approached looked an even more unrelenting plain than the one I had driven over. The horizon was perfectly level round most of the compass. A little east of south one almost indiscernible blue bump might be Mount Cecil, 120 kilometres away at the eastern end of the Musgrave Ranges. To face that way was like standing in the bow of a ship, faring forward, seeing the plains divide and fall away behind. I could see it like that because I could leave here at thirty or forty miles an hour (I hoped). For one John Ross, who had cut his name in careful copperplate in the soft yellow base of the Pillar on 22 September 1870, or for Stuart, or for Ernest

Giles, who started his exploration westward to Uluru and Kata Tjuta on 22 August 1872, such places were reached and left most arduously.

They seem to have been a psychological as well as a practical necessity. Fixed points were needed from which to take bearings in this unmapped terrain and they were best taken from a rise. The travellers also craved relief in the other sense of a mental rest from the sameness of the slow, hot trudge. If only they could find a locus — a goal, a marker, a kernel of aesthetic nourishment on which to feed! In his journal for 22 August 1845 Sturt, one of the most soldierly and detached of the explorers, wrote with a groan: 'It is impossible to describe the general appearance of such a country as this . . . We had then a level horizon all round us and a dark gloomy country covered with polygonum for miles . . . '

Ernest Giles had much the most feverish imagination of all these explorers. His intense introversion must have contributed to the character of Voss in Patrick White's masterpiece — and he expressed again and again that hunger for a landmark. On his third expedition, following the 19th parallel as closely as possible to reconnoitre new lands for stock, he records a characteristic moment: 'as the mountain to the south-west looked so inviting from here I determined to visit it (in spite of what the old blackfellow had said about there being no water) . . . It looked high and rugged, and I thought to find water in some rock-hole or crevice about it.' He failed, in the teeth of the advice he had received from Old Jimmy, at whom he had previously marvelled for being able to guide them unerringly for 120 miles 'by the recollection of spots which have no special features and no guiding points'. It was also forty years since Jimmy had last seen them.

On his journey west from Chambers Pillar in 1872, forty miles short of Uluru, Giles was 'delighted to perceive any feature for which to make as a medium point, and which might help to change the character and monotony of the country over which I had been wandering for so long'. He yearned for it. Kata Tjuta [The Olgas, twenty miles west of Uluru] became 'My old friend the high mountain [which] loomed large and abrupt at a great distance off.' When his horses sank in a large and brittle salt-pan, he became still more convinced that the mountain landmark would 'offer a route out of this fertile region'. He was obsessed — the sheer salience and shapeliness of Kata Tjuta's clustering bodies (on which he rhapsodised once he got there) convinced him, on no evidence, that they were the waymark: 'I have great hopes that if I can once set my foot upon Mount Olga, my route to the west may be unimpeded.' Weeks later he was in full retreat, his chief comrade

Gibson dead and he himself at his wits' end after a long solo walk with little food or water. Pierced all over with spines, maddened by deprivation, he finally snatched up a young wallaby and ate it alive.

Giles's wanderlust clothed itself in rational pretexts — the search for more and more spreads of farmland, an overland route for stock to avoid the dangerous and costly sea voyages. Other people who came past here were more soberly workmanlike. The telegraph line from south to north had to go through. So had the railroad. It never made it. When I got back to Alice Springs that night, I had a meal at Bojangles Bistro sitting on a bench made out of sleepers from the Old Ghan railroad. Dozens of names of the surveyors, engineers and labourers (but not the Chinese) are cut into the buff stone 'Visitors' Book' at the base of the Pillar which makes it the Inscription Rock of central Australia.

The native Australians had mixed feelings about 'these incredible bearded white men who dragged themselves along on their aimless journeys as though bewitched by some fetish'. Sometimes they dogged them, even coming right into camp with gifts of fish or cake and accepting old clothes in return. Sometimes they put on warlike displays with weapons and body make-up. For uncounted generations before that the Aboriginals had conceived of the pillar as a point in an epic journey. Iliktajara, a knob-tailed gekko forebear in the Creation-time, kept killing ancestors and having sex with women from outside his tribe. At last he was banished for it. He travelled north-west, growing into a giant as he went, and came up the Finke River, which rises some 250 kilometres south-east of here in the Gibson Desert. When he arrived with his last mate, Yayawaru, he turned to stone, creating the pillar. She turned away in shame and became the long narrow hill with a fretted red crest a mile to the north.

The two outcrops are perfect sexual ikons: the Pillar's white length and red gland, the mountain's twin paps, one quite breastlike from the west with its white slopes and pink nipple. Having thought this, I promptly realised that, for black or dark-brown people, this colouration would be all wrong. I was imposing my own fantasy. The cue for the myth can only have been the shapes. The Pillar is an 'old man' as in the Old Man of Mow in Staffordshire or the Old Man of Storr, Britain's tallest single rock tower on land, which stands on a mountainside in north-east Skye. Its true local name translates as the Big Penis of MacQueen — either a compliment or an insult to the bygone laird. What matters is that this part of Australia was once lived in, people frequented it, with their sexual worries, their need to warn young folk about difficult behaviour which threatened the community. The only indigenous life here now was the few pairs of doves that skim off over the bush, the occasional hawk prowling above its own shadow. We visitors were nothing but birds of passage, swarming briefly round a lighthouse.

It would have been good to linger here. Giles was sorry to leave it. He found an opossum in a small 'chamber of the pillar' (one of his rare jokes?) and when he set off, having broken a coating of ice off his blankets and pannikins, he wrote: 'We turned our backs upon this peculiar monument, and left it in its loneliness and its grandeur — "Clothed in white sandstone, mystic, wonderful" ' — imposing his fantasy in a nice variation on Tennyson. As I ate my bananas and drank my lukewarm water down at the *lager*, I couldn't turn my back on it, I had to look and look at the great upstanding snow and fire of it building themselves against the blue.

Flies were as thick on my hands and cheeks as on African children at a feeding centre. Other parties were having their siesta behind insect screens. It might be a good idea to visit Yayawaru — no, I was as reluctant to clamber over her flanks and tips as though the old taboo had been real for me. The return to Alice Springs had better be made before sundown.

The difficult dune was no easier and on the rocky downhill the suspension almost caught. The most ticklish obstacle was created by three other jeeps or pick-ups that came past me north of Maryvale. Each stirred up a cloud of dense bronze dust, more impenetrable than the worst smog. For safety I should have waited the minutes it took for each one to subside. I hurried on over the plain where the sun, low over the horizon now, was making a shadow from each stone, as in a Dali painting. The dust had turned the black jeep tan, inside as well as out. I repeatedly had to wipe the display clean to keep an eye on the petrol and the temperature. The little car had done well. After all those scarlet dunes it must have been seeing red — it certainly looked red, and by the time I got back to town it was fuming, the hot dust smoking from every rim and sill. I should have planned to drive the not so many miles direct to Uluru and Kata Tjuta from the Pillar, south and west by Indracowra, crossing the Stuart Highway and taking the Lasseter Highway by Curtin Springs to Yulara. That, as it turned out, would have been a more fitting approach to the great rock.

11   The Red Centre

Half an hour out on the flight from Alice to Yulara, a Japanese man stood up as much as he could beneath the luggage lockers and waved his camera at the window. 'There it is!' he crowed. Like a fool I had a look. Ayers Rock was turning below us, like a travel poster made to revolve by tricky work with a rostrum camera.

Although this shrunk and flattened image was more or less replaced by the actual massive presence over the next few days, it remained hard to sense Uluru as it is itself. It was named Ayers Rock by William Gosse on 20 July 1873, the day after he climbed it along with a camel-driver called Kamran, whose bare feet were an advantage. Ten scientists climbed it in 1894, and a man called Bill MacKinnon left his name at the top in 1931. Twenty-five Europeans climbed it in the next sixteen years. I reached the top one morning at half past nine, and there were already 240 names in the Visitors' Log, including Umberto Acerri from Trieste, who claimed to have had *'uno orgasmo psicologico'* — long intended and carefully prepared-for, I should imagine.

Here was the difficulty. We 'know' the Rock already — the 500, 000 of us who visit here each year. How to sense it directly through a bulky cloud made up of photos and magazine articles, noticeboards, new sealed roads, handrails, painted pathway, gift shops, hotels, T-shirts, leaflets, buses and hire cars, cameras, camcorders, and people, people, people . . . Kata Tjuta felt 90 per cent visible. Uluru was at least half blurred by its cloud of celebrity. I am adding to it by publishing this book. I could have refrained only by the utmost self-restraint, by which I mean the writing of a book about great rocks which ignored the most remarkable one of all.

The problem is focussed in the notice at the foot of the ascent, which is the only permitted way up. It is a cultural health warning: 'The Mala (hare wallaby people) had all this as their domain. When you climb it you are walking on the tracks of the Mala. The Anangu (traditional owners) would prefer you not to climb Uluru.' I almost wish they had taken the onus off us on to themselves and just forbidden us. The government made them an irresistible offer — 10 per cent of the box office receipts for admission to the Park. Soon after the brand new designer resort of Yulara opened, on the eve of Australia's bicentenary in 1988, it still looked as though the Rock might be closed. The media came swarming, scenting a row. The traditional owners took the money, as they did when the uranium lode was opened in Arnhem Land. Dilemmas remain. They kept cropping up as I walked round and through and, where possible, up the giant heads-and-bodies of these rocks over the next days.

The several hundred of us who climbed Uluru early in the morning of 26 August, in the chilly fag-end of the Australian winter, were strung out continuously up the 300 metres of steepness at the point where the western face angles into the north-western. We were *mingma*, ants, so-called because of our tendency to move about in long queues. Our way was eased by a chain strung out on stanchions driven into the red flesh of the rock. At least they had winnowed out some of us by leaving a break where the slope steepened at fifty metres, so that those not up to it were prompted to retreat at that point. If you trusted your balance and your friction, you could pad up unaided, especially if you lodged the balls of your feet on the lower rims of the blister-craters where the rock is perpetually spalling off its skin. The few who were already on their way back down were grasping the chain fairly grimly as they felt the urge of gravity upon them. One bright spark in expensive trainers was taking it at a carefree jog.

As the angle lay back, we entered a great undulating plain of dull-red stone, dimpled into hollows some of which held a scatter of shingle and a few tufts of bleached grass. A broken line of white paint suggested which line we should follow. Without exception we all meekly obeyed, for fear of straying into spaces sacrosanct to the hare-wallaby people. The deepest of the many furrows had sides high as a person at an angle of as much as 75°, because the mass of arkose river-grit which knit to form Uluru 600 million years ago tilted nearly upright 100 million years later and the layered cross-section of it was held up into the erosion of rain and sun. Now we had to run down the walls of the furrows to gain impetus for the run up the far side. By early afternoon, as rainshowers wet the surface, this was becoming quite hard to do. By 2.30 the Rock was 'Closed to Visitors.'

Five hours earlier the weather had been overcast, grey, uneventful. From the summit you could see a complete Hebrides of pale-blue bergs all round the compass. Furthest away was the Basedow Range, 157 kilometres to the east of north. The giant mesa of Mount Connor, where the Ninya (ice-beings) shed icicles that split the soles of people's feet on frosty mornings, stood 89 kilometres away east by south. Out of twenty mountains only one was named in its original Australian, the Katamala Cone. Mount Woodroofe in the Musgraves, the highest peak in South Australia, should be Yerimbi, the home of the honey-ant people; Van Doussa Hill is Kulpi Elli, shelter of the fig tree. For explorers to name these places after their friends and relatives was natural, but Giles could surely have done better than to obliterate Kata Tjuta (many heads) by imposing the name of Olga, Queen of Spain. From Uluru, Kata Tjuta is easily the most compelling sight, thirty kilometres due west, the massed bulbs of it like some visionary citadel of the future, or as John Pilger puts it, 'like mammoth figures that have died in each other's arms'.

From the Valley of Winds that penetrates them, a damp chilly airstream was flowing. A white blur of rain effaced one mountain or another from time to time. Then sunrays parted the overcast and the great plain suffused crushed-bramble colour, as though the juice of fruits were welling up from below. One of the Kata Tjuta domes glowed dull rose as though an opal were kindling its inner fire.

Fifty metres west of the summit panorama a gully led towards the brink. The water that must fill it after heavy rain had helped the growth of a grove of mulga trees with jade-green leaves, kurrajong shrub which remains sap-green even in drought, and clumps of spinifex stitched into the crevices. The foliage makes a green eyebrow on the forehead of the Rock. It would offer the only shade in summer. Even now, in a rising of the wind that stunts the trees and has laid low the twisted torso of a veteran mulga, it was a place in which to be at peace. Uluru was finding me at last. Its mass felt utterly central. It was its unlikeness to all around that did it. It stands out. It is pre-eminent. We need to rise above this infinite-looking plain, which makes us plod and offers so horizontal a horizon. It made Sturt feel as though he was 'in an open boat in the middle of the Atlantic Ocean' and even his horses shrank 'aghast from the stony wilderness'.

Uluru up-lifts us, locates us, makes us name the world and perceive its co-ordinates. The native Australians, who came here for the fine waterhole in the Mutitjilda Gorge and the fruits and brushwood watered by it, situated a fundamental epic here: the struggle between, on the one hand, the two groups of Sky Heroes who lived here, the Mala on Djindalagul (the sunny northern side) and the Kunia (carpet-snake people) who lived on Wumbuluru (the shady south side), and on the other the Windulka or Mulga-seed people who lived 'towards the sunset'. The Mala, who lived in Eden, were self-centred, complacent, and would not go to the Mulga-seed initiation ceremonies. The Mulgas created a hairless devil-dog who attacked the Mala and drove them forever from their garden of primordial delight, condemning them to wander. The Kunia set out for Mulga-land, then met the

Sleepy-lizard women at Uluru waterhole, and settled down with them. The Mulga persuaded their friends the Liru (poison-snake people), who lived at Kata Tjuta, to attack the Kunia and force them to flee eastward. In their grief they sang themselves to death. The entire conflict so troubled the earth that Uluru rock rose up out of the ashes of the burnt-out Sleepy-lizard camp as a monument to these cosmic wars between friendship and faithlessness, self and obedience, inviolable ritual and careless flouting of it.

The cycle of stories was chanted at length to the anthropologist Charles Mountford just before and after the Second World War, and to Bill Harney, the first Park ranger in the late 'fifties. The Loritdja people who knew them had nearly all left by the early 'sixties. Now the traces of the war, the glyphs which record it, are the erosion holes and mouths and grooves, the limbs and bony segments that mark the entire body of the Rock and are as marvellous as the titanic naked bulk of it. Meanings sprout from them even if you know nothing of the Aboriginal epic.

Starting before sunrise, a few of us walked the eight kilometres round Uluru with a zoologist called Neil Hermes. On the north or 'sun-over' side, the upper half of the 250-metre face was taken up by the indented black pattern of an uncannily lifelike human head more than a hundred metres high and as broad again. Tourists call it 'the Brain', and certainly the deep infoldings of the cortex are figured in the many dark slots and sockets. Equally you can see the base of the skull, the forehead and orbital ridge, eye-socket, septum of the nose, upper and lower lips, chin and lower jaw. The whole gigantic cranium is carved with the boldness of a master sculptor and sliced through to show the maze of its interior, where the thoughts form and the memories survive.

This was the *nguru*, the camp, where visitors from the shade side came and stayed. It is almost directly above a hole called Ngindi, which is the womb of the Earth-mother. The gutters on the summit were made by the feet of running Mala men. The segmented ribs which lie loose on the summit are legs, bodies, and heads of slain Kunia men and women. They look like some stones that have remained with me as the epitome of history frozen in its moment, such as the temple columns at Olympia in the Peloponnese which were felled by an earthquake in the seventh century and still lie there in sequences of fluted marble drums.

On Uluru nothing has been left meaningless or unnamed. A straight-sided round-headed boulder is Kalpunya the hairless devil-dog. A pair of caves are his footmarks as he stalked and killed Kedrun the eagle chick, symbol of perfect initiation. Most potent of all, along with the *nguru* head, is the broad low cave with a mouth fifty metres across, a great red gash or rictus, which Michael Andrews in one of his exquisite Ayers Rock paintings unaccountably calls 'Laughter'. Its stretched agony is that of the mourning Kunia woman Ingridi, whose son Ungata, leader of the Kunia, was mortally wounded by the Carpet-snake leader Kilikitjeri and bled to death in Mutitjilda Gorge.

As Neil Hermes walked us round the Rock, identifying symbolic features here and there, we came abreast of the *nguru* head. I stared and stared at it, photographed it, walked backwards looking up at it, wishing to remember it for good and not to lose the scale of it as it shrank in memory. When I caught up with the party, I asked him about it. He said at once, 'I didn't hear that . . . ' Then: 'I was hoping nobody would ask about that. The Aboriginal owners would prefer it if we said nothing about that.'

As we sat in a cave out of the wind to eat our breakfasts, he waxed explicit about the whole vexed question of lore which is known and which we must now pretend not to know. The Pitantjara, whose reservation we were on, are worried because their heritage is being leaked away to visitors, sapping their self-sufficiency. It was again what we had met with in Canyon de Chellay when Hoskee Begay said that 'the old guys *live* behind the stories' and therefore dislike the recording of them. Neil Hermes did not disguise the fact that the story-cycles are to be found complete in thousands of libraries, in the books of such devoted anthropologists as Mountford and Ronald Berndt.

'Of course you can get hold of them, if you like,' he said. 'Or you can decide to hold back. It's up to you.'

At this a black-bearded American in a flapping Packamack announced in a low, decided voice, looking at the ground, 'I for one will *never* seek out those books.' This high-minded ban seemed to depress us all and we walked on in guilty silence. My inner voice was saying, Can it really be necessary to bury forever these stories which carry the practical wisdom about sexual maturing, poisonous or nourishing plants, and the need for tribal solidarity of a people who no longer exist as a people — who no longer live here, or in any wild country any more?

Presently it turned out that some younger Aborigines are grateful to the anthropologists for recording a wealth of poetry and belief which would otherwise have been lost for ever. The intermediate phase, of the sixties to the eighties, saw the onset of terrible anxiety as tourism opened up the interior of Australia to millions of incomers — people

like myself, who do want to acquire what we see, in words and photographs and memories, and perhaps to exploit it, in books and articles.

On top of the great inselberg itself you can for a time forget all that.
The sides are so steep that the car parks, the buses large and small
cannot be seen or heard. Fifty metres away from the summit and you
can wander down channels and into major valleys from which the little
groups of sightseers at the end of the painted path are small and unreal
as spectres in a Giacometti drawing. Inch your way down a granular
red flank and they're invisible altogether. It is natural to walk down
beside the stone body of a slain Kunia person — not stepping on the
segments themselves — until the slope becomes prohibitive and you fill
with the rock-climber's longing to sprout wings, take off, and occupy
that air whose translucent planes exist a few metres out from the rock,
350 metres above the map-like countryside to the east.

Down there, out of sight, is Djugajabbi, the Women's Cave, where
women pregnant or hoping to be entered their own taboo domain and
sang fertility songs to the *kirakip* (hawk symbolising desire). Areas of
scrub at the foot of Uluru are now fenced off and notices tell you that
this is the Women's Place or the Men's Place. They would have been
much easier to reach than the Woman Stone on Ben Avon in the
Cairngorms where pregnant women went to sit in the natural kettle-
holes in the hope of easing their confinements. The black streaks of
algae on the wall nearby were left by the fires with which Kunia
women destroyed Liru warriors who had broken into their sanctuary.
A little further east is a niche, the nest-camp of Lundba the red-
rumped kingfisher who called out to warn the Mala that the devil-dog
was coming.

The stories would have meant that much more to me if I had heard
them from a singer who lived or had lived here, who at least half-
believed them. For me Uluru (Meeting-place) was coming to be the
finest conceivable evidence of what actually forms our planet. Here is
the world-mix. Of course it is everywhere; every dune and clod and
scatter of dust is that, but here it is salient, unmistakable, a pillar of
cloud-fire by day and night. Looking at it and treading it, we know
that materials were in place anciently, they had crystallised out of the
cosmos. Tectonic time ticked and struck. This part bulked and crested
and is now named Uluru or Kata Tjuta; that part buckled under and
lies as low as Uluru's foundation, 6,000 metres down.

The two great bergs formed in the same prehistoric river. Uluru is
the finer sand from nearer its mouth or delta, Kata Tjuta is the coarser
shingles from further upstream. Tracing back this geological flow, then,

we drove to Kata Tjuta before sunrise, in time to see the scarlet rays stream over the rim of the semi-desert a little north of Uluru. The wide sky, the latitude only 22° south of the Equator seduced me into walking in my shirt-sleeves. Soon I was almost too cold to speak or point the camera. The world was all 'hustle-farrant in windy light', in Hugh MacDiarmid's phrase, as the night-cooled air raced round the huge pink bells and eggs of the mountains.

As the yellow disc surfaced above pricking bushes and shocks of porcupine grass, it diminished, whitened, intensified. Black fingers grew westward from every stone, planes of shadow carved dark zones from the red cheeks and brows of the mountains. The wind spun furious metallic streamers in mid-air. They flourished round our heads, threatening to whip us like tops. They drove us round at a cower and a scurry into Walpanga, the Valley of Winds. The rocks, still cooling just after sunrise, were discharging their airs into the even colder atmosphere above the wild flowerbeds and drifts of ruddy soil. If soil is the word: there was only sand and clay here and it was up to the termites to recycle the withered foliage into nutrients. The meat-coloured shingle-stones that fused to make these bergs were being buffed to a dull glint, the boles of the ghost-gums resilvered with precipitate of moonlight, their hard green leaves glossed again as they shook like seaweeds in some accelerated tide.

In this pellucid medium everything stood out for the first time, new-created. How could this be, rocks and trees entering the world at the same time? Unless the dry land did appear along with the seed-bearing herbs and fruit-bearing trees, on that third day? Or according to a different Genesis, 'Inside the sun, the eleventh day modelled stone and tree . . . Thus it is remembered in Yucatan.' In the Australian Genesis, or *tjukurapa*, Wanampi the Great Snake left Kata Tjuta for Uluru because it was waterless here whereas the deep pool at Mutitjilda never quite dried up. The restless, continual blowings from the Valley of Winds are Wanampi's warning go-away breaths. Yet Ernest Giles remarked on Kata Tjuta's two good springs. Perhaps he was here after a wet time. These mountain shapes perfectly fulfilled his need for landmarks. When he saw the 'exceedingly high and abruptly ending mountain loom', on his first expedition, it drew him to it. On his second expedition he was reluctant to leave here.

His descriptions are exact at first — 'rounded blocks of bare conglomerate stones'. Then he seethes off into a welter of images — 'rounded minarets, giant cupolas, and monstrous domes', 'enormous rotund or rather elliptical shapes of *rouge mangé*', 'enormous pink haystacks leaning for support against one another', 'a gigantic pink damper, or Chinese gong viewed edgeways'. We feel his sensuous passion for the place — he would happily have been buried there — while wanting his metaphors to be less imported and less artificial.

The Aboriginal stories about Kata Tjuta, which are really sustained metaphors, are at home with the rocks. They were the birthplace of the Snake — a nice vision of their eggness. The south-west heads were metamorphosed bodies of kangaroo, euro, and little night owl, the eastern domes the old homes of Mice-women, and the double row of isolated pillars on the west side the camps of the Pungalunga men, allies of the Liru who were victors in the war at Uluru, beings taller than trees and faster than most birds. They played with boulders and came back at night with dead men tucked into their belts instead of lizards or young wallabies. Latterly, in the human epoch, a Pungalunga person lived here and hunted wallabies for lack of humans. He could step easily from one summit to another, misjudged his stride across Walpanga on a cloudy day, and fell to his death. There are no stone remains of him because he was human, not an ancestor from the Creation-time.

Giles got 300 metres up one flank before he retreated. We were forbidden even to try, although I went up ten metres, behind the guide's back, and began to feel the tension of keeping in balance with just two forefingers in little holes and the edges of my trainers slurring on the cheeks of embedded shingles. Yes, it's good that they will never be climbed now, or drilled, or encumbered with any hardware of radio masts or beacons. They are this terrain compacted into its own mineral monument, sprinkled with grasses and little bushes where seeds have lodged in the few seams of their great impersonal curves, holed enough for kestrels, swallows, falcons to breed inside them and mark them white with lime, lapped by the flowery wilderness where green budgerigars chatter in the trees and kangaroos and feral camels leave dung-pats and double footprints on the vermilion sandbeds. They are past event, time stopped, or slowed almost to motionless, and the leaves and the birds are the multicoloured flicker of the present.

None of us wanted to go back into our own present. Tim Lanyon, the guide, led us by a stony path that squeezed between stooping shoulders, then extended the normal journey by a wide loop of two further kilometres.

'They're going to make a new trail here anyway,' he said.

We walked in single file to disturb the surface as little as possible. This was the only permitted route. Nearly the whole of the range is taboo. Some of the animal droppings were black and fresh. Had they retreated into the shade already? There are sixty walleroo at Kata Tjuta — none were to be seen. The emu which had taken to snatching apples out of people's hands had probably been trapped and eaten already, according to Alan Fox, biologist and head of the guiding company.

Here we were in a sanctuary and would have stopped the sun rising if we could, to keep the enchantment of its peace. Inside their cleavages the huge bulbs had been shadow-sculpted — made to look still more sheer by the arcs of their profiles being so nearly parallel to the arcs of the shadows cast on them by their neighbours, as when the Earth eclipses the moon. Once the sun was halfway to the zenith, the shadows had shrunk to narrow black skirts around the mountain-torsoes, which now looked almost monochrome and monoform, so many blind snouts, unbreathing breasts, deaf lobes, in which nothing was going to happen ever again.

Back at Uluru a similar stasis prevailed, reminding me again of Mary Barnard's insight into the continent as being at 'the end, or nearly the end, of an evolutionary cycle . . . It was immobile.' A greyness was materialising in the sky. At night it was comical to see us all, on a Sunset Tour laid on by A. & T. King ($A16), pointing our cameras at the Rock and waiting for the luminous amethyst spectacular to happen. We leaned on the fences round the scrub (still struggling to grow in again after the unorganised tramplings of the sixties); we levelled our cameras and camcorders at the famous target as though waiting for a giant panda to give birth. Uluru did not oblige. 'It was sufficient unto itself.'

All night rain hammered on the tin roof of my cabin at the motel. By lunchtime next day cascades of every height and calibre were delivering the drench to the ground. Lusty white links joined the scalloped pockets in the rock. Threads that started in the middle of a broad apron and reached the floor or else originated at a high lip and were spent early or disappeared in the middle of a russet flank. Sluices like vehement lightning down major gutters. Few of the falls had tributaries; they were single whether they were thick as sinews or fine as nerves.

It was as startling as though a body long embalmed had come to life. Of course it was not extraordinary that a watercourse should start out of 'nowhere', in the middle of a slope. It happens all over our mountains whenever it rains, only in Britain the network is invisible, much of it, under peat or heather, grass or scree. On Uluru all was open to the light of day, as though the vascular system of a body were laid bare, the skin and fat peeled off. The mane of greyish cloud trailed slowly along at less than two hundred metres while below its fringe the white vessels pulsed and pulsed.

12   Waves in the Granite

Western Australia had mattered to me for one thing — Mount Augustus, 'the biggest rock in the world'. As I searched the stacks of regional and local history in the state library in Perth, other unexpected massifs rose slowly into sight, like broad grey moons — 'domes', the literature called them, 'great granite monoliths', 'splendid masses of primitive granite' — as distinct from the usual more civilised granite. These were dotted about the hinterland of the Darling Range, where millions of acres of farmland turned sandy near Wave Rock at Hyden, then blanked off slowly eastward into the Nullarbor Plain.

I scarcely knew what to expect of Corrigin Rock, Gorge Rock, Emu Hill, and Bruce Rock. Could they be landmarks at all when the woman at the filling station at Corrigin, 290 kilometres east by south of Perth, at first wasn't sure where their very own rock was? Then she said apologetically, 'It's only a small rock in a field . . . '

I drove on eastwards, having failed to find any jutting scarps. The map threatened to become featureless yellow. Settlements were rare on its mesh of thin black roads. In the lands that lay ahead round Lake Hope, south of Kalgoorlie, most of the placenames involved rock — McDermid Rock, Disappointment Rock (a dried-up waterhole, perhaps, or a lack of gold), Bull Rocks, Geordie Rock, Lillian Stoke Rock — hardly an Aboriginal name among them.

Morning and afternoon merged in one sunlit continuum as roads stretched straight lengths under a sky where the clouds were making pelmets, louring bluish–grey above farmland which might have been the Soke of Peterborough or the plain of Westmeath had it not been for the little reservoirs at the bottom of one field after another, created by piling up embankments of clayey vanilla soil. The other reminder of drought was the frequency of pylon windmills for pumping up water from the aquifer. A sequence of these filed towards a bedraggled wood and a little leaning sign said 'Gorge Rock'. I drew off into a copse and parked beside two corrugated tin toilets with 'Eve' and 'Adam' daubed on their walls. No 'great granite monolith' towered. Beyond a lattice of lichenous branches a convex surface sloped gradually, like the Laurentian Shield west of Ottawa.

I splashed up on to the reef through its fringing marshes and found that it was one of a cluster of broad, shallow-angled tortoise-backs, with life-size tortoiseshells scattered over them where plaques of the rotting granite were exfoliating. The rock, dark with its high content of coaly felspar, was clad inches deep in sodden lichens. Networks of trickling run-off forced me to turn this way and that as I made for the summit, and the summit beyond the summit. The reef was expressing the winter rains — 'expressing' as in drawing milk from a breast as well as in transposing from one medium to another. Ponds two inches deep nourished rose-pink branchy mosses and the willows round the verge of the rock stood ankle deep in bog-water.

Here was the function for which the domes were invaluable — their gathering in and slow releasing of the rainfall. Such, no doubt, were Woondlin and Koorikin Rocks. Such was Woorkakanin, which I found east of Kondinin. Such was Bruce Rock, which I reached the following day. Before the virgin forest was cleared, these domes had just enough height to give travellers an outlook, a chance to look for the next oasis and take a bearing on it. Travellers and itinerant craftsmen. John Rufus Bruce had been one of the sandalwooders. These men cut the wood for the rich Middle East market in temple incense for as long as the groves of it lasted (1847–1880). Their depots were linked by trails. 'Usually these led from one rocky outcrop to another, for at these points the sandalwooders had put down shallow soak-wells which filled with water seeping from the nearby rock catchment.'

The motor roads tend to bypass the old network and I had difficulty finding Bruce Rock, although it was within a mile of the settlement named after it. Eventually a winding track of yellow sand disclosed itself and at the end of it the wells turned out to be beautifully intact. One of them had a square stone parapet built up (recently) round its shaft, the other a circular one. The water in them still reflected the sky, thin shadows of willows and dwarf eucalypts dappled them. Lapped in their mild moist atmosphere, they seemed the gentlest reminder of a life for which the granite domes and their waters and copses had been essential — remote now as Hardy's *Woodlanders*.

Towards Hyden, whose Wave Rock was the other landmark I had heard of in Western Australia, the pelmets of cloud lowered, each one of them stretching its sombre level round as much as 40° of the horizon. Near Kalgarlin the rain came hosing down so densely that I lost interest in McGann Rock, somewhere down a dirt road between fallow fields, and pressed on towards the source of all this downpour with a growing sense of having passed through the looking-glass into a darkened dream. The road was still tarred, so narrow now that on one of the rare occasions when a muddy pick-up came towards me we would both play chicken, seeing whose nerve gave first and forced one into the thick brown dust of the soft shoulder.

At Hyden it was almost the Boorman/*Deliverance* experience again. In a minimal café where I drank an unwanted pot of tea and waited for the deluge to slacken, the tall scowling woman went on scowling when I asked for directions to the Rock — although its presence must have guaranteed her most of her customers — and gestured wordlessly eastward along the road where a shallow flood was gathering. Wet fields and the English language were familiar enough and yet, both now and that night at the hotel in Narembeen where sheepshearers were roaring jokes at each other and swigging Fosters, I was under-mined by a feeling that I had passed way beyond my own patch and would never see it again.

Wave Rock reared so imposingly in the photos — surely it had to be a section of a tall edge, like Stanage or Froggatt or Curbar where the Derbyshire gritstone juts out of the eastern Pennines? How could this watery plain, which at one point had me driving axle-deep for half a mile through permanent wetland, ever rise to any such thing? It didn't, exactly. One more turtle-back gradually rounded up — Wave Rock was the breaker of the granite swell on which I had been rising slowly for mile after mile.

The back of it slopes up through copsey woodland, the front of it steepens, hangs over in a lip which will never burst in foam, uniquely and classically beautiful, hollow-moulded by the leaching-out of metal salts from the rock. The trickling waters, held on by surface tension, perform their millennial curettage. The curve and the height of the Wave — only ten metres from base to crest — are enlarged by the vertical striping, barbarously beautiful as Aboriginal body make-up, in five colours from embrowned black through copper and peach to biscuit and lime-white. It curves from end to end as well as from lip to base, and the wings of it disappear behind thickets of wattle and casuarina. The incurve is wonderfully, improbably deep. The striping, like foam-streaks on the glassy face of the breaker along with the rearing-gathering shape of the whole, makes it seem to mimic, speeded up a millionfold, the event that swelled the igneous material upward in the crust of the continent.

Gold sun, released from behind the indigo rainclouds, was striking along the face of the Wave, making it gleam wetly although its over-hang had kept it dry. It was the last sun of the day and I was about to be benighted in this forlorn outback. I climbed the slope at the western end of the Wave and roved over the broad convexity of the top, between dozens of new-filled ponds and freshets. From here the beauty of the Wave was almost negated by a pair of walls made of stone flags set on edge. The one was a cunning use of the run-off, directing it into a little reservoir. The other, nearer the brink, could have no such use since it ended prematurely and allowed the water to pour down and waste itself in the sandy floor below. Could it be a safety wall, to save us silly tourists from ourselves?

I turned my back on the mean structure and padded down the steepest manageable slab at the east end, making for the Hippo's Yawn. The path threaded the forest at the very base of the outcrop — more stream-bed than path, floored in coarse-crystalled orange sand. Where the water deepened too much for comfort, I took to the glacis and tiptoed through the pulsing films of run-off. Blunt monoliths loomed in the bush ahead and revealed themselves as the skull-bones of the Hippo. She (or he) is gorgeous, a blunt jutting snout arching six or seven metres above a gullet as deep again. From a Jonah position inside, the curve of the palate or upper jaw shows unblemished for 140° of the 180°. At each side it rests on a thin process as well as on more massive ends, so that the whole skullpture is beautifully lifelike — you can almost hear the creak as the toothless jawbone starts to hinge down on to its marshy food. Only the size makes 'Hippo' inappropriate. Perhaps it should be the Whale's Yawn — the Whale and the Wave.

At the hotel in Narimbeen, where the ageless furniture and the aroma of tobacco and hops carried me back to hotels in the middle of Ireland forty years ago, I was delighted by evidence that the granite domes are cherished. The landlady, Jinty Toovey, turned out to have taught art at the very school in Dumfriesshire where one of my oldest friends had worked for many years. As we talked in her tiny office and I explained my project, she recalled that at Kwolyin, sixty kilometres west of Bruce Rock and a hundred from here, people were so incensed by a plan to quarry the granite from an outcrop nearby that they demonstrated with placards saying 'DON'T ROCK THE ROCK'.

When I reached the place I found a newish sign well painted in chunky letters naming it as 'COAMIN ROCK'. Nearby lay some raw-yellow boulders, as though off-loaded by a dumper interrupted in its work, with drifts of wild sunflowers already growing round them. The demo seemed to have succeeded.

I had also wanted to get from Jinty the whereabouts of Emu Rock, the nearest outcrop to Narembeen, and she was able to tell me that they knew it as Roe's Look-out. One dirt road led off at right angles to another and presently a weathered sign directed me to a place I might otherwise have disregarded. By narrowing tracks, which in the end were barely driveable, I gained height gradually. The loam and herbage thinned to nothing, the granite lay bare, and the summit was marked by a silvery monolith the height of a small person. Beside it a very old eucalypts with a weather-blasted trunk curved out into a last surviving branch. Roe might have seen it in his prime. He was a captain in the Royal Navy, Surveyor General at a time when military expeditions were being sent inland from the coast by the Swan River settlers to find out whether good land for grazing and cultivation lay beyond the Darling Escarpment. In 1836 he named the outcrop Emu Hill. From this viewpoint the land for the taking must have looked limitless — level, well enough watered, asking to be cleared of bush and turned into these green lowlands that now echo the England of huge fields and uprooted hedges in Lincolnshire or Wiltshire.

Roe's stay here in the autumn of 1836 was the first occupation of the site by people other than native Australians. He depended on the water springing beside the various outcrops he explored, but considered it 'temporary' until some Aboriginals directed him to 'an old native well close to a granite rock' at Mangowine. The invaders are still here, the original people have gone, overwhelmed by the likes of Lefroy, Superintendent of Convicts, a generation after Roe. He sounds as though he dabbled in real estate. In 1863 he wrote: 'Nothing could give a more unique and characteristic appearance to the future towns of this country, which undoubtedly is capable of maintaining an exceedingly dense population, than those massive and magnificent elevations of bare rock, projecting in their respective centres high above every structure raised by the hand of man, and doubtless they would contribute no less to the health and enjoyment of their future populations than to the beauty of their appearance.'

I wonder if Mr Lefroy, or his copy-writer, ever came here? If anyone succumbed to his purple hyperboles, he might have been baffled, or exasperated, by these most unassuming crags. In fact such settlers as there were chose to move east to Narembeen because its district, unlike Emu Hill, was open to the liquor trade, as Jinty Toovey told me with an Irish relish. The heyday of this region seems doomed to have been short-lived. The shabbiness I was scenting all down this far western fringe of the Nullarbor resembles that of another zone reliant on agricultural income, the American Middle West, whose produce is losing value in a world which would rather deal in currency, property values, insurance than in real things.

At the foot of the last granite mass I explored I came upon a poignant trace of this dying-back, in its turn, of the culture that had displaced the Aboriginal one. The little sign at the roadside west of Kwolyin said 'Kokerbin Hill'. The profile in the middle distance drew me by its much greater bulk and steeper contours than any of the other outcrops. Even Superintendent Lefroy would not have had to tell lies about this. It rose up out of pasture fields a few miles north of the road west from Bruce Rock to Quairading, sunlit under a blue-and-white sky, with that ineffable look of having once been the hub of a society that clings to many low isolated hills all over the world, to Bronze Age forts that still faintly roughen or flatten a skyline, to Dunadd, the Pictish capital in Argyll, to Glastonbury Tor in Dorset, to Ewaninga south of Alice Springs and to the Magaliesberg in the Transvaal.

On a fork of the trail that wound through open woodland to the base of Kokerbin, a sign said, 'This stone marks the site of the Kwolyn South No.1 School (Kokerbin Hill 1917). Serving the children of the area 1912–1928.' A few miles away, on a disused loop of the highway, a similar sign next to a burnt-out pub recorded the Townsite School, 1920–1956. Jetsam from a little social tide that had ebbed for good, baring the hill and leaving it to be itself again.

In the woods a sign or two encouraged visitors to follow a beaten path. I wanted to touch and know the dome itself so I forced my way between trunks and sprays of wiry foliage and picked a path along the line where the rock plunged into sandy earth. The flanks of Kokerbin were rough enough to tear your skin with their large crystals and were seamed and wizened as an Indian elephant's hide seen close to. No brown eye looked out at me. Gullies blocked with chock-stones invited climbing, then repulsed me by their steepness and lack of holds. The rock angled back more easily as it rounded into its western shoulder, at the point where I emerged from the shadow cast by the northerly sun. I padded upwards, babooning on all four limbs at first, then evolving a stage or two and becoming quite human as I stood by the panorama at the summit.

Bruce Rock (25 miles) was just visible among bush, like a grey sleeper's face upturned. Wave Rock was 127 miles away south-east by east, Perth (and therefore Kalamunda where I was staying) 167 miles west by south, and Port Hedland on the north coast of Western Aus-

tralia 1,430 miles due north. I would have to drive almost as far for
Mount Augustus in a week's time.

This curved field of granite was perfectly tranquil and high enough
up to help you see the millions of farmed acres with a buzzard's eye.
They looked like my native Aberdeenshire, especially the classic beef
and oats and barley country of Buchan north of Aberdeen, though less
affluent and less well-kempt. Boulders seven metres high — remnants
of the time when Australia was in Antarctic latitudes, being reft and
bulldozed by sheets of ice — had grouped themselves up here in little
herds, ruminants brown as bison, with nothing to graze on but stone. I
bridged up between the haunches of two neighbours, clambered with
difficulty and rasped fingertips on to the back of another, and perched
in breezy filtered sunlight. Tracts of sap-green and bluish-green Australia flowed into me and over me, steeping me in the mixture of exile
and expectancy that must have been felt by the people who came from
Barra and East Anglia and County Wicklow to this end of the earth.

The way off to the north turned into a track that bent back on itself
and passed between the breasts of Kokerbin by a shallow gorge. I
cleaved to the base of the rock again and found myself in the middle of
the half-shaded southern side, at one end of a wave as beautiful as
Hyden. The upcurve reared, striped in luminous Aboriginal colours,
charcoal and glowing ochre and darkest chocolate. The curled lip
rounded out eight or nine metres above my head, less high than
Hyden, tall enough to impend like a more daunting breaker than any I
have quite dared to swim into on the beaches of the Pacific in California or the Indian Ocean north of Perth. Hard up against the very point
where the wave burst out of the ground, bushes flourished more than
head high, their spindly grass-green foliage flourishing like seaweed
in the currents undersea. The children from Kwolyn School would
have played hide-and-seek here eighty years ago, and generations
of unschooled children for centuries before that, as free in their wild
playground as the girls and boys photographed among the rock labyrinths of the Musgrave Ranges in our own lifetime.

13   The Biggest Rock in the World

The last trawl of the voyage stretched so far, to the remote crag with
its pompous alien title 'Mount Augustus', that I had no clear sense
of what lay at the end of the line and whether it could be hauled in. It

was said to be the 'biggest rock in the world' yet nobody had heard of it or seen its picture, not even the man in the Perth climbing shop. The Japanese don't fly in to snap it, apparently; there is no hotel there, no railway, no plane, no bus. It is a spot-height far out on a map with few names, where the red vein of the road stretches so thin it looks ready to snap in a curfuffle of desert dust and die back into the earth.

Every staging post on our way north from Perth was a landmark where minerals had built into forms that were marvels in themselves, each more isolated and unfrequented than the last. We left the Brand Highway near Thirsty Point and drove south for a few miles, then inland again at Hangover Bay. Ahead of us, occupying a long reach of dazzling quartz sand called Nambung, a Chinese army of limestone spearheads rose up out of the desert, each fanged with its own black shadow. Some were blunt as molars, others sharp as assegais, tapering like specialised tools, or as squat and triangular as the dorsal fins of sharks. They were all sizes, from a foot or two to twice the height of a man. The crowding of them, running to many hundreds, and their consistent colouring, pale cheese yellow lower bodies and grizzled heads, made them a tribe, from tall elders down to dwarfy infants. They grew from mobile dunes that became soft limestone, were over-layed by humus and a layer of calcrete that finally split, disintegrated, and blew away again, leaving the original stone divided into these slim survivors. The rocks were not animal-like, let alone anthropomorphic, and seemed to have no myth, presumably because there was no water to attract the storytelling families. The place is outside culture, or was until it became a 'beauty spot'.

I was travelling with Nigel Gray, a long-time friend and co-author, who had emigrated from England to Western Australia some years before. Just as I was saying to him, 'I've seen nothing like this in my life,' I remembered that I had. In 1991 Anne and I had found a place called Cabarceno, in Calabria south of Santander. Here too hordes of stone spearheads stood up like *penitentes* in an ice-field. They were limestone, anything up to ten metres high, and Celtic or Roman in that this was a prime centre of copper and ironmining from the Bronze Age onward. The Celts made cauldrons and other implements from the metals until the Romans — excited by news of 'a high mountain which, incredible though it may seem, is solid metal' — came here led by Augustus in person. The Celts 'resisted utterly'. When they were at last defeated, the Romans cut out their tongues and eyes and enslaved them in hellish mines and foundries. Now the natives are fighting back again as Japanese theme-park developers try to buy this large piece of

Spain. The regional president has said Cantabria will not sell. Since he has also described his province as an *'infierno fiscal de Dante'*, perhaps the invaders will triumph once again.

At Cabarceno we wandered through an armoury of blades, each daubed with succulent brown earth. It looked as if it had been plastered on them in some magnificent conception of outdoor theatre. The reverse is the case. The brown is rust. Most of the iron-rich soil has been washed away, for smelting, from whole hillsides that were structured through and through by these huge fins of rock. The industry peaked before the Middle Ages and again to make artillery in the seventeenth century. The lode was last mined in 1989. A remnant of headgear still stands, for our interest, at the top of a chute down a spoilheap like a small mountain. Its slopes are coal-black with lurid orange veining. Down among the calcareous tusks you can climb on nubbins like the rust blisters on a submarine wreck, sidle round the tip to the hidden rear, and peer down into crevasses soft-lipped with dewy fern, the mouths of prehistoric workings or the graveyards of Celts.

At the north end of Shark Bay, just south of a seasonal lagoon called Lake MacLeod, we again turned off the North West Coastal Highway. Two miles from the ocean a lighthouse with a white stem and a red tip, like Chambers Pillar, stood abandoned on the last bluff before the coastal plain. A stack of dead twigs adorned the platform round the extinct lamp, the nest of some large raptor. At the shore, from a pavement of fretted sandstone ten metres above the sea, maddened bassoons blew suddenly on several notes. Spume thrilled straight up, fifteen, twenty metres of it, a shimmering feather which flung sideways on the gusting southerly and pelted the reef with fusillades of white rain.

We approached with difficulty. Salt-gust had tooled the rock into dragon spines and pockets with toothed edges. The prickliest area dropped three metres into a pit pocked all over and filmed with gelatinous green weed. In a little geo at the back the master blowhole raged. A fifty-centimetre mouth belched white water. Above its soupy bubbling thick jets of spray flared off northward. Near it two lesser holes signalled a spasm by shrilling furiously. The sound hit the nerves with a shock. A hollow dunt from the invisible depths could be heard as the droplets hosed upward, the stream of them shuddering, giving out an accelerated lion-breath.

It was like a weird steam-engine, violent vapour bursting up the cylinders, finding no piston-head, fleeing into the sunlight and blowing away in short-lived rainbows. As we watched and listened, its rhythms became clearer. The mouth breathed only, ejecting no water. Or a heavy cauliflower of foam spilled and roiled round the pit. This happened four or five times. Then, with no apparent heavier sea, or correlation with the waves, the mouth spewed a full storm of spume, signalled by the fastest, hoarsest scream and jet from the twin lesser holes, giving meaning to Pablo Neruda's extraordinary lines from 'Rider in the Rain' —

> steam like a demented milk accompanies
> the hardened water with fleeting doves.

I wanted to see down into the mouth itself. If I crept up to its verge from the south side, surely the bulk of its spew would whisk away from me? And Nigel could take photos with the long lens, out of reach of the salt-gust? I stripped to shorts and trainers and clambered down the painful spines into the pit. The ear-impact of the jets starting up was still unnerving me, making me want to back off. The amount of water coming out of the rock couldn't be dangerous — could it? I padded nearer, set my feet on flat rock next to the mouth, keeping one hand on slimy spikes. The holes hissed fiercely. I jumped back and up, bruising a finger. I had missed a chance. I crept down again, into jet and dazzle and breathy roar. The mouth volleyed its utmost, sea climbed the sky and fell back on to me with a mass weightier than mere liquid. I clutched the nearest rim and braced myself. Water ran off me, off rock, seethed like new milk in a bucket, and ebbed down the mouth in glistening falls. Then all this happened again, cold water avalanching out of the sky, thumping and shaking me, doing no harm.

I must look straight down the mouth. I darted to the edge. Intense white boiling. I flinched. The holes hissed and roared but no water volleyed upwards. I looked in at a braiding of rills, pouring back down into the dark. Suddenly the mouth vomited, flared, water crushed down on to me. I was inside the event now, accepting its threats and shocks. Had I really seen right down there? I hung on to the spiny edge, trying to suss the rhythm — it couldn't be done, not while I was in mid-maelstrom. On the blackish back wall of the geo, yellow was moving — I'd no glasses on — what *was* it, a spastic banana, some yellow husk, a guinea-flower calyx washed in from some jungle source? I tried to focus — they were crabs, a pair of crabs with crocus bodies and ebony-and-amber claws, brandishing and sidling on dimpled gleaming rock. Had the jets blasted them up? Were they lurking, waiting for the tide to flow?

I balanced quickly over to the verge and looked deeply in. As usual nature was complex. It was no more 'a hole', a straight shaft, than our throats are. The ebbing water was dropping not straight down but sideways through a kink in the runnel's gut. As air plus water pulverised to spray came hissing up yet again, I forced myself back and out of the frenzy — sorry to leave this elemental focus where a human could live for a time, mingling that pure force with his own capacity to exult.

These were morsels of rock, reminders of its versatility on our way to the Big One which lay somewhere up there among ranges with disappointing map names like Waldburg, Kennedy, and Gooch. Here the roads were following the rivers. Between the Nambung pinnacles and the blowholes at Quobba we stayed overnight at Kalbarri and walked in the morning on reefs at the mouth of the Murchison estuary, watching an osprey fishing fruitlessly in the waves where the fresh water met the salt. At Carnarvon we turned inland up the Gascoyne, northward up the Lyons, and east again at its bend at Minnie Creek where it flows between the Waldburgs and the Kenneths. At Carnarvon I negotiated uneasily with 'the owner of Mount Augustus' — big Jim, senior of the Edneys, on whose tribal land the rock stands. In his son Ernest's office at the Aboriginal Cultural Centre the two huge men listened courteously to our plans. Jim's eyes were whitening with age. Ernest's skin was smooth deep brown and he was obviously in his prime and on top of the game.

'Yes, sure,' he said, 'my father will meet you there, at the station, and he will tell you the stories about the mountain.'

'Three hundred dollars,' put in Jim.

I settled quickly for this when Ernest seemed to be taking my agreeable smile as a sign of weakness and started to raise the price to $A400.

Back on the continuum of the red roads, it felt as though speeding along their ruts had become a permanent condition of life. A corner was an event. These roads are rectilinear as the boundaries of the 'blocks' and 'stations', the quickest way from A to B in a 4-wheel-drive. They are the antithesis of the traces left by explorers like Giles or Sturt, whose efforts to steer through the oceans of dune and the crumbling sandstone ranges look on the maps at their most baffled like the webbing of a spider deranged by insecticide.

So we scooted along hour after hour in the little red hire-car. There seemed to be no other car in the region and not more than four or five jeeps and pick-ups in a day. The corrugations made us jump like an ear of corn in a hot frying-pan. Grasshoppers five centimetres long kept hitting us — well, we kept hitting them — with a phuttt-phuttt-phuttt.

They died in the windscreen wipers, the grille, the radiator itself, on the number-plate, sidelights, headlights, in there on the battery leads, washer-bottle, engine cowling, distributor cap — grasshoppers daffodil-yellow, mauve, cigar-brown. When I picked one carcase off the windscreen, its huge bent hindleg slowly flexed. The smell of the pâté of baked grasshopper on the front of the car was like fermenting hay — naturally, they were grasshoppers, but where was the grass, apart from the harsh wires of the spinifex?

The desert floor was upholstered with flowers, short-stemmed yellow 'daisies', long-stemmed clumps of lavender 'scabious', purple flowers unknown to me like upright pincushions, drooping scarlet heads of the desert pea named by Sturt, with its fine myth of the woman whose warrior lover made her a cloak of red parrot feathers. When he went off during a drought to search for food, the tribe moved on, she wouldn't leave, and when the rains came and the tribe returned, the red-and-black flower was blooming where she had sat and waited . . . The massed colour of the flowers vibrated and dazzled — so many because pollination is hard to achieve and each plant multiplies to avoid the danger of missing out. From time to time majestic emus flounced through the gold and purple flowerbeds, once crossing the road in front of us from covert to covert, picking their huge feet up delicately as though to avoid dirtying them in the churned vermilion gravel. Once they were safe, fifty metres off, they raised their black hooked heads on erect necks and surveyed the bush while I stared entranced, as though looking through a telescope into prehistory and its great swaying animal forms.

Between Mount Sandiman and Mount Thomson a kangaroo, rufous as a fox in its new coat for the summer, bounced athletically off between mulga bushes, one of only three I saw alive compared with fifty or sixty dead — furry brown mounds if they were fresh corpses, one of them reduced to spine and rib-cage prostrate in the middle of the road, its bones stained stale butcher-red with soil and dried blood. Around noon we overtook the grader as it levelled the gravel and piled its little rampart at the verge. Now that we had outstripped it, there were continuous pink and orange flowers in the middle of the road. The land on all sides lay in a trance. The rivers had stopped running and existed as separate pools. On their banks the boles of the river-gums shone silken white, serenely beautiful as though they could live forever without rain, their narrow sickle leaves dangling like earrings.

As we ate and drank beside a bumpy cement ford across the Edmund, fire-colour flashed and bobbed on a skeletal tree — a Red-rumped kingfisher, remote descendant of Lundba at Uluru who warned the Mala people that the devil-dog was coming. The sun was lowering into the north-west haze by now, making no difference to the colour of the land, which was ember-red at every hour of every day. When Mount Augustus raised himself at last, his western limbs glowed amethyst as coolth stole over his hot recumbent body, the slopes of his flanks, the cliff which made his ribs and hip in the middle of the northern side. He was every inch a tall, felled being. It was perfect that he should turn out to be, in the eyes of his own people, Burringurrah, Sleeping-man.

Where were his own people? We were staying in the Langs' guest-house on their rough little farm at Cobra Station, just out of sight of Burringurrah to the west. When we called for Big Jim at the shop and trailer-site at Mount Augustus intersection, there was bad news. A phone call from Carnarvon the night before reported that he had fallen asleep somewhere on the 450-kilometre drive, plunged off into the bush, and been admitted to hospital with injured ribs. So we must climb Burringurrah first and hope to learn his stories later.

Our rudimentary sketch map showed that the only trail to the summit struck up the mountain — already we were calling it 'the mountain', not 'the rock' — from a creek called Beedoboondu near a disused cattle-pound at the western end. Years of harsh drought drove the Aboriginal people away for good some forty years ago. The rainfall here is very low, little falling as either monsoon or winter showers. Today, yet again, the high white flecks of cirrocumulus looked painted on the blue. Between boulders and pendulous trees a thread of trodden path snaked into the base of the mountain past a deep stream, clearly unfailing. Its pools were verdant with fat water-weeds and mantles of algae. As the slope set in, a broad gully led gently upward by spillways where spates must sluice over boulder-chokes.

This natural causeway was naked except where clusters of flowers with mauve bells created a primal garden. Coarse sands streaming down it in the rare floods have buffed it to so glossy a patina that it was often too dazzling to look at. It was a dream ascent between jambs of rock as massive as the Lion Gateway into Agamemnon's citadel at Mycenae. For two hours our feet never backslid an inch, or kicked up dust or took in painful grit.

When we turned on the top of a boulder and looked out southward over the land-sea, two hills had mounded into sight as though the body of the continent, lying supine, had breathed in, raising its breasts. They could have been Mount James and Mount Gascoyne, ninety kilometres away. Francis Gregory, who named Burringurrah Mount Augustus after his brother, had been able to take bearings on mountains more than 150 kilometres away. Now the gully was narrowing and twisting off westward where we wanted to head south of east for the last three kilometres of climb to the summit. A dusty trail led through dense bush. Where it became wearisomely indirect, we slanted upward by natural steps in red and brittle strata. The bare-swept character that seems the essence of summit at home is replaced in the tropics by luxuriant skylines. So here the higher we rose the thicker grew the bush until, 1,105 metres above sea level, a strongly-built drystone pillar cairn as tall as a tall man stood up on the final reef. I climbed it to see out over the dense acacia foliage. The vista was as large and blue as an ocean, wild land all round the compass, so visible and large a sector of our planet that it became at once, and I think will remain for me, a classic image of

> the very world which is the world
> Of all of us, the place in which, in the end,
> We find our happiness, or not at all.

I never met Big Jim again. A few days later he spoke to me from his hospital bed.

'Yes, I run off the road that night. My ribs not too good. Be alright.'

Then he told me about the features of the Sleeping-man.

'That mark right across the west end of the hill — there they caught up with him and they hit him with a big stick. He got away from his tribal camp, see, and he walked off, so they speared him. He runned away, from the Carnarvon ranges, and he came along the top end of the Gascoyne. He made his way down there by Lyons River, where it turns, five mile back. We call him Burringurrah — that's Sleeping-man.'

So the rock gully was his great slant wound? Other points on the rock each had their story. 'The knoll at the end [a flat-topped spur at the south-east corner], that where the stub of the spear broke off in his thigh. It got my name now — Edney's Look-out, they call it. And he lost his big toe at Beedoboondu, and at Mundee a cart ran over his leg, it cut his leg off. They knock you out with a stick, to cut your leg off . . . '

Every mountain had its story. Ranging over the hills and rivers sixty kilometres to the south, he described one as 'pointy' and another as 'long' and told their stories with a brevity that was acutely tantalising — fragments from the epic of this country.

'The Mount Gould,' he said, 'he came down the Murchison; and Yarlarweelor, she came down the old river [the Yalgar?]. He wanted them to get married. She turned him down. So, now, one is facing the north, the other is facing south-east. The two rivers met there, that's where they divide.'

Both confluence and separation — it was a beautiful case of the naming and characterising habit with which the native Australians (and Americans, and all other original peoples) accounted for every landmark made by rock on the face of the Earth, even the smallest. A Navajo story about fossils sees them as bits of monsters brought back by Naayee'neizhghani the Monster-slayer to his father the Sun, 'wing feathers and hairs, eyes and innards'. He buried them as best he could but 'sometimes if we look very carefully we can see small parts of them protruding out of the rocks: a finger here, a claw there'. So on the north-east coast of England fossils were seen as snakes cast over a cliff at Whitby by the Abbess Hild or as rosary beads forged by St Cuthbert on dark stormy nights at Lindisfarne. In the eastern Mohave Desert the pre-Paiute, the Chemehuevi, saw waterholes as the result of spills from jugs carried by a giant as he stepped over the ranges on his way to visit Ocean-woman.

Uluru is a comprehensive archive of the great war of the cosmos in the Creation-time. Although the pocking and grooving of its colossal form were bound to arouse supreme imaginative efforts, they were of a piece with landmarking as created by the nomads all over Australia (and world-wide). Consider some motifs from the Flinders Ranges in South Australia. A bumpy mountain called Mudlunha [Mount John] is where two spirit-men or heroes cooked a kangaroo and threw away its hip bone. Traces of copper in the ground beside a creek are where they found their emu meat was going green with rot and threw it away. The mountains enclosing the Frome River are the mud walls some Yura people built round their place and two points of rock are the heads of snakes their rivals sent to attack and which ran into each other. Black rocks at a cave-mouth are where Wildu the eagle scorched some crows who were mocking him, making magpies half black and the others black all over. It is a matter of seizing upon outstanding features and allowing a story to blossom which will imprint these invaluable points of reference in a culture without maps or texts. So on Half Dome in Yosemite the black lichenous streaks on a big white dihedral were made by the tears of an Indian girl called Tis-Sa-Ack.

The Flinders Ranges themselves were made in a struggle between a buck kangaroo and a buck euro. Mandya the euro got a sore hip, took a stone out from the sore and blew on it, and hills started up from the plain. When Urdlu the kangaroo saw what his rival had done, he 'pushed the ranges back to where they are now' with a 'big sweep of his tail'. You can see it beautifully from the air as the mountains show themselves like crumples in the earth's brown hide.

The stories are a brimming-over into free or playful invention of functions inherent in the human brain, or at least in our culture since *homo sapiens* evolved, if not before. We must name, to make landmarks unforgettable in the wilderness of kindred features. We must explain — we can see how very young children actively want to tell one bird, say, from another. We must let into our consciousness, and our ethics, the conflicts between forces (person and tribe, youths and elders, sun and water, water and rock, congealed rock and the molten magma beneath it) which frighten us — which we know are permanent and come with the territory. It is striking to see how many of the Flinders stories (and they are typical) hinge upon conflicts between groups, impulses, species. They are social as well as elemental. Iliktajara the gekko-man who became Chambers Pillar was a runaway from his tribe and so was Burringurrah the Sleeping-man. So in the Flinders Ranges the marks across the goanna's tail and the white spots in the fur of the wild cat are seen as the scars where the elders' spears thrust in to punish two lovers from different tribes who eloped.

The nomadic groups had to hold together, to ensure that everything necessary was catered for, breeding, child-minding, food-getting, initiation. The last archetype they were likely to value was the lone wanderer who has been so charismatic in west-European culture since the factory system split and dispersed the peasant communities.

As we climbed Burringurrah, drove round it, walked some way into it to find its springs, look-outs, and painted caves, we were playing at stories ourselves. 'That must be his head,' Nigel would say, looking up at the stepped northern brow, or 'Those are his hands folded on his stomach.' Of course the features of the great rock-beings need not be likenesses, though some are stunningly so, the 'Indian head' on the side of Great Gable in Cumbria, for example, or the Cailleach [Earth-mother] I found on Glen Einich-side in the Cairngorms.

Many features were, in the original Australian vision, so subtly rooted in their practices that invaders were bound to fall foul of them or violate them. In Yiwara, in the Gibson Desert, all rock alignments were sacred landmarks or transformed totemic beings, bound into the cult of initiation at puberty. In what Giles named Glen Cumming, the totemic penis, Yula, pursued the Seven Sisters and split a cliff trying to reach one of them. The water dripping from the ceiling of a cave is his semen. Hollows in exposed bedrock were caused in the Creation-time by a marsupial Cat-youth as he sat waiting to be carried to a site for circumcision. The rock-walls on the sunny side were Sun-men, the opposite walls were Shade-men, and these were acted at recent (now extinct) ceremonies by two groups of singers. After the rite the Cat-men turned into stones, 436 of them, which until the middle of this century were kept carefully in a serpentine alignment and cleared of weeds and rubble. It is possible that when Giles was attacked by men with spears at Fort Mueller, wantonly from his viewpoint, it was because the Aboriginal men were afraid he was about to interfere with, and maybe use for shelters and campfires, 135 boulders in a mulga grove — a mere rickle of stones to him, to them the bodies of totemic possums from the Creation-time.

Burringurrah had looked and felt in every sense a mountain. Is it 'The biggest rock in the world'? Does it matter? It — he — could almost be one of the lion-couchant mountains in the Mounth that divides Aberdeenshire from Scotland to the south — if the rock were grey, not vermilion, if the bluey-green foliage were pine, not mulga, melalenca, and red-gum. True, Burringurrah is a monocline — the rock is homogeneous (apart from some thread-like veins of quartz) and there is no split or change of age in it, vertical or horizontal. He is all one being and both longer and higher than Uluru. Only everybody perceives Uluru as a rock, as *the* rock, supremely salient and naked, durability incarnate. Burringurrah's dense coverts (through which we bushwhacked for an exhausting hour in a fruitless effort to look straight down the northern crag and suss it for future climbs), his bones showing through in broken ribs, his skin scruffy with scree and dusty soil — these are so much the lineaments of what is usually called a mountain that 'rock' is finally a misnomer, a term for the geologists and the promoters of tourism.

They are developing this mountain. We could have done without the five-centimetre spots of white paint that show the way up the gully, since this is perhaps the most unmistakable mountain route in the entire world, and the plastic tags on the trees along the ridge, which wipe out the pleasures of way-finding and getting lost. Spurs off the road that rings the mountain are signposted to 'Edinye's Springs', a fine rocky path to the knoll where the spear-stub sticks out, and the painted cave, scooped cliffs glowing lurid flame-orange, with simple designs of serpents and rows of holes. The hand-out promises 'The Biggest Rock in the World', '100s of kinds of wild flowers', and 'Much More'. It is 'fast becoming a Mecca'. No, it isn't. On a flawless late-winter day, with a light breeze and the thermometer at 80°F, five other people were on the mountain. Two of them gave up low down. Not more than a couple of off-road vehicles used the Mount Augustus trailer site at night and the Cobra Homestead family were stoical about the tourist situation.

'No, there haven't been many visitors coming through. It's the kangaroos we're depending on. They've been quite good lately.'

The farmers and professional hunters shoot them and sell the carcases for pet food and the American burger market.

Francis Gregory climbed Burringurrah on 3 June 1858 and named it after brother Augustus, who was off in South Australia 'conducting the expedition in quest of the remains of Dr Leichardt'. He himself was on a quest for fresh pastures, sponsored by settlers following his success the year before. It strikes me now that many of these outlands which the explorers found and the pioneers opened with such travail are places in which, really, the human race can no longer live. In a barely credible diaspora we came here out of the industrial slums and the ravaged peasant communities. How delectable the abundance of both land and independence looked, and were, to crofters cleared from tiny rented holdings on the shell-sand meadows of the Western Isles, to labourers earning twelve shillings a week in the flea and cholera-ridden backstreets of Glasgow and Liverpool. To move still further out, from the well-watered grasslands surveyed by the likes of Captain J.V. Roe, was something else again.

The Langs at Cobra Station are making a life of sorts on their station called Cobra because it is a hundred kilometres long and only ten across. Their homemade plank house and wing of little bedrooms, originally an inn for the first prospectors here in the 1890s, was trellised with bougainvillea. At the back a poinciana tree spread its shade across a lawn so coarse it felt like walking on brushes. The place was all cosy contrivance. To soak the grasshopper pâté off the radiator grille I drew hot water from a Heath Robinson outside boiler. Its little furnace was fed by the burning end of a four-metre tree-trunk which was being slowly consumed. Nearby a galah in a cage said 'lo cocky', 'lo cocky' over and over again in a sugary simper, then gnashed a beakful of its own feathers as though desperate to build a nest.

We were served very English meals of stewed meat and vegetables in the parlour. The family ate at another table — the farmer, his wife, four fair-haired daughters, and a grandparent, the elders in aprons and dungarees. Grace was said before the soup was brought. Mr Lang had steel-rimmed spectacles, short steely hair, and fingers thick and used as the hafts of old tools. In front of a board wall the Langs would have made a classic portrait by Dorothy Lange or Walker Evans from the Dirty Thirties in Oklahoma or Tennessee.

Outside, in a yard of beaten earth, shagged-out bulbous cars from the forties and fifties, earth-caked trailers, and a truck with 'Cobra Station' on the door stood about like items in a folk museum. It was hard to tell which were in use and which were derelict. I utterly wish that family well. I wonder if they haven't perched in a place where human-social life was never more than barely on. The water is too deep down and bitter — one station may have fifty water-windmills to maintain. The summers are too hot, the winters too thirsty, the leafage too hard and narrow.

Big Jim Edney translated Warrarla, among the trees on the north side of Burringurrah, as 'Paradise'. He said, 'That was the dancing ground.' He spoke with nostalgic fondness about Goolinee, the cattle pool among silver-trunked gumtrees on the Lyons halfway between Cobra and Mount Augustus. 'The bullwhacker grass at the sides of the pool,' he said, 'it was white tucker, real good.'

Now his people have left. Their paradise is empty. Maybe this place is fit only for the mulga bushes and the ghost gums, the kangaroos with their trusting curiosity and their ears alert as red deer, the goannas scuttling between the grasses like dusty dragons, and the pairs of powder-blue doves we saw at the roadside whose eyes are said to have been reddened by weeping for their lost millstones.

H. M. S. Victory *being towed into Gibraltar after the Battle of Trafalgar in 1805.*

PART THREE
The Straits of Gibraltar

---

14   Stone Poles of the Earth

All over the world, in Mongolia and the Arctic, in North Africa and Palestine and Scotland, stories were told about clashing rocks or pairs of rocks like the jambs of a gateway. Often they flanked the door to the Otherworld. They were the Jaws of Death, or a miraculous gate beyond which lay Oceanus, the Isle of the Blessed, the Realm of the Dead. According to the Karens of Burma, 'in the west there are two massive strata of rock which are continually opening and shutting, and between these strata the sun descends at sunset.'

The space between the rocks could house the water or the bread of life. Any being, whether animal or human, who passed through in a quest for the most valuable things, or as a test of prowess, was in danger of failing to get back unscathed. As the gates clashed shut, they could crush or cut off the ship's stern ornament or the hindlegs of the hero's horse, the hare's scut or the stork's tail-feathers. In the Navajo creation epic two heroic 'children of the Sun', who are bidding to supercede 'the old gods', only manage to pass through 'a narrow chasm between two high cliffs' by repeating words taught them by Spider Woman. The rocks keep trying to snap shut on them, they quickly draw back, and the rocks relent when the special words are spoken.

In my search for sites or surviving tangible symbols of these myths, I was looking for pairs of rocks that would be remarkable in their own right, monuments to elemental forces, with a gap between them which was frightening to jump, a seaway which was stirring to sail across. The prime site of that kind in Europe must be Gibraltar, its straits, and its African counterpart. Hercules, god of strength, for his tenth labour had to steal the red oxen of Geryon, grandson of Medusa the Gorgon, who lived a hundred miles west of Gibraltar at Gades (now Cadiz). He annihilated the Libyan Amazons and the Gorgons in North Africa, then came to a rock barrier on his journey west and tore it apart, leaving two pillars between which he passed. That is to say, five and a half million years ago the ocean broke through the limestone reef between the places the Phoenicians were to call Calpe (later Gibraltar) and Abyla (later Ceuta).

The Mediterranean was then a desert basin, deeper and hotter than Death Valley in California today. The shifting of the plates in the Earth's crust had cut it off from the primeval ocean which geologists now call Tethys, after one of the Titans. Over two million years it had dried out, leaving a few brackish lakes like the Dead Sea. Then the melting of polar ice and glaciers after an Ice Age raised the oceanic levels and salt water poured in from the west in a waterfall five kilometres high. It poured for at least a hundred years. The waters came brimming up crags the colour of old bones, all round the rims of what are now Spain, Corsica and Sardinia, Italy, the Ionian Islands, what was Yugoslavia, mainland Greece . . . Our own species had not yet evolved. Tribes of erect hunters, australopithecines, lived in what is now Morocco. The roar of the falls, the teeming mists, the rainbows making their arcs will have formed a pillar of cloud by day, marking a place where the peoples could no longer pass on any sally northward as they followed the bison and the musk-ox.

That waterfall and the sea-way, whose current still flows at over four knots and roughens the surface between Algeciras and Tangier into a welter of whirlpools and overfalls, must have been unsurpassed as a display, both intimidating and inspiring, of the world's primal force. Gibraltar itself is so tremendous a landmark that it makes a fit house for all those stories in which destruction by water or fire is kept at bay and a way through to the light of the west is kept open.

As Anne and I flew in down the Spanish coast after the sun had set — compelled to come in by a circle over the sea because of the continuing grievance between Spain and the United Kingdom — a black island seemed to float among the swarm of yellow and orange lights. The plane dipped. The black island grew — was it island or mountain? The plane banked, west and north and east again, and we were skimming past a scarp of haggard rock that tapered two hundred — three hundred — five hundred metres into the sky. A few days after we arrived, on our first visit, the air roared and out of it came a wing of RAF Tornadoes painted in yellow desert camouflage. They had just completed their Herculean mission to destroy all the bridges, all the power-stations and waterworks, and all the conscript soldiers in modern Babylonia — that is to say Iraq.

The Herakles/Hercules power of the Aegean cultures had its counterpart further east and south in Melkarth, Sesostris, and Baal, in Sandon the lion-god of Tarsus, in Attis, Tammuz, and Vishnu. Hercules, like the giant cut into the chalk downland at Cerne Abbas in Dorset, wielded a club and leaned on it when he was tired. Freudians would interpret the club as phallic. The Graeco-Roman (also the Babylonian, Egyptian, Indian, and Scottish) myths emphasise more the whole gamut of powers, in the Earth, the waters, and the skies, which set the conditions for our lives.

The Rock of Gibraltar is not much like a pillar, Monte Hacho in Ceuta still less so. The upright symbol was crucial and sucked into itself many different natural shapes. In ancient Babylonia pillars embodied the 'world spine' or 'world tree' and pillars for worship carried stone heads in the shape of a lion, a ram, a lance. At Calpe/Abyla, now Gibraltar/Hacho, the notion of pillars or twin jambs of a great portal was especially potent because what lay beyond was the impassable and unknown. When the Spaniards followed in the wakes of Columbus and Magellan and set out across the Atlantic for El Dorado, the land of gold (and silver), they dropped the negative from the old motto *Ne plus ultra* and moulded into their coins the confident phrase *Plus ultra*, asserting that there was more beyond. Modern empire-building had begun. The symbol they chose for their pieces-of-eight and doubloons was the twin Herculean pillars with ribbons entwining them and waves rippling round their plinths. So the almighty dollar-sign was invented. No doubt it is far-fetched to see anything in the fact that recently the dollar-sign has lost half its substance — one of the two uprights — and retained the mere ornament, that sinuous ribbon — $. The two decorated pillars and the motto still figure in the Spanish coat-of-arms.

Hercules' winning of Geryon's cattle is especially rich in meaning because it is an occidental myth. For people in the Graeco-Roman and North-African worlds the sun set in the straits between the Pillars. Geryon's red cattle were the light and heat of the westering sun. Hercules reached Geryon's hide-out by setting sail in the golden bowl of Helios the Sun, which was shaped like a water-lily, and sailing westward in it along the river of Oceanus. His defeat of Geryon and his ally Cacus, a fire god and son of Vulcan, was a victory for light and water over darkness and drought. In India the victory was Indra's, the Vedic thunder god, over Vritra the Obstructor, a drought demon.

Indra sets free waters and sunbeams, embodied in cows, from the demonic cave — that is to say, from the dreaded possibility that benign suns and rains might fail and kill off the cattle. When Indra broke open Vritra's cave with his club, he 'slew the dragon lying on the mountain, released the waters, pierced the belly of the mountains'. The ruddy rays of sunrise are cattle coming out from the dark byre in which they have been imprisoned.

The whole island of Gibraltar — for that is what it feels like — is a prodigy of fire-work and rock-work. A few hundred metres down the eastern shore from that highest cliff and the airstrip laid over the narrow sand bridge linking it to Spain, you can touch the last remnant of the dunes from the Mediterranean's Dead-Sea phase — a bluff of hard sand striated in layers of pale brown and yellow. Above it slopes the biggest 'roof' in the world — the thirty-four hectares of corrugated iron sheeting which were laid over the Great Sand Slope to make a water catchment.

To explore the warrens of streets between Rock and sea we walked down Bomb House Lane and passed beneath jutting bastions built from the biggest blocks of stone I have seen other than the Inca masonry in Peru. Here were Casemates Square, O'Hara's Buttress, and Lord Airey's Battery, Tank Ramp and ramps named after Kavanagh, Hargreaves, and Cratchett — NCO's, or so I imagined, with smoke-stained faces, scorched moustachioes, and several fingers missing. The colossal limestone chunks to make the likes of Stanley's Tower and the Orange Bastion were blasted and crowbarred out of the Rock itself, of course. The big wound in it bears an angelic name now — St Michael's Cave. For those who lived here after the Phoenicians and before the Moors it was the entrance to Hades. Concerts are held in it now. Rows of plastic chairs stood on the rock floor, wetted with drips from the naked rock above.

In the dusk at the back it looked hellish enough, an entrail twisting out of sight, no longer explored by cavers since a heavy rockfall. What we could see was horned and frilled with stalactites, stalagmites, and unnameable formations like growths in a diseased gut. The more pil-lared forms were shapely with rippled collars like the more conven-tional craft-shop candles. Most of the calcite secreted by the fistulae in the walls was coagulated in long drools and stretched membranes like images dreamed up by Dali in a morbid parody of the weathered limestone in the halcyon world outside.

It is still possible to penetrate parts of the Rock in the steps of the Pioneers. In the summer of 1782, after three years of the Great Siege, the Company of Soldier Artificers tunnelled towards the Notch, a col between the main face and the spur called the Devil's Tower. Their aim was to mount a gun there and blast the Spanish infantry. The tunnel was the brainchild of Warrant Officer Ince, who must have been Herculean in his cunning and hardihood. When the smoke in the tunnel became unbearable, he ordered holes to be blasted sideways to let in fresh air from the north face. How many of his men had been deafened, blinded, or mutilated by then?

We walked downward at a shallow angle. Light broke in from our left and we stepped into a bay seven metres wide and four high with a vaulted roof hewn out of the rock. Its mouth was barred with iron rods. Mediterranean light dazzled us. At our feet space dropped sheer two hundred metres to the airstrip. Alpine or Pallid swifts skimmed shrilling past — it was April and it would be almost exactly a month before their distant relatives arrived in our village in south Cumbria.

The drill-holes grooving the walls were often barely a foot apart — it had been as hard as that for the Artificers to shift the rock, planting all those charges, dinting with sledgehammer and iron bit, working on minimal water rations, shielding their eyes and ears from explosion after explosion. I was remembering the one controlled explosion I had seen in Shilbottle, the most northerly pit in England — the shotfirer saying quietly and distinctly, 'Torn yer feaces, laads,' his hand turning the brass key in his leather pouch, the bomb-like crump and the coal-smelling gust that hit us a second later.

Gibraltar had been a whole sub-culture of kindling and shattering, of man-made earthquake. The two look-out boys with the sharpest sight were nicknamed Shot and Shell. When Ince realised that the vents they had opened would make good fire-posts, Lieutenant Koehler designed a carriage from which 24-pounder guns could be directed more steeply downward than ever before. The Spaniards threw a quarter of a million rounds at the Rock before the final truce in February 1784. In the later stage of the siege, thanks to the Artificers, they could be answered with red-hot shot poured from the mouths that still gape from the rockface as though it had been visited by the marsupial mole that burrowed through Uluru in the Creation-time.

Gibraltar became a strongpoint by virtue of the intense slow force that produced it — a section of primeval seabed, hardened by aeons of pressure, forced up at last by tectonic buckling. It then attracted fire and the terrible hammering of the Spanish smiths and gunners. One of Hercules' antagonists at Gades had been Cacus, a son of Vulcan. That body of myth is fraught with rock and fire, rending and re-shaping. The first Herculean labour was his mother Alkmene's in giving birth to him: 'the weight of the baby stretched my womb . . . Why, even as I speak to you now, a cold shudder runs through my limbs, and it hurts me to remember. For seven nights and as many days, tortured and worn out with agony, I stretched my arms to the sky . . . Lamenting in words that would have moved flinty stones, I prayed to die.' Melkarth, his Babylonian counterpart, burned himself at Tyre — just as Hercules burned himself on a mountain after the poisoned shirt had stripped his huge bones bare — and children were sacrificed to him, according to Isaiah, 'in the valleys under the clifts of the rocks'. Gilgamesh, the Sumerian Hercules, who like him wrestled with a lion, passed through a mountain on his journey to find the Water and the Plant of Life. Hercules also made rocks. When he suspected Lichas of giving him the poisoned shirt, he flung him into the sea: 'His body, as it went soaring through the air, hardened into stone . . . fear drained away his blood and all his moisture, and he was turned into a hard flinty rock. Even now there is a little reef in the Euboean sea that juts out of the waves and keeps traces of human shape.'

Now that the British Army has gone from Gibraltar and it is losing its importance as a fuelling depot for warships and fighter planes, its hellish aspect can be effaced a little. Its paradisal population of birds and apes and flowers can begin to gentle and beautify the ugly war-mask. To explore the wild garden of the east side, I took a path signposted 'Mediterranean Steps'. It twisted off into the maquis between an army steel-mesh fence and a blockhouse. Flowering bushes rooted in the limestone scree closed behind me in aromatic coverts. Giant candytuft held up their broad rosettes of pink petals, butcher's broom sparked yellow like little bursts of flame. The leaves of succulents with purple flowers shone darkly green as though varnished. Tall yellow umbellifers were putting out fat new shoots, still unfurled. Dwarf palmyra palms cut spiked green discs out of the kingfisher-blue expanse between Europa Point and the Moroccan coast.

The path, a narrow channel of rubble and dust, led under the white faces of the Levant Cliff, past the twin mouths of Goat-hair Cave. Now and again I couldn't avoid re-entering the social world, by cement steps, under the walls of a bricked-up blockhouse festooned with old barbed wire, coming out on emplacements still armed with obsolete guns. When I climbed the seventy-metre cliffs of Buffadero Bluff with an army instructor who was about to leave the Rock for good, we had to regain the foot of the cliff after each route by down-climbing the *inside* of an iron ladder that had been lovingly twined with wire. It was a struggle to save our thighs and elbows from the rusty barbs.

The cliffs themselves were a hanging garden. Every ledge brimmed with mauve and orange blossom, with yellow daisies whose coronas of petals printed circles of pollen like little suns on the legs of my climbing trousers. As we pulled over on to the level at the top of Sawtooth Slab, our fingers grazed gulls' eggs of pale turquoise with brown blots like gravemarks on the back of a hand. They were lying on dusty ledges among wisps of fluff. Below us freighters and small tankers and the fast 'Winston boats' that smuggle cigarettes into Spain plied to and fro. The fuming blue berg across the water was the shoreline between Ceuta and Tangier, piling up into the limestone mountains of the Rif. It was there we would have to go to find the other Pillar.

15   Traces of Hercules

As the hydrofoil from Algeciras bucketed across the snaking and whirling currents of the Straits, limestone massifs began to rear and show a vertical grain. The mountain range on the eastern Moroccan border near Ceuta rises more than seven hundred metres above sea level. Should not the southern Pillar of Melkarth/Hercules be there? The pier of rock called Monte Hacho that makes the foundation of the 4,000-year-old castle is a much lesser thing than Edinburgh Castle rock, hardly a fit jamb for the gates of the Sea of the Middle of the World. Where else to look?

Outside the shipping office on the quay, a small dignified leathery man, bald and aquiline, appointed himself our guide. He was dressed in a meerschaum linen jelaba with a hood, a silver medallion on a chain, and white leather slippers with no heels, and he decided instantly what we wanted to see.

'You want to go to Titouan. Is market — only twenty-five kilometres. All very typical thing — these Berber people, Bedouin, they bring all-kind thing. Dancing you will see, playing for the snake. This man, he drive you. Is all correct. I am Morocco Tourist Board. Six thousand pesetas — whole thing.'

I was utterly intent upon Hercules. I named him, adding several other words with no pretence at sentences. 'Hercules,' I said many times. 'The Pillar. Abyla? The Pillar of Hercules?'

Our man twirled his hands helplessly. 'For that you must go to Tangier. One hundred kilometres.'

I repeated my simple demand: 'The Pillar of Hercules'. If I had known more Spanish, or any Arabic, I might have been less single-minded. As it was, I held my ground, saying 'The Pillar' from time to time and pointing eastward at the pale-blue masses of mountain lifting and scooping among steamy cloud. A compromise emerged: the driver would take us all to the mountains, and then to the market.

We drove through dusty suburbs, between stands of umbrella pine and eucalyptus, past barracks of the Army and the Spanish Legion. 'All they do,' said the driver over his shoulder, 'is eat and sleep.' Well, thank goodness for that. The mountains had disappeared behind their foothills. After half an hour they reappeared near and high, the skyline hanging between shapely peaks, a kilometre inland from the coast. Opposite a gap in the eucalyptus forest the driver pulled off the road, stopped, and pointed. 'The woman — is like a woman. You see?'

On a col between summits features jutted. A brow, tilted back almost to the horizontal. An orbital ridge, the bridge of a nose, the lower jaw. They composed the face of a head lying back, turned up to the sky. White hair of fine-weather cloud skeined over the features, slowly unravelling. Set in between her brow and her broad-ended nose with its open nostrils, a dark socket hollowed and yellowish scree wept from it down the mountainside. The grain of the limestone, drawn down from the profile, gave each part of the face, forehead and cheek and jowl, the look of very old skin sagging, of muscle whose tone had gone forever, a face in a hospital bed, sleeping its last sleep.

'Is called Dead Woman,' said the driver. 'Monte Muliere Muerta. Hercules marry this woman. In the *mythologia*. The wife of Hercules. *Mythologia*.'

I gaped at him, amazed by the apparition he had conjured. 'Could I climb the mountain?'

'No — is in another country.'

'Well — could you drive us along the coast road, so we can get nearer to her and see her better?'

'Is prohibited. Military zone.'

Up there on the skyline, dapples of sun on the cheeks and forehead suggested bygone smiles. The shreds of cloud sank and thickened — the face was grave, expressionless. The cloud lifted, evaporated — in full sun she was calmly asleep.

The Monte Muliere Muerta makes a much worthier counterpart to Gibraltar than Monte Hacho. It lacks the singleness of a pillar but the massif as a whole is a fit gatepost for the Straits. Really it's pointless to pose the question, Which *was* the Pillar of Hercules/Melkarth, since the matter isn't on the plane of verifiable truth. No more can we decide which was the place on the shore of Ithaca where Odysseus landed to take his wife's suitors by surprise or in which cave Eumaeus hid his herd of pigs. Historically speaking, the Phoenician sailors pointed to one or another rock as they sailed past and credited it with the legend. That is beyond our knowing. The naming of mythic or sacred places happened on the tongues of the people — at least until the stories sung by the Homeric and other bards were written down — and was bound to change, die away, and reappear, as do the lyrics of folksongs.

Later that same day neither Anne nor I could be quite sure whether or not the Dead Woman was the wife of Hercules. Had the driver not once called her his 'mother'? As wife she would have been either Megara, whom in his madness he killed along with their children, or Deianira, who unknowingly gave him the shirt steeped in the Centaur's poisonous blood to win him back from Iole. If the mountain was 'really' his mother, then this would agree with Ovid's story of his birth and the infant crag a few kilometres east in Ceuta could have been seen as issuing from between the great stone hips of the Moroccan mountain.

A day or two later, as we crossed on the slower boat to Tangier and shuffled along in unending queues on various quays, another Herculean rock came to light. We kept sharing space with a tall old Englishman in a beret, who looked like a minor character in a Graham Greene novel. He had worked for shipping and trading companies in Africa and seemed to be spending his lonely retirement revisiting the depots of his prime. We looked together at his French Michelin map and noticed a feature called Les Grottes d'Hercules, just south of Cap Spartel where the Straits expand to become the Atlantic. After saying goodbye to our friend, whom I now think of as Mr Gatwick because he lived near there, we drove west from Tangier and stopped to explore the Cap before going south to the Grottes.

The headland was a fine crux, perfectly fitted to mark the turn south of the continent towards the tropics. The bulges of hard sandstone on its landward face were not hard to climb and I could perch above the fifty-metre drop into the ocean and stare northward across glittering sea towards Trafalgar. Most remarkable of all was the little colony of people living here. The strip of ground between the westward-facing bluff and the shore was the most precise and skilful cultivation I had ever set eyes on. The light-brown earth of plot after plot had been ridged and patted with the spade in readiness for vegetables. Each pattern was different, deeper or narrower or more slanting, making an exquisite fabric out of loam.

A white horse carrying twin creels full of dung was walking between a small square flat-roofed whitewashed house on the slope above the Cap and the area of crofts below.

'Who lives here?' I asked our driver.

'Gitanes,' he answered, then paused and looked grim. Was he about to condemn them in the usual way for being gypsies? Not at all. With evident bitterness he went on, 'Soon they must leave. To make way for the bungalows.'

As I came back up from the Cap, the white horse was returning to the farmyard for another load. A black-bearded man walked beside him. I so valued his place and felt for his predicament as yet another peasant about to suffer clearance that I broke for once my taboo on pointing my camera at people and prepared to take his photo. He held up his hand, palm facing me, and came towards me, saying nothing. As I started to make some excuse, he took the camera from me, pointed it at me, took my photo, and handed it back to me with a smile.

A few kilometres south another white horse stood above a hollow near the shore, statuesque except for the swishing of its tail. A cave-mouth opened in the face of the hollow. A guide in a hooded brown jelaba led us underground and repeatedly lit a petrol-soaked cloth in a bottle to show us the rock-walls. Where the chamber bent seaward, light like molten platinum blinded in from a westward-pointing entrance shaped like Africa. On every side the rock was hollowed as though stacks of coins or lids, each half a metre in diameter and twenty centimetres thick, had been pressed into malleable stone and left their shape in it. Each disc had been a millstone chiselled out when the place was a mine — 1,500 years before the Romans, according to our guide. The querns were used to grind maize and olives. In places a stone had been cut on the vertical. In others the initial circle had been made with a compass, then cut in deeply but the stone left *in situ* — perhaps when demand fell away, as happened to the millstone trade in England early in the nineteenth century.

*

Here in the Grotto of Hercules even the natural walls at the mouth were scooped and groined, as though Melkarth leant against them when they were still plastic and left the impress of his muscles. The large-crystalled rock, like north of England gritstone, had a coarse open texture, which would have let the air permeate and kept the grist cool. Outside, from the 25-metre level down to the water's edge, hundreds of circular scoops marked the sites of cut-out stones, some of them worn by the sea into natural-looking kettle-holes. Bosses showed where a stone had been cut round, then left, and the salt water had worn away the surrounding rock. Men with long bamboo poles were fishing, or dozing in hollows above the reach of the waves.

It would have been pleasing if Hercules' labours had included some mention of mining or grinding. It was pleasing in another way to find that any well-shaped site along this coast, any evidence of the forces human as well as superhuman that threw up and shifted, reft and sculpted the world's hardest stuff, could be symbolised in a vivid story. A story is an extended metaphor and if it lasts, if it is retold over generations, its essence must matter very much to the teller and his or her fellows. The passage between stone sides, the circuit between stone poles, not only fitted terrain all over the world. It also worked as a metaphor for a crucial test or a deed that mattered and was hard to achieve. In the Scottish Highlands a couple could make a 'handfast' marriage, for example, by clasping hands through a hole in a monolith. There are not many of these about, which may have deterred young people from going into these things too lightly.

I had heard that on the shore beyond Sligo in the west of Ireland, near the village of Iaskaigh or Easkey, there was a split rock called the Fingerstone of Finn Mac Cool. What we found was an elephantine silver-grey bulk, a granite erratic four metres high, ten metres long, and seven metres across. A glacier must have dropped it on the low ground not far from the sea after rafting it from the mountains fifty miles south. Now it crouched in a field full of mown thistles and portly sheep. So little has happened to it since Finn hurled it and it broke on landing that the innards still match each other. The story is that you must pass through it three times, and if it doesn't snap shut on you, then you are a just person. An amiable idea, since it enables absolutely everybody to pass the test — unless of course unjust persons back away from damnation, as Brendan Behan put it, and show themselves up.

Anne and I risked the test, and passed it. It was a squeeze and the earth floor was well trodden by previous pilgrims. A camper full of Americans drove up before we left and when I asked them their version of the story, one of them said, 'This giant came up from the sea, and took up a huge stone to throw at his enemies, and this is where it landed.' They were delighted to hear of the test and hadn't known that the giant was Finn himself.

In the Ossianic cycle Finn MacCumaill was a hunter, a popular hero roughly equivalent to Robin Hood, and like Hercules a slayer of monsters. What he incarnates is the strength or potency that makes offspring and the shapes of the land. A lake is a hollow where he scooped up a handful of earth to throw at an enemy, a grassy place on a mountainside is his bed, a rock is a missile he used to kill a rival giant — young Diarmuid, for example, who went off with Grainne when she was betrothed to the ageing Finn.

Herculean energies resonate in the story of Finn's last battle. War-cries 'rang in woods and rocks, in cliffs and river-mouths and the caves of the earth and in the cold outer zones of the skies'. The armies threw 'hard, mighty stones . . . huge stones to break each other's helmets and skulls'. As Finn exerted his last effort, he 'circled the Battalion of the Pillars like honeysuckle hugging a tree or a mother her son, and the crushing of thighs and shins and halves of heads was like a smith beating an anvil, or the shots as withered trees crack, or sheets of ice under cavalry hooves'.

So great rocks are the most durable evidence of the world's energies, and if they are twin they become two principles, or principals, that need each other even as they conflict. Hence the King and Queen rocks on Bredon Hill south-west of Evesham; hence Adam and Eve on the ridge of Tryfan in Snowdonia with a gap between them which inspires us to jump across it.

In the Highlands of Scotland, at the head of Glen Einich on the slopes of the Cairngorms above Strathspey, a pair of rocks are called A'Cailleach and Am Bodach, the Old Woman and the Old Man. They face each other across the head of a long loch. Such natural 'totems' are all over the Highlands; a pair in relation to each other is uncommon. A *bodach* was an old man; the word also contains *bod*, penis. One blunt, dark spur across the mountains on the Aberdeenshire side is Bod an Deamhain — cautiously translated by the Victorian Ordnance Surveyors as Devil's Point. *Cailleach* means 'old woman'. The connotations of the word branch out into nothing less than a fundamental vision of how this land evolved.

The Cailleach was the Earth-mother. She trampled to and fro across the northern lands with a creel on her back full of rocks and earth. When it tipped, mountains were made. According to Norman MacLeod of Leverburgh in Harris, from whom I had heard biting stories of the Clearances, a Cailleach called Lochlannaich lived in 'the isle in the west'. In old age she wanted to return to Lochlann but could not bear to part with her island. She started ripping it into pieces, to carry it with her to her last resting-place in the north. 'Only by this time she wasn't as tough as she'd been and she not only couldn't lift it but kept dropping bits as well — hence Barra, South Uist, Benbecula, etc, etc — and Hirta [St Kilda].'

She took many forms. In the Cromarty Firth she was the south-westerly gale that came 'yelling round the Heel of Ness with a white feather in her hat'. She was the flood that drowned travellers in fords. When she forgot to close her well on Ben Cruachan with her stone slab one night, the water brimmed over and formed Loch Awe. When she washed her plaid in the strait north of Jura, she stirred up the contrary tide-races called Corrievreckan, the most turbulent round Britain, with their fierce flow and spinning overfalls (that nearly drowned George Orwell in 1948). The Cailleach's day is 25 March, virtually the equinox, when winter's last cold gales arrive. At that time her son, who has fallen in love with a beautiful young woman kept prisoner by his mother, runs away with her on a white horse. The Cailleach drums up a storm to forestall them, then thrashes the grass with her rod or hammer to stop it growing.

The land was the ground of our being — it was full of rocks that broke the plough. The wind was a necessity, to fill the fishermen's sails — it could sink their boats. The water was equally necessary — it could flood and drown. So the people faced the difficulties of the land to which they were committed by embodying the whole mixed nature of it in the one giantess or god. Her looks were in keeping, her face blue-black, her hair 'white as an aspen covered in hoar frost'. A Gaelic quatrain from Argyll, 'Bha aon suil ghlumach 'na ceann', creates this definitive image of her:

> In her head was one deep pool-like eye
> Swifter than a star in a winter sky;
> Upon her head gnarled brushwood
> Like the clawed old wood of an aspen root.

To find the Cailleach and the Bodach, to gauge their stature and their character and feel our way into how they might have been perceived by the people of the place, Jim Crumley and I came at them from every angle in five days of walking and climbing. The head of Glen Einich is Coire Odhar, dun cirque. Grassland a quarter-mile square spreads out at the head of the loch. This was a shieling, where the people lived with their herds and flocks in summer. Three huts are still visible on the true left bank of the burn, their plans showing as boat-like enclosures of boulders in the lush grass. At the back looms a 400-metre headwall split by a chain of white cascades.

My first view of this was as though from the air. We had come in by Glen Feshie, the next glen to the west. From the headwaters of Allt Fhearnagan we skirted the northern slope of Carn Ban More, big white hill, and entered on the Moine Mhór, the great moss, a prairie at a thousand metres above sea level, bounded in the east by the ranged peaks from Braeriach to Cairn Toul. They stand in huge calm silence, their summits hoar as though with age, because nothing will grow at their height and they are bald above the russet shag of heather on their flanks.

We made for Sgor Gaoith, rocky peak of the wind, and were amazed to come upon a seemingly unrecorded building in the neuk of Fuaran Diotach, the well of food. The remnant of it was a palisade or wall of big stones, the end of it set into a peaty bluff. Its back would have been the ground; the front of it had gone. At 1,000 metres above sea level, it must have been one of the highest permanent structures in the country. Speculating that it might have been the summer pad of someone who didn't get on too well with her neighbours down at the shieling, we worked our way north along the brink of the glen above the south end of the loch, then down a narrow headland jutting towards the water. It narrowed, falling away on either side. One slip would send us bouncing down gullies ending in chockstones, then nothing, then the rasped-metal surface of the loch 500 metres below. A fox had been here — its turd lay on short heather, charcoal black speckled with white bone shards. A chasm faced us, twenty-five metres deep, cleft north/south through the rib.

It would have been hard to cross safely without climbing gear, but it was not necessary. There she was, in full view, A'Cailleach herself, her profile louring against the shieling pasture far below, frosty grey against briefly sunlit green.

Her cranium is low, her aquiline nose a metre long from bridge to nostril, her grey eye the size of a melon under a brow cut in a perfect shallow arc — another of the Cailleach's names was Mala Liath, grey eyebrow. Under her nose her upper lip purses deeply in to a mouth that has been empty of teeth since she was young. Her chin recedes into her squat neck and shapeless trunk. She is acromegalic, her flesh is built up in blebs of lichenous granite, as though a sculptor besotted with the grotesque had slapped on handfuls of clay and left them clinging to the armature of the skull. She is aboriginal — if we accept the civilised disdain in that word. She is a titanic squaw who grimly supervises the pastoral work of the little people down below, tacitly challenging them to smirk at her deformity.

As for the Bodach, he was hard to identify, in spite of the seemingly exact instructions in Seton Gordon's *The Cairngorm Hills of Scotland*, which put Jim on to the pair in the first place. Several broken pinnacles tottered along the ridge to the east across the loch. As rain began to storm horizontally across the glen, we skirted the top of the headwall and struggled through a torment of hummock and bog and lochan, passing amphitheatres floored with boulders like charnel pits full of old men's heads. We contoured north again along collapsing slopes strewn with clumps washed down by incessant rains, peering up at each crag, willing it to shape itself in a rough human likeness. Could it be this one where two lateral rocks make a mouth or an eye, or that stack which merges back into the broken cliff and never quite makes a body or a head?

In the next few days, approaching southward down the whole length of the glen to follow in the track of the shieling people, we scarcely managed to see a male totem among the rocks. The Cailleach was never in doubt, a superbly salient Earth-mother who had needed some kind of counterpart for the completeness of the myth. She had her handmaiden or daughter, a slender blade standing her ground amongst the barely stable scree halfway down to the loch — A' Phocaid, the pickaxe. Perhaps the Bodach, worn out with the effort of sustaining his erection for all those millennia, had drooped and collapsed at last, in the seasons since the Great War when Seton Gordon saw him.

The Cailleach's relation with the Bodach was teasing. Both 'resented a mortal entering their domain after certain hours'. They were also rivals. If one was angry at an intruder, 'the other would at once encourage the offender with friendly cries'. When no humans were about, they threw boulders at one another. This is fairly whimsical, so much so that it almost smacks of a fancy made up on the spur of the moment to please a scholarly visitor in a kilt, such as Seton Gordon . . . On the other hand not all myths are fundamental, they are also a seedbed of story available to people at play, pleasing themselves, letting their imaginations loose on their surroundings. So a stone in North Roe, Shetland Mainland, is said to be a missile thrown by a giantess from Yell at a rival on the far side of the sound, and the Vee Skerries north-west of Papa Stour in St Magnus Bay were boulders tossed playfully out to sea by a giant called Atla.

Certainly those stories of the Cailleach and the Bodach quarrelling would have been told at the evening ceilidhs down in the shieling houses. A Speyside man has testified that around 1890 he heard a story of the Cailleach turning into a grey stone to escape harassment by her son and that this was associated with a place on the side of Loch Etive called Horse Shoes. The people traditionally went to the shielings at Beltane, May-day, the great summer festival of the Celts. 'Women knit, sing, talk, and walk as free and erect as if there were no burdens on their backs, nor in their hearts . . . All who meet them on the way bless the trial, as it is called, and wish it a good flitting day.' The men would see their families on their way, then turn back to resume their work at the fishing or at harvesting in the Lowlands.

In Glen Einich the animals were sent up a few days before and a herdsman went with them as far as Craobh Tillidh, the tree of the return, then left them to walk the six miles by themselves to Coire Odhar. The tree, or its scion, can still be seen between the track and the river of Am Beanaidh, a pine with dense bunches of needles and a hefty trunk and limbs which glow bronze at sunset. It is the last tree on the trail, an outlier from Rothiemurchus, the plain of the great trees, down in the strath. Five miles south, as the Cailleach and the Bodach came into sight in the jaws of the glen head, the shieling women moving up from Inverdruie and Coylum Bridge would know that their long trek with children, animals, and dairying tools was nearly done for another season.

In the mellow days of May, June and July, hunger and the weather ground the people less harshly. During the time of the Big Sun, from Beltane to Halloween, the Cailleach was transformed into a grey boulder and stayed that way, always moist, until the time of the Little Sun came round again. While she was in abeyance, the young folk in the shieling could play and flirt and twine stories round the baleful god-heads waiting up there in the crags. A Gaelic quatrain, 'Ann am bothan an t-sugraidh', evokes this time which was the nearest the Highlanders got to an idyll:

> In the bothy of courting,
> With birchwood stopping the door,
> The cuckoo and the ring-dove
> Sang for us on the trees . . .

Their myths were not moral — concerned with right and wrong. Like the religion of the Phoenicians, they were inspired by the powers and processes of nature, which by and large must be accepted or worked along with. This is true along the gamut from the Scottish Highlands to the Near and Middle East. In Tyre Melkarth was Baal, chief of the 'primitive groups of nameless deities' — the oldest gods, most deeply rooted in nature. I found the signs of them again at Delphi. Baal was a storm god, nourisher and destroyer, lord of wind, earthquake, and fire, personification of sun-heat. The Egyptian Baal was Shu; his consort Tefnut, like the Cailleach, was a rain-spitter, plague-spreader, and blower-up of gales.

So there were no temples to the Cailleach. She is found in the earth itself, she emerges from it in certain places. These were 'sacred' in that people saw there an epitome of the powers that were beyond them — that preceded them and outlasted them. To form them into a myth, to embody it in a human likeness as in the Scottish or the Moroccan mountains, or to suppose that a being with some human likeness shaped those pieces of your world, was to gain a hold on reality through your imagination — to see it as that much less random or amorphous, that much more intelligible.

These powers continue to play upon our world, quaking, eroding, fertilising, although the cultures that imagined them as godheads have passed away. The sites themselves are not everlasting. The Cailleach is slowly, slowly splitting off from the Peak of the Wind. When she goes she may take her scion with her to drown in the loch. The Bodach may well have gone already. In the Mediterranean basin the tectonic plate that carries Africa is inching northward again.

In the meantime Gibraltar stands where it did — just. Two years ago I set out to climb the North Face with my youngest son, in the teeth of its reputation for being 'very loose'. The most baffling part of the climb was getting to the base of the Rock. Or so we thought until we embarked on the face itself.

16   Rock Haulage

On a Saturday, around noon, a yawning wiping-of-hands-on-oily-rags time in Gibraltar, we started to ask our way along the limpet-horde of wrecked garages and scrapyards that encrust the base of the reef. Nowhere does the 500-metre soaring triangle of raw limestone actually sprout out of common ground. These rusting corrugated iron shanties shut us out. At Rock Haulage Ltd. in Devil's Tower Road, a tanned and stubbled man was standing in the doorway of a den stacked up with cannibalised cars. When I said 'We want to climb the cliff here,' he said at once, 'Are you sure?' — looking me full in the eye. He was friendly about access but would have to clear it with his boss, who 'should be back by six'. As we talked, the crag leaned over us hugely, its average angle looking impossibly beyond the vertical — an optical illusion, none the less intimidating.

For a few hours Neil and I worked out at the other end of the Rock, on the sun-warmed and flowery tiers of Buffadero Bluff, familiar from two years before. As the mountains of Morocco grew more distinct across the water in the filtered glare of early evening, we drove back round to the North Face by the east side, through the tunnel coated with filthy dust which I first saw from the cab of a beat-up gravel wagon. I had hoped to get right along the shore by scrambling paths. The cliff turned impassably sheer and a driver picked me up and took me through the tunnel to town again, with a stop to tip his loads of rocks and earth into the sea under the black, burnt-out stare of a tall Arab in a dirty green jelaba.

Today, when we returned to Rock Haulage, we found the door padlocked shut. At Rock Services Ltd. next door another tanned and stubbled man, younger and with a bigger paunch, was sharing a brew in the doorway with a stoned-looking man whose lower face was invisible behind a luxuriant walrus moustache. They too must wait for the boss, who 'should be back soon'.

'I wouldn't have the guts to climb that,' said the Paunch. 'Or the brains.'

At this my own guts turned to water. The sun dipped, more tea was brewed among the scarred limbs and torsoes of unidentifiable cars. Presently we were shown the sights. Paunch took us through to the back and gestured at a great sagging hole in the roof.

'A big rock came through there,' he said proudly. 'Whole place was fuckin' shakin'.' He grinned, pleased by his desperate environment.

Giving up on the absent bosses, I wandered along Devil's Tower Road to what looked like the only other feasible access, a pair of open steel gates in a solid, well-painted yellow wall. It was apparently Royal Navy property. A young serviceman in a blue uniform and beret had been here earlier. Now the yard inside the wall was deserted, seemingly disused. Nothing could be less shipshape or Bristol fashion. The bare concrete was littered with stones from fist- to skull-size that had rained down from the face above. A reinforced concrete walkway led to a painted metal door in the base of the Rock. As I walked about eyeing the drifts of nettles and sagging mesh fencing at the boundary with the cliff, the young rating came out of the door.

'Can I help you?' he called.

'Yes,' I said. 'We could do with a strong boarding-party, preferably with helicopter back-up.'

Actually I uttered my usual request for access and he beckoned me to follow him into the Rock. Inside, a few feet from the seeming dereliction of the yard, were passage after passage lined with immaculately maintained consoles, generators encased in metal, vents and piping and wiring and needles in dials quivering with massed voltage or tonnage or whatever. From here, I supposed, were powered the instruments 500 metres above our heads with which the Forces monitor all shipping and aircraft movements in the Straits. A flight-lieutenant in the RAF had already given us clearance (by letter) to finish our climb beside their thicket of masts and pylons on the summit. A major in the army had given us clearance to approach the base of the cliff. The face itself is owned by the Gibraltar Government, which did not seem to care what we did. Now only the Navy stood in our way.

Deep inside the Rock, entrenched in his phalanxes of generators, a less junior naval officer sat at a desk in a cubby-hole, under a closed-circuit TV monitor, entering figures in a ledger. When his mate explained my mission, he looked openly derisive and phoned some distant superior.

'There is someone here, sir, who wishes to *climb* the Rock, because he, er, likes doing that kind of thing. Can we give him clearance to access the cliff? No? Very well. No chance at all? Thank you, sir — very good — g'bye, sir.'

He raised his eyes to mine with the studied sardonic pity of Kojak briefing his boss and said with biting relish, '*Nobody* is *ever* allowed use of the yard, not even our own vehicles. Rockfall is much too frequent. You saw the covered way? We built it to cover ourselves against rock-fall.'

Then they left me to find my own way out through this nerve-centre of NATO.

Paunch and Walrus sportingly agreed to open up for us next day and let us through to the Face, which had grown huger (though not steeper) as dusk thickened. We were 'armed only with an old photograph', as they say in adventure stories. Adrian Cabedo, the Gibraltarian most expert in the Face, had lent us his print of the photo used by the first recorded ascensionists to note their routes. Broken lines in ink marked the Metroway on the left, climbed by Smiler Cuthbertson,

Don Whillans, and D. Coward, and Regina Mater on the right, climbed by Ben and Marion Wintringham. Adrian had told me two years before how his arm was broken by a falling block while he was in the Regina Mater party. He had to be rescued from the Notch, the col between the massif and Devil's Tower.

On the phone before we left England Cuthbertson had been encouraging. 'Our line was very good,' he said. 'It's an Alpine-type curving crack. It's about VS [Very Severe grade], with a Hard VS bit where it goes through an overhang on jugs [big holds].'

'Was it loose?'

'No — not all that loose. Only near the start, where the weight of the whole rock is cracking it a bit.'

On the other hand the people who work in the firing-line, in these repair shops and scrapyards, had been stressing that 'a lot of rock has come down in the last few years', dislodged by heavy rains.

On the light-table in Adrian's artists' shop in Irish Town, his big slides of the Face shone glamorously silver and proud. The details of gully, groove, and vegetation which the slides were too small to show were more or less visible in the grainy murk of the large black-and-white print. Next morning we saw detail in plenty — the curving crack, perhaps 300 metres up, blocked by a rugged eave (the HVS crux?), the steep groove which is the entry to the upper Face, with its bristling ilex copses, the lower part where smeared-looking brownish walls must be outflanked by puzzling a way up labyrinths of cracks. The Face hung over us, scoured by the dawn wind whisking along the coast from Algeciras. Hordes of gulls 500 metres straight above our heads were gyring in brilliant sunlight which turned their flight-feathers into ermine fringes.

If the Face was loose, so was this backyard. We waded waist-deep through jagged layers of car-body and collapsing drifts of rotted timbers from demolished houses, then geared up and uncoiled our ropes among beds of nettle and corn marigold which had been turned into a rock garden by dozens of chunks showered down from the Face.

I led off up easy, flowery ramps, then a series of rounded rock-steps and bollards. When the drag of the rope started to hobble me, I looked for a belay and could find only a crack between an unstable rock and the shoulder from which it was parting. I jammed in a wired nut and yanked on it to test it. The lips of the crack splintered, so I replaced the nut further down. What was the logic here? Did I really think the stone became stronger the nearer it was to mother Earth?

Neil reached me and climbed on through, then belayed surprisingly soon. I found him eyeing a steep cracked slab which steepened into a wall before fading back into the ilex groove. The rock of the steepest part was suspiciously discoloured. We had noticed when we put up a new route at Val Canali in the Dolomites that only white or grey limestone is strong limestone. The brownish-orange areas aren't even for the birds. Below us the scrapyards were starting to shrink, so directly underneath us that stones nudged off by our feet plummeted down on to the rusty roofs and aroused the car company guard dogs in No. 26, a brown Alsatian, a white Alsatian, and a pair of dusty blackish mongrels. They barked furiously, fought each other in little circles, then settled down again in the shade.

As I did so myself for the next half-hour, hour, hour-and-a-half. Why was Neil so slow on that comfortable angle? There must be a reason for it. He was trained and fit and very much at home on vertical Spanish limestone. As he put in yet another nut and stood staring balefully upward, I called to him.

'What's it like?'

'It's horrifying,' he shouted back. 'And I can't see where I'm going.'

He kept on going and reached the steep discoloured area. I was encouraged to see his feet, as he stepped up on protruding wafers, disappearing almost completely. I had been expecting mere toe-holds. He still gained height at the speed of a tendril unfolding on time-lapse film and kept looking all ways, across to right and left as well as up. Then he disappeared — always a bleak juncture for the second climber on a steep and problematic route. Time passed, and the dogs wrestled, and the wind died into the warmth of noon.

Down in the car park Anne got out of our hire car from time to time — almost too miniature to be recognisable — and a man mooched across the road and back again, presumably Walrus, who emerged frowstily from the Portakabin where he slept. The ropes were taken in invisibly by Neil and vague shouts from him told me when it was time to go.

Now that I could see the bulk of the pitch, the stature of this climb became unmistakable. The 'slab' was fairly steep, and blank apart from the black cracks that split it — all too closed to help us except the one Neil chose, which was wide enough to take a boot. The fissure of it was choked with rubble, precariously lodged. The right-hand edge was strong enough to act as a handrail while the bounding rock was not too steep. When it reached nearly 80° I was forced to search for lodgements for my feet and found only small bevelled facets.

The steepness experience was setting in now. I felt like a frail bubble of flesh, inhabiting thinned air, levitating with next to no attachment to this rock-element which was so close to me. At home it would smell of earth and moss. Here it had the fish-and-distemper whiff of gull guano with a sweetish-resinous under-tang of the wild candytuft and corn marigold which adorned the face in solitary pink and yellow clumps.

These tiny footholds might have done if the handrail had continued solid, but it was in places cuttingly sharp, and the fissure was stacked up with big wedged blocks half a metre square. They had fine edges, and my fingers itched to clutch them and heave up on them. They would unpile like a child's bricks. I could lay-away to the right but the rock was so steep that I started to lose it and my toes slipped downward. Sink your hand in the crack, I told myself, and feel up as far as you can — there must be something! My forearm disappeared up to the elbow and my fingertips touched a little upright edge. If I laid away from that it might put less of a destabilising stress on the wedged block and the one above it, and the one below it. This was madness. Nobody and nothing could live in all this totter and collapse. I made the move. I remember a moment's grating, like a tooth starting to come out of your jaw under the dentist's forceps. Everything stayed put. I could not trust my full weight to this block. I did, and it held for another year or so. I left this place of barest equilibrium and stepped thankfully up beneath the 'rusty' overhang.

Those fine big shelves on which Neil had stood were cracked right round. One of them looked to be lodged in a lateral crevice about as securely as a packet in a letterbox. As though slow-motioning through a repeat of a bad dream after nearly waking up, I repeated Neil's steps, trying to perform the trick of withholding half my weight, making myself lighter, weightless even. There was no downward lurch, no crash of rocks or bodies on to the rusty roofs. I eased myself out of the perpendicular world and stood in a brief daze among more or less solid ribs upholstered with little flowerless plants. Neil's dirty white helmet, borrowed from Adrian, came into sight above the threshold of the ilex groove. He had found a roomy stance, thank goodness. I ensconced myself, tied on, took off my helmet and let sweat pour down my forehead.

The debriefing was terse. We both wanted out of here.

'I just carried on,' Neil said, 'because there was nothing else to do. Nothing was strong enough to rope back down off. It's horrific. D'you think it'll get any better?'

I peered upward, knowing I could tell nothing from down here.

We had climbed about eighty metres. So how much more was left of Cuthbertson's 'start'? I nibbled melting chocolate and took a swig of lukewarm water from my rucksack (heavy also with camera, spare film, rock-hammer, and a bunch of pitons).

'If only we could get to that tree . . . ' Neil said. 'D'you want to lead this next bit?'

'Want' was hardly the word. 'Okay,' I said, and added some of Neil's gear to my own rack of nuts and slings before stepping up on to the solid left rib of the groove. A small ilex was growing in the middle of it, shading a gull's nest containing two turquoise eggs blotched brown. In this dizzy place they looked especially precious. I had to step into the bed of the gully, which was hard, without breaking the eggs. The rock of the bed was made up of arrow-heads in a crazy paving and I tried pulling up on them. Each one shifted and could easily be lifted out. The left rib was vertical and blank.

When I gave Neil the disgusting news, he said with little emotion, 'What d'you think, then?'

'Shouldn't we go down?'

'What about your book?'

'That's okay — this is just one aspect of Gibraltar. And anyway, isn't all this interesting, in its horrible way?'

'Is there anything to go off up there? What's the tree like?'

The tree was hard to suss — its base was defended by huge nettles. I seized it as low down as possible and gave it a shake. It was so thin it trembled, and it was only rooted in such soil as had gathered here, dusty-gravelly, shallow, friable. Respectfully I lifted the nest a little, trying not to send the eggs rolling down among the guard dogs, and saw that the root was a rusty rod — not a tube, a rod, planted at a slightly upward angle in the bedrock of the rib. It was a dream anchor, which Neil scarcely believed in after his trials with various wands and brackets lower down. I put a sling round this memorial to long-ago sappers, another round the tree-stem, and climbed back down to our eyrie. There we set up our abseil and retreat.

The Face gave one last grimace. As I planted my feet on a plaque of rock near the overhang, it shattered and a fusillade hit the roofs with the biggest crash so far. For the rest of my backward-downward journey I was staring up at the edge where the rope came tautly over, wondering furiously if the strain of it was about to burst the stone, twang the rope on to a freshly jagged edge, cut it right through and . . .

When we rejoined Anne, it turned out that ours hadn't been the only danger. Walrus had invited her in for a cup of coffee, then bolted the cabin door. She had laughed and talked her way back outside.

I will go on rescreening that day for as long as my memory lasts, re-editing the film to picture us deciding to climb on, managing to get up the Face (as we could have done technically), exulting and celebrating before we flew back north, Neil to Newcastle, ourselves to Barcelona . . . Unlike the heroes of the various epics, we had not squeezed through the stone poles and made it to the Isle of the Blessed. And if we had, would the rock have snapped off our tail-feathers, even our hindlegs?

Some sanity and consolation was offered by Peter Greenwood (most fearless and agile climber in Cumberland forty years ago) when I told him all about it. 'Well,' he said, 'you're back in one piece.' And at least it turned out that our hard pitch was on hitherto unclimbed rock, since we had strayed too far left above the ramps.

That colossal triangle with its soaring, skyward-reaching grain is one of the most handsome shapes in Europe. We have done our best to ruin it. No great rock in the world has been so hewn, mined, drilled, blasted, shelled. It has been shaken through and through, by the Spanish cannonballs and the gunpowder and dynamite of the British sappers. If charges were to be set off inside it now, I should think the whole North Face would shake and the cracks all over it would spurt out dust like smoke. Will it ever settle down again into solidity, having shed all its man-made debris? Or will its racked body give off shards for millennia until it is transformed into unimaginable shapes, or no shape at all, as it takes the shocks of the African tectonic plate on its grinding voyage — which has moved the Pyramids 53 metres north since they were built — and the doors which Hercules opened five and a half million years ago are closed again?

PART FOUR
Africa below the Equator

---

17   High Towers and Refuges

'The White people, the Honkhoikwa, the Smooth-haired ones, are still strangers to these parts. They still bear in them the fear of their fathers who died on the plains or in the forbidding mountains. They do not understand yet. They have not yet become stone and rock embedded in the earth and born from it again and again like the Khoikhoin.'
— André Brink, *A Chain of Voices* (1982), p 21

A few months later I was standing at the foot of another such cliff, as high and as steep — so soaring that, once again, it appeared to reach out well beyond its 85° and project a great eave that would have fallen well behind us if it had sheared off and fallen. This was the North Wall of the Blouberg in North-west Transvaal. Behind me, as I stared upward and tried to accommodate my bodily imagination to something so tall and so sheer, embrowned wintry plains expanded north and north and north to the Limpopo, and beyond it into Zimbabwe, and beyond that . . . From two thousand metres above sea level the tracts of the veld looked huge. They were only a fraction of a land mass I may never get to know, but which I have at least locked on to here and there by the pulps of my toes and fingers.

Our ways had led from a thatched chalet on an asparagus farm south of Johannesburg, folded round by pale gold hills as softly recumbent as the limbs of sleeping lions. Here I had climbed up to a ridge of tawny sandstone and looked through a hole almost as handsome as Window Rock in Arizona. The hill was called Nyakalesoba, mountain with an eye. Leaving this valley in its late winter trance was a mental wrench and suitably chastening or awakening for the darg of the twelve-hour trek down to the Cape. In the Great Karoo a ferocious brown dust-storm made the headlights almost useless and the land feel as featureless and unstable as an ocean churned by cyclones.

Cape Town waited with its European cultural style, its botanical gardens, its tiered campus, its Visitor Centre at the docks reminiscent of San Francisco or Liverpool. Here I would climb in cool sunshine on the towering curtain-wall of Table Mountain, then drive north to the Cedarberg for a long walk in through bush to a secluded precipice. Or so we had planned. After weeks of calm a gale was blowing up out of the Antarctic. The faces of the mountain showed dark streaks of weep from the previous night's downpour. Freighters were gathering off the harbour mouth, riding at anchor as they waited for the swell to become more manageable.

As a gesture against the omens, Mike Loewe and I took the stepped stone path from the cable-way car park up towards Venster Buttress and climbed a route on the sandstone plinth of the Mountain as dusk came on. Out to sea past the haunch of Lion Peak, a low-lying island showed barely clear of the water, its lights sparkling feverishly through the blown moist air. Robben Island, which both blacks and whites gazed at with dreadful fascination for three centuries, is now a tourist attraction. It looked like a stingray floating dead on the face of the ocean.

Turning our backs on it, we pulled up on brown ledges which in places jutted airily. When it came my turn to lead, the dusk, the alien land, the seeping crevices combined against me. I spent many minutes motionless as a rabbit caught in headlights before I nerved myself to inch left along a ledge made by a bedding-plane. The rockface above it threatened to breast me out and off. The final trouser-splitting stride felt hideously precarious. And this was only the doorstep of the mighty building.

Next day, as gale, swell, and deluge intensified, the Harbour Master closed the port, for the first time since 1978. We abandoned the Mountain, now invisible behind its wrack of cloud, in favour of the lodestone which had drawn me this far south in the first place — *the* Cape, originally of Storms (*dos Tormentos*) to its European discoverer Bartolomeo Dias, then renamed 'of Good Hope' (*de bon Esperanca*) by his monarch, Don Joao II, who was never there himself.

A captivating new myth called *The First Life of Adamastor*, by the novelist André Brink, had helped me to envisage the Cape as the bones of a giant who took part in the Titanic rebellion against Zeus. Adamastor is not usually listed among the twelve Titans, who were conceived by Gaea with her son Uranus at the first peopling of the world. Perhaps he was one of the Giants, Zeus's antagonists in the second cosmic war. The first had lasted for ten years. The scooping out of whole lands to use as missiles created the islands, mountains, and valleys that form the present Aegean — the Vale of Tempe, the mountains of Pelion and Ossa, the island of Nisyros. At the end of it all Zeus the God-father imprisoned the members of his mutinous family in great rocks and headlands around the world. Their surly and forbidding character is the repressed aggressiveness of those original powers.

Brink's originality is to see that the repulsive character given to Adamastor in European myth is the reaction of white people overfaced by an alien continent. In the Portuguese epic called *The Lusiads*, by Camoens, the giant headland is

> Of stature all deformed and vast and tall,
> The visage frowning, and with squalid beard;
> The eyes were hollow, and the gesture all
> Threatening and bad; the colour pale and seared;
> And full of earth and grizzly was the hair;
> The mouth was black, the teeth all yellow were.

In fact the multiple headlands at the Cape rise in majestic brown prows, their dip slopes tilting steeply behind them, their faces lined with galleries high above the burst of the ice-white combers. We can enjoy the luxury of perceiving such extreme terrain as beautiful because we are armoured, more or less, by steel shells and petrol engines, against the elemental destroyers. Dias lost a third of his fleet on his second voyage round the Cape — searching like so many of his kind for a city built of gold. For us, as we drove through the *fynbos* or luxuriant scrub of Cape Point, the storm was just 'bad weather' — violent squalls that darkened off eastwards across False Bay in a metallic shadow like clouds of iron filings and soaked in five seconds the thin silk suits of the Japanese tourists.

Among the *fynbos* an ostrich grazed beside two offspring, the feathers of her vestigial wings wafting like lace curtains at an open window. Much of this bush was destroyed when F.W. de Klerk came to visit the Wildlife Reserve and his security team, casing the peninsula before the great man's visit, managed to set fire to the undergrowth. Now the leafage was growing in again and the crowns of the protea bushes were luminous yellow-green in the rainy half-light. From the granite saddle near the Point the gables of the mountains ranged northward in line astern, dip slopes building up from the Atlantic into shapely summits, dropping in haggard scarps that faced east along the southern coast of Africa — graphic evidence of the Earth's buckling that lifted the continent above the waters.

I scrambled down massive natural steps to just above the sandstone masonry of the lighthouse. The usual elation of reaching an end of the Earth sharpened to ecstasy as I saw a spearhead of foam running south from the point. It seemed to be making from east to west, trailing combed white foam-skeins, cresting enough to make a trough on the Atlantic side. Seals were sporting in it, black sides glistening, flippers angling out of the seethe like dorsal fins of sharks. It was the precise meeting of the two great currents — a fundamental nexus of the world's waters — the Mozambique or Agulhas flowing down eastern Africa from the Equator, the slower-moving Benguela running northward from the Antarctic.

Adamastor fell in love with Thetis the Nereid, creator of kingfishers, born of Doris, daughter of Ocean, and Nereus the Truthful, son of Gaea the Earth and Pontus the Sea. He had caught sight of her naked and white as foam. When he tried to embrace her, he found in his arms

> a rugged mount,
> With harshest wood and thorny thickets faced;
> Standing before a rock e'en front to front . . .

The giant and the nereid could never mingle. At this juncture, or lack of it, Zeus turned the rebel male into the outcrop that we call the Cape —

> Into hard earth my flesh converted lies
> My bones are turned to rocks all rough and strange —

while Thetis was reabsorbed into her ancestral waters and forever causes him 'redoubled anguish of his woes' by flowing round him and passing on beyond him.

This magic of waters and rocky sources was given a further lease of life in the most unexpected way. We tired of waiting for the South African winter to relent and went up into the clouds to gain at least some experience of Table Mountain, however soaked and darkened it might be. We were four — Anne, myself, Mike, a sub-editor on Johannesburg's only black-owned newspaper, and Barbie Schreiner, a writer who had taken an M.A. in Creative Writing with me in the 'eighties. We followed the stone staircase, built to save erosion, like the new-made ways up High Stile and Scafell back home in Cumbria; skirted the crags of Venster Buttress; followed a gully to below the west wing of the curtain-wall; and contoured round its cliff inside the darkness of the cloud until only our African friends appeared to know distinctly whether we had travelled 180° of the circle or a mere 18°. The path was the twisting thread where the *fynbos* was not impenetrable. Occasionally a yellow-painted footsole on a boulder confirmed that we were still on route. Steep clefts between rocky masses yielded to pulls and heaves on their grainy surfaces. The angle eased and we were staring out over a misted stony heath like some more growthy Dartmoor.

With Mike I walked round below the base of Africa Cliff to refill our water bottles at a pond he knew. Above our heads the Cliff was a mere deepening of the dripping dusk. Cracked ribs overhung the path — the first pitches of routes that would have been a delight to climb on a dry day. A rill coursing down a white rockface fed a waterhole surrounded by thickets of succulent leafage, scrolled like kail. It could almost have been English, had it not been for the immaculate creamy horns of two wild arum lilies, their mouths filled with rain or dew.

When we rejoined the others, we found them looking with eyes of wonder into the mist. Two people were coming near. As they became more than silhouettes, we saw that they were a black African couple. In the gale the woman's robes were blowing, butter-yellow and white, a sun-wraith in the gloom. Her hair was crowned with a circlet woven from grass and the sockets round her eyes were smeared ash-white with ritual make-up. He had the look of a retired citizen, shabby and respectable, in a felt hat with a crumpled brim, a thin brown linen jacket, and a baggy blue pullover. When they had come near enough to greet us, we saw that her feet were bare. His were shod in black town shoes with flannels turned up above them, as though he were going for a paddle. Each carried a peeled stick with an oxtail plume attached to its end with coloured plastic tape. They were not young — they were Anne's and my age. She looked like pure traditional Africa, he more like the half-Europeanised Africa of shitty jobs in industrial conurbations.

And so they were. They were brother and sister. He was Hitler Magwaza, plastics-factory worker at the U.S.A. Brush Company in Nyanga Township north of Cape Town. She was Nomama Mbobi and she was a *sangōma*, a traditional healer, who specialised in water. As Barbie and Mike translated from the Afrikaans, we gathered that she often prayed beside the sea, or over water to enhance its healing properties.

A few days later the *Weekly Mail* reported that a veld fire in Soweto had laid bare an old house nobody had seen before. It seemed to have been unlived-in and it was now being rumoured that it was a ritual centre for student *sangōmas* who 'told people that they stayed under water for months before they qualified as traditional healers'. Was this one of Nomama's practices? We would probably never know, not even if we went to Nyanga to consult her.

'I am the one who can see through people,' Barbie interpreted her as saying, yet she laughed and laughed when she heard Mike describing her as a *sangōma* to us. The two of them were on a quest to find the source of the waters on the top of the Mountain. They had never been here before, in this place now given over to tourists and bronzed young climbers. For five days she had eaten nothing. They had hoped to get up by cable-car but the gale had closed it. The broad soles of her feet were coping sturdily with the grating stones of the path and her brother seemed unruffled by the dimness and the howling winds but she was getting seriously cold. Her robes were impossible to manage in the gusts and she gladly accepted a nylon-pile jacket from Mike.

'Do all the water-healers come up here?' I asked her.

'No, no — the others are too scared.'

Without Mike's guidance they might well have lost the path. As it was the six of us trudged on and up beneath crags like ogres in shrouds, past blossoms whose sunflower faces were ringed with petals like flakes of salmon-flesh. At last the ground flattened into the great table-land, most familiar of mountain landmarks, recognisable even in this premature dusk. Two water-tanks came into sight, small round metal reservoirs built over wellsprings. Quick talk in Afrikaans and Barbie translated, 'She is going to pray.'

Nomama Mbobi held up her right hand like someone about to testify and burst into passionate utterance. Each sentence (or verse?) peaked in a near yell, then diminished in two or three pattering syllables. I could have listened indefinitely, as though to some headlong aria. After perhaps three minutes she delved into the tapestry shoulder bag carried by her brother, took out some beans and yellow mealies, and threw them up and over the rim of the nearer tank. They pattered like hailstones on to a metal top. The source, however, had been reached, and it had been blessed.

As we picked a path across the level reefs, in a small circle of the visible bounded by featureless cloud-wrack, we made an extraordinary crew, a little assembly of the nations, people from (ultimately) Zulu-land, Germany, England, Scotland, cast by all manner of currents on to this makeshift raft of friendship, or at least co-operation. I was beyond surprise when we finished up in the terminal of the cable-car — where we had gone to shelter our stove from the tearing wind — eating egg and vegetable curry at the invitation of a coloured lad in a linen Muslim cap while the other half of the engine-house maintenance team, a shy white youth, lay on a trestle bed in the next room watching rugby which was being transmitted live from a sunbaked ground in the Transvaal.

From the mouth of the building steel ropes looped downward into a grey gulf. We gathered that our way off the mountain was by Platteklip. Only the Boer name distinguished the jagged gutter at our feet from a thousand of its kind that funnel off into the steaming void below the ridges and plateaux of familiar mountains in the Scottish and English highlands. This had been the route taken by the first white person to climb the Mountain — Antonio de Saldanha, who came up here in 1503 to find out whether or not his fleet in Table Bay had passed the Cape of Storms, as his pilot alleged. In the first description of a Table Mountain climb 130 years later, an Englishman called Peter Mundy was awestruck by the Platteklip, 'like a valley but wondrous steep, the rocks on each side upright like monstrous walls, from which there is a continual distilling water'. This much had not changed, although there was no longer any need for a fire 'to drive away lions and other wild beast'.

In this rock and water world Nomama Mbobi was at home, out of the wind now and warmed by the food. When we stopped beside a cascade to rest our legs, she said with a laugh, 'Of course it is raining! God is here, he is taking care of us. In the fog the thugs will not be able to see us, or harm us.'

What dangers from the desperate daily life of the townships did she have in mind? Cape Town looked genteel and peaceable, and the seething heart of its black quarter had recently been torn out, razed, turned into a wasteland ready for 'development'. A few weeks after we left for the Transvaal and Malawi, the new habit of drive-by raiding hit the city. A Protestant congregation was sprayed with automatic-rifle fire: twelve dead. The event was later celebrated at a Pan-Africanist congress to chants of 'One missionary one bullet! One church one bomb!'

In the violent post-colonial culture disturbing cults flourish. When we drove to Cape Agulhas, Africa's southernmost point, on a louring day of rain squalls blowing up out of the Antarctic, armoured cars crouched round the fringes of the squatter camps and soldiers with guns stood at the ready. The shanties made of brushwood and flattened tins were marooned among sheets of floodwater and on muddy hillocks a few young men sat, coats turned up against the rain, cheeks ashen with ritual make-up. 'Teenagers waiting for circumcision and initiation,' explained Barbie and Mike. The daily paper carried a story about a university lecturer who was alone in his room, preparing for a chemistry seminar, when a group of students with knives burst in, intent on circumcising him. (He got away.) Without this rite, the zealots are increasingly feeling, a man is not a man and is unfit for power in society.

In conditions like these Nomama Mbobi's honouring of the wellsprings seemed benign, a natural human practice not yet overgrown into morbidity. We knew we could fathom only a tithe of her beliefs. And such things are complex. It is possible that the sexual partner of a circumcised man is less likely to get cancer of the cervix . . . You could say that our journey down the teeming obscurity of the Platteklip Gorge was a symbol of our wayfaring and wayfinding through alien lives that were vexingly hard to interpret.

The place itself turned out to house a story — a history? a myth? — which was typical of rock after rock, range after range, in southern Africa. The wood at the foot of it is known as Verlatenbosch. A Cape governor in the Dutch period had quarrelled with a citizen. The man made a flute from bamboo, gave it to a leper to play, and then left it where the governor's young son would find it. After playing it he caught the leprosy and was isolated in a stone hut at the foot of Platteklip, near 'the bush of the forsaken. At twilight his flute sounds among the leaves, "*Verlaten, verlaten*" . . . '

Although the story ends in schmaltz, it is rooted in the real harsh life of the early colony, when one great rock after another came to be used as a refuge. In the middle of the eighteenth century Table Mountain, then heavily wooded and the haunt of leopards and hyenas, was a haven for runaway slaves. Their fires could be seen at night by the burghers living below, in reassuring proximity to the gallows. For the incomers, the colonists, the mountain had been the seamark for a haven ever since 1503, when Antonio de Saldanha veered into the bay by mistake and found the Mountain's sweet-water springs ideal for replenishing his tanks. For Africans the colony became a place of dread where slaves were flogged, then branded and sent to Robben Island for retaliating; 'broken on the wheel without administration of the death-blow';

Impression of Cape Town and Table Mountain in 1812 by an unknown artist

facially mutilated, impaled up the anus, flogged again, then strangled after they were finally hunted down in the thickets.

In primal times, during the world's innocence, rock could figure as the first stuff of life. Ma-Rose, tradition-bearer and story-teller of the Khokhoin, the People-of-People or original dwellers of the Cape, could refer naturally to a stony place as 'the rocky spot where in the beginning of the world the stones had come tumbling down the mountain'. Her Genesis story goes like this:

> In the beginning there was nothing but stone. And from the stones Tsui-Goab made us. But then he saw that we couldn't live without water, since it's water that makes the grass sprout and the trees grow and which is drink for man and beast. The inside of a woman is water; her children swim from her into the world. And whenever the earth gets dry and threatens to turn to stone, it's rain we pray for . . .

With the coming of slavery stone turns into the instrument and symbol of captivity. In prison the slave-hero of Brink's *A Chain of Voices*, Galant, meets a huge man who has been in irons for many years. He hears from him the story of a runaway slave, a Malay woman, who is finally chained to a rock for good,

> far enough from the house so no one would hear her screams. Once a day a child was sent with some food and water; and they even put up a small shelter on poles to keep away the worst rain or sun. There

163

she stayed all her life, and the people say she lived to a very old age. Chained to the rock she remained, and never spoke another word to anyone. At last she died, and the beasts of the veld and the vultures devoured the carcass and scattered the remains. In my time there was no one left who'd known her. But the rock was still there, and the piece of chain.

This nameless woman fuses Andromeda, chained to a rock because she was too beautiful, and Prometheus, similarly punished because he was too independent. The crime of both was lack of submissiveness to the overlord. In Africa such myths became reality. André Brink tells me that he took the chained woman from an historical record, where she was 'cited as a specific instance of extreme cruelty'. In his novel, the huge man often sits on that rock and fantasises about the people who have made it to the country beyond 'the Great River', where there is freedom. If we think of this as the Orange River north of Cape Province, the story becomes all the more poignant, because of course freedom did not prevail there either, except for the Boers. When we went north again to explore the great rocks of the Transvaal, one after another of our landmarks had a history as a refuge in the epic struggles of the peoples.

18   The Road to Moonshadow

On our way south from Johannesburg, making for the asparagus farm near Ficksburg, we had stared eastward into Lesotho, trying to identify among the mesas of the Maluti Mountains the one called Thaba Bosiu, mountain of the night. Here the Sotho chieftain called Moshoshoe had rallied his shattered clans in 1824, reaching it in darkness after a forced march through cannibal country, and set up the nucleus of the Basotho nation among the spring-fed pastures on the summit plateau.

Such were the desperate shifts of the Africans as they struggled with fearsome forces. When the British fixed or 'closed' the frontier of South Africa in 1825, 'the crowding of tribal land disturbed the pattern of Nguni life deep into Natal among clans who had never encountered the white race far to the south of them'. Their heartland 'was filling with people behind the closed frontier, and as this disrupted the ancient pattern of movement among the clans, competition increased for the overstocked grazing lands and for the water sources. Warfare was becoming incessant.' The Difaquane, or forced migration, gathered terrible force as millions fled before the newly-organised Zulu armies under their commander, Shaka. Clans fled south and west, ousting other clans. 'Waves of refugees rolled forward like animals before a band of hunters.' People crazed by famine turned cannibal. At last three million people were 'stumbling back and forth . . . across the length and breadth of the central plateau' where not one permanent village or kraal remained.

Another bastion of survival in this devastated land was what had drawn me as I read the mountain literature Mike had sent to England the year before. In the safe centre of a range called the Blouberg, not far from the southern boundary of Matabeleland, a chieftain called Maleboch (or better, Malebogo, in his own Sepedi language) had refused to recognise the laws and taxes of the Zuid-Afrikaanische Republiek, which therefore declared war on his Hananwa tribe in the spring of 1894. During a long siege of the stronghold in the Blouberg the Staatsartillerie bombarded the Hananwa with dynamite and Cayenne pepper and killed off the women with sniper fire when they tried to run in water to the parched defenders. When at last they surrendered and turned out to be so few, they were left to maintain their tribal enclave, where Malebogo's descendant is counted chieftain to this day.

The North Face of the Blouberg is the 'big wall' to Transvaal climbers. It is a kilometre long and more than four hundred metres high, and the first route up it was named Maleboch after the chieftain. This at once became my Mecca. The great rock, darkly glowing greenish-bronze in the photo I had seen, had become in my imagination as much an ordeal as a goal. It should not get like that. It does. Sunlit days limbering up on the lesser walls of the Magaliesberg, 70 kilometres north-west of Johannesburg, were subtly shadowed for me by the Blouberg's darkling presence 350 kilometres to the north.

The kloofs of the Magaliesberg made a kind of linear Eden garden, deep-cut in sandstone that still seemed to glow with the fires that once hardened it. Its colours and forms were so succulent that they looked carved from papaw flesh. Late in the day the bronze and salmon, cubic and pyramidal crowns of its buttresses might have been the sunlight solidified. If I went blind, these would be some of the incarnations of the visible world it would be most heartening — or maddening — to remember.

I suppose an Eden should have had more animals. They hid, from us and from the sun. One area was named Stench Gorge after the depth of baboon shit in it. We never saw the animals and the only turd we found was odourless and broke into dry crumbs like very old parkin. Approaching from our chalet in Mountain Sanctuary Park, we startled three klipspringer, which took off from a red reef as though they had charges in their hooves, then sprang and levitated away between totem rocks like massive chess pieces, as though they were improvising the most gymnastic of ballets. In the evening, as the sun set and the cliff-tops turned from peach to pollen, cliff-swallows flocked screaming in a mad circus, hunting the last of the insects wafted upward by convection.

The glory of the gorge's life was in its plants. Tree-ferns grow down there, apparitions from prehistory, with the extraordinary contrast between their hairy trunks, like the legs of dwarf black mammoths, and the sudden arcing of the frond-fountain at their tops. Soft ferns curved their asexual green fingers sideways above our heads, semi-transparent lettuce-green in the piercing rays of the tropic winter sun. It looked like the first plant to be perfected after the aeons of electric storm and scorching drought. We hauled up the split bulges and cracked lips of the crags like apes; we abseiled, sharing space with the cliff-swallows as they tore into a new-hatched swarm; we bridged and slithered down water-rounded boulders between pools where the water still pulsed although no rain had fallen for months.

The main gorge was called Tonquani, after the Bakhatkla chief Tenquaan, who took refuge here from Mzilikazi, a captain in Shaka's army who tried to set up his own dynasty in the Magaliesberg. So history had burned and hacked its way through here too. On our first visit to the range, gaining height slowly from the south, we had followed a track past a long low rickle of stones — clearly a ruined building. It had been a blockhouse in the second Anglo-Boer War, built to contain the commandoes and enforce a scorched earth policy by razing every farm. Among the stones I found one reminder of the soldiers' terror and boredom under an alien sun a century before — the rusted iron strap from an ammunition box.

The peace that reigned here now, among peach and orange orchards, was still uneasy. As we trekked back down to the car well after dark, a dog bayed from the nearest farmhouse. By the time we had stowed our gear, the farmer had arrived in his 4-wheel-drive, with a dazzling flashlight that he shone in our eyes and a heavy-jawed mastiff on the seat beside him. Mike needed to talk fast in his jokey Afrikaans to persuade him that we were *bona fide* climbers.

Ensconced in the Sanctuary Park, belaying on ledges fifty metres up the glowing rock-walls, we could forget all that and pretend we were still tree-creatures — smoothing the dust off the wild-fig leaves with our fingers, penetrating the clefts of the sandstone like the root-systems that were gradually prising the strata apart. Where Cedarberg Kloof entered the main gorge, I climbed the Corner Route straight up, reaching and reaching a full arm's length and never failing to find some dream edge or pocket for the fingers. On Dom's Party, I terrified myself by failing to lodge in a tall split with rounded faces — feeling myself spewed out as though a giant were vomiting a piece of gristle — swarming up the right-hand face on big crystals with the last of my energy. A renowned Yorkshire climber called Robin Barley had pion-eered routes I struggled up back home in Malham Cove, then emi-grated to Africa and helped develop the Magaliesberg for climbing. On his classically beautiful route called Hourglass we tiptoed up a twenty-metre cut above the waist where two perfect niches touched apexes, two slim triangles cleft into the rockface, one of them inverted. The tall elegance of the forms seemed to infuse our limbs with gracefulness, or so it felt inside the looking-glass world of my own head. In Boulder Kloof, on Red Column, whose erect tall body and brow it was imposs-ible not to see as the tutelary god of the gorge, I felt a strong inspi-rational upward surge in me at last and managed to edge out and out and out again into airy space above the tree-ferns, along a hand's-breadth ledge and round a blind corner which Mike said had detained his previous partner for a good half-hour. We even put up a new route, an ambling slab like a baboons' playground, and I called it Kei after the child about to be born to Mike and his partner Sheena. She is in the world now and they have promised that the slab will be her first route.

Meanwhile Blouberg North Wall was rising into sight above the leaf canopy — it could not be stopped. When we took off north along with Chris Benner, from California, we travelled via Pretoria, skirting the expensive-looking concrete of the Central Prison where at least two ANC guerrillas were executed every year throughout the 'sixties and 'seventies — where Steve Biko arrived, dying, in a prison van from Port Elizabeth. Our goal was the Spinal Unit of the hospital where a friend of Mike's called Dominic Souchon, a worker with the National Com-mittee for the Rehabilitation of Political Exiles, was lying with a broken back. He had been climbing, boldly and too fast, up a route called Phoenix in the Magaliesberg Grootkloof. When he fell, his highest protection point, an *in situ* piton, pulled straight out and with

Mike Loewe abseiling in Tonquani Kloof

the force of his fall his own lower protection nuts pulled too. Mike, out of sight nearby, heard the dreadful thump as Dominic hit the ground and rushed along to find him in agony, bloodied, but still composed enough to warn them against disordering his broken back.

Now he was paralysed and incontinent, waiting for an operation to repair some vertebrae with bone from his hip. In bed he was an emaciated figure, white-faced, beak-nosed, black-bearded, his eyes glittering with witty intelligence. When we came through the doors, he raised his stem-like arms, one cased in plaster, and said, 'This [the unbroken one] is normal South African malnourishment. And this is Somalian malnourishment.'

Mike had been a surfer when he lived on the east coast before moving to Johannesburg. He was looking for a change of sport when Barbie Schreiner gave him a copy of my book about climbing, *Native Stones*. This was what had turned him on to rock. Dominic had read it too and now said courteously, 'I enjoyed your book very much.' At this a qualm of responsibility added itself to the excruciation of seeing someone almost destroyed by climbing. A black jagged edge had appeared on the Wall ahead of me — although I knew with the rational part of myself that I had neither the nerve nor the skill to climb as fast as Dominic had apparently been doing.

Our way hammered on northward across plains of dun dust, seared grasses, low hard-leafed trees with the tufts of weaverbirds' nests in their crowns. This was the savannah of the old hunting tribes, seized for 10,000-acre farms by the Voortrekkers after the Difaquane and after their own Great Dispersal between 1838 and 1847. When we drove through the occasional market towns, I could feel my radical friends bristling against these heartlands of the Nationalists, the backbone of the apartheid culture, and I could imagine that the farmers on the sidewalks were looking stonily at Mike's hippy hairstyle or at our little beat-up car from Rent-a-Wreck.

In the leafier areas outside the towns, high steel gates barred the driveways to hidden homesteads and black 'boys' dozed in the shabby porters' boxes. The service town here was Potgietersrus. Presumably it was named after Hendrik Potgieter, Transvaal leader of the Great Trek in 1838. For me it connoted also another Potgieter, Hermanus, whose slaving raids aroused violent conflict between the Boers and the Ndebele:

> Potgieter and his men spanned out their wagons at the foot of a rise
> with a village on it. Presently two Africans came down and greeted

him. He took out a ramrod, stuck it upright in an anthill and pointed to it, saying nothing.

The men went back to the village and came back presently with a couple of slaughtered goats. Potgieter said nothing, looked hard at them, and pointed to the ramrod.

They went back and fetched an ox. Potgieter still pointed to the ramrod. So they went and fetched two tusks of ivory. The ramrod remained erect.

Then Potgieter and his men mounted their horses, rode round the hill and up to the kraal, and shot some Africans. After a time he came back to the camp, driving cattle and children.

That was the requirement when the ramrod was stuck upright.

Where were the Africans now? A few still live in round thatched huts built higgledy-piggledy along the edges of the forest. Most have been 'resettled', recently, in big grid-plan townships at one point or another on the waterless, shadeless plain. No trees had appeared as yet, hardly one garden-patch, or a chapel or a shebeen. How could a person, or a family, put down a root of belonging in these pitiless conditions?

Presently the mountain refuges came bulking up round the horizon. As we turned off west into the long straight dirt roads, the range of the Soutpansberg raked away to the north-east. Here the Venda fled from the ravages of the Difaquane and beside a sacred lake called Fundudzi built kraals out of stone brought as offerings to the Ditutwane, the ancestral spirit-guardians of the mountain. Isolated mountains, epochal remnants, lay stranded across the wide levels like whales on a beach. Our own goal, the Blouberg, was starting to show its stature, a cluster of steep massifs with something of the look of Kata Tjuta in the middle of Australia — less sculpted but equally a landmark by which any traveller would want to steer.

Beyond a desolate re-settlement, where a few goats nibbled at the rubbish heaps, we reached a homely kraal among red boulders. Well-fleshed longhorn cattle browsed, goats herded in compounds made of branches. A polished stone beside the road marked the grave of David T. Njana, died in 1959, aged 104. In a minute we were being greeted by his son Frans, the present headman, an acquaintance of Mike's previous Big Wall trips. When he proffered a Visitors' Book, Mike said, 'We'll sign when we come back.' Somehow this sharpened my foreboding. Then we checked our packs and walked off into the wintry woodland.

The way followed a dried-up drift. Above brown tatters of leafage we could see humps of cliffy mountain, called donjons in tribute to Malbogo and his resistance from this stronghold. Droppings littered the path and as we rose up a toilsome gravel slope we came upon their source, a brown donkey and a grey one. Later we learned that they are used to carry down the crop of *dagga* (cannabis) from fields hidden on the plateau above. So the Hananwa were still a law to themselves!

The limbs of the Blouberg were starting to enclose us, the most northerly of them high up on our right as we headed south, whitened over large areas by the guano from two colonies of Cape vultures. Another refuge, for these vultures are threatened by the growing number of settlers who shoot them, supposedly to protect their stock. (Much the same is happening to the Golden and White-tailed eagles in the Scottish Highlands.) The way led between lofty broad-leafed trees, a hummocky path mired by cattle-hooves. Among mud and mossy boulders a plastic tube split lengthwise poured a stream of sweet water from a spring and we filled our bottles before setting off into a drier zone where glades of lustrous golden grass had the look of clearings for living in long ago. The one human remnant was a wooden spade, grained with age, handle and blade roughly carved out of the one piece, lying in the grass.

By the time we entered a boulder field made of laval rubble, the donjons had disappeared. Where was the Big Wall? I would rather have been having a sight of it. Or perhaps I wouldn't. At least some goal would be nice to make for as dusk came on. As we gained height by rock steps above a gorge, Chris pointed ahead and said, 'There's our cave.' On an upper tier of a cirque of crags a black eye with pointed corners had opened, its pupil a green tree. For the next two nights we made a home in this perfect refuge, sleeping between its lids, the rock ceiling half a metre above our faces, our bags put down on the thickest drift of dust to cushion our hips.

From sealed oildrums concealed in the rocks nearby Mike produced tins of tuna, peanuts, spare sleeping-bags to use as mattresses. When we left we would replace what we had used with whatever chocolate or sugar or dried fruit remained in our packs. After we'd eaten — sitting on stones and setting up the stove on stones — Chris produced from his gear the parts of a saxophone. With his legs dangling over the lower lip of the cave he played his music while from across the way the gallery of the cliffs echoed and trebly re-echoed his notes — not the wistful '*Verlaten, verlaten*' of Platteklip but 'Streets of Laredo' and 'Hey Jude'.

At dawn the animals were awake. Hyraxes (hare-sized relatives of the elephant) were chattering somewhere in the gorge below us, shrill notes above the ground-bass of waterfall. On a flat boulder-top a pied raven couple were billing and nuzzling — no doubt, like our pure black ones, they mate for life. I was focussing each detail to weave a fence of homeliness between here and the Big Wall. For me, though probably not for Mike or Chris, even washing up was a pleasant domestic distraction. Then it was light enough for wayfinding, though still chilly at 2,000 metres, and we were climbing still further up the glen and surmounting a col to look along the north face of the mountain.

A bronze brow dropped, and it dropped, cleaving the blue horizontal that planed off across the southern tip of Zimbabwe into Botswana. I didn't have to be told — this was the North Wall. We worked our way down between the massif and a donjon, hugging the cliff. As at the base of Fairview Dome in Tuolumne, wasted bushes and freshly scarred trunks were evidence of rockfall and I looked up with a qualm at broken overhangs where the sandstone had been plucked out by gravity, its strength gone at last after the hundred million years since Africa was uplifted as an entity.

The cliff enters the ground in massive pink timbers held together by blind joints, with few cracks or jutting handholds. So how do we climb this thing? A tufted ledge walks us out beneath the climbs. The rim where we will finish — if we make it — is exactly 369 metres above our heads and has that deceptive look of leaning way out beyond us like Gibraltar North Face. A daunting omen. At least this section of African rock looks solid as cast metal.

Our route is called Moonshadow. Its first pitch starts up a route called after Chris's tune of last night, Hey Jude. He leads off, up the gap between a huge curved flake and the mother-rock. I fix my eyes on him, hungry for know-how. I'll wedge a haunch into the gap and . . . no I won't — he's swinging right *across* with his hands on some invisible edge. So I'll be able to repeat the move I practised on Table Mountain . . . no I won't –

'That was wild,' Mike is muttering beside me. 'He should have crossed lower down.'

When I get up there, impossibility sets in. The dusty ledge Chris reached with his fingers is inches beyond me. There's nothing here, I probably called out angrily. There is, though; there's a rough-lipped cavity an inch deep which I must lever on with my left toe-tip. It can't be done, can't not be done, can just be done and I'm mantel-shelfing on to a narrow ledge, fraught with a renewed sense of rock's sheer hardness (in every sense) that cramps my brain for the next two hundred vertical metres.

For three hours the trampled sand we started from is almost directly below us. As we geared up down there, the air sussurated as though with strummed strings or rubbed drums and thousands of swifts, paler and larger than our summer visitors, cut the air with their blade wings in a morning celebration of furious energy, then disappeared. From the semi-jungle excited yelps spoke of a hidden troop of baboons.

'Sounds like an orgy,' I suggested.

'More like rape,' said Mike grimly, as though he knew a thing or two about baboons.

Sunlit quietness returns as we rise. The treetops below turn slowly into bushes, then into fretted green blobs on an architect's plan. An oval clearing shows yellow and umber among the green. Mike remembers a hut there, now deserted, perhaps for good. Each pitch we climb is nearly a full rope's length. The leader tows two ropes, and the followers (either Mike and I or Chris and I) then climb closely one after the other — a great help to me, since absolute loneliness might have been crushing. Each time I have to leave a stance and take off up the rockface, my back feels stripped naked, even dissected, by awareness of the vacancy behind out there and below. I am fragile, transparent, the core of me laid bare to life-threatening forces.

Any tigerish climbers among my readers, accustomed to the grades we call Extreme 2 and upwards, are welcome to laugh at my fuss about a route which was a mere Hard Very Severe, mostly 4c, a good deal of 5a, some 5b moves round short roofs which taxed me to the utmost. We all have our technical limits, and though mine is slightly beyond Moonshadow on the Blouberg, the giant stature of the crag expanded my brain until the stress felt only just bearable.

The ledges are quite roomy, which helps. Water can be drunk, the camera used, a film changed. These stances are so homely that launching upwards again is almost too much of a douche, a drenching in cold space. I find I'm latching on to details as mental lifebelts. That vulture cruising a few feet out from the upper rim, the crook of its neck and the tapering of its wings distinguishing it from an eagle. This pile of swifts' droppings behind a flake on a ledge, the only nest of theirs I have ever seen close up. Lying on it is a single feather, grey as smoke, probably the narrowest in the entire bird world, since the swift, the supreme aerobat, is so slim-winged that it cannot use the buoyancy of the air and must fly-fly-fly continuously for the first two years of its life, until it mates . . .

Contemplation is broken into again by shouts from above. Then the ledge must be abandoned — thankfully in the case of stance 5, which was cracked in many places along its length and will surely break off soon. At the end of pitch 6, 283 metres up, the stance is broader than the usual bare metre and at its east end (its left end facing outwards) a yellow-wood sprawls its limbs and bristles its yew-like foliage. It makes me feel at home just looking at it. It's like the yew through and off which the climb on pitch 3 is begun on the route called North Crag Eliminate on Castle Rock of Triermain, near Keswick in Cumbria. I hang my helmet on a branch to let my head steam off, my small sack with camera and trainers from another, and allow the ambience of the tree to cocoon me like a nest. At last the hollowing air out there no longer feels as though it could evacuate me at any moment with its destroying suction.

Is this a fool's paradise? The guidebook advises, 'Carefully move through the yellow-wood and step off it on to the thin face.' 'Thin' is climbspeak for 'very small holds'. The branches of the tree resist like tangled wire. I stare up at the face. What do you *do?* The rock here is very beautiful. In my contentment I forget to watch as Chris forges on upwards. Lower down it is as though a master of gouache (John Piper, say) has painted sweeps of mustard yellow on a copper-cinnamon ground. Above me now is an almost vertical sheet of grainy stone, tea-rose pink, dotted with knobs nearly as small as the features called chickenheads by American climbers. And that's all — no other holds and all that fall below my footsoles.

'There's nothing here,' I call to Mike, yet again.

'Just go straight up,' he suggests.

How limpid, how undeniable! And when I do, it's *all right*, the vertical world has accepted me at last, or rather I have accepted it. I have advanced on what I call the fear barrier, neared it, found it (yet again) to be an illusion. I'm fingertipping on two knobs at fullest stretch, pulling up with my toes smearing on friction, reaching for a knob higher up the sequence, lodging my toes now on knobs so sharply moulded they are as secure and fine as features ten times their three-centimetre diameter.

Bliss flows. No super-muscle is needed, no technique of leverage beyond my simple powers. Let the lithe levitation happen, trust that the holds won't run out — however could they, Chris has been here and there are his benign spectacles, shining down at me from the upper end of the fifty-metre umbilicus.

After that, for the final five pitches, pure pleasure was free to brim up and fill us to the fingertips — a mix of the achievement now behind us and the gymnastic joys of the moment. The last pitch overhung for twenty metres and was covered with blackish bulges like tarred skulls. Grasp one, pull up hard and reach for the next, stand where your feet were a moment before, grasp and pull up again. The glycogen in my arms was running low now. The summit rim was visible — was tangible — it was just a matter of doing this thing that was so natural, and shared with all the other primates.

At the top I whooped like an owl, divided up the last of my chocolate-covered Kendal mint cake, and turned to take in the spread of central Africa. Behind us was the high point of the Blouberg, Ga-Monaa-Sena-Moriri, Man with no hair, and I could identify with that. Beyond, a little south, we could make out the stubble-fields of the Hananwa. To the north, through rifts in the puckered slaty cloud, the declining sun splayed out its light in shafts, making harvest-yellow dapples on the parched brown land. In the furthest blue zone, not a hundred kilometres distant, the Limpopo was (in principle) visible, and beyond it South Matabeleland. The western sky was flushing magenta in the direction of the Kalahari desert — a barely thinkable tract, a panel of the map with no names, which I would never cross.

Presently we would overfly all this to Blantyre in Malawi. Flying at altitude doesn't count, not as journeying. It is a suspension in mid-air while even the 250-kilometres-an-hour jet-stream is rendered impalpable and the world revolves below, its great rocks shrunk to two-dimensional orts. The stars seen from the cave-mouth that night were as conceptual as the jet-stream, or the Kalahari or Zimbabwe beyond the Limpopo. At least for ten hours we had known height close-up with our own bodies, our own eyes.

19   The Stone Writing of Mikolongwe

In Malawi we were heading for a fastness that may have been a refuge only in fantasy — the colossal inselberg called Mulanje, near the border with Mozambique, and its soaring single neighbour to the north, Mchese. 'Little men' are said to have their home on Mchese. An Englishman who used to farm in the Fort Lister gap between Mchese and Mulanje, near the old strongpoint built by the British to block a slave route from the interior through to the east coast, told us that his servants would point to sunset light reflected from the weeps on the rockface and say, 'There are their fires', and they left bananas for them in the forks of trees.

How much was this a case of wanting to believe in earlier inhabitants, so as to people a wilderness and make it less daunting? So we have our trolls and trows and wodwo's, the small squat hairy humans that can be glimpsed in half-hidden nooks of the stonework or woodwork of medieval cathedrals. Of course there were, and are, small forest-dwelling people in Africa, whose 'voice' or symbolic language speaks to us from faces of the rock. My Mulanje informant, John Killick, pointed out that Mchese is too steep to hold water and is therefore uninhabitable. No artefacts have been found up there. What has been found are Late Stone Age axe-heads and scrapers on the Mulanje plateaux, where the montane forest and grassland would have made a rich enough, though arduous, habitat. According to the rock-climber Frank Eastwood, who pioneered 1,600-metre routes here, using grass tufts for holds and belaying on the stems of liliaceous shrubs: 'the massif has been a place of refuge throughout history, and has been occupied sporadically by groups as diverse as Stone Age hunters [the Batwa] and 19th century refugees from the slave trade'.

This bloodstained face of the past stared out at us briefly from the smaller inselbergs between Blantyre and Mulanje, with their woeful names — Namitembo, place of corpses (its several tops looked like upturned toes), Nsomi, sorrow, Madema, darkness, and Ntawaira, runaway hill. In this district of Chiradzulu, named after a mountain, John Chilembwe, an African converted to Christianity during his time working in America, had led the first rising in Nyasaland against British rule. Once he preached from the pulpit with a planter's head on the lectern in front of him. Ntawaira was where the rebels' courage failed them and they fled.

Now, after Independence, the country — renamed Malawi — is peaceful, very poor, congested. The population of ten million includes about a million recent incomers from Mozambique, many of them refugees — although definitions are tricky here because the Malawi/Mozambique boundary is an imperial invention and has been migrated across habitually by east African peoples for millennia. Our own essential image of the place came to be the crowds of people walking along the verges of the narrow roads between Blantyre and Mulanje, indeed on all the roads, at all times on all days. It looked as though a football match had just finished somewhere nearby. It was the normal state of a country with few cars and not so many bicycles, where everybody walked the miles to work, whether they were carrying briefcases or bundles of sugarcane — where somebody with a bike was liable to push it, heavily laden, the ten or twelve miles home from the shrinking wild lands where he had been cutting small trees to burn or sell, or grass for thatch.

The eastbound roads skirted the lesser inselbergs, homing on Mulanje. At Likhubula, a short way up one of its western valleys, we rented huts from the Forest Department. Here I found I was expected to employ a boy as mountain guide from among the little crowd that gathered to solicit work, whether guiding or posing to be drawn in pastels by our host and friend, Robin Broadhead, a doctor in Blantyre.

From a distance the multi-headed mountain had bulked and glowed as though a whole summer's light were embodied in the one mass of granite and syenite. Although it was more broad than tapering, its upwardness was accentuated by the vertical grooving of its flanks, which must engender lightning-forks of white water when the summer rains run off it. With Frank Jalli, a slightly-built barefoot lad of fifteen or so, I set off up the Skyline Path, between the 2,500-metre peaks called Chambe and Chilemba. Our height gain would be about eleven hundred metres.

Under our feet the way was dusty, biscuit-brown, the stones laid bare, the hollows between tree roots gullied deeply with use. Steel ropes in mid-air arced far up the mountain, linking a clearing stacked with sawn timber to some unseen headgear in the higher forests. It was not in use. Presently, above us, we saw long yellow pieces of timber tilting and slipping down towards us, like hogweed stems in a stream (in one of Goldsworthy's nature-sculptures) or rice grains borne along on a column of ants. Each piece was a cedar plank, flexing and bending on the head or shoulder of a man. They were about six metres long, seven or eight centimetres thick, and twenty-five or thirty centimetres across. We stood aside to let the men pass as they strained with spread toes to keep their grip.

Their eyes were enlarged and intent, their faces unmoving, like people deeply alert, listening. Shiny paths of sweat ran from their necks to their bellies. They wore ragged shorts or cut-offs, ragged shirts or no shirts at all, usually no footgear. Each man gave off a reek of cheese and smoke, the smell of wood fires and their bodies.

A few said 'Hullo' to my 'Hullo' and some added 'How are you?' with a tinge of trying out or parodying polite English. Once a couple of them, chatting and resting beside their loads, said 'Hullo', and when at once I got in with 'How are you?' just before they did, one held up a forefinger to signify 'Nice one!' or 'Snap!' Mostly, they were silent.

One man had a ten- or twelve-year-old walking beside him and had added the lad's four-by-four to his own plank. Another, the only one with well-developed biceps, was carrying two planks — each probably weighing sixty kilos. Just below us he bent at the knees, let down the front of his load against a tree, stepped out from under it, and began to remake his head-pad, pulling the thongs of beobab bark through his teeth to supple them, then retying the grubby bundle.

It was all utterly salutary. I was 'working' hard enough, climbing as fast as I could to get up and down before the sun set, at a latitude 16° south of the Equator, and the sweat was streaming off me. This was perfectly voluntary. I could turn back at my own sweet will, chat with Frank, stop to swig springwater from a bottle or admire and photograph the view. The plank-carriers were climbing and down-climbing the mountain for a living, or less than living, wage to exchange for kerosene, salt, and sugar, or for a school uniform. Frank would not be allowed back to school in September unless his parents bought him a new uniform. The statutory daily wage was 5 kwacha, or 90 pence, and each man was expected to make two or three trips laden before climbing the mountain again to his home, a Forest Department hut at 1,900 metres in the Chambe basin.

When the logging of mountain cedars started in 1901, the wage was 1/3d for five trips, or nine pence to carry a load across country the fifty kilometres to Zomba, the colonial capital north of Blantyre. One mountain was known as Ninepence. In *Venture to the Interior*, published in 1952, Laurens van der Post says that it was hoped this desperate labour would finish soon, when the cable-way was built. Evidently the company I saw at work, called Shiré Limited, could not or would not afford the charge to hire it from the government. So this hawser spun from human will and muscle continues to twist its way down and up the mountainside, between clumps of mauve and scarlet balsam flowers, over outcrops that have been moulded into foot-shaped hollows inches deep by nearly a century of effort.

We were given cups of smoky black tea by climbers in a hut next to the old bungalow of the couple who had come to grief in a storm in van der Post's atmospheric book. Between the trunks of monumental conifers we could glimpse sweeps of cliff fledged all down their vertical corrugations with beards of shrub and lichen. From a high point on the Skyline Path, as dusk came on and forced us to trot and jump downhill, we looked westward over a plain breasted with hills and printed with cloud shadows like unknown animals surfacing in a sea, in the direction of Mikolongwe between Blantyre and the broad moist plain of the Shiré lowlands. A hill there called Mwala Lolemba, Stone writing, was said to bear traces of the aboriginal people, the Batwa hunters, who had made paintings in a cave.

Down there, a few days later, Mwala Lolemba began to seem elusive as the tarmac ended, a dirt road stretched brownly ahead, and settlements thinned to a scattering of huts. We retreated, then turned off up a rutted track, beguiled by a sign that said 'Veterinary Research Association'. Cautiously we drove through a concrete trough of disinfectant, beside which a young mother sat suckling her baby, and turned into a compound. Here a man gave us detailed advice in good English.

'Go back to the tarmac,' he told us. 'Turn left — go over a stream. Approach the railway line — do not cross it. Later you cross it, and there is a police post. Ask there. About seven kilometres.'

All was as he had said. At the police station, in a hamlet of breeze-block bungalows, the national flag was fluttering above dusty, well-kempt lawns. Inside, a massive sergeant with the jowl and jutting nose of a stage dictator was finishing a phone call in front of a concrete wall decorated with one thing, a pair of handcuffs hanging from a nail, next to a doorway with the word 'Interrogation' stencilled above it. The 'dictator' was helpfulness itself. He knew of the paintings — 'Over there, five kilometres' — and went across to a bungalow nearby to find us a guide. This turned out to be the Chairman of the Local Congress Party, no less, a tailor by trade, called Lastoni Mponda. Mr Mponda, in a beige jacket and immaculate trousers, went inside again to fetch a plastic document case and we set off again for Mwala Lolemba — joined at the last moment by Constable Paul Zeta, summoned from the guardroom by his sergeant.

The road was like a garden path of clean sand, side-stepping between mud-brick houses the size of toolsheds, little orchards with papaw trees and banana palms, round the edges of clearings floored with earth, past fields where the maize harvest had left a few bleached and tattered stalks. Children ran out to stare and wave, black goats bleated, women sat peeling sweet potatoes beside cloths spread with newly ground white flour. We parked the car in the yard of the one modern bungalow for miles around and set off, the four of us, Anne and I and our guard of honour, towards a craggy skyline.

The path stepped round little fields, became an earthen gully deeply grooved by run-off, and climbed between badges and shields of grey granite. Where a British eye expected moorland to take over, the ground levelled out and more fields, recently ploughed, stretched along the hillside. Each half-acre of arable was used. Here, I was thinking, was what the Scottish Highlands had been before the allotment into crofts and before the Clearances, when the people 'lived companionably together in loosely clustered settlements' and their siting was 'entirely a matter of immediate conditions of slope, shelter and aspect'.

Mr Mponde and Constable Zeta led continuously onward, talking non-stop in Chichewa, pausing solicitously to say in English 'We go this way now', or 'It is not far'. The southern upland of Malawi, dappled brown with winter fields, expanded southward towards the shapely isolated cone of Chiperone, which has given its name to a rain-bearing summer wind, south-east into the furry green jungle of Mozambique, and east to the blue citadel of Mulanje. A broad boss of crag on the skyline of Mwala Lolemba was opening a wide dark mouth. A smaller slit gaped lower down. Which was the ancient Pygmy shelter? From closer up the cragface showed speckled brown and black and orange, the ingredients of the rock. The wider mouth opened inward to a cave eight metres deep from lip to innermost recess and we could begin to read the signs of those who had been here.

The middle of the back wall was scribbled with burnt stick — 'BIZAAR WAS HERE' and 'BANGWE BABY' and 'CHETESBAYO' and dozens more. There were a few big circular glyphs, like a breast or a CND logo on some wasteland wall in Britain. Among the black graffiti small red symbols came into focus, faded vermilion, carefully painted. Bunches of short thick stripes hung down like the Mohave 'rain-storms'. There was a rainbow', four parallel semi-circles inside each other, in white as well as red, and a horizontal blunt 'egg', in white and red. I spotted a fine 'sun', a double circle with stubby rays all round it, and a 'pod', lower end open, with a stamen-like shape sticking up into it — very sexual. We were seeing the last traces of a people, almost the least noticeable remnants of a presence on Earth. An earth-tremor could close the cave for good. Some more graffiti could complete the substitution of our culture for the older one.

Staring at the red symbols, seeing them glow calmly into sight, was like catching a clear signal amongst static or phrases of music amongst the babel from foreign stations. It is no wonder that students of African rock painting have spoken of 'a voice from the Drakensberg' or 'a voice from Kahlamba'. What do these voices say? Their language is hard to read. The most skilled decoder of Amerindian petroglyphs has proved that they are not art, in the sense of an imagery representing people's perceptions, memories, visions, and so on. They are a pictography, whose symbols work not by obvious likeness but by a highly conven-tional code. He shows that the Navajo rendered what we could call 'prosperity' by a group of concentric circles — the symbol for 'holding' multiplied several times. The so-called horned sheep pecked out on rocks all over North America are usually symbols of 'direction', varied to denote running, walking, climbing, even lying down. The 'rain-storm' symbol that particularly appeals to me stands for 'broad down-ward movement'; in Dakota, if it is slanted, it means 'blood flowing'.

The more elaborate African stone-writing is as apt to be symbolic as the simpler glyphs. If I had seen the superb eland scratched on rock in the Calvinia District of the Cape, I would have taken it for hunting magic and the many slash-lines for spears. Actually it was made for a rain ritual. Southern Bushmen saw the rain as 'an imaginary animal, which they called the *!khwa:-ka xoro* . . . It was the task of the shamans of the rain, *!khwa-ka !gi:ten*, to enter the spirit world of trance and there control the rain.' The columns of falling rain 'were said to be the "rain's legs" that "walked" across the land'. A shaman said, or chanted,

I will really ride the rain up the mountain on top of which I always cut the rain. It is high so the rain's blood flows down, for the Flat Bushmen live on the plains.

Rain mattered not only because it supplied drink and food but because it 'brought life, harmony and happy relations between people'.

At Mwala Lolemba we were seeing not sumptuous images of animals but those smaller, most enigmatic glyphs. It is so tempting to read rayed circles and concentric semi-circles as suns and rainbows. They are probably the entoptic phenomena that dazzle and flicker in a migraine and also when people enter a trance by dancing, hyperventilating, or by concentrating intensely. Among Amazonian peoples those 'nested U-shapes' represent 'the thought of the Sun-father'. Among African Bushmen, and possibly among the Malawi Batwa, they may have stood for wild honeycomb — a favourite symbol of potency. It seems that in Malawi especially, red paintings, as compared with white ones, were symbolic, not lifelike, and they may have been used by later peoples for their own ritual purposes — throwing stones at them, for example, in rain-calling ceremonies.

A voice spoke from Mwala Lolemba, then, in a language we could only just begin to understand and which was the more poignant for that. What made even this much communication possible was the rock itself — its plane dry surface, its durability. The sheltering roof and clean floor must still be attractive to people. Rounded stones were obviously in use as seats and round them were scattered yellow peelings from the sugar-cane pieces that Malawians love to chew and offer for sale in little bunches at every roadside.

If only Bangwe Baby and Chetesbayo would concentrate a little more and turn their stories and fantasies into symbols, instead of leaving it to the media to do it for them. Then people who came this way in another thousand years might get some inkling of what matters to us, as garbled and tantalising, no doubt, as the body-shapes, element-shapes, and entranced glimpses left on rock by the Mojave and the Navajo, the Warramul people of Nourlangie, the Crô-Magnon hunters of Cantabria, or the Batwa of Mikolongwe.

PART FIVE
Eastern Mediterranean

---

20   Doves in the Cleft Rock

Israel, the physical place, flowed naturally out of Africa and into Asia with little sense of continental divide. In its simmering heat, the nakedness of its rocks, it was all potently not-Europe, as against my lax Eurocentric conception of it as an outcome of post-Holocaust history — of terrible events in Poland, Austria, Czechoslovakia that had imprinted fear even into my insular childhood.

Now that we were actually surrounded by waterless lands that dimmed off into a sick greyish-yellow haze, where Bedouin living in ragged khaki tents herded their long-eared goats and sheep on hillsides where not a green blade grew, I was reminded of a conversation in a Cairngorm bothy five years before. Outside a gale was blowing the rain horizontally out of the pass of the Lairig Ghru. Inside, among filthy concrete and raw stone, a young man with a haggard face and an almost empty rucksack conversed weirdly with Bill Brooker and me as we shared out our chocolate and fruit juice. He said he was spending 'a few nights here to see what happens on the mountain' — by which he meant its elemental changes, not any kind of human event.

'Where are you from? I asked him.

'I am Asian — from Asia,' he answered, giving us a fixed look that challenged us to understand and accept this title in the teeth of his obviously European appearance.

'Turkey?' I guessed. 'One of the Soviet Asian republics?'

Each time he shook his head. It took us some time to think, by elimination, of Israel. He was an idealist from Jerusalem, determined

183

that his new homeland should be thought of as itself, in its own physical place, and not as some outpost, invasive and temporary.

The air, as Anne and I stepped down from the plane in Tel Aviv, was clothy with humidity, faintly touched with some alien aroma — dew on flowering trees? — among the aviation fuel and hot rubber. Two hours later blossom and foliage were a withered memory as we entered the desert east of Jerusalem — called Yerushalayim on some of the signposts — between dun hills terraced with crumbling whitish crags. Quite suddenly there were no cypresses or vineyards, no fields of vegetables, no suburbs like pale Cubist abstractions in the morning twilight. The road wound and climbed, wound and fell, reached Sea Level (according to a signpost) and kept on going down. A Transit van, pressing me from behind on the otherwise deserted highway, gave me a qualm. It was packed with Arabs in dark glasses. The words of the woman at the car-hire desk came back to me: 'Best to avoid the Occupied Territories . . . Arab villages along the Jordan . . . Jericho' — which was now signposted ahead, left for Jericho, right for the Dead Sea.

We turned right and made for the kibbutz at the oasis of Ein Gedi, wellspring of the kid, by the western shore of Yam Ha Melah, sea of evil. For mile after mile the beach was posted with signboards in Hebrew, Arabic, and English: 'MILITARY ZONE. NO SWIMMING. DO NOT ENTER THE WATER I HOUR BEFORE SUNSET OR I HOUR AFTER SUNRISE', emphasised by a skull and crossbones. At a roadblock a soldier with a rifle in one hand came forward between charred oil-drums, then waved us on. This highway too was empty. In 65 kilometres we met half a dozen vehicles, one of them an army jeep with three men in it and a light machine-gun pointing across the cobalt water towards Jordan.

As in Death Valley, the crumbling mountainsides, featureless in the hazy glare, threatened to burn off into faint images of themselves, mere thickenings of the dust. In these conditions you crave oasis almost as much aesthetically as physically. Amidst the searing and stunting of this desert, the date palm, wonderfully named *Phoenix dactylifera*, was bound to become a chief symbol of nourishing beauty, with its single naked limb, its genital cluster of fruits, its swaying green tresses. 'I grew tall like a palm tree in En-Gedi, and like rose plants in Jericho,' it says in the poem we call *Ecclesiasticus* — the Apocryphal book of the Old Testament which was found in manuscript among the ruins of our goal, Herod's stronghold of Masada. There were solid cultivated ranks of date palms on the shelf between the mountains of Judea and the

Dead Sea, appearing abruptly and finishing abruptly on a plain as dry and brown as biscuit, the masses of fruit bundled in bags against the stabbings of crows.

Here for centuries there has been luxuriance amid drought. When there was a culture here, it was based on the growing of balsam for the perfume trade. The richness of it feeds into the luminous eroticism of the *Song of Solomon*:

> This thy stature is like to a palm tree,
> and thy breasts to clusters of grapes.

> I said, I will go up to the palm tree,
> I will take hold of the boughs thereof;
> now also thy breasts shall be as clusters of the vine,
> and the smell of thy nose like apples . . .

and again:

> My beloved is unto me as a cluster of camphire
> in the vineyards of En-Gedi,

— corrected in the new translation to 'a cluster of henna blossom', with its beautiful suggestion of hair and fingernails dyed dark crimson.

A few kilometres south of the first date plantation the oasis has given rise to a kibbutz. We entered it past ugly sheds of chicken-batteries, through a gate of sheet steel and barbed wire. The man on duty with a revolver at his belt checked that we were booked in at the guesthouse before wishing us 'Shalom' and waving us on through. Up the hill chalets and public rooms stood on terraces among a whole arboretum of perfectly tended trees — an oasis still, perched above a gaping sand quarry where camels came at the end of each day to stand tethered and honk gently into the dusk.

Twenty kilometres south, between a range of mountains like heaped cinnamon and the ghastly reaches of Yam Ha Melah with its lemony glitter under a brazen sun, one rock mass stands up and out from the east flank of the Judean highland: Masada, once called in Arabic es-Sebbah, most perfectly 'the Great Rock in the weary land'. So it must have seemed to Herod the Great, who built his stronghold there in the first century B.C., and to the Zealots a century later who made the last Jewish stand against the Roman Empire in Judea. Here is a Gibraltar of the desert, a great flat-headed mesa which has become the paramount symbol of Israel's power to withstand hosts who prowl around the Promised Land. 'Masada Shall Not Fall Again' is overprinted on the postcards. Recruits to the army are sworn in each year on the bare summit.

I knew which route to the top was the one for me — the Snake Path up the eastern cliff, which was rediscovered after centuries of erosion and earthquake by Zionist youth commandoes during their campaigns against the British. Later I would be able to visit a veteran from among them at his kibbutz north of Jericho. In *The Wars of the Jews* Josephus describes this harder access, 'from the Lake Asphaltitis, towards the sun-rising . . . called the Serpent, as resembling that animal in its narrowness and its perpetual windings; for it is broken off at prominent precipices of the rock . . . and he that would walk along it must first go on one leg, and then on the other: there is also nothing but destruction in case your feet slip; for on each side there is a vastly deep chasm and precipice . . . '

It sounded as though the Snake Path would give us some direct touch with the rock, even in the new age of guidebooks, air-conditioned buses, and cable-cars. Just before sunrise we skirted the Visitor Centre and set off across dusty sand and rubble towards the start of a whitened trod that zigzagged steeply up scree between shattered outcrops. Gaggles of teenagers from Europe, Australia, America were already coming down after sunrise-watching — 'disappointing', they said. Yet another great rock, like Uluru at sunset, had failed to deliver on the day . . .

Outsize ravens with wing-silhouettes like vultures took off, coasted, and alighted again. The steel hawsers of the cable-car sagged in space beside us. In places steps had been made of limestone blocks cemented together, obliterating the old footway. Often we could see it as it was at the time of the siege in 72–3 A.D., and on through the centuries of Byzantine tenure of the site until the earthquake of 1927. A length of metal railing held a sign saying 'No Passage'. Beyond it a runnel of scree angled between crags, steeper and more direct than the new tourist version. Where the crag became continuous and vertical, and must have looked impregnable to the Romans, the old secret way had been obliterated by the girderwork and concrete foundation of the cable-car station. The compromise, in the years after Yigael Yadin's famous excavation in the 'sixties, was to refrain from building on the skyline. Lucky Uluru, sacrosanct and therefore immune to all but the minor violation of the handrail.

Before Yadin's workers dug away the rubble to expose a complete citadel of workshops, houses, quarries, cisterns, palaces, the summit must have looked like a desert in mid-air. The mother-rock crops out in places, the elephant-grey of dolomite, seamed with rough-lipped cracks, a hide cured by centuries of sun and electric storm. Buildings reconstructed from the original stones stand up here and there — storerooms, a bakery, a Zealot leather-worker's shop inside the double casemate on the western side. At the north end the great rock peaks, tapers, and steps down 35 metres in three tiers. On the lowest, short rows of broken columns, monuments in cream and pale gold, stand with that silent presence, that entranced stillness, that comes of having lasted epoch after epoch. They were cunningly made — drums of stone built up in segments, then plastered and moulded to look like single sculptured pillars with Corinthian capitals. Remnants of lavish crafts-manship showed everywhere — the base of a plastered wall painted to simulate veined marble, scrolls of stonework painted gold.

Herod bathed here, refreshing himself in a cold room, a tepid room, and a centrally-heated hot room. Cleopatra could have banqueted in the marbled hall during one of the periods of detente — if she had been rash enough to venture into territory harrowed by wars between unstable alliances. A century later the grandees had departed. Canny bargains were being struck — Josephus himself, once Governor of Judean Galilee, had gone over to Rome. These wild outlands between Judea and Moab were being fought over by warlords. On Masada the Zealots set up a short-lived and ramshackle society, re-using a bath-house lintel with its magnificent carved flower like a sun-burst for rough building at the other end of the rock, applying kohl to their eyelids with the slim spoons that Yadin's people dug out of the rubble.

On the steps down to the cold pool they found the skeleton of a young warrior who had worn armour with silvered scales, the scalp of a young woman with her hair in braids, and the skeleton of a child — people who died in the collective suicide on Passover, A.D. 73, the night before the Romans broke in through the west wall. The men put their own families to the sword after embracing them, chose ten by lot to kill the rest, then one of the ten to kill the other nine,

> and he who was the last of all took a view of all the other bodies, lest perchance some or other among so many that were slain should want his assistance to be quite dispatched, and when he perceived that they were all slain, he set fire to the palace, and with the great force of his hand ran his sword entirely through himself, and fell down dead near to his own relations.

From the west side we looked down on to a huge splaying white ramp built of small stones, stretching up nearly to the rim of the mesa beneath the wall. It clung to the massif like some stingray or white shark guzzling at the innards of its prey. This was the perfect Roman subjugator. To breach the wall after the months of siege, ballista were dragged up the slope. The temperature today was rising past 40° C. In such heat thousands of PoWs toiled with baskets on their sweating heads to bring up the megatons of rubble and pile it, month by month, in full view of the defenders, each foot of height making the end more certain.

On floors of excavated rooms boulders have been found, fallen through burnt roofs where they had been stored ready to roll down on the attackers. The desperate stones they trundled down on to the ramp-makers, archers, and catapult-operators will have merged back into the desert long ago. In the bakery soft-stone vats still stand and in another workshop a large vat whose inside is stained faded damson. This was the only visible trace of the old use, the old life. It was at the other end of the rock, and of the social scale, from the marbled and gilt pavilion. It was also easier to feel in touch with over the centuries.

The heart of the stronghold is none of these. Near the south end we came upon a ragged breach in the ground. Thirty steps cut in the mother-rock led down into a colossal chamber. The walls were plastered smooth. The ceiling, of integral limestone, was seamed with shallow cracks. Through a window-hole high up on the west wall sunrays beamed and made an orange blaze on the wall opposite. This was the main cistern, an artificial oasis four hundred metres above the desert floor. Flash floods would have filled it — like the one that temporarily halted the excavation in 1963 — and the beleaguered Zealots will have been able to survive on its water even after the Romans sabotaged the aqueducts that gravity-fed the smaller cisterns halfway down the north-west cliff.

The slow-rising, slow-dipping yellow wasteland littered with stone heaps is the most desolate image of a gone life, of lives scraped and burnt and hacked and terrorised into extinction. Not that the latterday occupants of Masada were purely virtuous victims. In the decade before the final siege the faction under Eleazar ben Jair withdrew from the war against the Roman Imperialists and controlled this part of Judea by terror. At En-Gedi more than seven hundred women and children were slaughtered. Such was the leader whose last oration rings so proudly in Josephus:

'I cannot but esteem it as a favour that God hath granted us, that it is still in our power to die bravely, and in a state of freedom, which hath not been the case of others who were conquered unexpectedly. It is very plain that we shall be taken within a day's time; but it is still an eligible thing to die after a glorious manner, together with our dearest friends ... Let our wives die before they are abused, and our children before they have tasted of slavery ... But first let us destroy our money and the fortress by fire ... and let us spare nothing but our provisions; for they will be a testimony when we are dead that we were not subdued for want of necessaries, but that, according to our original resolution, we have preferred death before slavery.'

What an ambiguous martyrdom to have become the symbolic focus of a nation! Yadin was an ardent patriot, proud to think that his team included 'the young generation of newly-independent Israel'. His book, with its huge circulation and status, says nothing about Eleazar's bloodstained record — without which that leader's reference to 'our manifold sins, which we have been guilty of in a most insolent and extravagant manner with regard to our own countrymen' must sound like a token gesture of self-criticism by a polished orator.

Each day we were there, the roar and rahl of jet-engines cannoned through the mountain passes and the crump of unseen weapon-testing made the air quake. Across the Sea of Evil, among the mountains of Moab, were the forces of Saddam Hussein's uneasy semi-ally, King Hussein of Jordan, whose gunners had strafed the Jordan valley kibbutzim in the late 'sixties. How understandable it is, and how unbearable, that a nation which lost millions of its people in the death-camps, and in their turn expelled 800,000 from their homelands in the single year of 1948 and destroyed 400 Palestinian villages, should find its ikon in the site of a breached stronghold and a collective death.

In this light Masada stands up like one great altar stone designed for human sacrifice. To know it more as a mountain, a piece of nature, I set myself to walk right round it, with no assurance that there was any way out of Wadi Sinein, the gorge to the south. Its western exit, if there was one, had been invisible from above. After a few hundred metres the track was destroyed, evidently by flood, and never resumed. The way became a trod, twisting between huge grey boulders, in and out of entrances made by their undersides.

From the scree just above me to my left came sharp clicks — a male ibex, horns curved back to the mid-point of his spine, was picking his way along. We walked abreast for a while before he headed off up one of the many threads of path where others of his kind had contoured

Tipping's engraving of the southern end of Masada

along the wadi–side. A little later something rasped on a boulder and I turned in time to see a Syrian hyrax, like a large light-brown guinea-pig — cousin to those we heard chattering from the cave in the Blouberg. It scurried about nervously, then whisked out of sight — answering perfectly to the description in Proverbs, 'The rock-badgers are but a feeble folk, yet make they their houses in the rocks.' After that nothing moved for an hour and the heat and glare intensified towards noon, forcing my eyes almost shut.

Wayfinding was becoming interesting. I hauled repeatedly into the neuk between touching boulders, bridged up on niches chipped out of them as they hurtled down the hillside, then found myself in a blind alley, retraced, and picked a different way through. Every ten minutes I stopped in the narrow shade of a crag for a drink of water. In its insulated bottle, taken from the fridge an hour before, it was already very warm. Now the slope beneath Masada's south-west corner was looking more manageable. Might it be possible to gain height up it, then contour round it to the west? Shattered outcrops stood up from the scree like stacked spears and battle-axes. Everything looked brittle and ready to collapse. Captain Warren, who rediscovered the Snake Path in 1867, faced the same difficulty: 'We commenced scrambling up by a path more dangerous than difficult, for the natural lay of the rocks is such that they crop out perpendicular to the steep side of the hill, and thus each stone you scramble up is overhanging and ready to topple over and crush you, should your weight be sufficient to over-balance it.'

I carried on low down. Ahead a prow jutted northward from the bank of the wadi to my left. If it continued till it met Masada moun-tain, I would be balked and must turn back. If I could round it, then perhaps I could get on to the scree slope round Masada's back. On all sides bluffs and hills of stone enclosed me. Light breaths of air reached me from behind — Dead Sea wind, better than nothing, faintly cool-ing in the throat. A two-inch galvanised pipe had followed me all the way. Now it climbed the scree towards the col at Masada's south-west corner. I followed it up a sweep of loose stone barely at the angle of rest. When it threatened to avalanche, I used the pipe as a banister. It was almost too hot to grip. Boiler-plates of rock sloped upwards, polished by feet. So this way was used and presently must deliver me to the ground behind or west of Masada. Now I was level with the sheer cliff rising to the casemate wall. At the col the ground levelled out. I could see a path coming through from the mountains to the south, converging with mine.

Among all this raw stone one tamarisk tree had found a footing, its trunk no thicker than my arm, its light-green spindly foliage making a shadow the size of a hearth rug. I remember it now with the affection you have for a pet. It offered company as much as shade. I pulled a flat triangle of limestone under it for a seat, hung my sweaty hat on a dead branch, and swallowed water in gulps. Perhaps I should have poured a little of it into the ground beside the roots of the tamarisk.

The pitiless, subjugating ramp was ahead of me. Maybe it took less work than one might think — that is, it was merely Herculean — because the forced labourers would have been able to heap their stones on to one of the many natural scree fans that pour out of the gullies. The ramp reached the cliff a little north of a slight break in the belt of rock. The attackers must have had some cragging to do as they scaled the last twenty or twenty-five metres. On either side the natural hol-lows or cavelets in the rockface were much deeper than the others of their kind nearby and had distinct roofs. Perhaps the Roman artificers deepened them to make shelters for the men working the ballistas and mangonels and for archers keeping up covering fire.

The ramp remains monstrous, a slaves' graveyard, a monument to imperial force, a blotter-out of the fine grain and fall of the natural cliff. My feet were reluctant to walk on it. I climbed it for a few metres, then turned off down a path to the left. It led to a gallery cut and built precariously along Masada's west face. A ravine threatened to block my passage north and round. At the foot of the cliff it had been bridged by Herod's engineers with a handsome rounded arch, like the single one left standing (or rebuilt) up on top. Beyond it entrances gaped in the rockface, two metres high and four across. One could be entered, the stair inside descended. The chamber was a cistern, smaller than the master one on top. The whole of it was plastered with lime, fifteen centimetres thick, still smooth as paintwork. The ceiling was integral limestone. The gallery outside was built along a supporting wall many metres high. After two thousand years of flash flood and earthquake everything was intact, except the ductwork bringing water by gravity from wells in the mountains, destroyed by the Romans to parch out the Zealots.

Back down on the plain to the west, I climbed a brown cone like a moraine reshaped by the spade. A well-made stone stair led to a terrace with a blue notice which said:

> On Monday 21st of Tammuz 5729 (7 July 1969) the remains of the last defenders of Masada who had fallen three years after the destruction of the Temple were buried in this place. They were buried by the decision of the Government of Israel with full military honours.

A way round the north end had still to be found. The ravine below the cisterns cleaved on and on. Its walls looked impassable without ropes. I found a way through the galvanised fences where audiences gather for the Yadin lecture-film and the Son et Lumière, past ogreish replicas of the Roman ballistas and catapults, climbed a last fence, and walked off northwards. After half a kilometre a path came into sight among the broken rock some hundreds of metres below and I was encouraged by a notice, uprooted and lying on its back, which said in English only, 'Dangerous Path. Do Not Descend This Way'. It picked an excellent hairpin line steeply downward by natural rock steps between crumbling outcrops — very much as the Snake Path must have been before it was tidied up.

The triple-stepped prow of the north end rose in its pride. Below the pillared pavilion on its breath-catching eyrie, three buttresses slanted up to the left, the gullies above them sloped right, the grain of the cliff slanted left again, and the prow jutted finally sheer. As I rounded it, it turned from blocky to pointed, a classic upstanding mountain-shape, a giant craft riding northward parallel with Yam Ha Melah and the mountains of Jordan lost now in the eastern haze. I slogged back down the length of the east face, inside the noose of the circumvallation built by the Romans to enforce their siege, now shrunk into a low worm of stone which presently will die back into the desert. Above me the Snake Path zigzagged, the white track of it empty of people in the crushing heat of the afternoon.

A few days later we found our way through the barns and fine dairy herds of the kibbutzim in the Beit Shean valley north of Jericho to meet Jacob Noy, nicknamed 'Czech', once a member of the youth movements that 'started trekking to Masada and sought to fathom its secrets' even before the freedom struggle against the British had come to an end. Jacob had injured his leg badly in a fall from the Snake Path in 1947 and now, in old age, was being given therapy by a graduate student of mine, an Alexander-method teacher called Joan Diamond. Czech was a barrel-chested veteran, retired, a father-figure at the kibbutz of Kfar Ruppin. His legs were badly bowed and a long neat scar ran down the front of his left leg from thigh through knee to shin. He had fought in the Free Czech Army against the Wehrmacht in the Western Desert, had retreated to Alamein after the fall of Tobruk and been interned in Mauritius, where he learned scouting — ropework, bridging, climbing walls and crags — from an English missionary. He came illegally to Palestine in 1942 and then, as the Zionist campaign gathered momentum, he organised treks from Jericho to Masada as part of commando training.

'I was fighting in Jerusalem in '48. We knew we must open the road — we were surrounded by all Arab villages. We were nine hundred people. So tired we marched in sleeping. Marched twenty kilometres. Ten people of us would have one rifle. We would surround a village but we left always one side open. So the people could escape.

'All the songs we sang were saying, what brave people they were against the Romans. Masada is the Mountain of Heroes.'

He had first heard about Masada through the commando groups. 'Nobody was living there. Nobody but Bedouins in En-gedi, Masada. It was not in the plan to take En-Gedi. In the end we took all we could.'

He first saw Masada in 1944, by which time he had risen high in the chain of command through his skills as a scout, in spite of being born abroad and laughed at for his faulty language. The youth groups were competing to rediscover the Snake Path, which had been ruined in the earthquake of 1927. After his group had found the old line of it among broken rock, Jacob fell and rolled some distance, crunching his knee almost beyond repair. We could feel how for him emotion of all kinds clung to the mountain. In a voice that trembled a little towards the end he told the story of how after the digging out and restoration of the North Palace they took a man there who had a bullet lodged in his spine. He was in a wheelchair and had to be manhandled down the precipitous steps.

' "I am rich! I am rich!" he kept saying. "*Shmulig* — rich!" "What is rich?" we ask him. "I have friends," he tells us.'

Jacob entered ardently into the motives of the Zealots and their refusal-unto-death to be captured: 'If I am killing myself I am not a traitor and I am not a slave. If I am a prisoner they do with me what the Japanese did with the English. They wanted to take them to Rome, to sell them like slaves: "Look, we brought you monkeys," ' and he grimaced, miming derision.

His belief in the present and the future of his people was unshakable and felt unforced. He guided us round the fishponds which the people of Kfar Ruppin have built a few metres from the west bank of the Jordan, where blue herons and egrets stalk fishing among the reedbeds, and pointed across the river to a roofless two-storey house.

'In the days of the Terror,' he told us, 'in '67, they were sniping at us from there. My friend was hit, he was driving a tractor and it went on into the river. It was hard getting him out.'

Our track was parallel with three features: a broad zone of rutted earth — the minefield; then a dense entanglement of razor-wire, which Jacob had helped to build after '67; then the green pools, low, not quite exhausted. On the east bank Jordanian soldiers with rifles watched from look-out towers on metal stilts. Beyond, before the flood-plain rose into the mountains of Moab, green farms basked in sleepy heat.

That afternoon in the Beit Shean valley we had no means of knowing that the accord between Rabin for the Israeli government and Arafat for the PLO had just been made public. Extreme Zionists were demonstrating against it in Jerusalem. Jericho, when we drove through it, had been quiet not because it was siesta but because a general strike had been called in support of the accord. Unaware of what may yet turn out to be either a 'symbolic handshake' or 'a first step towards reconciliation or real peace', I was still struggling to see any kind of fair face in this land. It looked barely habitable, politically or physically, whether by Jews or by Arabs. Even the Dead Sea is dying some more — fallen fifteen metres since the start of the century. The only access to its stinging waters for ordinary bathers and swimmers is by strips a few yards wide between Military Zones. Such is the sheer adversity of this place where kings and monks and farmers have carved out the narrowest foothold over the years. I found escape and solace in the valley of Nihal David, a few kilometres north of En-Gedi, where a tunnel of giant reeds led us into an Eden between the lips of a great rock.

We set off from a car park through a turnstile (four shekels each). The path led under the fine-mesh shade of a tamarisk grove where wild ibex were bending their muzzles to something wonderful — a covering of green grass. Beyond the trees the ground was too harshly sunlit to look at and side-paths were signposted 'Use In Case Of Fire'. A Calcolithic people left their dead here in caves in the crumbling dun bluffs above the dried-up stream of David (*nihal* is Arabic, *nachal* is Hebrew). This place was settled almost uninterruptedly, by Israelites, Persians, Hellenes, Hasmoneans, Romans of the Byzantine period, early Muslims. The sole reason was the stream, which dazzled suddenly into sight from a tunnel in a reedbed, a full juicy water, two metres wide, fast-flowing.

The path tunnelled too, between stems like bamboo, under a ceiling of criss-crossing green blades. Ibex lairs, like caves in the reeds, smelt of goat and mouldering hay. Masoned steps climbed over a rock rib and we could look down over the roof of reeds, a forest of green knives slanting and straightening again in the hot wind from Yam Ha Melah. We stooped below reeds again, a few inches from the rapid glisten of the river, and became aware of a roaring and hissing somewhere upstream.

On either side the crags steepened to a height of thirty metres. We emerged in a cove which kept its full height round 180°, enclosing us. From a great mouth in the rim of the headwall the river was volleying. Beyond and up, through the dark rock barrier, we could see the full sun lighting the upper waves of it. The water purled headlong down a rampart at an angle of 60°. On the left bank a parallel watercourse, shrunk by the summer drought, was letting fall fringes of rills like spun glass from clumps of dewy moss. In the main course shining bursts leapt out at us and we walked straight towards them, through the shallow pool at the base, and let the cool lave our legs and breasts and faces.

The few people there were virtually worshipping the water. Two German lads lay on their backs against the rock in mid-fall. An American boy aged twelve or so sat down fully clothed in the pool and looked round happily at his parents, at his more inhibited teenage brother. An elderly Jewish woman stood staring up at the cascade, crossed over the river for a different angle, and was still staring upwards when we left.

The air-space of the cove was hoarse with crows, chattering with starlings which flew out into the sun above us, showing the copper of their wings. Rock-doves flew round and back to their perches through the spume and one milky feather twirled down into the pool. In the sunlit green canopy up on the rim, ebony crow-bodies clambered like gorillas glimpsed in rain-forest and two of them were billing on a coign of the highest crag below its cinnamon towers. Wild figs spread their leaves like hands, creepers dangled in festoons past blunt stalactites and sockets like gutted mud nests, though no martins were flying. That morning a swallow had sipped on the wing in the swimming pool at En-Gedi.

The place was a small paradise, a single artery of growth/colour/ motion in the middle of great vacancy and dereliction. It is no wonder that people have wanted to locate hereabouts, though without firm evidence, the origin of the *Song of Solomon*:

> The fig tree putteth forth her green figs,
> and the vines with the tender grapes give a good smell.
> Arise, my love, my fair one,
> and come away.
>
> O my dove, that art in the clefts of the rock in the secret
> places of the stairs,
> let me see thy countenance, let me hear thy voice;
> for sweet is thy voice,
> and thy countenance is comely . . .
>
> His eyes are as the eyes of doves
> by the river of waters,
> washed with milk, and fitly set . . .
>
> Thy neck is as a tower of ivory;
> thine eyes like the fishpools in Heshbon . . .

I had thought of this poetry as springing from a wide land flowing with milk and honey. Nihal David was showing me that its richness was all the more precious for being one of the very few sources of life in a dry wilderness.

2I   Formed of the Dust

The eastern Mediterranean from twelve thousand metres up was a
waking dream of beauty. Nobody before the present generation
could have seen this. The islands patterned across the Aegean are
limestone cut-outs as finely curved and spined as though fashioned by
great jewellers or sculptors. Each one gives off the shapes of its shallows
like tissuey turquoise angel-fins, paling and twisting off into the ultra-
marine of the deeper water. And each is a great rock, of which we see
only the summit. This is a trick of words, untrue to our experience.
Only the fishes, the squids and the lobsters, can perceive Ithaca or
Lesbos as a great rock. Only the deep-sea creatures of the Pacific can
perceive the Polynesian islands as mountains. And yet, if I were a
diver . . . Given that two thousand metres of Uluru is underground, as
against the four hundred we can touch and see, how can we say that we
know the great inselbergs any more than we know these islands?

We were heading now for a world in which rock was not pro-
digious, a refuge from extreme turbulence and suffering, but commonplace, the medium of domestic life: the tufa dwellings, steadings, and
churches of Cappodokia in the heart of Turkey. The only thing that
was commonplace about this rock was its uses. We lived in a hotel
converted from the house of 'the richest man in Göreme'. Its southern
wing was supported by a twenty-metre tower of compacted volcanic
ash, as round and straight and goat-cheese-white as the stem of an
edible mushroom, with a grey goblin-cap of basalt that leaned rakishly
eastward and little doors and windows, their wooden frames long
gone. The windows had been cut out of the soft creamy stone by the
obsidian axes of workmen centuries ago. In the lane at the back a cow
nosed at some husks that had been thrown down for her, as though she
would have preferred hay. Over the wall behind her two more grey
caps stood up together in the sunlight like the dorsal fins of a pair of
basking porpoises.

Seven of the original rooms had become usable bedrooms. At night
we found our way to the dining room through a tunnel in the mother-
rock. The north wing of the building was destined to become a labyrinth of rooms — I believe the owner mentioned the visionary number
seventy. Just now, and possibly for years to come, it was a skeleton of
grey concrete. In the naked sun- or moon-light that shone down on us
continuously, it was all cutting angles and intense black slots of shadow

like a painting by di Chirico. We breakfasted alone on one of two stark stone terraces. Would nobody else ever come? Were we spellbound? Suddenly a reception was to be held here for an ecological conference in Ürgüp, the Provincial Governor would attend. The few staff strewed maroon and gold and burgundy carpets over the terraces. Armed police arrived and took up their positions. A crowd of extras material-ised and made noises like ecologists as they drank their aperitifs. The Provincial Governor came up the steps, chunky, well-groomed, impassive, like a senior detective. At one point I shook his hand, or he shook mine. In the morning the carpets had disappeared again. Perhaps the Governor had soared off on one, skimming the goblin-caps, the creamy towers.

In front of us the Valley of the Doves led southward towards Urçhi-zar, less than a kilometre away, with its crowning citadel, a stub of tufa seventy metres high, slotted all over into a Gruyère of doors and windows and random erosion holes. On its summit a white pole flew the red national flag with its crescent moon and star. Guidebooks and reputation focus on the multitude of churches hollowed out and painted in the Byzantine epoch, the 'caves of God'. You could spend many days here and content yourself with the secular buildings, the barns and byres and dovecotes, houses and threshing floors and garages, the entire condominiums once housed in the stems and caps of the mushrooms and the greater cliffs of Göreme and Çavuşin, Zilve and Urtahizar.

Day after day we looked out past a derelict dwelling — a small cliff that looked as though it had been poured, then eaten by giant mice, under the direction of Gaudi. The flat floor of the vale was patterned densely into plots. Between the boles of the petrified goblin-forest, fruits and vegetables flourished. The cliff that made the opposite or west wall of the valley looked, from here, as incongruously soft as a Dali watch. How could stone appear to be a new-washed blanket a kilometre long, draped over giant knees and hips? or the world's entire output of zabaglione, poured out in a lavish swathe from some paradisal sweetness-mine?

Up on the far rim huge tourist buses drew up at ramshackle stalls that sold onyx eggs (crafted in tiny cave workshops in the cliff at Uçhizar), and cheaply overprinted T-shirts, and Kodak Gold film, and reproduction Seljuk figures of squat bow-legged men clutching enormous erections. Below, the honeyed cream of the tufa cliff was permanently sunlit, a backdrop for the towers whose tops looked sombre, a stone version of the ice-blades known in the Andes as *penitentes*, or the cowels of inquisitorial abbots come to police the sweetness-world. In Ürgüp, a short way to the east, the *peri bacalari* or 'fairy towers' — each a further-eroded pinnacle with its cap reduced to a boulder barely balanced on the stem — have been seen as the homes of demonic powers that retaliate if humans flout them. If they desire a young person, they wile her or him away forever.

When I set off to explore the valley, I made for a section of the bluff which had been the back wall of a church carved out of the rock. The front and most of the roof had fallen away and left two storeys of round arches, like a backdrop representing a church in some opera by Verdi. A maze of trodden earthen paths led between the crofts. In a café in a cave retired men in the dark jackets and flat caps of old Anatolia were playing cards under the apricot trees. Nearby a solar heating panel was fixed to the rock, marking the one extant dwelling, the weekend cave-home of a businessman from the nearest city, Nevşehir. Each morning the woman who looked after it watered and weeded in the flower-garden between the rock and the path.

The plots were still locally owned. 'This brother owns this place, this brother that place, another has another,' said Shermen Ataman, our landlady. 'All Göreme people.'

The little, thriving plots were a slight, tough sprig of the old peasant culture, still alive in a capitalist world. The volcanic earth is rich in potassium, excellent for crops. The crofts brimmed with vines, not wired up but allowed to spread. The green grapes, already plumping and sweetening, would be harvested in a month or so to make the oaky Cappadokian white wine. Prostrate tomato vines were heavy with reddening fruit. Yellow squashes lay on their sides like boats at low tide. A little wheat or oats, already reaped, had left patches of golden stubble on terraces beneath the hardened dune of the bluff. Here subsistence farming has turned into a kind of useful hobby. I was reminded of the Scottish Highlands and Islands, where the profit from crofting itself averages 7 per cent of the crofters' total income.

Until the earlier part of this century, all this produce and its pro-ducers were housed in the rock that had been poured out sixty million years ago by the three volcanoes, Erciyes Dag, Hassan Dag, and Göllü Dag. Presently we must seek out those great sources. In the meantime we strolled through an enchanting maze. Not a fraction of a cubic metre of this place was blank. Never was an environment more used. When Kemal Ataturk — whose photo is still in all the cafés — nego-tiated a treaty on minorities with Greece in 1923, the Turks from there came home and the Greeks in Turkey went back. The hundreds of

199

Greek Orthodox churches were closed, many were lost among the cliffs (the Greek guides having gone), and many others were turned into dovecotes, for the sake of the guano. Now the storeyed arches of a church on the far side of the Valley of the Doves make shallow eaves above rows of little black mouths, the entries for the birds. Another nearby has been decorated specially. The entries are surrounded by a horde of paint marks in ox-blood red, as though a flock of pigeons were exploding out into the air or converging to feed and brood, printing a burst of scarlet shadows on the stone face. It is the same red as in the invariable two colours used in the simpler rock-church murals from the seventh or eight century onwards — red for happiness/wealth, green for Paradise.

In Urçhizar, at the end of the valley, we parked beside a boarding house built into the rock, near the onyx workshops and just off the spiralling old main road paved with basalt setts. I followed an alley, then a footpath into the apparently derelict old town round the foot of the citadel crag. Mouths opened into the tufa bluff, at first with tyre-tracks leading into cave-garages, then with no tracks at all. The wooden doors had rotted away, one cart stood bleaching in the sun — the kind still used among the endless rolling wheatfields of the plateau, painted daintily with garlands of flowers and the owner's name.

I was among goblin towers. Five or ten metres up their shafts the fronts of rooms had fallen outwards, leaving half of each chamber as a pock in the face of the stone. A chunk had fallen down out of a cone top and rested in the shadow of the gaping chamber below, like a polar bear's head at the mouth of her snow-lair. Many lower storeys were intact and I pulled up into a system of rooms one of which had been built as a dovecote, with 88 cubby-holes for the birds to nest in, cut in the walls, and in a long balk or pillar left *in situ* when the place was delved out.

The sunlight reflected from the *meerschaum* surfaces all round me was so warming, the crumb of the stone so palpable, its tops so crusty, it was like walking about in a world of bread lapped in the heat that baked it. Some of the ground-floor chambers were, or had become, cellars. One was floored with onions gone to sprout and the air was redolent as soup. In another tower I looked through a hole in the rock-wall dividing one cellar from its neighbour, felt cool air on my face, and smelt a gummy liquorice odour from the herbs spread over the floor.

As I walked across a tussocky slope to the next tower, a tall, handsome, hawk-nosed man of forty, who seemed to be standing doing nothing in particular — or perhaps wondering what on earth I was up to — said 'Welcome' in English. I thanked him and he said, 'It is good — yes?' He gestured round the enchanting scape.

'The only one in the world,' I agreed. 'Beautiful!'

'Good — yes.'

'When did the people leave these places?'

He shrugged and said one word in Turkish with a tone of '¿ *Quién sabe?*'

Presently I reached an area where the towers, being more accessible from a good track, were still fully used, as steadings, not as homes. The doorways were still furnished, with doors made of three broad planks, some faced with oil-drums hammered flat. Most were padlocked. Some were numbered in blurred white paint on red tin labels — 79, 78, and next to it 125. I had arrived in a square space walled round with tufa blocks. Horse or donkey droppings were scattered among stalks of straw. The chambers opening on to it had open doors, some of them showing well-stacked straw. Another door was caked from top to bottom with dried dung and opened to disclose a battered, dirty manger. At the back of the walled space a reef of tufa spilled thrashed chaff on to the floor in a cascade of light gold.

This used environment was wholesome beside the dereliction of the churches, which were weird in their profusion and perhaps morbid even in their heyday. By the eighth or ninth century the Byzantine imperial army was managing to hold back the Arab invasions, peace broke out, and 'the most important activity in the region had become the building of churches'. One man could carve out two to three thousand cubic feet of rock in a month, with an ease that surpassed building. 'His structure stood, a monolith, before he started work on it.' The foundation was already there and the engineering was simple because 'loads and thrusts were negligible' — although we would have to say that a high proportion of the arches and roofs have now fallen in, undermined by gravity, and have proved weaker than built ones kept up by keystones, beams, and buttresses.

What the soft stone seems to have enabled was a sustained frenzy of craftsmanship. Outcrop after outcrop was hollowed out into a church, often of the size we would call a chapel. Walls, ceilings, cupolas, the surrounds of arches were painted, first on to naked rock with pellets soaked in pigment, then on to plaster with more advanced tools. Some historians cannot quite stomach the fever of religiosity. 'Prayer to holy images had become a sort of cult' — well yes, thinks the unbeliever, isn't that what it's all about? — 'and one which neared idolism according to some attitudes. The figure of Christ was portrayed in various ways, almost to the point of disrespect.' Presently Constantine V forbade the worshipping of ikons and restricted imagery to the cross. Taste and philosophy swung back again and in 843 Theadoria reinstated figure-painting as a pious activity and caused disfigured churches and pictures to be restored.

Centuries later it is hard to tell whether the grievous damage done to the paintings — the eyes of saints scratched out, the red of robes or blue of skies scribbled through to the original white of the rock — was due to the Iconoclasm of a thousand years ago or the more random vandalism of recent times. Either way it was almost as though a disorder seized on human nature in this place, whether in the constructing of escape-hatches from this life or in the turning against a previous generation for having done so. I was beginning to relish more the 'caves of God' in which the signs of sacredness were very old and plain and cool.

A kilometre up the Ürgüp road from Göreme we found ourselves one afternoon at a café dug out of a cliff. As we parked, a man with a stubbly aquiline face came out and offered to guide us to the 'hidden church' — Sakli Kilise. Sometimes the thought of a guide is wearisome. This man, whose name was Hikmet Aydinoglu, was neither pushy nor insidious. Over the next few days we spent good hours with him drinking apple tea in the shade of the café rock and listening to the rapid, complex music he played on his *saz*, a stringed instrument with a long neck and a bowl-shaped sound-box.

The way to Sakli Kilise was by yellow-white paths between tusks of tufa and the softly moulded meringue-like flanks. After climbing perhaps seventy metres we came out on to a ridge and saw Urçhizar's citadel rising in the west. A steep little gully with heavily worn rock steps led down to a ledge. Behind a buttress carved out from the mother-rock lurked a doorway fitted with a green-painted door of metal bars. Inside was the simplest chapel. The small cupolas mined out of the roofing rock were naked, flour-white, stretching down to the floor in pillars like the earthed-up stems of leeks. The saints and apostles on the walls were faded, still visible in their robes painted 900 years ago in fluid vermilion lines. The figures were static, inexpressive. Only a believer steeped in that symbolism would be able to perceive their postures and gestures as differing significantly from any others in the repertoire of meanings. What endeared them to me was the way they had been painted directly on to the tufa. No ostentation, no striving for merit or kudos through expense. A few craftspeople had brought their tools up here and made a place of worship for a very few others, where they could hope to achieve 'concentration within themselves' — the psychological goal of the Byzantine movement called Hezychasm through which, in fourteenth-century Bulgaria for example, people 'withdrew to live in distant inaccessible niches and caves which they turned into churches and monks' cells by additional labours'.

Here in Cappadokia the rock favoured the movement. Anchorites' cells flowered into chapels or full-fledged churches, often sponsored as an act of piety by the wealthier people locally, and the place became 'a rapidly developing centre of minor pilgrimage'. Because they were not grand buildings they were never razed by invaders and could endure 'as material evidence of a generally unchronicled Byzantine class: monks who lacked hagiographers; soldiers too low in rank to be given credit for victories; minor officials who did nothing good, bad, or important enough to bring them to the attention of historians'.

As for the worship that had gone on here, we can no longer know the distinctive smell of the incense or the elaboration or simplicity of the vestments. What we were seeing at Sakli Kilise and at the 'hospital monastery' to which Hikmet led us next were churches from which the ardours and odours had long since drained away, like marrow from bones or sap from furniture. No incense, no flame of votive lamp or candle, no chant or murmur or sweat of a distraught believer. All that was left was a bare dignity that looked 'eternal' because it was finished and done with.

The monastery was at Hallaç Dere, the fluffed-cotton stream-bed, so-called because the tufa was lightly mounded, hardly like stone at all. Among old orchards of walnut and apricot, whose fallen dusty fruit we chewed as we walked, a kind of arena opened back into the hillside, made rectangular by cutting out and squaring-off the rock. The long side was chambered into chapels. Earth-tremors had breached the walls between them and we looked through perspectives of holes and doorways, past white jambs and columns like the forest of pillars in the great Moorish mosque at Cordoba. Trunks of rock had been left by the delvers, plinths continuous with the floor, capitals merging with the roof five or six metres above our heads. Integral columns like these look like guarantees of permanence, of connection with the world.

The cliff that made the monastery at Halaç Kilise turned through 90° and rose to a height of seventy metres. Its face had been shaved high up into perfect planes, pierced with little squares for pigeon entries and bigger ones for doors. I climbed ten metres up it, first on hand-jams between the blocks of a masoned parapet, then on cup-holds carved in the rock. On a sill I pulled up and squeezed through into a loft smelling of guano. New wooden perches had been nailed to the walls and a new wooden lintel fitted above the door-hole. Looking out I could see further valleys with sides like dunes of petrified zabaglione, clusters of the slender *peri bacalari*, and the squat towers with goblin-caps. Immediately below, fourteen blue beehives stood between nut-trees and stubble-crofts, the last in the row carved out of the rock with a modern blue front set into it. In this cosy bird-home I felt for the first time part of, or at least close to, this foreign world. Fortunately it happened again when I went to find the reputedly oldest caves of God in the cliffs behind Çavuşin, up the valley called Güllü Dere.

The way led off from the old village by a track through dust as soft and white as powder snow, past a graveyard where plain stones with minimal inscriptions — 'F. 1774' — stood up amongst bronzed late-summer grasses. A path forked left, hugging the bases of twenty-metre rock cones that almost touched each other. For some reason, that is for no reason at all, I expected the ancient churches to face me at any moment. After a hot kilometre the rocks remained inscrutable, unworked, themselves. At the verge of a vineyard a man with a leathery tan and eyes the colour of prune-flesh was folding away a tent.

'The kilise?' I asked, pointing to the nearest cliffs.

'No. By thees way,' he answered, making curving gestures west, then south.

I pounded on, encouraged presently by a notice on a tree that promised 'Aya[illegible] Church. Cold Drinks Tea'. Now the path was as deeply entrenched as the central way in the Valley of the Doves, so it had to be old, with something worthwhile at its terminus. It tunnelled through small crags and entered a wetland phase. Frogs ruffled the surface of a stone trough. Then things dried out again and I noticed that the water-pipe beside me had been broken off, which presumably put paid to Cold Drinks Tea.

Now I was squeezing between the pink torsoes of many tall abbots, who punished me for my longing for cold drinks by grazing my elbows. Boulder chokes and rock ramps blocked the gorge and I pulled up them by rudimentary cut steps. These died out, and the way was becoming improbable as the access to anything at all. The abbots had become a mosaic of pointed heads below me. The skyline ahead and above was the rim of a layered roseate cliff that ranged along for several kilometres. When I reached the base of its buttresses and corries, the quietude of the upland world sank into me and I thought for the first time about the sheer silence of rock. On this dry Anatolian plateau, lapped round by hundreds of miles of cornland, with hardly a lake or a river of any size, there was almost no water-vapour to make the air hiss or moan. The nearly impalpable convection breeze was no louder than the soughing of my own blood in my own scarlet tree.

It seemed a shame to go down again into the wicked plain. But churches must be found. Near the broken pipe I had noticed a sign lying down amongst parched grasses saying 'Hacli Kilise' and left it for later. Now I retraced my steps, took this turning, and scrambled steeply up slopes of oatmeal dust. There was a pleasant feeling of having passed through the looking-glass into the duneland of some forgotten or undiscovered sea. Presently, on a barely-stable earthen slope that seemed to have been tilled, fourteen sunflowers stood forlornly, withered leaves crepitating. Behind and above them a shapely tufa cliff faced the west, a glare of white gold with a pointed top like a small Matterhorn. Two rounded archways cut into the rockface were blocked by steel doors. They were shut — padlocked. I banged one angrily with the flat of my hand and heard an echo grumble from the dusk inside.

It was bitterly frustrating. Here I was at what could be a wellspring of the rock-church culture (not that it can be assigned to a single spot) and it was impossible even to see inside. The earliest church paintings in Güllü Dere have been dated c. 550 A.D. and the first hermit-caves were delved out long before that. The local martyr, St Hieron, was persecuted under Diocletian at the end of the third century. When the Roman soldiers chased him and thirteen fellow believers through the vineyards where they were working, he managed to hide for a time 'in a mighty cavern in the flank of a hill, which had been carved out of the rock with great skill'. This rockscape owes much of its charisma to having been the home of very early Christians, long before hierarchy and panoply, when worship sprang from nothing but authentic need.

In a cone nearby a barrel-vaulted chapel was found by a French scholar in 1912. The most recent experts have failed to locate it, so it is as well that we have Jerphanion's transcript of the epitaph which the hermit painted for himself in red characters on white plaster:

> I was formed an infant in my mother's womb.
> For nine months not consuming normal nourishment,
> I was nourished in the flow of liquid.
> I came out from my own mother.
> I saw the creation, and recognised the creator . . .

Still living, I prepared an excavated grave;
So, tomb, receive me too like my namesake the Stylite.

So the cycle of life is compressed into one lyric utterance — the vision that Beckett took further in Pozzo's drastic epigram from *Waiting for Godot*, 'We give birth astride of a grave.' The hermit's poem resonates for me as the essence of this extraordinary culture of cells and chapels because its central symbol of womb-enclosure springs so directly from the sac-like, even egg-like spaces with their curving white interiors and their small, bright openings into life which the devotees carved out of the tufa.

Unwilling to accept the impasse, I cast about and saw a faint trod mounting the col between the Matterhorn and its neighbour. I followed it and came out in a byway where the first and last church lay open to the sun. It was cut out of a tower just below the level where the basalt cap sat on the tufa shaft. The grizzled basalt showed reddish where the eyebrow of the doorway had fallen out. It was just possible to friction up a tufa ramp to the door-sill. Inside, the ceiling was a single cupola. The decoration was mostly abstract, curlicues wreathed round a central reddish-brown cross painted on a circular white ground. Where the arc joined the vertical, a broad reddish border showed ancient graffiti in Greek lettering, carefully scratched through to the white of the rock.

The heart and beauty of the church was in the painted walls — images not of saints or apostles or anything explicitly religious but of grapes. Tendrils of branch issued in plump bunches of fruit. The centre of each grape was rendered in Prussian blue, the rest of it in light purple-black. The leaves were stylised, pointed, their centres turquoise, the rest red-ochre. Nine bunches showed on the right-hand side. On the left, traces of the same colour made little glints on the worn whitish stone.

These were the only unmistakable figuring of this country that I had seen — a virtually totemic honouring of the native crop — the fruit St Hieron was working with when the imperial soldiers came to get him. A much more crudely and less sumptuously painted vine than the one I was now looking at on the ceiling of Uzumlu Kilise (Church with the Grape) at Zelve north of Çavuşin has been interpreted as a Christian offspring of a Dionysian ritual symbol, adapted to signify Jesus himself. Such images are many-layered. The point for me was that this church, whose stone was gradually returning into the land, celebrated the very fruits that teemed in the valley below. I admit to feeling justified, not guilty, when I picked a dozen ripe green grapes from a wayside vine to slake my thirst on the long walk back to the village.

We had still to see the two great sources, the volcanoes called Erciyes Dag and Hassan Dag, which rise more or less equidistantly to the east and west of the Göreme/Urçhizar hizar heartland. Twisting hill roads east of Ürgüp dropped us abruptly into a plain as different as could be from the calmly rising-and-dipping cornlands we had travelled for hundreds of miles between Ankara and Nevşehir. Here, chemical deposits have given rise to ugliness and jobs, a suppurating canal, villages devoid of leafage where women were building up roadside parapets with a mixture of breeze-blocks and big round cakes of dried dung. Solace was at hand — in most of the settlements new mosques were arising, with glittering aluminium cupolas.

Above all this Erciyes Dag rode pale-blue and serene, her furious days long past. For most of the afternoon a white cloudlet was suspended above the summit, like a ghost of extinct fire. The only sign of old violence was in the broken skyline. This mountain had not risen up in the gradual tectonic way and was liable to sudden changes. North of Develi we climbed a long, long hill past stubble fields pasturing herds of sheep and goats mixed — restoring actuality to the Biblical phrase — and other fields where sheaves were still being hand-gathered by women and men living in white tents like British Army bell-tents long ago. The east face of Erciyes Dag bore scabs of dirtied snow.

The summit stood up in splintered shafts, and from due north at Haclar a huge wound was scooped out where the mountain had blown and beheaded itself, like a colossal egg hatching. We turned west again at Kayseri, once Caesarea, bishopric of the Cappadokian churchman St Basil the Great, a levelling aristocrat who did more than anyone to further the ideal of the *coenobium* whereby isolated hermits were drawn into communities from their fastnesses in the rock. Hassan Dag to the east was smoother in outline, less obviously a mouth that had spouted enough lava, cinder, and ash to create an entire terrain. In either case it was awesome to think that they had haemorrhaged enough between them to make deep strata (now cleft into gorges), lesser hills, and millions of hectares of the arable soil itself.

For us Hassan Dag was the landmark signalling the Ihlara Gorge, whose sides were said to house a rock-dwelling culture as remarkable as Göreme's. A hundred metres of new-made concrete steps led us down into a long, sinuous paradise of running water — the Mendeliz never fails — and stands of poplar and willow whose foliage spired up and trembled like green spray. Rock churches with beautiful names might have detained us here — the Church of the Serpent, Hyacinth Church, Honeyed Church, Church of the Tree, and also, it is true, the Smelly Church. Undoubtedly many saintly figures gestured stiffly from within these cells, looking out on the modern world from eyes hollowed darkly underneath. My own purpose was more to perceive as nearly as possible those moments when the moth of civilisation just broke from the chrysalis of the rock.

We walked downstream by a made path which struggled now and again through ruckles of boulders fallen from the cliffs. These were phalanxes of upright members like bronzed girders forty metres high — columnar basalt, standing on a layer of tufa. Surely the dwellings, barns, and anchorites' cells would have been mined out of this softish base? For two kilometres nothing could be seen up there and we walked contentedly in the channel of vibrant sound and light. All day 'By cool Siloam's shady rill' sang in my head. The relief of energetic water was as keen as it had been in the Canyon de los Frijoles after the shrunken streams of Arizona and New Mexico.

At a right-angled bend in the Mendeliz a family of women and children were cooking on a fire of sticks beside a patch of potatoes ready for lifting. Further on a flock of long-eared sheep with luxuriant yellow and white fleeces couched placidly in the dust and didn't fluster when we walked through them, presumably because, unlike ours, they are herded continuously by people, not chivvied on special occasions by impatient dogs. A woman passed through the flock with a pot, looking for a ewe to milk. A man was walking along the track with shears in his hand. Nearby, women and youths were piling sacks stuffed with fleeces on to the saddles of their donkeys.

Now rows of mouths were showing in the lower levels of the rock-face, round and square and oblong, mostly on our side, the true-left bank, which was much the shadier. I climbed up to them through scree and stravaiged along the base. Three metres above the ground an oval mouth a metre high could just be reached by delicate footholds. I pulled up and in, expecting a room, and found myself at the bottom of a well-like shaft, smoothly cut out, with cup-holds in the sides all the way up to the light and a roomy circular exit. Ten metres of easy climbing and some tricky moves on much shallower cups took me into a dwelling three-and-a-half metres across, the height of a tall person, and twelve metres deep. Its broad mouth looked straight out over the woodland canopy to the basalt cliff opposite.

The chamber had five entries on one side, four on the other. Two were dummies, nicely hewn recesses not half a metre deep, and one was the entrance. Opposite it another shaft bored down into gloom. A pebble dropped down it took some seconds to hit bottom. An exhausted well? The remaining five were cubicles, presumably bed-spaces. The stone partitions left between them were thin and in one there were two little openings like knot-holes in a fence. For parental supervision? or chipped through by frustrated lovers?

The fine domestic detail of this place continued right along the cliff to the village of Belisirma. Material fallen from the cliff had banked up against the face and grown over with shrubs and grasses, leaving the round tops of three arches just showing. They had been a church. Some decorations in the red-for-happiness paint made a zigzag round one curve where the ceiling dropped in a canine tooth, the remnant of a broken pillar. On a strip of whitened wall three Maltese crosses had been roughly cut and reddened. In the next entry two coffin recesses had been carved out of the floor, the size for children. Next door was another with a cross in bas-relief above it, set in a chipped-out circular recess and whitened. One brief life, leaving this clear signal across, what, ten or eleven centuries? You could almost hear the father's or the uncle's chisel striking the rock, the day of the interment. Again the place came over as perfectly authentic — long before inquisitions and confessionals, before the *auto da fe* or the mass baptism of con-quered peoples. The very crosses still looked alive: the antlered ends of their limbs suggested a totem-world of trees and deer as much as martyrdom.

Nearby I climbed the rockface by a 'stairway' of worn pockets and entered a system of rooms and alcoves running inside the rock for fifty metres, with window-holes every so often. This was repeated in a still longer system down at river level when we came back along the other bank a few hours later. Were these in effect arcades, for comfortable access in all weathers to rooms, stables, and chapels?

The other explanation for these rock-settlements stresses the fought-over history of Cappadokia, the constant raids and not infrequent invasions and wars. The literature is full of this and emphasises the secret nature of the passage systems, the doorways well above ground, and so on. In fact these are not typical. Both in Urçhizar and here in Ihlara you can walk easily into many of the chambers. Doorways are far from usually on the first floor as they are in, say, the round towers of Ireland. Nor was this land exceptionally fought-over, as were Lom-bardy or Belgium.

Stone towers and hidden caves and entries up shafts may remind us of sieges and wars. In a rockscape they were the most natural medium of habitation — weatherproof, enjoying (as caves do) a fairly steady temperature, the stone both strong and workable, the place already half-made by nature. One chamber at Ihlara clarified the issue for me. It was at ground level and its floor was strewn with dead grass. It could have blown in. It looked like bedding for animals and it made me think : if all this honeycomb of dwellings was for defence (against the waves of Romans, Parthians, Seljuks, or whoever), what did they do with their valuable flocks and herds, when the humans were hiding one or two storeys up?

Nearby I found a chamber at ground level which was divided into what looked more like stalls than rooms. They were narrow. There were very few binks or cupboards cut into the walls and no lamp- or fire-black on the ceiling. The hewing-marks were rough compared with the beautiful hatching of curved cuts made by stone axes on the walls of the human homes. Surely this place was a byre, for winter use on this plateau a thousand metres above sea level, with a long snow-time (November till March). I believe I was looking at a settlement made for use in normal times, employing the material that volcanoes had supplied so abundantly, and leaving the slopes and bottomlands for pasture and for crofts, whether flat or terraced. Like the Anasazi at Keet Seel or the Sinagua in Walnut Canyon, the people had found a place wonderfully equipped by nature for living in, and adapted it much more thoroughly than the native-Americans because the rock was much more workable.

The theory which makes much of warring and defensibility has one more trump card in its hand — the *yeralti sehri*, or 'underground cities' at Kaymakli and Derinkuyu, thirty kilometres south of Nevşehir. These are hardly great integral rocks standing up from the earth's surface. They are labyrinths burrowing ten storeys deep into the thickness of the volcanic stone, linked by kilometres of passageway: a marvel, or a monstrosity if we believe them to be bunkers mined by the Hittites for refuge in times of invasion and massacre. They may be cool-stores — fruit and vegetables can keep for more than a century in such conditions. And difficulties of water supply and sanitation would have made it impossible to live in them for more than a few weeks . . . At least one such prodigy of rock-work would have to be explored.

We turned west at Kaymakli off the road south towards Tarsus, down a side street crammed with mule-carts and snorting tractors, and wondered for a time if we had gone wrong as the way crossed a level area of corn and potato fields. Then the low range of Erdas Dagi came into sight ahead, evidence of rock and therefore of mineability. In a village called Özlüce women were working on the threshing floor, throwing up shovelfuls of corn, scattering it sideways. We followed black arrows smeared with tar on the ends of barns and houses and halted in a yard full of dust and dung. Children gathered, giggling and saying 'Hullo, money' and 'Bonbons'. A small stone building, unmortared, with a flag roof, had the word 'UNDER' tarred on the curved lintel of the door, which was padlocked.

As we wondered about giving up the quest, a middleaged woman in woollen pullover, baggy trousers and headcloth, with broad dusty feet in rubber flipflops, came down the lane, holding a torch and a key. She was Sakure Sivritepe and we gathered from her vigorous mime, hands and arms swinging a shovel, bunched fingers tapping her breastbone, that she herself had worked at the digging out of the labyrinth below our feet.

In an ante-room a few stained old jars, with high shoulders and narrow bottoms, stood against the wall. Then the maze led off into a darkness of holes, tunnels, shafts. Half-shut black eyes stared from the passage walls, byways left unexcavated, choked with dust and rubble. The passage sloped gently downward like a drift-mine and Sakure explained that now we were two storeys down, now three . . . A chamber with shallow half-metre holes in its floor, like cauldrons cut in the rock, was for washing, which certainly suggests occupation — unless the fruits and vegetables were washed before storing? In another place a manhole gaped, two metres across, and a shaft funnelled downward, with cup steps chipped in its sides, shallow and filled with dust. A well? As I lowered down into it, the rubble my hands were planted on started to give, my toes slithered, and I climbed charily back out while Sakure looked on, amused and appalled.

Whatever the function of these catacombs and however we explain the vast communal labour that must have gone into their making (echoed in the past thirty years by the toil of people like Sakure to dig them out), the single feature I found most striking was their use of massive 'wheels' carved from rock, like convex millstones, to make doors for the chambers and passageways. They could be stowed in a vertical slot in the wall or rolled back into position, filling the space, biding there like an immovable shield: the rock removed, trimmed, and returned to its own place in nature.

Here again, as with the mixing of the sheep and the goats on the slopes of Erciyes Dag, we were seeing a Biblical phrase restored to its full actuality and resonance:

211

And when Joseph had taken the body, he wrapped it in a clean linen cloth, and laid it in his own new tomb, which he had hewn out in the rock: and he rolled a great stone to the door of the sepulchre, and departed . . . And behold, there was a great earthquake: for the angel of the Lord descended from heaven, and came and rolled back the stone from the door, and sat upon it.

For the early Christians in the Middle East, these sentences would have been that much less fantastic, that much more real and telling, because they would have known the safe strength of such a door. They would have stared too at its impassive face and wondered what might be coming at them from the other side.

The final phrases that recovered their meaning, as we walked by paths and tracks and tunnels that had never been concreted or tarred, were all those turning on the word 'dust'. It had always struck me as a feeble word, in a modern northern society where the stuff exists mainly as a film of textile particles on the surfaces of furniture or hovers in the air as motes. How could this paltry substance be taken seriously as the life-component that it stands for in one ancient poem after another?

> And the Lord God formed man of the dust of the ground,
> and breathed into his nostrils the breath of life;
> and man became a living soul.

> . . . he knoweth our frame;
> he remembereth that we are dust.
> As for man, his days are as grass;
> as a flower of the field,
> so he flourisheth.
> For the wind passeth over it, and it is gone;
> and the place thereof shall know it no more.

> All go unto one place;
> all are of the dust,
> and turn to dust again.

Dust originally, after all, is the hardest stuff in the world — rock — reduced to its smallest state, milled finer even than sand. In the hot byways of Israel and Turkey, climbing between the slowly-wasting crags of Judea or slurring through these trails of Cappadokia like inland beaches, we could perceive through our own footsoles that dust is everywhere and is the last, lowliest detritus of the earth we inhabit.

22   Ladders of Divine Ascent

As the little train, trundling between fields of vegetables and cotton, neared its terminus at Kalambaka, where the plain of Thessaly tapers to its northern end among the enclosing mountains, a gang of bald ogres with naked shoulders rose to their feet. The rock towers of the Meteora were sunned grey and weathered black like African and Indian elephants. Their howdahs are monasteries — six with roofs now, eighteen in their heyday 300 years ago.

To see them as giants has long been natural. Behind the westernmost rank of them a tall cave with multiple mouths gapes in the tower called Ogla or Phylaki. It is ghastly — rotting woodwork dangles from the walls with a look of disused torture instruments and an underlook of Florestan's dungeon cell in *Fidelio*. The beams and ladders on the verge of collapse, the pitiless enclosure of the rock-walls, catch exactly the spiralling hope and slumped defeat of the momentous aria in which Florestan tries to imagine freedom and his beloved, then fails, exhausted. It turned out that Phylaki was the prison where erring monks were shut up. A copse of stunted oaks grows below its mouth. A villager from Kastraki was cutting them, a giant came out of the cave, the man died of fright, and 'since then no one has dared put an axe to the giant's oaks'.

On Sunday in Kalambaka we woke up to a concert of bells and amplified baritone chanting. One bell was giving out a blacksmith's hammering notes, a steady 'ding, ding, ding-ding-ding'. A tenor bell sent shimmering pulses over the tiled roofs. Because the sources were mostly invisible, somewhere up there in the forest of towers, it was as though the music was issuing from the domes and rounded sides and embedded clapper-stones of the rocks themselves. Presently the 'joyful noise' died down in a long rahl. We were free to follow the sounds to their wellsprings in the monasteries. Some of the bells were huge, with shallow bas-reliefs of apostles and saints processing round the rim. In the idyllic peace of the very small monastery of Anapafsos, the late afternoon convection breezes roused the bell to the occasional clangour. In the big and much-visited monasteries at the summit of the cluster, the Great Meteoron and Varlaam, we noticed clubs of wood hanging on the walls beside lengths of iron — substitutes used under Turkish rule (which lasted in Thessaly from A.D. 1394 to 1881) when proper bells were forbidden.

Montserrat, near Barcelona

The towers of Meteora were compacted from the shingles of an ancient delta where a river drained out of unimaginable mountain ranges and its current carried the finer materials on into the sea, providing the silts for the perfectly flat and fertile plain of Thessaly. All this was before the Mediterranean became a dead sea and its dunes drifted up the flank of Gibraltar, before the gates were opened again to let the ocean pour in to make a sea for Odysseus.

For me the towers linked the two ends of the Mediterranean. We had spent hours with my daughter and her partner walking between and round and even a little up their distant relatives in Montserrat, north-west of Barcelona — cones and columns of conglomerate even more anthropomorphic than Meteora, torsoes of sumo wrestlers, a rounded Titan which Anne and Marian saw as an elephant and I saw as a silverback gorilla with a massive paunch, and giant foetuses with eyes folded shut, and faceless Buddhas and fennel bulbs and goats' udders. The teeth in the word 'Montserrat' had led me to expect jaggedness. All was rounded and benign. Slopes could be frictioned up even without the help of cracks or flakes and the gullies were fledged with dwarf conifers and heathers that grew head-high.

As the light yellowed at sunset, all the westward-facing countenances smiled, and the massive bulks resonated, ringing tenors and baritones, joined soon by basses deep as sea-caves. Vespers was about to be celebrated at the monastery three hundred metres below and several chimes of bells were sounding together, as though the skirts and flanks of the rocks were cast metal and their round cross-sections were the ringing hollows of bells and the expanding circles of their sounds.

Next day I found a map which told me that a huddle of monoliths at the west end is called the *Frares Encantats*, the chanting friars. The rocks of Meteora resound to the same music and they filled the same function as a refuge and a heartland of national resistance. Caves at Montserrat were used for secret worship during the Moorish occupation. In 1811 Napoleon's soldiers looted the monks' treasures at Montserrat, vandalised their buildings, and 'hunted the hermits like chamois along the cliffs'. A hundred years later the Abbot set up a press to print the Bible in Catalan and illegal publishing and demonstrating was centred here during Franco's dictatorship. So rocks are not only the evidence of extinct or dormant powers, they also make a sanctuary from the powers-that-be.

During unrecorded centuries anchorites had lodged in the caves that honeycomb the great round mass of Doupiani at Meteora, between Kalambaka and Kastraki. They found them with the help of goatherds, then gradually turned them into something more by building up walls of stone along their lower lips. This rockscape, 'where no one lived except birds of prey and vultures', was ideal for the practice of hezychasm, which cultivated *hesychia*, the peace of solitude, as a means towards *ataraxia*, freedom from anxiety — paradoxically attained, as rock-climbers do, by breaking through the often intense anxiety of the climb itself. 'Mountaineer', in Greek, was a common synonym for 'monk'.

We can only imagine the mystical ecstasy of those first hermits. A latterday form of it breathes like a perfume from the writing of Sister Theotekni, the nun who has written a devout history of Meteora: 'on bare grey rock which stands facing other stony giants surrounded by threatening space . . . you imagine yourself on wings and your soul delights in your flight and the embrace of the soft blue world . . . if you have in you the wings of the Lord's love, your soul yearns to fly alone together only with God's adorable Company.' Her innocent lyricism belongs to the tradition of the early Meteora hymn –

> We pay homage, Father,
> To Thy ladder and net,
> Wise instruments uplifting
> To the spheres of purity
> Souls drawn to the Holy Light.

Behind that again lies the Psalm which describes believers coming to their god 'as a little bird finds a nest for itself'.

Now, six hundred years after the first recorded occupation of Meteora by a brilliant and energetic young monk from Mount Athos called Athanasios, the climb up the pillars is no longer a 'ladder of divine ascent' but an innocuous routine. It is the last place you would go to find 'the peace of solitude'. Athanasios' abilities ran to organisation. Funds were raised; plots of land for fields and vineyards were acquired by agreement with the feudal rulers; fine churches, dormitories, bakeries were built on these 'great high rocks set up by the Demiurge at the creation of the world for just such a purpose'. By the end of the fifteenth century the Great Meteoron had become tyrannical. Its monks attacked the monks of Pantokrator nearby with knives and sticks when they tried to build a new water-mill on land they had thought to be at a safe distance. A Turkish court decided in favour of the Big One and Pantokrator lost its land, its vineyard, and its water supply.

In 1616 the Meteoron itself was pillaged by Turkish soldiers posing as 'innocent tourists who only wanted to take the air and see the viewpoint from the top of the rock'. In 1812 the monasteries became a haven for five hundred women and children, refugees from Turkish persecution. A little later, an aristocratic visitor from England remarked with the fascist wit of the grandee that 'the anchorites who burrowed in them, like rabbits, frequently afforded excellent sport to parties of roving Saracens; indeed, hermit-hunting seems to have been a fashionable amusement previous to the twelfth century'. After Independence the monks had to struggle to save their archives from being commandeered by the new central government. Early in the 1920s the Archbishop of Trikkala forced the brothers to replace their 'ladders of divine ascent' (rickety wooden ladders and a net hauled up by windlass) with staircases cut in the rock.

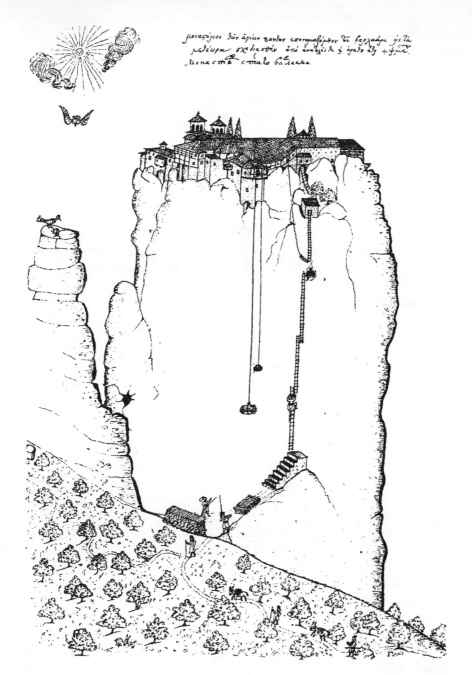

Barskij's drawing of Varlaam (1745)

It is as though every kind of social force was hellbent on destroying the solitude which had been the *raison d'être* of the place. No wonder Athanasios had seen demons flying round his first cave — and he had come here from Mount Athos for safety from Turkish pirates. Now the invaders are no longer soldiers disguised as tourists but tourists as organised and invincible as soldiers. We are transported up a newish hairpin road in huge Volvo and Atlantean buses with on-board television. The queues of us, often at a standstill, choke the staircases built by decree of Polykarpos. The files of us pack the small dark churches to be lectured, usually in German, about each martyr and apostle and crucifixion and transfiguration painted on the walls — only we can't pause there, to think or feel, because the next platoon is already being marshalled in.

I was reminded of our efforts to linger over the murals by Mantegna in the palace of the Gonzagos at Mantova. Each square foot was dense with painted behaviour and, given time, would have yielded meaning as richly as a page by Tolstoy or George Eliot. We must keep up with our party, whose regulation minute in Salon No. V has come and gone and must instantly be followed by a minute in Salon No. VI. We try lingering, to savour Mantegna's image of a feudal grandee smiling officially to a suitor while leaning a little backwards to catch the briefing dropping into his ear from the lips of a consultant in a black cloak — no good — the next party has caught up with us, and when we try merging with it, we're glowered at by two heavies in Mafia suits . . .

The Meteoron and the Varlaam were not as bad as that. We could sun ourselves in a little garden orange with marigolds, sombre and peaceful with the stone crosses of monks' graves. We could spend as long as we liked in a library which happily was suffering a power-cut and peer by candlelight at ikons fretted with woodworm and illuminated Bibles and Orders of Service. Most memorably, just above the dairy and the kitchen with its massive blackened utensils resting on beds of ash, we could look in through the small square unglazed window of the ossuary and return the black-eyed stares of the monastic dead, a library of skulls above a shelf stacked with femurs and tibias.

What was missing was a functioning way of life, which we might (or might not) have been invited by its members to share for a time. No Henry VIII has dissolved these monasteries. They have just been overwhelmed and denatured by the tourist industry. A rare flicker of religious life occurred at Varlaam, when a very old monk was walking slowly past a woman lighting a candle at a shrine and she asked him to bless her, which he did. At Anapafsos, which at least was bypassed by the buses, the single monk was sitting at a table selling admission tickets and reading a tabloid. He was handsome and sardonic and seemed bored out of his skull. Certainly he had no bread to bake or crofts to till or books to copy or illuminate. He and his house were there primarily to be looked at. I felt *de trop*. So, in another sense, was he — living in a house built with the utmost difficulty and courage, its walls dropping straight down a fifty-metre cliff, whose reason for existing could only be its almost impossible access, its solitude, and which now finds itself committed to maximising customer throughput and the turnover of consumer goods.

Down at the road, where the zigzag path to Anapafsos made off through dense coverts of ilex and scrub oak, not a car was parked. A woman in widow's black sold us half a kilo of sweetly fragrant Muscat grapes, which she sprinkled with water against the dusty heat. By turning our backs on the tarmac road and taking the stony path down the mountain from the larger monasteries, we had found our way through to a time when this place was still itself. The path, no longer a thoroughfare, petered out down aprons of crag and had to be retraced to find a way round bulges of conglomerate, a pudding-stone whose cobbles looked like mottled goose or ostrich eggs embedded in greyish dough. The bellies and hips of the outcrops stood out from the profile of the rock like pre-Christian totems, for example the chunky stone 'Venuses' from southern France which emerged along with cave paint-ing and refined tool-making at the start of post-Neanderthal humanity 40,000 years ago.

The sheer outlandishness of Meteora reminds you that Thessaly was a heartland of myth, the home of the Centaurs, and that in the days of the first anchorites the Christian and the pagan were still parts of one vision. The huge cave under the rock of Varlaam was the lair of a dragon, which terrorised the countryside until the hermits prayed up a black cloud, a thunderbolt burst from it, broke off a piece of the cliff, and crushed the monster. In retreating here from ordinary social relationships — Athanasios was extremely ascetic and referred to women as 'slings' and 'afflictions' — the hermits remained at risk from outward demons as well as those of the mind. Athanasios had escaped from the pirates ravaging round the peninsulas of Khalkidiki. When the Byzantine regime collapsed and before the Ottoman was estab-lished, Albanian warriors and looters terrorised northern Thessaly and at least four of the monasteries at Meteora were built as refuges from them.

The one survivor of these, Hypopanti, attracted me because it was 'inaccessible', rarely visited, and approachable only by a path. This was supposed to leave from near the road-end where the buses backed and turned to the irritable signals of a white-gloved policeman with a revolver in his belt. A woman in widow's black who sold me films at one of the many souvenir stalls gestured into the scrub, put her hands edge to edge, and said 'Cross'. She also seemed to say that the monastery key mentioned by Sister Theotekni was not available.

After a false trail through the bushes we found a gully that looked like a very old path eroded by run-off. It slanted up the ridge and divided at the watershed. Here a battered and illegible sign had been smeared with a red arrow, pointing south. To the east was a wooded basin, its hollow peopled with great trunks of rock, its sides softened and shaded by woods like those that must have covered Cumbria, Kerry, Wester Ross before the felling to make charcoal for the cannon foundries, before the locust munching of the sheep and the red deer. We could just make out, on a promontory at the far side, a white cross, a flagstaff, and some kind of statue.

We followed the path downhill for a kilometre. Among the parched grasses of late summer, autumn crocuses flared mauve through rustling brown leafage like a woodland floor in a very dry British winter. Somewhere in the trees the bells of a flock clanked. Between the trunks a mean-looking brown dog glared at us and barked, shadowed by his black twin. In a minute or two the shepherd appeared, an old man with bright brown eyes in a face sunburnt to a ruddy flush. He had a sprouting blond moustache, a peaked khaki cap on his head, and a rough stick in his hand. He introduced himself as 'Gregoriou' in a voice so hoarse that the name was all rasping gutturals — 'Hrehoriou'. He assumed we were German and in a pidgin version of that language, much better than mine and learned perhaps during the Occupation, he asked us our names and how many children we had. When we said no thank you to cigarettes, he gave us cherry-menthol Tunes and mimed with a smile that his dogs were there to do the shepherding when he was sleeping in the shade.

By now his goats and sheep had strayed off northward on a newly bulldozed track and he followed them, waving to us over his shoulder, a husky figure in the sunlight between the trees who looked as though he would live forever. Above us, in the lateral crevice of a deeply groined and layered crag, Hypopanti was ensconced, a row of tiled and balconied buildings with what looked like solid new varnished doors — part of the recent restoration after nearly two centuries when only bats lived there. Soon, I suppose, a monk or two will be installed to sell admission tickets and mass-produced ikons. In the meantime it perches there, perhaps seventy metres from the ground, like a *rifugio* in the Dolomites waiting for the snows.

A staircase cut in the rock slanted up the face. Where the parapet had crumbled away, two of Gregoriou's goats were tearing mouthfuls of leaf from young oaks and wild fig-trees. As I neared them, they panicked off beyond the brink of a seemingly sheer drop, then re-appeared on the track far below and sauntered off after their master and his dogs. At a ledge where a ravine sliced down from above, an entry to the monastery had been tunnelled through the rock. The steel door was locked, presumably with the unavailable key. The 630-year-old place would have to be left to itself.

The many decades of vacancy at Hypopanti were the result not of peaceful decay but of desperate events. Sister Theotekni tells them in her devoted way. A twin monastery round the east side of the rock, built by the same fourteenth-century founder, had 'played an import-ant historical role during the years of the Greek Revolution. It was used as the headquarters of our national hero, the priest Thymios Vlahavas.' The less committed historian puts it that this man 'formed a celebrated klephtic band among the Meteora rocks and bullied all the monks into supplying his men with food'. Such is, such has to be, the way of guerrilla freedom fighters.

The man is honoured now, not only officially. Gesturing at the cross and the statue up on the promontory, Gregoriou called him familiarly '*Papa*', priest. On the upright limb of the white cross black Greek lettering told us that it was put up in 1988, to the honoured memory of Papa Thymios, on the 108th anniversary of the rising. The statue itself looked wonderfully stern and unforgetting on its stark natural plinth of rock, with the fields of Thessaly brown and golden far behind and below. The man himself, two and a half metres high in dark bronze, was dressed in a soutane and a tall round hat of the kind we remember from Makarios of Cyprus. A pistol was stuck in his belt and his right hand was reaching round to draw a short sword from the scabbard on his left.

The flagpole was bare. Another, at the end of the monastery crag, carried the Greek flag, Mediterranean blue-and-white, hanging in the windless heat. Here was the monastery of St Demetrios, fortified by Papa Thymios, left in ruins by the Turkish cannon in 1809. Scaffolding had been reared up to the level where the courses of ancient stone-work clung to the lip of the drop like wild bees' honeycomb. It was weathered but sound and a homemade ladder led up to a couple of steep catwalks lashed to a tree with thick wire. This was not quite too hot to grip and helped me stride over on to the precarious rubble of the end wall. Up above I found the last throes of a building that had once rambled all over the top of the hummocky crag. A cistern two and a half metres square had been cut in the rock, with runnels to lead in the rainwater. Now it was filled with virulent green fluid. Broken tiles were mixed with the heaped stones, mostly unmasoned, that choked the shells and alleys of the monastery and buried almost out of sight the fine rounded arches of doorways. The stacks of rubble, untouched for generations, reminded me of the Boer War fort in the Magaliesberg — yet another site of mayhem committed under the sun by people much too far from home.

Down at the foot of the crag, a small shrine built of stone, with a gable and a cross on top and two niches in its front, showed the usual traces of respect for a memory — charred pastilles in the niche, a few coins, a little brass vase with six or seven withered wild flowers. Papa Thymios was tortured to death by the regional governor — son of the renowned Ali Pasha — and his quartered body was hung on plane trees at the entrance to the provincial capital at Ionnanina, a hundred kilometres west across the mountains. So it goes. Three generations later the Turkish colonists left and Islam withdrew into its eastern lairs again, for a time.

In the forest, as we climbed the path again, acorns were turning tawny on the oaks and the summer's sun had gilt the thistles. On the limed ledges of the outcrops above the trees, the vultures had raised their broods and the young birds were learning to ride the thermals. Dwarf cyclamen were unfurling mauve scrolls again as the sun blazed less fiercely, reminding me of the first time we saw them, ten years before, on the great citadel prow of Monemvasia at the south-east tip of the Peloponnese.

On the other side of the mountain the monastery called Rousanou, above the valley called Skaphidakia, had the most perfect look of a secretion from the rock, continuous with it as coral. Nowadays it is immaculate, tended by a convent of nuns who have planted flowers in every coign and terrace. When Curzon was here in the 1840s, two old women screamed at him that the monks were away and the ladders could not be lowered to visitors. Nowadays tourists are never turned away. We crossed the abyss between the massif and the slim rock tower by a well-maintained bridge and passed through the looking-glass into a miniature world, as though entering the obsessed head of a devotee.

A nun with a greyish complexion like very old bread sold us our tickets with her eyes downcast. The murals in the church were a display of atrocious martyrdom. A Roman soldier was hacking off a saint's foot and letting the blood pour into a funnel. Four martyrs were stewing in a huge pot above scarlet and orange flames. Two torturers were cutting into a saint's head with a double-handed saw. In the land of Papa Thymios and Mukhtar Pasha, who can say that these images are exaggerated? In the tiny church, with two windows barely thirty centimetres square opening out into the sunlit valley, the scenes darkled and seethed like nightmares.

In other of the monasteries the life in the murals was more of a wholesome mixture. In the church at Anapafsos the surrounding landscape was celebrated, stylised, in painted forms like massive rock eggs whose thick shells had been broken open to show all manner of scenes. A seated man shaped spoons with a hammer. A very old cowled man with a snake draped over his knees received the respects of two kneeling men who were offering him necklaces. A man with a belted tunic ran a spokeshave along the edge of a timber, shaping it perhaps for the monastery's own gallery from which the basket used to be lowered. In the foreground, an elder peered at the bandaged face of Jesus in his grave-clothes, his eyes slitted in suspicion.

This epic mixture of the domestic and the magical has affinities with Bosch and Brueghel. It was painted by a monk from Crete called Theophanis who flourished a few years after Bosch's death and during Breughel's heyday. Although he is more stiffly devotional than either, more bound by orthodox models, his big frieze at Anapafsos is pregnant with delight in the animal world. In the upper panel the Saviour, seated among flowers under an orange tree, blesses an arkful of animals: griffins and lions, crested magpies in a tree of pomegranates, an elegantly couched stag, a snake threaded between an elephant's legs, a hare and a brown bear peacefully coexisting.

As we walked down the valley looking for the re-emergence of the path below the motor road, Roussanou rose above us like a figurehead as it would look to a swimmer towered-over by a sublime ship with a prow forty metres high. Ahead, on the other side of the valley, stood Anapafsos on its narrow pier and a twin pier topped by the stones of a monastery shaken to bits by an earthquake in the last century. The path, in summer, is free to follow the dried up river-bed. It wound past outcrops like those in Renaissance paintings whose drama is heightened by posing the holy figures among beetling crags that look cast in plaster or metal. Our goal was a final chapel from the group founded as refuges in the 1360s. We had been seeing it, decorated with a line of what looked like flags, in a mouth in the rock high above Kastraki. Its patron saint was St George the Tropeoforos or Mandilas. When a Turk started cutting trees in the little forest at the base of the cliff, St George fixed him motionless to the ground. The man promised to offer up his wife's finest scarf. The saint released him and he duly brought the scarf and hung it outside the chapel.

Nowadays local people bring scarves and hang them up there. How do they do it? The face looked impossibly sheer. We approached through the forest and craned our necks to see the cave with its many-coloured flutterings, fifty metres above the ground. The display of tokens, the wishes they represent, were what I had seen on the roadside near Cromarty, north of Inverness, where hundreds of rags have been impaled on twigs near a clootie well, a rag-well, to bring good luck.

Here in the Meteora you must survive a deadly rite of passage to win your luck, if I am right in taking this, as much as the honouring of St George, to be the meaning of the scarf-hanging. After all, only the most daring lads of the village would have the nerve to make this climb. And I am no longer a lad, far from it.

I started up the rockface with intense curiosity and little hope. Flat-bottomed horizontal grooves had been cut for many metres along the lumpy conglomerate. They made traversing easy and nerved me to climb from one to the next, edging on cobbles as I had done for a few metres up the roseate face of Kata Tjuta. The grooves ran out. I teetered upwards as the face steepened to sixty, seventy, eighty degrees. Bridging on two rounded shingles the size of baseballs, I placed my palms against the nearly vertical face and gazed longingly up at the cave with its line of scarves. Just ten metres above me, on the apron below the cave, a modern metal stanchion stuck out of the rock. So the lads from Kastraki abseil off after passing their ordeal and hanging up their scarves — or their sweethearts' scarves. It was so tempting to go for the stanchion. I could feel my upper arms and calves tensing for the move. Crazy, *crazy*! The ripple soles of my fell-trainers were frictioning barely enough to hold me on. Down-climbing all this would be even worse. Any cobble might pull out — there were plenty of empty sockets near at hand . . . When so many no-no's come swarming into your head, you've lost it. With the utmost care that I could muster, I balanced back down from the steepening, reached the grooves, traversed along them, and made the last downclimb, not without difficulty.

Talking it over with Anne at the café in Kastraki, my eyes still magnetised to the huge sunned limbs and foreheads towering above

224

the rooftops, I confessed to her the ignominious fact that if there had been a few others with me I might well have gone on, with no objective security whatsoever, 'protected' by the safety of numbers. Oh dear, oh dear — how completely I had failed to climb the ladder of divine ascent into the state of *ataraxia*, freedom from anxiety. I could have achieved it only through the intense anxiety of climbing steeply on small holds, fifty metres above the ground, without a rope, at risk of disablement or death — at risk, too, of preventing myself from visiting Delphi and Machu Picchu and therefore from finishing this book . . . Such are the rationalisations of fear, a fear which had fixed me to the spot as immovably as the Turk who broke the taboo and violated the forest of St George.

23   Greek Underworlds

For days we had been living, at Kalambaka, within a few yards of the battered north-south highway along which massive trucks snore and chug, hauling their loads of cement and timber and crack cocaine to all points in Europe. The road and the railway are forced here to follow the course of the Peneios between the mountains — a fabled river which gave birth to Daphne the Mountain-nymph and priestess of Mother-Earth at Delphi, our next goal. The Peneios flows into the Aegean a hundred kilometres to the east, after flowing through the Vale of Tempe, where Apollo took a cutting of laurel to plant at the Castalian Spring near Delphi. And so on. Still lurking in me were some ironical feelings about these gods and their doings. In my boy's-eye view 'gods-'n'-heroes' had come to seem like elders, and ruling-class elders at that. Jupiter was the headmaster and his emissaries were prefects — all too like the young Spartans at Gordonstoun, where we went to play rugby, with their stainless-steel manners and their cruel naked knees.

My deeper feelings of empathy or solidarity were bound up with the mythic underclass, with trolls and hobgoblins and wood-kerns, and with other mythologies from less prestigious homelands — the Scandinavia of Thor and Loki, the England of Robin Hood. Never mind — perhaps, at Delphi, the high and mighty Classical ethos would take on reality at last, the eyeballs of the gods would be unblinded and their blanched limbs would warm with blood.

The waves of mountain running off west from Thessaly towards the

Adriatic are limestone — old seabed sediments compressed into layered stone and buckled upward into ranges by the shifting of the Earth's plates. So Parnassos was formed, which we travelled round now by train, then bus, on the long journey to Delphi.

Our movement towards it was almost primitive, a drawing towards one of our civilisation's oldest centres. It had been sacred to Gē, Mother-Earth, and Poseidon, who was the Earth-Shaker, maker of quakes and wellsprings, before he was the Sea. The site might well be rocky but there was no reason for me to expect to be impressed by the actual stature of its crags. I was not prepared for a setting so tremendous, terraced high above the ravine of the Pleistos, flanked by the white-and-silver wings of the Phaedriades, the Shining Rocks, oriented towards the south-west and south-east — Phleboukos, flamboyant, and Rhodini, roseate.

These cliffs have fine slant skylines. They pile formidably, three hundred metres high. The vertical grain of them parts here and there in pink rents like wounds. As we approached, they converged, directing our feet and our eyes to the precinct of ancient magic which they enclose as the wings of a stage frame a performance. And of course it was all wonderfully, classically Greek. The battered drums of the columns at the east end of the Temple of Apollo, six of them set erect again, their fluted sections flushed white as magnolia petals, stand for lastingness and vulnerability both, assuring us that meanings can reach us, garbled and obscure no doubt, through aeons of historic time.

In the theatre the arcs of seating spread outwards and upwards from a stage which spectators would have watched against a backdrop of the limestone ravine plunging off towards the Gulf of Corinth. It still brings out performance in people. A small lad in black T-shirt, green shorts, and a white sunhat was scampering about on the battered flags of the floor and the cameras and camcorders were treating him like a star. At the apex of the site the stadium between its banks of seating, with crags of integral rock still in place behind the athletes' starting line, still feels so 'Olympic' that duos and trios of visitors were running it from end to end, happily re-enacting the ancient contests.

Among all these grand symmetrical structures, handsome even in ruin, what stood out for me was a pocked and bulging outcrop below the polygonal south wall of the Temple of Apollo. It was only five metres high, with a green and yellow apron of ivy swarming halfway up it out of the sandy ground. To make it obviously remarkable you would have to lie down in front of it and photograph it against swelling white cumulus-bodies with dark-blue sunrays breaking from behind their heads, as I did later with the Puma Rock above Cuzco in Peru. This Delphic outcrop was the Sibyl's Rock, centre of the most ancient cults. The Sanctuary of Earth, or Gē, was here — a circle of rocks surrounding a natural cleft and guarded by a snake, Python, mate of the monster Delphyne after which this place was named. Before Apollo was named, and before the Trojan War which she foretold, the Sibyl called Herophile prophesied from this rock.

The replacement of the autochtonous — deep-rooted, local — divinities by the new pantheon is storied in the slaying of the dragon-snake by Apollo when he was still a baby in his mother's arms. His rape of Dryope, once he had become old enough to have his way with females, has been understood by Robert Graves as standing for the supersession of a cult of oak by a cult of poplar. The Muses and the other oldest powers were descended from the Titans, the unruliest beings of all, and they were not wholly ousted by the deities brought in by Aryan invaders from the distant north and east in post-Neolithic times. Apollo is not widespread whereas Dionysos, one of the most animal or organic of the powers, sprung from the lightning, turns up everywhere and seems to have spread with the spreading of the vine and wine-making from its wild origins in northern Turkey. On Parnassos, a few kilometres north of Delphi, he reigned during the winter and women were brought in from Attica and Phocis to take part in cultic orgies lit by flaming pine branches.

Near the Sanctuary of Earth, on a circular terrace called the *halo* (or threshing floor), a play was put on every eight years re-enacting the killing of the Python. In many mythologies, right round the world to Arnhem Land, the great snake is life itself. To act out its periodic extinguishing would seem to symbolise its ongoing, as in old British rituals John Barleycorn was thrashed to pieces annually, then rose again in next year's crop.

How convincing the whole thing ever was is another matter. Before she prophesied, the Apollonian propehetess Pythia bathed in the Castalian Spring and chewed a laurel leaf. Then she sat on her tripod above the crevice, got high on fumes coming from it, and uttered incoherent sounds which were turned into forecasts — artfully ambiguous ones — by poets hired by the temple management. And rich and powerful people consulted her before setting up their wars! Perhaps it was no more misleading than being briefed by GCHQ Cheltenham or spooks in the employ of the Pentagon. The system which was run at Delphi in its most famous and profitable time smacks of an imposition on the cult which had grown out of the ground here almost as naturally as its oaks and laurels.

The older divinities *were* the place, not personages arbitrarily supposed to have been here. It was inhabited before the start of the Mycenean period (1450 B.C.) and nomadic herdspeople went on living here after the collapse of the Mycenean culture in the twelfth century B.C. A goatherd called Coretas is credited with being the first to see the vapour steaming out of the ground which showed the presence of Gē. 'Rain and thunder', according to Plutarch, could disperse the fumes and 'earthquakes can cause it entirely to disappear'. The cleft can no longer be found — closed perhaps by an earthquake — and the spring the Python coiled round has dried up. So the superceding of those oldest powers symbolises the changes forever going on spontaneously in the Earth itself.

All this was embodied in the rough grey outcrop like a disinterred skull, with its socketed features, its abrupt emergence from the dust, the green snaking of the creeper up its lower body. Although the other rocks in the circle were destroyed when the extremely expensive Temple of Apollo was built, this uncouth limb of the ground has been left in its place, still able to water wild plants with its run-off, while everything else on the site was laid out and masoned on geometrical patterns. It would be wonderful to see the cleft again, and the mist smoking above it. Their disappearance is the evidence of their original reality. They were themselves, not symbols — statues, ikons, regalia.

It was a relief to find at least one of the autochthonous powers still alive — the Castalian Spring, a kilometre back along the Livadia road, not far from the Sanctuary of Athena. Living, but only just. This was where the Pythia bathed and munched a laurel leaf before prophesying. For generations before that ritual was concocted, the well would have supplied water and confirmation of a life principle to the herdspeople. Now, at the roadside, water pours from a marble mouth. We refreshed our faces with it and drank from it. Nearby was a small pond lined with stone — it looked like a reconstruction of something very old. Behind was a wire-mesh fence, blocking entry to a gorge with soaring walls, its mouth filled with a copse. The cliffs were clad in the highest scaffolding I have seen apart from the semi-permanent rigging on some English cathedrals. More of it towered up the neighbouring crag immediately above the road from Livadia and, ultimately, Athens.

This was the cliff that twice fell on to invading Persian armies, at exactly the right moment. Clearly the Greek government is determined that this won't happen to the new invaders by coach, car and service bus. The Spring itself was overwhelmed by rockfall in the earthquake of 1873 and dug out again by Greek archaeologists. Now the gorge is having to be stitched together with steel bolts. Cement coloured to match the pinkish, most brittle faces of the crag is being poured down it to glue it together.

So we could not get to the wellspring itself — not unless we trespassed. As we drank chilled fruit juice at the café beside the Sanctuary of Athena, the barman seemed to suggest with a wink and a lowering of his voice that the fence was not impassable. We went back, stepped round a stanchion on the bank of a duct where the springwater had been diverted from its natural course and made to run into the marble fountain, and picked our way through the copse to the ancient source.

Dark green spires of juniper, or 'Italian cypress', matched the soaring verticals of the gorge. A headwall perhaps forty metres high looked formed to pour down cascades after heavy rain. The supply is unfailing. Even in this summer that had the Athenians gasping and complaining, a shallow rill spread over shelves of limestone. It was filmed with green. Flies buzzed and a fritillary opened and closed its wings as it tried to sip at the edge of the water. A deep cut led back towards the crag on the true left bank and here the water ran between the rock and an ancient barrier built of stone. A thread of water showed clear of scum, barely moving, and when I leaned closer I saw the tremors in it as it pulsed from beneath the mother-rock — the exact source of the legendary water. Above it, in a recess in the main cliff, a drum of limestone sat in shadow — the base of a statue of Gē, Mother-Earth.

It would have been marvellous to see how she was figured in stone — a non-personal shape, no doubt. Even the emptied plinth was striking, a last bone of the old Power, and as such it linked up for me with a crucial stone in the Delphi museum. This is a bulb of marble less than a metre high, which was the *omphalos*, the navel, the core of the fundamental cult. It was found in the south wall of the Temple of Apollo and was believed to be 'the point where the eagles of Zeus met at the centre of the known world'. On it (or the original of it) in the Oracular Chasm under the Temple sat the Pythia as she uttered her prophetic noises. Its top is flattened (to make the woman more comfortable?) and its sides are carved with a deep bas-relief of netting in braided wool, the strands between the knots so fat and grooved that they look like coffee beans.

The *omphalos* was 'traditionally the tomb of the hero incarnate in the serpent', the hero being the sacred king or cult leader who ceremonially killed his predecessor. A snake hatches from an egg and the marble *omphalos* looks more like an egg than a birth-knot. My guess is that the archetype of the *omphalos* was the most sacred cult-thing of the tribe, carried from place to place in a woven bag — much as, still earlier in prehistory, hunter-gatherers carried fire from place to place in a pot. Even now in western equatorial Africa, chimpanzee families carry their most precious thing, their nut-splitting stone anvil and hammer, from one part of the forest to another.

I had gone down under the Temple of Apollo through a low stone door, knowing that movements of the earth had long since destroyed the Oracular Chasm, still curious to get as near as possible to the root of the chthonic cult. Built passageways made a labyrinthine basement. At times it was pitch-dark, then daylight glimmered ahead and I emerged from a door further along the south wall of the Temple. The Shining Rocks towered above against sheer blue, the restored pillars stood up in their broken beauty, and the Sibyl's Rock cropped up a little way downhill — the undestroyed physique of the place itself.

This was what I wanted to find in Athens too, on the Acropolis. On our first visit there ten years before we had seen it more as the site of the West's most illustrious and classic culture. Socrates had walked in the arcade near the market-place, posing his questions. Euripides and Sophocles had had their plays performed in the Theatre of Dionysos below the southern cliff. Demosthenes had made his speeches and the citizens, those who had the franchise, had balloted on potsherds, some of which survive.

In the smog-filtered brownish sunlight, or floodlit at night, the long walls, files of pillars, and triangular pediments of the buildings on the summit of the great rock glow golden and symmetrical, floating above the city on invisible foundations — monument to the systems we know as Democracy and Philosophy. They look ideal — the realisation of a Platonic 'form' — and that is what they are: concepts fully articulated in people's minds before they were made actual by masons and labourers.

Reading that perfect guidebook, Stuart Rossiter's *Greece*, in order to make sense of the Peloponnese, Ithaca, and Athens, I had found intriguing sentences about the Acropolis before the Golden Age:

Natural springs have attracted man to the slopes of the Acropolis since Neolithic times (c. 5000 B.C.) . . . opposite the seventh N. column of the Parthenon and protected by a grating, is a rock-carved dedication to fruit-bearing Earth (Gē Karpophoros). Here stood a personification, rising apparently from the ground, of Earth, praying for rain to Zeus . . . The discovery here [on the north-west slope] of a 7C polychrome votive plaque portraying a Chthonic goddess flanked by snakes perhaps locates a *Sanctuary of the Semnai* in a nearby cleft. This accords with tradition, which places the Cave of the Furies beneath the N.E. brow of the hill. A spring here was locally credited with medicinal virtues in recent times . . . the precinct of the cave was a recognised sanctuary for murderers and fugitive slaves . . . conspirators were killed within it in abuse of the right of sanctuary. Persons acquitted by the court of the Areopagus were wont to sacrifice at the cave. Within the enclosure stood the tomb of Oedipus . . .

Snakes — the Furies — a healing spring — murderers — slaves — sacrifice — Oedipus: here was a cluster of deep-seated habits and beliefs, bound up integrally with the rock and its waters. This felt altogether different from the purified high culture of the textbooks. The realisation that the Acropolis had this underside was a crucial stimulus to the writing of this book.

We prowled round the rock at sunset, eager to find the outcroppings of those older ways before the guides lost patience and herded us all out — grizzled veteran couples, Japanese with Sony camcorders and Nikons, young Americans or Australians in trainers and cut-offs. Once you looked, the mother-rock thrust up everywhere, pitted round heads of it under the squared courses of curtain-walls, cliffs topped by parapets, pavements of naked limestone under your feet. On the western slope we climbed a flight of rock steps in the valley of a reef and sat on its ledged and knobbly summit with forty or fifty other tourists. The lights of the city sparkled orange in the broad brown basin of the twilight and the beams of a light show played on one façade after another round the Parthenon. This rugged grandstand was the Areopagus. Demosthenes was tried here. Five centuries later St Paul preached a sermon here on 'the Unknown God'. Was there ever such a site for a seat of government and trial? Here the aristocrats held their Senate; here people were tried for murder, treason, and desertion.

Round on the eastern scarp we walked up a stepped lane past bars and restaurants. Above us on our left a black iron fence guarded the famous buildings, running between the ancient wall round the plateau and the steepest cliffs of the rock itself. I climbed up to its parapet by a slithering slope of dust between bushes. A man was following his terrier along a trod. In an angle of the fence, below a fringe of preventive spikes, a young couple were throbbing silently together. Smells of beefburger and onion wafted strongly from the kitchen window of one of the small shabby houses a few metres below.

Above me in the face of the cliff a black mouth arched high as a sperm whale's jaw. The upper lip of the limestone gathered and curled over like a breaker seething to its fall. We know that 'tradition places the Cave of the Furies beneath the N.E. brow' not of this rock but of the Areopagus. It should have been here in this big, dark crater. It is hard to believe that so good a shelter was not a favourite resort of murderers with bloodshed on their consciences or of slaves trusting that piety would work more strongly than greed in their pursuing owners.

Like the wild land round Arthur's Seat in old Edinburgh, or Table Mountain in the time of the Dutch, this wooded, spring-fed, rocky massif was a zone of escape for people from the constraints of their society. It was unimproved, ragged, still half in nature yet exactly on the boundary with civilisation.

The terrific sculptures that have survived in cracked chunks embody the two: the blue-bearded monster Typhon, with triple human heads and bodies ending in a snake; a snake wound round a horse, bringing it to its knees, strangling it. In the century before the classic heyday, a Dionysian festival was set up and choruses of satyrs dressed in skins sang 'goat-songs' round the altar. A little way along from the Theatre of Dionysos on the southern slope, a hollow in the ground was either a pit where sacrificial blood was poured out in worship of the chthonic powers or the lair of the sacred snakes.

We used to be told that this place was 'the origin', or the cradle or the fountainhead, of pure Thought and Democracy. Looking round this great rock, with its symmetrical buildings balancing on their narrow rough-hewn pedestal, we can see that there was no such thing. Gradually the cults allowed human nature to count as much as nature. Gradually the leaders saw that, from time to time at least, they must let the rest of us choose and decide for ourselves.

PART SIX
Machu Picchu, Peru

---

24   'Los Tangibles Dioses Andinos'

Making for Machu Picchu in the Peruvian Andes was like going to the home of rock, or so it had been in my perception for the thirty years or so since I first found Pablo Neruda's 'The Heights of Machu Picchu'. We can read it now in its complete context as part of *Canto General*, a poem that feels to have the whole continent in it. Reading it is like traversing ranges, following river systems, looking for a place to live:

> And so I scaled the ladder of the earth
> amid the atrocious maze of lost jungles
> up to you, Machu Picchu.
> High citadel of terraced stones . . .
>
> Mother of stone, sea spray of the condors.
>
> Towering reef of the human dawn.
>
> Spade lost in the primal sand.
>
> This was the dwelling, this is the site:
> here the full kernels of corn rose
> and fell again like red hailstones.

Not that it is hard to reach now. When Hiram Bingham rediscovered it in 1911 with the help of a farmer called Melchor Arteaga, it was heavily overgrown, invisible from the nearest used track 600 metres below in the sinuous gorge of the Urubamba. A generation ago, when friends of mine went there, they still had to climb the ancient path from the railway station through jungle where Bingham's party had had to crawl on all fours. Now you can take the little bus up a dirt road with thirteen hairpins and no safety barrier, while the maintenance men hack down scrub with their machetes and throw the branches on to the pitted and muddied surface to help the tyres grip.

Every bend increased the exhilaration of height, of being buoyed up in a crystal atmosphere, and this had been with me since the plane touched down at Cuzco in a basin of brown mountains with the white teeth of snowy *cordilleras* looking clear and near to the south. In wholly alien country, among people who spoke the old Inca language, Qechua, rather than the language of the European invaders, I felt as physically at home as though I were surrounded by the Cairngorms.

My acquaintances in Cuzco, Victor and Peter, friends of my youngest son, who had worked here, said that I must also go to see Qenqo and Saqsahuayman. Of course I took their advice and stone worlds opened out. On a terrace of the mountain 400 metres above Cuzco was a broad corrugated shield of limestone, so familiar from Cumbria in its maze of clints grooved by grikes that I half expected to see the familiar hard-fern and herb-Robert, dwarfed ash, even violets and primroses, since October in Peru is the counterpart of April in England and hailshowers were duly dropping out of the skirts of the cumulus clouds. A few days later I was equally endeared by the granite at Machu Picchu, exactly the Aberdonian mixture of white quartz, black felspar and glassy mica.

There familiarity ended. Qenqo was once an Inca temple. In the centre of the outcrop, above a crevasse in the floor of a cave, a shelf had been cut square along one wall with a massive stub of rock left *in situ*, carved in the purest Inca style with several smooth upper surfaces at subtle angles to each other and angular shoulders. Seen in deep shadow, from three or four metres below in the crevasse, the expressionless gravity of the piece was the very face of an uncomprehended other culture. The Incas carved gnomons like that, and shrines, and the most sacred sun-stone or *inti-huatana*, which I would see at Machu Picchu. This stone in the inmost penetralium of Qenqo looked like an altar and may have been a focus for rites of divination and rites venerating the dead. An equally remarkable thing up above declared its purpose unmistakably. Near the northern rim of the outcrop a cup had been either found or carved in the rock. From it a gutter, jagged as a branch of lightning, ran downward to the brim of a deep grike with fluted sides. This was an offertory channel. The blood of sacrificed animals ran down it into the underworld.

234

This sounds 'barbarous', and as I looked at the zigzag gutter and its ending in a dark sump I was perceiving it as 'sinister'. Such rituals were civilised and turn out to have been integral to the farming practices of the Andean peoples. On the *altiplano* on the border between southern Peru and western Bolivia, the Aymara people still sacrifice a llama for the sake of the potato crop. The children plough a terrace to the rhythm of a flute and drum band, the ritual leaders embrace and kiss the animal with tears in their eyes, and say farewell to him for his journey to *uma pacha*, the highland shaped like a llama's head which the people see in the mountain ranges. The Elder prays:

> Small and large valleys, grant us abundant food. This we ask of you, Mother Earth, and we give you blood with all our heart. Today the children break the earth for potato planting, and as fine children we will work and we will break the earth.

Then the herdsman who owns the animal leads it to the west side of the field so that its body faces 'the place of origin and return', twists its head back 'to face the place of the sun's birth', and its throat is cut deeply. The heart is taken out, the blood is caught in a basin, and everyone fills little cups with it and sprays it over the ground in all directions while the heart is still beating.

This was taking place among poor hill farmers a few years ago and shows their totemic respect for their animals, and a not unthrifty use of them. Things could get lavish and wild in the metropolis, no doubt. At Saqsayhuaman, a few hundred metres from the carved outcrop at Qenqo, Manco Inca fought the last battle of his dynasty against the Pizarro brothers. One of the Spanish soldiers had seen the Inca consult an oracle at Saihuite, 190 kilometres down the road from Cuzco to the coast. A thick pole banded in gold was ornamented with 'two golden breasts the size of a woman's' and mantles fixed with gold pins. This idol, and rows of smaller ones, were 'bathed in blood' from sacrifices. 'The [Indians] said that the devil spoke to them from the large idol.'

Inside the monumental precinct of Saqsayhuaman today the energies of that potentate and his culture are still palpable in the stone lineaments of the place. My guide, José Quevedo, told me to hold the hem of his jacket while he led me through an unlit labyrinth below the ground, to emerge in an area of sacred reservoirs which has only just been excavated.

'Water is male in the Inca mind,' he said. 'The earth she is female.' He was vehement and full of what he knew, turning to look me full in the face as he spoke and pausing for me to show that I had understood.

'So the water, it comes to the earth like a man comes to a woman. And these walls' — he pointed to a newly excavated foundation — 'they have this shape' — he mimed their zigzag line with his hand — 'to be like the lightning.'

This was also his meaning for the western wall of the fortified temple with its cyclopean wall of forty-two recessed or jutting angles that make a lightning-plan on the ground. The salients it forms would have meant that assailants always had to expose one flank to the defenders' fire. José said nothing of this. His meaning for it was that the angles were puma's teeth, since Cuzco, the Inca capital, has the shape of a puma's body stretched along the valley with its head at Saqsayhuaman. The meanings fuse in one — the flashing-white line of teeth with their power to rend and crush, coming furiously out of the mountains.

I had seen a puma rock already without knowing it. The outcrop rearing from the prime point at Qenqo, with a low plinth built round it, had looked phallic in its readiness and aggressive dominance. In the Amerindian vision, from Mexico to Bolivia, that shape, squat on its haunches with a slant backbone and a thrusting rounded head, is the great cat, the shaman's *alter ego* and epitome of cosmic power, whether it is the Olmec jaguar from the southern tail of Mexico or the Inca puma of Peru and Bolivia. On islands in Lake Titicaca puma rocks were oriented on the sun: 'Nevertheless that rock, and not the sun, was the principal fetish,' wrote Bandelier, whose gorge we had explored near Albuquerque.

José was committed to these totemic meanings and wanted next to show me 'the eye of the puma'. This was the foundation of a round tower called Muyuc Marca at the high point of the temple. A circle of masoned stones is embedded in the ground with ducts leading into it from twelve points of the compass. The waterways are blocked, the tower has been razed, pillaged for building stone in the four centuries since the Spaniards sacked it. José had a beautiful explanation for it.

'The Inca filled the bottom of this tower with water, and the top of it was open, so that it reflected the sky at night. They could see all stars in the surface of the water, and this way they could tell the seasons.' He was reluctant to leave this place and when he saw that I had had time to take it in, he said with emphasis, 'Esoterical persons come here. They come to receive the energy. In this place. They can feel it here. There is an echo.'

Then he made me stand in the centre of the circle. What nonsense!

How could there be an echo on a flat hilltop? I said some words and heard each one a millisecond later with an enriched resonance.

We stood for a time on the rim of the rampart looking out over Cuzco and José identified streets and buildings. 'That is Conquista Street,' he said. 'The conquerors came in this way. From the west.' He named church after church with their handsome brown-tiled domes.

Finally I ventured to say, 'José — really I don't want to see the Cathedral. What I feel, in my heart, is that the Spaniards should not have been here at all.'

'They destroy everything,' he answered instantly. 'Buildings. Our culture. The minds of the people. Everything!'

We had spent two hours walking round Saqsayhuaman, sheltering from violent icy rain in the angles of the cyclopean walls, noticing the columnar phallus four metres high set into a corner and the twin rounds of breast on the stone beside it, where barren couples came to make themselves fertile. On the way out there was a consumer opportunity. Women in superb scarlet-and-mauve woollen capes and felt hats were selling knitwear and carding wool from the alpacas and llamas grazing nearby. A condor was tethered to a perch, rather tattered black wings half-spread in a crucified position, waiting to be photographed. I hated the sight and asked José, 'Does the condor have a meaning for you?'

'Yes,' he said. 'It is the people's heart, in the sky.'

In that case the people's heart has been brought low, and this is true. When the Pizarros recaptured the fort from Manco Inca's army in 1536, drove him into permanent exile in the jungle to the north-west, and installed Spanish rule for good, they slaughtered at least fifteen hundred men. Next day the condors came down in flocks to feast on the dead. To celebrate this great event, when the Spanish regime granted a coat of arms to Cuzco four years later it featured eight condors circling a tower.

As the sun set, his day's work finished, José pushed his peaked cap back from his forehead, put away his bundle of closely written notes and took me down through the city by flights of steps, past floodlit waterfalls and little stone sculptures of animals, into the craft quarter. Here we visited the workshop of a great maker of ceramics, recently dead, who had specialised in monstrous figures of women with elongated necks. The Virgin Mary was flounced and furbelowed like a seventeenth-century *grande dame*, with holes in her bodice to expose her glazed pot breasts and a white neck a good half metre long. My eye was caught by something less sophisticated — a tile quite crudely painted to represent a Calvary, with a black wooden cross pinned to it and a *brown* Jesus with long black hair and pieces of red material hanging down to represent the blood dropping from his pierced hands.

Had I been on my own, I would have been baffled. José explained that it was a copy in miniature of the *Senhor de los Temblores* in the Cathedral nearby. The Lord of Earthquakes. It seemed a marvellous way of taking the Christian cult from the conquerors and remaking it to satisfy a people who worshipped the actual powers of the mountains, the snows, the rivers, the rocks: what the exiled Inca in his jungle hide-out affirmed to be *los tangibles dioses Andinos*.

On my way to see the original Lord of Earthquakes I walked past rows of shrines, all unlit and gloomy behind closed gilt grilles. The doors of the shrine to the brown Jesus were open. About 150 people were worshipping, mostly women. Batteries of candles in gold sconces stood amongst flaring ranks of scarlet carnations and gladioli. Jesus was flanked by two grandees, female and male, in sumptuously embroidered black cloaks, standing in front of alcoves upholstered in crimson velvet. He himself was naked, emaciated, dark chocolate brown, with a crescent wound under his ribcage, face gaunt as a Modigliani, eyes profoundly shut, feet displayed straight downward, each bone in them a ridge, big toenails rimmed with blood, the three nails through hands and feet crusted in red so bright they looked like dahlias, the crown of thorns a glitter of gold filigree set on a tattered wig of black ringlets.

As I watched, the crowd started to sing. Their voices rose in solid unison — a mounting, almost catchy melody, buoyantly rhythmical as 'Guantanamera'. At the end of each verse one or two voices carolled out in clear vibrato above the rest. That was the end. The group dispersed and an elderly man began to fuss round the Lord of Earthquakes, snuffing some candles, replacing others, shifting vases, opening and closing little doors.

Nobody knows when or where the *Senhor de los Temblores* originated. When an earthquake began to shake Cuzco to pieces in 1660, he was carried in procession round the plaza and the quaking stopped. Pablo Meija of Calli in Colombia tells me that there is another swarthy Jesus in his country. An Indian found him near a river, dressed in a loincloth with Indian designs. When people crowded to see him, the priest decided he had been sent to confuse them and reintroduce pagan customs. A fire was made, the image was thrown on to it, and as it burned it became bigger, and darker, and was not consumed. Now it occupies its own basilica, in Buga.

José had said that the swarthiness of the Cuzco Jesus was caused by smoke over the years. It looks to me as though it was made that way. This Jesus is not an imported gewgaw from the Jesuit catalogue of church furniture. It is the embodiment of *les damnés de la terre* themselves, the wretched of *this* earth — condemned to invasion, massacre, and slavery (the Indian population fell from six million in 1500 to little more than one million by 1585) — to eviction, starvation, death by mudslide and earthquake. Now the tortured Indio hangs in the shrine among a plethora of blood and gold — the gold for which the *conquistadores* ravaged Tawantinsuyo (the Inca empire) and converted its last leader, Tupac Amaru, to Christianity immediately before beheading him in the plaza.

A few days later, as the train trundled through Izcucacha on the way to Machu Picchu, I saw a graffito on a mud-brick wall: 'TUPAC MARO VIVA' in thick black letters. Ever since his martyrdom the lost leader has had this half-life as an ikon of Indian liberation, especially in these areas of the harshest and poorest life. The railway had twisted west-north-west through the *pueblos jovenes* or 'young towns' of Cuzco — brand new mud-brick slums perched on collapsing terraces of earth, grooved out by gutters full of refuse and discoloured water.

At an altitude of 3,500 metres, just before sunrise, a white-haired farmer and his wife were stooping their way up the steepest field I have ever seen, a roof of black earth, and putting in plants by hand. In the gorge of Huaracondo, where the railtrack barely squeezed between mountain slope and river, the first blue smoke of the day was fuming through the thatched roofs of isolated farms.

This journey goes from the dry brown mountains of the *altiplano* through the Pampa de Anta, where the Inca armies defeated the Chanca people at the start of their empire-building, down into the cloud-forest. High above the mossy tapestry of the jungle, the spires and pyramids of the *cordillera* wore their snows like ermine. The country was all natural glamour and the human squalor of lives lived in the merest crevices of arable ground. This train, the tourist train, counted as luxurious in comparison with the crammed and battered standard train. We could buy excellent books from the attendant, infusions of coca, which he recommended for 'the altitude' with a knowing gleam in his eye as though he were pushing an illegal substance, and a faintly sour bottled drink called IncaCola.

The rolling stock looked to be on its last legs. By the time we had lost a thousand metres of height and dropped into the stony gorge of the Urubamba, something was amiss with its innards and an engineer kept opening a door at the end of the carriage, once with a coin and once with the end of a spoon. Then he brought old coffee tins full of water from the lavatory and poured it into the depths. The brakes were overheating, and the problem wasn't solved until we stopped at a rushing mountain stream near Ollantaytambo and the man scooped up bucketful after bucketful and threw it on to the cables between the carriages while families sat and watched from the doorsteps of their huts next to the track and the mothers combed lice from their children's hair. Beside the line, mile after mile,

> The torrential silver of the Urubamba
> . . . crystal and cold, pounded air,
> extracting assailed emeralds.

A few years before, it had taken the life of the nephew of my agent, Deborah Rogers. The bank broke and he slipped into the violent mint-green water and was never found. The ground here looked permanently temporary, a stramash of freshly scarred boulders. Above our heads the crags were covered with old sad beards of lichen a metre long and grey as fog. Crimson flower-tassels drooped from ledges where a little humus had been able to form. At times the air-cushion in front of the heavily breathing engine wafted aside butterflies as large as finches. Then we were running into the station at Aguas Calientes, a riverside village of perched homemade houses that looked as Bavaria or Switzerland must have done two centuries ago.

On its hog's-back between two mountains 600 metres above, Machu Picchu was almost invisible and you could understand that it might never have re-emerged from oblivion. That afternoon, as I walked through its streets between steep gable-ends and trapezoidal windows, the staircases, doorways, and walls were so perfectly in place, one massive smoothly-bevelled stone upon another, that it came alive again as a working town. The roofs had been thatched with dried grasses laid on timbers lashed to carved stone stalks protruding from blocks in the walls. The few that have been restored domesticate the place and knit it back into the coca-growing, poncho-weaving life of the surrounding highlands. You feel almost at home. Then, so far below that it looks more map than actuality, the darting green snake of the Urubamba glitters and the terrific balance and declivity of the site reasserts itself. Across the gulf the narrow triangular peaks climb like the gables, tall tents of jungle bound to the earth by stays forged from rock and feathered with leafage.

Above everything is Huaynapicchu, the slim mountain jutting from the north end of the saddle. I had been looking at it in the photographs for years: a tusk, round-shouldered on its left side, sheer on its right, matted with green and yellow tropical hair. It had always looked barely accessible, climbable only with equipment. It turned out that a staircase led right up it, part built, part hewn. So Machu Picchu was not doomed to be one more showpiece of antiquity, dropped in on, toured, left behind in the half-known. I could explore with my own feet the luxuriant surroundings, the actual terrain.

Huaynapicchu also promised relief from the busier tourist scene. Bus after bus was bringing people up the hairpins. The Inca Trail which twists along the mountain ridges was delivering gaggles of walkers in cut-offs and heavy sacks, many of them sounding all set for the big New Age experience. In front of the hotel one young woman was saying to another, 'Y'know, this place is *really* something! When I got in here, I felt, y'know, it was my kinda place. So I sent this postcard to my friend and I put just word on it, "Rainbow". And when I got up this morning — I saw a rainbow! *Wow!*'

I made for Huaynapicchu through the maze of streets and plazas, looking for forms that grew directly out of the rock. Between the centre and the south end, where the Inca Trail enters the town down Machu Picchu Mountain, the underlying granite breaks through the turf in a thicket of fangs and stumps. Perhaps these too would have been cleared, or used, if the place had lived for more than its brief century (mid-fifteenth to mid-sixteenth century).

Mostly the granite has been crafted into shapes which are austerely beautiful in the abstract, pregnant with meaning once their functions are known. A low tower called the Torreon rose straight out of a deeply undercut reef. The scalp of the rock, ringed by the only curved wall in the town, had been cut into shapes like three-dimensional doodles by some engineer of genius, brooding on ideas for spacecraft, dreaming of turtles and sharks. A straight edge in the centre was aligned through the nearest window on the point where the sun rises over the mountain on the June solstice, also on the rising-point of the Pleiades, which were (and still are) associated with weather forecasting and the fertility of crops.

You could not wish for a stronger example than these grey and silver planes of how humans situate themselves, pushing outward from the natural reflexes of the senses to an exact and intricate understanding of how the universe works, through sundials and clocks, maps and star-maps. The place opened out also into less rational linkages with the material world. The stone nipples at the upper corners of the windows have not yet been explained. A trapezoidal doorway opens into a void and its base is surrounded by granite block pierced by holes. Sacrificial fluids may have flowed out of them, or sacred snakes, or they may have been used to attach the *punchao*, the golden image of the sun at daybreak.

Working my way north along the western rim of the town, I reached the high point where the *inti-huatana* stands in its own plaza — a low square-cut pillar rising out of bedrock. *Huata* means a year. The same vocable, used as a verb, means to tie: 'Hence, *inti-huatana* is translated as "hitching-post of the sun" — like the great masts used to moor airships.' Nobody knows quite how the *inti-huatana* was used. Apparently it symbolised trust that the sun would not go on disappearing from our world with the shortening day but would come back in its fullness after the June solstice. Such stones were central to most important Inca sites. This one is the sole survivor, the Spaniards having smashed up all the others.

Its base is carved in the shape of a mountain, with ledges and slopes. Its top is a conning-tower, leaning on the west side, vertical on the east, very much like Huaynapicchu a few hundred metres due north. At the equinoxes the sun rises behind the highest summit of the Veronica range to the east and at the June solstice it sets behind the highest summit of the Pumasillo or Saqsarayoc range to the west. Such mountains were worshipped as embodiments of supreme powers, controllers of the waters, 'owners' of the potent products from the forest (coca leaves, cane alcohol, coffee, cacao) and also of the animals (pumas, bears, snakes, birds).

Whatever rites centred on the *inti-huatana*, it remains absolutely a focus — mountainness concentrated into a single angular form that still emanates a sort of contained power. Clearly the *conquistadores* knew them to be central to the way of life they were determined to root out and replace with their own extraction of metals, their own coinage, and their own god. As I spent my time in the plaza, nobody else was there except a black-headed kestrel with his streamlined forehead and his fierce fixed stare. He perched on the parapet unconcerned for several minutes, then took off, suddenly folded his wings, and plummeted into the gulf of the Urubamba.

My other special goal was the condor stone, somewhere in the warren of buildings on the lower east side. It could wait until I had been up Huaynapicchu, since I had no means of knowing how long the blue sky would last. The way to the mountain led past the Sacred Stone — a feeble name that hid a revelation. At one end of a little plaza, next to a thatched *masma* or three-sided hut, a straight-faced rock five metres long, four metres high, and one to two metres thick rose like a titanic shield on edge. It had been set up like one of the great liths at Stonehenge. The steep shoulders of it, rising to a peak, almost exactly matched the mountain skylines on either side, Yanantin to the east and Saqsarayoc to the west. It could have been found providentially; it could have been sculpted to the right shape in homage to the mountains. As you look at its profile, then miles beyond to the crests of the *cordillera*, then focus near again on the beautiful shield, you feel the invisible connections between one rock and another, between rocks and yourself, stretched through space like beams, transparent, everlasting, the co-ordinates of the universe.

To enter the mountain you sign a book at a little kiosk and the man in charge offers to sell you a Coke from the stack of bottles he has hauled here in a sack. Since the beginning of August 2,000 people had been here, 51 today, mostly before noon. I met the last of them coming down, chattering and bright-eyed with the elation of hours spent on this sublime crag. Or mountain. It is on the very cusp between rock and mountain; it *is* the cusp. To the left of the great tusk a smaller child or sibling of it climbs out of the Urubamba gorge. To the right Huaynapicchu is the culmination of a ridge structured almost vertically by six huge strakes of granite, the lie of them still enacting the tectonic buckling-up of the entire mass. The western face is a tangle of bushes, creepers, trees. The eastern is starred with bursts of yellow, as though swarming canaries hovered there permanently. They are succulents found only on the sheerest rockfaces, yellow as bananas or crimson as sea anemones. Down this face the gaze falls irresistibly river-ward in a falcon-stoop, on vertical lines redoubled by the black streaks of water-weep and pointed plaques of moss.

The air simmered gently, the way was shady. Under moist rock-walls wild begonias glowed pink among their glistening leafage. The steps were well made out of squared stones, with a few short sections up seams in the mother-rock. Slowly the summit was coming into focus as a hanging garden, elaborately terraced nearly to the highest point. On the north-western skyline a steeply angled gable-end was pierced by the clear blue oblong of a window. The staircase headed for a tunnel cut through the mountain, or you could climb round more tamely by flights of steps. Before choosing, I noticed stone steps dropping down the sheer east face, linking terraces each narrower than the one above. The steps were drifted thickly with leaves. Nobody came here to this forsaken garden which looked English until the focus widened to take in the glinting jade links of the Urubamba four hundred metres below.

Why did they build so crazily, forcing their craft out to the very edge of the air? Purely for the delectation of Pachacuti Yupanqi, we must suppose — the Inca potentate who commissioned Machu Picchu, or for his son Topa. Oh, the hubris of the élite who could order a garden for a mountain-top 2,700 metres above sea level, and tell a gardener to climb 300 metres to pick them an orchid, while not seeing through the brothers Pizarro when they came bringing gifts!

The steps ended in a little heap of split rocks — debris left here by the builders five centuries ago. I slithered through a slit in the mountain, making for a lanceolate 'window' where ferns and flower-heads made fretted silhouettes against blue sky. The floor tilted towards a sheer drop and I turned back, reclimbed the stairs, and walked up through the final tunnel to the summit. Below, the garden terraces were layered steeply downwards, roughly cleared, clad in rusting weeds. The highest point was a nest of grizzled boulders, shattered by lightning and weathering, unshaped by humans except for a blunt arrowhead two metres across, carved into a spur, pointing towards Salcantay (5271m.). Its permanent snowfields merged their pure whites with the cumulus clouds.

Rush-hour had more or less finished. A middle-aged couple with their teenage son arrived and asked me to take their photograph. Two tanned young Australian globe-trotters swigged cans of Pepsi and discussed where they had been last night and where they were bound for next. A plump Peruvian, sweating and breathing heavily, accepted a cup of papaya nectar and told me about his management studies for a Masters degree in Miami, then hurried back down to rejoin his wife. For the next two hours I perched at my ease, revolving with the sun.

Pairs of leopard-brown butterflies flirted and blew past. A black one perched on a glossy green leaf, sucking beads of sap. When it opened its wings, they were luminous sea-blue. A flower-pecker green as a mallard's head hovered in mid-air, then dropped down the cliff. My gaze swooped down and up the serrated slopes of forest, like a bird, or like a boat bucking over a green sea, and settled again and again on shining white Salcantay. At the root of its name is the Qechua word *salcca*, wild, uncivilised. It is the brother of Ausangate (6372m.), highest peak in the department of Cuzco; or else its twin summits, Urco and China, are a male and female couple.

These mountains are named first in the rituals practised hereabouts, and their permission is sought to make offerings to other mountains, for good weather, or fertile livestock, or for health and prosperity. The snows of Salcantay feed the rivers that water this region. The Milky

Way was seen as a celestial river 'actively involved in the earth's hydrological cycle', and the Southern Cross, seen from Huaynapicchu, is at its highest point in the sky on the morning of the December solstice, exactly above Salcantay. Annual pilgrimages are still made up the glaciers to increase the fertility of crops and herds. Was I worshipping the white peak as I looked up to it again and again? I had worshipped nothing since my Presbyterian boyhood fifty years before and I was certainly not hoping that anything would result from all this contemplation — nothing but the contentment that comes from being in a perfect place.

On the way down I noticed again that a path forked off the main one and disappeared into the jungle on the west flank of the mountain. It was well trodden and it had no signpost. It turned out to lead round to the Templo de la Luna, noted for its outstanding stonework. Stones are not rocks, in my definition, and I almost gave up on the Temple of the Moon. An apparently banal saying of Solzhenitsyn's, quoted to me last year in New Mexico by Donald Wesling, had fixed itself in my brain, 'Always go the extra mile,' and this actually moved me next day, after a night of drumming rain, to trek round to the *templo*, just in case.

At the gateway into Machu Picchu guides were waiting to be hired. One of them, a young woman with a stout peeled stick almost as tall as herself, had a warning for me.

'You want to go to Templo de la Luna? Path is very overgrown. And there are snakes . . . ' She brandished her stick to suggest a need for weaponry.

This morning I wanted to go at my own pace and think my own thoughts. Also I slightly resented the local system, which had left that one path nameless to try and worry us into hiring guides. I set off alone, taking care to pick out a strong stick from the slashed brushwood beside the path and whittle it smooth with my knife as I walked.

The air after the rain caressed the face and was fragrant with odours of asparagus and curry. When I picked up a fruit like a damson and squeezed it, green flesh like avocado oozed out. In this paradise extraordinary plants flourished. A miniature banana palm sprouting blood-red poniards whose stems looped down and up again like candelabra. Tree-trunks plumed all over with saprophytic ferns. Just out of sight through screens of leafage two birds, dark and hefty as capercaillie, blundered from tree to tree with a clatter of wings, never clear enough to be photographed. Occasionally from a clearing I could see out above the treetops to the opposite wall of the Urubamba valley. Clouds were condensing in the forest canopy, shrouding the shapely peaks of the Cerro San Miguel.

When the trees thinned after half an hour's gradual descent, the granite cropped out in a small cliff to my right and overhung in a broad-mouthed cave. Exquisitely jointed Inca walls were palisaded against the rockface deep inside, with the trapezoidal niches that were used for idols or mummies. If only the idols were still *in situ*, embodying the old civilisation of the place in their broad noses, their wide thick-lipped mouths, their staring eyeballs. As it was, I could feel almost at home in this glade of temperate sunlight, among bracken and white granite and clouded mountain-tops.

The shrines here would have been ornamented with silver and served by priestesses. The Inca himself represented the Sun. His wife, the Coya, represented the Moon, *Mama-qilla*, wife of the Sun and controller of the months. When the moon was eclipsed, a puma would be trying to swallow it — a fine vision of animal force very nearly prevailing over the more measured movements of the planets and their satellites. Crouching in the dusky penetralium of this temple with my back to its masonry, I could look out through the frame of the rock and see the blue and green world whelm up like a tide. Or a black and silver world as the Indians waited until the moon was shadowed, a copper mask covered its face, the forest darkened as though black smoke crept through it, and the whole moon-blanched scape wiped into invisibility as though death were destroying their senses.

Down the slope to the north the end of a wall showed unexpectedly through the undergrowth. From a terrace in front of it a dwindling path led down further still. Going the extra mile, I found another temple in a cave, its masonry much cruder, and an even more overgrown path beyond that again. The path tunnelled through dense bracken, seemed to peter out, then brought me on to a ledge in front of a cave with one word painted on the rock beside its mouth — 'FINAL'.

I had to stoop to get into this last low temple with its scrappily designed and masoned walling at the back. Turning to look out and keep in touch with the sun, I saw between wings of rock, as though in a viewfinder, the white apex of an outcrop, like a miniature Salcantay, in head-high bracken. Using my anti-snake stick, I thrashed down the bracken until the rock rose clear, an ice-floe tilting through the surface of a choppy green lake. Its shape was familiar, mounting from steep lower slopes to easier shoulders and a breasty peak — the shape of almost every mountain visible from here.

When I went outside and climbed it, at once I found it natural to perceive its little crests as the ridges of some classic mountain nearer home — the limestone Towers of Sella in the western Dolomites, the quartzite heaps and cones of Beinn Eighe in Wester Ross. Just four metres above the ground I was looking down great sweeps of slab into the hollows of corries as big as Lochnagar's, or Birkness Combe in Cumbria.

No other boulder-sized outcrop had ever given me these sensations, the droppings and risings and contoured massings of an entire hill. Then I noticed that the crests of this mini-mountain had been whitened and roughened. Long ago it had been worked, to shape and liken it to the real ranges all around. I looked up towards Cerro San Miguel to check the match. It couldn't be done — the cloud was still trailing its fleece along the skyline. I knew it was right, though. These *cordilleras* had become almost familiar. This mass of granite was a final sacred stone.

A human vision of mountain and rock had reached an acme here. Out of necessity, a complete stone culture evolved. Its most practical needs were met by terraces, ducts, walls, stairs, trails. Its morale was fulfilled in all those symbols and rites where rock was central. Throughout the Andes 'oral tradition speaks of the divinities as incarnating into rocks . . . *Pachamama*, Mother-Earth, is always toasted before any Andean drinks a beverage.' The *ayllus*, the hill peoples, 'claimed their descent from prominent landmarks'. So the Inca people (and very probably the Chanca whom they defeated, then governed) honoured this place, 'the very world which is the world of all of us'.

Such were the beliefs the Jesuits set themselves to destroy, in accordance with a manual published by Father Pablo di Arriaga in 1621, fifty years after the first *auto da fe* in Lima. Questions were to be put to the Indian communities: 'Whether you know of any person or persons, men or women, who have worshipped or adored *huacas*, hills or springs; or Sun, Moon, Pleiades, Morning Star, or Lightning.' People calling their children by a *huaca* name were to be given 'one hundred lashes through the streets' and must call them not Manco or Curi or Libiac 'but Diego instead'. The same penalty, plus a haircut, applied to drumming, dancing, and 'singing in their mother tongue', also to dancing the *ayrihua* with ears of corn fixed to a stick or playing drums made from guanaco skulls. All this to root out the worship of high hills and huge stones and the telling of fables meaning that 'they once were men who have been changed to stone'. To kill off ancestor worship, mummies were burnt or thrown into the river or the sea. In a last resistance the Indians transferred their veneration from the grave sites to the rivers — which, in any case, they believed to be the means whereby relics were 'returned to an original time and place'.

By what right were the European beliefs deemed superior to the Andean? By no right at all — by force of steel breastplates and helmets and muzzle-loading guns. At least, when they tracked down the last Inca to his hide-out deep in the labyrinth of the mountains, they failed to find Machu Picchu on its ridge, and its gables still rise in parallel with the edges of the mountains, and its *inti-huatana* is intact. So, when I found it, was the condor.

In spite of maps and site-plans, the maze was difficult. A seeming way was blocked by a doorless wall, or a crag, or an archaeologist's rope. I went up and down long stairways, parallel with grassy gullies in which scarlet gladioli blazed. I revisited several plazas several times. Then I found the right level and was looking down from a terrace into a sunken precinct in which caves like cellars lurked beneath slants of granite with walls full of trapezoidal niches built into their upper layers. On the floor an exposed facet of the bedrock had been found, or chiselled out, in the shape of a triangle, making a bird stylised as a single wing. The leading point was grooved round to give it the look of a bird's head tapering into its beak. Two brackets of paler stone had been embedded round the beak in a perfect image of the condor's distinctive white ruff.

What was it for? This precinct has been dubbed the Prison Group, and so the niches may have been tiny cells. They have also been seen as housing for royal mummy-parcels. When the experts disagree so widely, who can say? The stone bird itself looks like a shrine. The grooves that shape the head could be offertory channels, and the caverns closely resemble the shrines to the underworld and the dead at Qenqo. I do feel sure that the condor sculptor was inspired by the natural granite. Behind the bird-floor the rock fans up in a pair of giant wings, the left one (as you face the condor) upright, the right one aslant. They are at least five metres from attachment to point. Their surfaces are feathered black-on-white with algae and weathered into shallow dimples and cracks, so that each spread seems to swither with life and the muscles that work the flight feathers are flexing like those of hen harriers as they exchange food in mid-air.

If the wings are romantic in their naturalness, the totem on the floor is classical in the practised way it stylises nature for cultic purposes. It is so perfectly as it left the sculptor's hands that under your eye the prime of the place is visible again. Condors spread their wings above the triangular mountains. Springwater from Machu Picchu mountain runs down the aqueduct and channel into terraces brimming with coca and maize. The Inca's gardener climbs the stone steps up Huaynapicchu to cut sheaves of arum lilies and gladioli. The idols and mummies are sitting in their niches. Beyond the horseshoe bend of the Urubamba the mists tear apart and rise off San Miguel, laying bare a skyline whose shoulders and peaks exactly echo the white rock in front of the last temple.

The 'Sphinx', Great Gable, Wasdale, Cumbria

PART SEVEN
The British Isles

---

25   Land's End to the Rock of Ages

There is an entrance through rock at either end of Britain, or an exit: Durdle Door off the Dorset coast, Dore Holm off Shetland Mainland. 'Durdle' comes from the word 'through', 'Door' means what it says, and 'Dorset' has behind it the Cornish word 'dorn', fist. The limestone arch with one strut in the English Channel west of Lulworth Cove is therefore the 'door through to the land of fist-play people'. This ancient ruggedness reaches you again as you stand on the highest point of the arch, balancing on its two-metre width, feeling a strum in your legs as the drop gets to you, and gaze inland as an early incomer from Gaul or Iberia might have done. After landing on the shingle beach, how to get past those tall chalk cliffs, siblings of the Seven Sisters further along towards Dover? Will there be timber enough? is anyone living already among those furzy coverts?

The valley still looks much as it must have done before it was settled, a sinuous hanging combe folding this way and that, hiding its inland depths. Now it is named — Scratchy Bottom, between Swyre Head and Hambury Tout. The headland to the west, also arched through, is The Bat's Head. The rocks nearby are The Bull, The Cow, The Calf, The Blind Cow. The narrow, almost landlocked sea between here and Lulworth Cove is Man o' War Bay. So many are efforts by the generations to bring wild rock inside the pale by naming it.

Here is the exact rim of England, also a boundary between earth and air, between stability and jeopardy. A notice on the path warns you to 'KEEP CLEAR OF THE CLIFFS'. Some day this span will fall, leaving a white stack like one of The Needles fifty kilometres to the east, off the

Isle of Wight. As you approach Durdle Door westward from its parent headland, its crest seen end-on looks like the slimmest horn sticking up. The strata forming it have been tilted from landward through 85° or so. In the crevices along the grain of the bedding-plane, now pointing skyward, various evidence has fetched up. The incisor of a rabbit — was the head brought here for eating by a black-backed gull? A bird bone, like a clay pipe stem barely a millimetre in calibre; two pebbles the size of peas, one split open, showing the mushroom colour of the flint; a stone the size and thickness of a gold watch, chalky white tinged with bruise-blue, like a piece of dawn sky solidified — how did they get here? Could the blue stone be part of the original rock, smoothed by the wind's grinding, not the surf?

Some dry fine humus has gathered, just enough for the rooting of sea-kale. Its leaves are as savoury to chew as any brassica from the garden. I can see thornless, yellow-flowered sow thistle, and a dwarf umbellifer, its splayed spokes shaking in the dawn wind. We've been here since six, to catch the orient light on the landward faces of the arch. We had better leave soon, on the haul westward to Land's End, Sennen, Zennor. First, another attempt to swim through the Door. It's no distance. Only the heaving of the swell thwarted me last time. Today the sea is barely breaking on the jambs. Andy and I swim boldly out from the pebble beach — less boldly as we feel the current's thrusting. At the base of the upright the waves are easily a metre from trough to crest and my body is thrown about like flotsam. We retreat simultaneously from just below the arch, Andy doggy-paddling for dear life lying on his back while I struggle along from one lacerating reef to another on the inside of the headland.

Later that day Anne reminds me of the sequence in *Far From the Madding Crowd* in which Troy, a few yards east of here, 'well-nigh exhausted himself in attempts to get back to the mouth of the cove, in his weakness swimming several inches deeper than was his wont, keeping up his breathing entirely by his nostrils, turning upon his back a dozen times over, swimming *en papillon* . . . '

As Troy was rowed to safety by the sailors who picked him up, he saw across 'the wide watery levels' to the south-west 'a long riband of shade upon the horizon' where the shore-line curved round: Portland Bill, the high-bridged, sharply tapering beak of limestone, barely joined to the mainland at the eastern end of the great shingle rampart which is the storm-beach of Chesil. The Isle of Portland — but everyone calls the whole peninsula by the name of its tip, The Bill — stood out for me by virtue of a small black-and-white photo I had long treasured. Was it a postcard or a cutting from the art columns of a paper? It showed an arrangement of flat stones piled in the shape of a straw hat worn by a farmer transplanting rice in the paddies of south-east Asia. It seemed to be divided by a path which changed direction at the point of the hat. There was nothing to give it scale. It was all abstract elegance, grounded and naturalised in its limestone home by having come together out of rough pieces found nearby.

So we set out to find 'Portland Sculpture Park'. At the Tourist Information Office a mile away little could be learnt. 'It's along there on the cliff — I think — quite near the road,' said Deborah (or Jennifer, or Lucy). Luckily a man on a ladder painting the hotel wall was able to point out the right path. He warned us that the place had been vandalised. It had not — not at all.

The root of the Bill is all one disused quarry. After generations of blowing up and cutting out the fine-grained oolite, or freestone, to form great public buildings such as St Paul's, the Ashmolean Museum in Oxford, and town halls and mansions across the ocean in colonial Virginia, low cliffs remain, and palisades three times the height of a man where unused blocks have been built up to keep the loose soil in place. We wandered through canyons, one of them bridged by a wall with a key-stoned archway through it, built in 1834 according to a tablet, massive as the gateway into a Corsican citadel. Presently there was nothing but spoil-heaps that looked like scree, hewn faces that looked like crags, thickets of bramble, ragwort, ivy, winding the workings back into nature. Sculpture park? Had anybody really worked here since the quarrymen and convicts knocked off for the last time?

As we looked about at a loss, a white hand hailed us. It had been ground out on a natural rockface and glared as flour-white against the weathered drab as a piece cast out of a mole-heap among the limestone dales of Yorkshire. Amid so much dereliction it said to us 'I am here' with the startling human presence of hands I had seen stencilled in blown red ochre on the wall of the cave called El Castillo at Puente-viesgo in Cantabria, or the crowd of hands on the overhang of the rock shelter at Nanguluwur in Northern Australia. It was as though a vanished species, a dodo, an archaeopteryx, a Neanderthal man or woman, had perched for a second and would flicker out of sight again as soon as we turned our backs.

Now that we were alerted, it kept happening. An ibex with back-curved horn framing its ear had been cut into a boulder with a power-wheel. Nearby was a chough's head, reminding us of this rare crow's cliff-dwelling habit — we had seen it only near Port Erin on the Isle of

Man — and a hawk hovering and a horse with a jagged mane. Then, in a shallow dell, I saw the straw hat itself. It was five metres across. The path through it was floored with yellow flints. It asked our feet to step through it, which we did, and on and on into a wonderland where rock had been made to blossom into flowers, jokes, ikons, visionary moments, petroglyphs, dreams in stone. On a face a fossil mollusc a metre broad had been carved in bas relief to remind us that this stone itself was a mass of tiny animals petrified. In one outcrop at Portland you can find white spirals that are fossil moulds of a slender snail called *Aptyxiella*. A sculpted flower like a rayed sun looked out above the real yellow flowers of ragwort. In a quarried face a human figure with arms close to the body dived steeply downward, turning the pit of shadows and ivy into a pool. Elsewhere a fluted form had been cut in the rock, a cactus-like trunk ending in a capital with curlicues. Stretching away from its foot lay a broken trunk which matched its 'mould' in the rockface. The moment of its fall is so exactly mimicked that it seems to have only just happened.

A few yards away in a little gorge all this playfulness gathers into a master-work. On a 5-metre face bounded below and above by the joints of bedding-planes, a human figure steps upward from a natural plinth, twice life-size, naked. Its right side is taut with effort from heel through calf-thigh-buttock-ribcage-armpit. The other side is a stylised vertical which bends to disappear over the lip, as if the figure is climbing the rock from which it is formed. The right side makes the edge of a deep crack, perfect for jamming. I wedged my hand into it, painfully, securely, pulled up, and lodged my left foot on the hip, then on the rounded cranium. My right foot I stuck deep into the crack and twisted for better grip. Finally I pulled up some more and mantelshelfed on to the ledge above. Looking back down, I could see that the hand had been chiselled out of the top in deep relief — which is exactly what you feel as you complete a climb.

Portland Bill is the southern tip of the 'great swathe of the Jurassic which runs north-westwards to the Cotswolds and thence northwards to divide the Midlands from East Anglia', ending on the coast of Yorkshire. The age of the rock, a little under two hundred million years, makes it a chronicle of animal prehistory, from clams to squids to ichthyosaurs. When history set in, it was a bleak one. Forts were mined deeply into the hillside against invasion by Napoleon's forces. Convicts toiled at blasting and stone-breaking on the bare, wind-scathed ridge. Now the place has metamorphosed yet again and surprised us with a transformation scene in which rock can play at being other things as well as itself.

West-south-west of Portland, 220 kilometres as the gull flies, juts the end of England, West Penwith, from which you can sometimes see those very last stepping-stones, the rockbound little paradises of the Scillies. The granite welled up in six great bodies, making what are now Dartmoor, Bodmin Moor, the uplands north of St Austell and south of the tin country at Redruth and Cambourne, Cornwall's fist of an extremity west of Penzance, and (split into little bergs) the Scillies. What could be more a piece of earth's mineral depths than these plutonic rocks, which crystallised deep inside the planet's crust and were exposed by erosion aeons later? Now they are so part of our own world that I feel at home among them as though I had been born there, and in some ways more at ease than in north-east Scotland. Aberdeen granite is colourless — unsmiling even in fair weather. Its fine-crystalled surfaces, whether planed by ice or diamond saw, offer little hospitality to human toes and fingers. The Cornish granite is rich in pale-gold crystals and embedded whitish bonelets large as macaroni. Salt fogs and spindrift have tooled it rough. The result is crag whose surface is, in the phrase coined for millstone grit by the climber Johnny Dawes, 'all one hold'.

So we have played and played among these Cornish buttresses and towers. My son Neil and I clambered unroped down to the base of the cliff at Sennen called Pedn-men-du, between pinnacles wind-sculpted into lizard heads, bananas, shawled women and cowled men, then squeezed and swung upward to the rim on the climb called Demo while bursting waves wetted the unwinding coils of rope. A few miles away at Boleigh, 'the Field of Blood', where the Saxon Athelstan finally defeated the Cornish, Anne and I lay awake all night while the Force-12 gale that was sinking thirty yachts in the Fastnet Race shook our tent as an orca shakes a seal between its teeth and moon-shadows writhed on the cloth beside our faces. Next morning we stood at the top of Pedn-men-du, 25 metres above sea level, watching the turmoil of the sea until we were forced to run for it. Spray from a monstrous wave volleyed out of the air above us and fell like cloudburst rain, foaming back down off Demo route and wiping out the seamark of Longships Lighthouse, three kilometres offshore on Carn Bras.

From Land's End the island of Lundy seems remote, 150 kilometres north-north-west, lying off Devon in the blue mouth of the Bristol Channel. The rock is the same, part of the granite batholith that surfaces as tors on Dartmoor or the boulder near Bodmin called the

Cheesewring. Further north again, at St David's Head on the tip of Wales, another plutonic rock, the gabbro, is shaped and textured to create the same atmosphere — purified by the westerlies, ribbed with buttresses, lit by bell-heather and tormentil, shaken at the foundation by the ocean swell, laid bare to the whole wide world by the opening out of the Atlantic. As the pioneering climber Pete Biven put it, 'beyond the crest of the ridge ... "nothing but sea, America, and night".' It feels impossible to face anything but west when you are here and almost physically baneful to turn back east, towards the fume and dusk of Europe.

If you must go by the helicopter from Scilly to Penzance, at least it flies you past the entire granite display and you can contemplate it as a gannet might. Here is the furthest west climb in England, Capillary Cracks, where you have to jam your hands into the split in the very nose of the land's end, like a quarryman stinging the rock with his chisel to make it break as he wants. Here is Pordenack Point — to me it means climbing Zeke's Route in the mid-winter trance between gales. Mild sunlight is diffused through cauls of moisture and everything looks newmade, unawakened, the world on the second day, with a firmament dividing the waters, an evening and a morning and little else. Here is Carn Les Boel, where Anne and I still have a date with Pinnacle Traverse, a dragon's-back peninsula first climbed by George Mallory, who died on Everest (and whose grandson has made tremendous routes on the Blouberg), and Geoffrey Winthrop Young, who had a leg blown off in the Great War and still went up mountains.

Now Chair Ladder cliff flows past below the coastguard station, properly called Tol-Pedn-Penwith, looking out over the surf on the Runnel Stone fifteen kilometres to the Wolf Rock and the thin black finger of its lighthouse. The keepers used to blench when the light was reflected through the highest window by spume bursting thirty metres up from the sea, filling the room with lightning-glare. Finally comes Lamorna, the artists' valley between Boleigh and the sea, where the granite resurges after the greenstone intrusion at Tater-du. Here I found an immaculate crack on the face of a huge bevelled boulder, climbed it, and named it Flying Enterprise because a lifebelt from that famous wreck is in the pub nearby and because I jumped off from four metres before I finally got up it and walked about for an hour or two with the balls of my feet buzzing.

And if the helicopter were to bank north-east and fly up the coast towards Cape Cornwall and St Ives? Here lies Bosigran's tall headland, where Anne and I were still on Ledge Climb, another of Mallory's, after the sun had set and made the last hard moves as Longships began to throw its brilliant javelins into the dusk. Here too is Wicca Pillar, where the granite starts its long dive under the Bristol Channel. There is still enough granite to have made the great rough stones round the edges of the oldest fields in England: above the road, towards Zennor, where the painter Patrick Heron has fought to stop the RAF vandalising the moors; below the road, near Tregerthen, where Lawrence and Frieda, Katherine Mansfield and Middleton Murry had their epic rows and conversations before the government's paranoia closed in on them and drove the Lawrences out of England for good.

Then the greenstone prevails, forming a gigantic corner on the south side of Gurnard's Head, making you downclimb to wave-wetted levels before you start up a right-angle, climbing a soaring line to a notch where I and my son Neil and my stepson Rob surfaced one after another as though we were being reborn.

Every hour, every thing in West Penwith seems to be cut so that it flashes and each experience becomes precious. Lundy brings this to even more intense focus because it is one small wedge of granite in mid-sea. The west side is all cliff, a bulwark, covered (like West Penwith) with Stilton-coloured whiskers of lichen, the faces of the Great Cheese Giant. The east coast, called the Sidelands, is a soft world of humus under groves of feral rhododendron. Cinnamon kestrels steady in the updraught above the broad sunned ledges of a seal nursery. Seals are the peaceable companions of the south-west coasts (and of the north-west, off Eriskay). They are our best mates. One followed us for over an hour along the North Cornwall Coastal Path until at Whitesand Bay it went down into the sea at the same time as the sun. Another swam beside me right across the bay called Ward's Landing, on the east side of Lundy, and didn't even take fright when I held on to the orange float of a crab pot and sang to her (or him) the 'Garton Mother's Lullaby' —

> Eval from the grey rock comes
> To wrap the world in thrall . . .

Lundy is dangerous. The map of wrecks has no more room for names round the jagged line of its shores. Montague Buttress is called after a brand new battleship wrecked there in 1906. The steel hawsers used to retrieve the guns and other valuables still loll down the cliff. When I tied on to one to bring up my climbing partners from down below, the thrumming (in a Force-10 gale) unsettled me, as though the planet was shaking in its orbit. At the north end I found myself, alone, hand-jamming up a very steep route called Eveninawl, on a granite gendarme called The Constable, and realised that, if I fell, I would bounce off the grass slope into an inlet thirty metres deep.

For a week one autumn we lived in the Old Light, a tapering hollow bone of granite, beaten by gales that make you run madly or stop you dead, and blow the skeletons of rats like leaves across the courtyard. The lighthouse was decommissioned because hill fog shrouded it when it was most needed. Now it is beautifully refurbished for self-catering, and I'm sure that the green heaps of poison round the rat-holes in the skirting boards have gone. On the high point nearby, more than a hundred metres above sea level, an elegant windmill revolves its arms with that look of a benign Titan signalling to his friends on another island — on Burgar Hill in Orkney, perhaps. The wind is rarely at rest. During one Indian summer the sea temperature rose to 59°F and for the first and last time in my life swimming in British waters was not an ordeal. We roosted in the lee of the island, in the brown wooden fisherman's house called Hanmer's, above the landing place where there is no slipway and you have to jump ashore when the outboard hits the shingle. The sea was roughened only when the tidal currents passing round either coast met and tangled, as they do at Corrievreckan off Jura in the Inner Hebrides. The balm of September gave Lundy the feel of a big, gentle mammal:

> Basting in light and oxygen,
> Sated on glowing krill, the greatest whale
> Becomes an island, folding into itself
> The opposing poles, the female and the male.
> The blowhole rounds, the oily eyelid rises,
> Each softlipped orifice becomes a well
> And feeds its essence to the flowers and grasses.
> Still headed northward with its bony brow,
> While the twin tides seethe past in overfalls
> It holds the same position under the Plough.

Follow this whale and you are steering up the Celtic Sea between Wales and Ireland — the right place for me, since the south-eastern half of England, to one side of a line from Bristol to Flamborough Head, can never keep me happy for long. It does its best but it is just too like the bed of the North Sea lightly clad in silt and humus. The geological map makes the sad case plain. This terrain is layers of clays and limestones, sands and shales and mudstones. Formless stuffs on the whole, and so raw — some of it, from the coast of East Anglia round to

London and the Thames valley, a mere sixty-five million years old. No chance there of mountains like couched lions lifting their heads to look time in the eye, or red scarps permanently stained with sunburn.

The southern limestone has its moments, especially in the gorge north of Cheddar where it towers so high that only a small channel of sky is visible. Here I feel no longer in England but somewhere on the Continent, in the Vercors west of Grenoble, perhaps. You want to lean back, stare upwards, and climb it with your eyes. If you did, a car would knock you down, or you would stand on someone's foot. Tourism has sucked this tremendous piece of nature out of the real world and turned it into a theme park. All it needs is plastic dinosaurs. You could escape, up one of the skyscraping vertical routes, Sceptre or Coronation Street — no you couldn't, climbing is forbidden in the summer months in case you dislodge a stone and brain a taxpayer.

You could go further, drive round to Bristol and climb in Avon Gorge, on the more or less natural crag that supports the north end of Brunel's suspension bridge. Downstream the huge sweep of slabs and hammered-looking walls were reft with crowbar and gunpowder to produce ballast for merchant ships in the heyday of Bristol's trade with America. Here you can find yourself monkeying happily from one quarryman's iron stake to another, or so we thought until it was put out of bounds in the early 1990s to be stabilised for the safety of the road below. And the Cheddar cliffs were closed for a month in the winter of 1993–4 so that workmen could abseil down and prise off rock that had become precarious.

To think that the hymn whose first phrase has become a by-word for rock as everlasting security — 'Rock of Ages' — was written a few miles from Cheddar across the western end of the Mendips. A local vicar, the Reverend Augustus Toplady, had his vision while he was sheltering from a storm in August 1775. His refuge was a cleft in a strange slant limestone crag beside the road running down the flank of the hills south of Blagdon. Perhaps it was as drenching then as when we went to explore it. Files of school students were embroiled in Outdoor Pursuits — trudging along in waterproof gear and helmets with head-lamps towards a pothole entrance, abseiling off an ash tree with many a cry of '*Sir!* Can't *do* this, *sir!*'

The crag wasn't vastly impressive, or high or continuous, and must impress even less the bus parties who come for a meal at the nearby restaurant with its sign showing the cleric looking staggered under a beetling cliff. They are then driven past the Rock of Ages while the driver talks at them through a microphone. You can feel Toplady's awe a little more nearly by scrambling round to the top by a path of slithering brownish clay, then clambering down through stumps and pockets of limestone to peer between writhen ash tree branches into the slit below. Or you can climb up the cleft from the valley floor, then turn to face outwards and wedge yourself with back and foot between the walls. Now you are in the hand of nature, if not of God. You feel like an animal at bay, all eyes for what may come at you from the woods above the terraced crag on the far side.

Toplady's own thoughts were mixed, as we can feel if we get past that ringing first phrase which has become proverbial:

> Rock of ages, cleft for me,
> Let me hide myself in thee;
> Let the water and the blood,
> From thy riven side which flowed,
> Be of sin the double cure,
> Cleanse me from its guilt and power.

I had never sung this hymn in my Presbyterian boyhood and had long taken its gist for granted. Discussing it one night in Aberdeen with my cousin, Annie Craig, a churchgoer, we began to see how alloyed the vision is. The rock in Christian vision was always strength itself — Mary Cameron's 'Great Rock in the weary land', the psalmist's 'The Lord is my rock, and my fortress, and my deliverer'. For people who hid in the rocks from the press-gang or the evicting bailiff — whose great-grandchildren had told me these stories on Barra and South Uist — those Bible verses rang utterly true. The Rock was whole, it was the strongest conceivable refuge.

For Toplady it was split, it was not God but the crucified Jesus, wounded by the centurion's spear. The godhead has become personal and mortal, like his flock — who then want to bathe in the plasma and serum flowing out of him. The morbid lusciousness of the emotion, with its tinge of the erotic-masochistic: this is the fevered mind-set of the Evangelical, craving to be 'washed in the blood of the Lamb'. If you read the framed manuscript letter of Toplady's a few miles down the hill in Blagdon Church, you can see how liable he was to treat his least dizzy spell as a revelation of God's power — and of his mercy, because he got better, didn't he? Everything can be both a judgement and a blessing. Such is the supple logic of the true believer.

26   Heading North

Only the Rock of Ages could have turned me aside from the northbound track into the dank enclosure of this particular neuk in Somerset. Wales across the water was drawing me now by the salience of its headlands, the little Cornwall of St David's Head, the array of sea-cliffs at Pembroke. Here with a student friend called Branton I climbed deep into an inlet a few yards from his house at Manorbier and brachiated across to the bottom of a shaft. We finally squeezed out head first into the sunlight like foetuses. We called the route Boca del Madre, Mother's Mouth, but never bothered to record it or claim it for the guidebook.

Water pours down Welsh rock when I am there or glazes it with ice. As I climbed Outside Edge on the Great Slab of Cwm Silin one fine March day, the amphitheatre was echoing with the light clatter of ice-plates parting from the rock. At Castell Helen, below Holyhead Mountain on Anglesey, Terry Gifford and I swung freely up Lighthouse Arete while the rest of Wales smoked and streamed with rainfall, then barely escaped off the next route, Blanco, by traversing precariously over unknown rock while fat snakes of water wriggled down the cliff towards us.

The rains seemed to have become permanent on the shortest day of 1984 when I embarked on A Dream of White Horses, on the quartzite face of Holyhead Mountain, with its originator, Ed Drummond. A Force-8 gale was blowing threads of waterfall sideways and upwards in such a chaos of wetness that I seemed to pass out of my own head and swither in mid-air like a kite in a squall. The rational part of me shrank but held firm, just, as I kept clawing crabwise from hold to hold. At the far end of the rope on the 50-metre traverse, the unshakable strength of the maestro gave me courage. For hours his salmon-pink balaclava glowed through the gusting moisture like a Belisha beacon — not actually going on-and-off, it is true, but an empowering symbol of safety all the same.

The mental helicopter is swinging me now from St David's up the long bight of Cardigan Bay, round Lleyn past Anglesey and Snowdonia, east along the North Wales coast past the grizzled limestone heads of the Great Orme and the Little Orme. Here we stayed in a converted lighthouse and looked out of the window into air crossed by seagulls, some seventy metres above the waves. Back into England

Penrhyn Slate Quarries, North Wales

again the imaginary flight skims past the red sandstone scarp of Helsby with its green patina, following the Mersey estuary. These heads and limbs and arching sides of Britain are so familiar, it is as though the British Isles had to be like this. The Lleyn peninsula bowing like a branch heavy with fruit, Cumbria's lumpy knuckle, the angular shoulder of Aberdeenshire, Skye's triple-tongued north end — what other form could our coasts have taken?

It is their form only at this time. There is a magical book called *Witches' Point*, containing photographs by Paul van Vlissingen of one shingle spit on Loch Maree seen over thirteen months. It is always there, always changing. If you bound the photos into one of those little books that can be flipped quickly to simulate the frames of a film, the nebs of the spit would dodge and point this way and that, like a dog's nose twitching or a cormorant surfacing and shaking the water from its head. By the same token, if you took satellite photos of the British Isles at intervals of fifty or a hundred thousand years, slender features like Spurn Head would not only twitch, they would grow out from the land, then disappear again. Bigger changes would happen under your eyes. If global warming became extreme and the Polar icecaps melted, you would see peninsulas separate into islands. The rias or drowned valleys of Argyll and Kerry would finger still deeper into the highlands.

Ennerdale, Wasdale, Windermere would become fjords. If the world's water shrank, by cooling and the concentration of the oceans as ice at the Poles, you would see Lincolnshire and East Anglia swell out towards the Netherlands and the great offshore rocks, Rockall and Hirta, Ailsa Craig and the Bass Rock, would rise up greater still.

By such standards, or those of the American canyons, the rocks that are magnets for me in the north of England are dwarfs. In themselves they are powerful totems, quirky characters. I am drawn to them, but never quite at ease with them. I am thinking of the Old Man of Mow at the south-west limit of the millstone grit — a Cubist sculpture fifteen metres high left in a quarryhole above Biddulph on the boundary of Cheshire and Staffordshire — and other prows or pillars left sprouting from the ground by the quarrymen out of respect for the stuff of their livelihood, impressive as the Yggdrasil trunks of Cappadokia and Cantabria. Tegness Pinnacle, Rivelin Needle, and Wharncliffe Prow are members of an international family stretching at least as far as El Medol in Cataluna north of Tarragona where a jointed finger stands made of the golden stone from which the Romans built the nearby city and the aqueduct. I'm thinking of Higgar Tor, alone on the moor east of Hathersage near Sheffield, a leaning heavyweight veteran, determined not to fall, which even a hardbitten climbing guide allows to be 'both a notable landmark and a crag of remarkably distilled technical difficulty'. In the cold of an autumn day soon after sunrise, the lean and bulge of this tower repulsed me with an obduracy which

The author leaps from Wharncliffe Prow

almost made me think that flesh and rock were insurmountably at odds with each other.

These rocks are refugees from another epoch. They stand about in corners of our society with expressions on their faces that we make out with difficulty. In woodland north of Leeds lurks Adel Crag, Henry Moore's first inspiration. North-east of Otley, Almscliffe is stranded on its hill above Wharfedale like the Ark on Ararat. And near the north end of this series, the vertebrae of England's gritstone spine, Brimham Moor above Nidderdale is home to whole families of stone trolls and deformed birds, and a dancing bear, and squat wrestlers sidling up to each other, outstaring each other from the single eyes in their fore-heads — rocks so biomorphic that people in past centuries honoured them in their own way by supposing they had been conjured there by Druids.

Prehistoric rivers created them. They stand on our skylines like things reared up and not what they are — the remains of thick beds of material reduced at last to these grotesque stumps by millennia of erosion. The commonest rock in Britain is carboniferous limestone, laid down at perhaps two-thousandths of a millimetre per year in shallow seas — 'sapphire blue when there were reflections from white lime sands forming shoals in lagoons'. The end of this clear, tropical ocean was signalled when a delta of shingle, gravel and sand began to build up over its bed.

The red and brown highlands that went to its making must have been much smaller than the Uncompahgre Uplift which erosion ground down to make the sandstones of Utah, New Mexico and Arizona. Thirty metres is high for a gritstone crag, compared with the two hundred or more of the American canyons. Millstone grit is strong, its sandgrains cemented together by quartz. It is tough and also porous, making it ideal for millstones, since the surfaces of the two querns grinding on each other do not overheat. The quarry at Mow Cop sent grindstones as far afield as Oxfordshire at least as early as the fifteenth century. When the French Wars ended in 1815, millstones imported from France undercut the English price and our craft and trade was snuffed out. To this day half-finished stones lie about in the bracken and heather below Froggatt Edge near Sheffield like planet-missiles scrapped after some Titanic war of the worlds.

The origin of limestone was calm, tropical, glamorous; gritstone was spawned in conditions altogether more turbulent. It is the latter that strikes me as beautiful now. The limestone terrain is bone-grey and grass-green summer and winter. The pasture is a homogeneous shroud draped over the chins and hips and feet of all those submarine corpses. A few flower colours scintillate here and there — pink primroses and yellow globe-flowers, for example. By and large it is a monotone of green, kept short by sheep who make a population as dull and unvarying as the grassland itself.

Where limestone is pallid and pasty-smooth, gritstone is as nutty as whole-grain bread. Its flora is vivid; the flourish of it ripples in the wind and changes seasonally. Russet of withered heather ignites to purple in July. Bracken unwinds its croziers through the peat until it fills up deep and green and choppy as the incoming tide under a breeze. Silver birches sport their wine-red branches in winter and swaying lattices of leafage in the balmier times when the rock dries out and is fit to climb.

I never set eyes on limestone till I had grown up. In Scotland, north of the rift valley whose edge runs from Stonehaven to Garelochhead, the bony stuff is a rarity. The patch of it at Rassal near Loch Kishorn in Wester Ross nourishes a shrill green of verdure and a grey of ash tree bark that look exotic in contrast with the gingerbreads, clarets, and bottle-greens of the peat-moss and heather, Torridonian sandstone and Scots pine that surround it.

Near Durness on the north coast of Sutherland, at the far end of the limestone series that starts at Rassal, the rock round the monstrous hole of Smoo Cave has a cheesy, structureless make-up in contrast with the monumental schists and gneisses that build the mountains of that county. Even the soil of the limestone country lacks structure, or fibre. It runs to fine mud compared with the textured peats and grainy sands of the lands where granite and gritstone are the foundation. Prejudice, prejudice — how would I survive if I had to live on the black soil of the Donbass wheatlands, or the sticky, uniform gumbo of the Alberta prairie? As it is, in a whimsical way I am fantasising a sort of Scotland down south when I travel across the Pennines from my home in Cumbria and feel gladdened by the weave of the Yorkshire moors, with their coarse-crystalled rocks and wiry heathers, like tweed compared with silk or granary bread with Suncurst or Mother's Shame.

At Brimham the whole bestiary of rocks is so lively that people are quickened into play, mimicking the liths or responding to them as to partners in a dance. Craning round corners. Bobbing up, then down again behind noses and knees and brows that bulge from the mass. Putting heads through holes. Striding gaps two, five, or fifteen metres above the ground. Sidling through clefts by drawing in the ribcage and turning the head to one side. A nicely-edited film made any day at

Brimham would look like a cross between the Goons' *Running, Jumping and Standing-still Film* and *Monsieur Hulot's Holiday*.

The last time I was there, I found myself clambering up into a chamber in the side of a pillar and crouching, facing out, to feel the womb-like enclosure of it. A couple with a two-year-old boy came past. The little lad stared, then turned to his Mum and Dad, pleading to be lifted up when I got down. It would have been perfectly safe, and there were delicious peep-holes to look through. Certainly not — the family in its spruce blue and grey rainwear walked firmly on, the child's hand clutched. I almost offered to lift him up. Then I held back, deferring to the parents. Should I have risked flouting them, for the sake of the boy's getting some inkling of how we can be at home in the rocks? His spirit was as visibly rebuffed as a snail's eye-stem recoiling from a hard rough surface.

Thousands pass through Brimham every week. Cared for by the National Trust, it is unscathed and keeps its own purity of rock and heather, birch scrub amd peaty pathways, unspoiled by either fences or foul litter. Twenty kilometres south, Adel Crag is nearly as disfigured as a strong, hard thing could be. Nature battered it to start with. The narrow sandstone reef seems to have collapsed as the ground eroded round it, giving it its lasting look of a tanker or dreadnought run aground, its back broken, its bow rearing in a last appeal. Now it has been chiselled and cut into, hammered, daubed, aerosolled. 'KICK Rony,' it says on the bow in virulent blue spray-paint, and 'Damy [squiggle] HERE.' Some time last century 'W. RAINE' was no less brutal when he cut his name on the sloping fore-deck, for all his fine square lettering with serifs.

Each time we go there, more harm has been done. The biggest oak nearby holds sandstone chunks between its roots in a clench that will never relax until the tree falls. Now fires have been kindled against it, charring it deeply, maybe by the same people who have hammered off flanges of rock, disclosing the brick-rose sunset colours of the unweathered stone. All this is normal. I hadn't expected to find, when I climbed on to the top, a swastika daubed in oil-based white paint that looks as if it will last for quite some time.

Henry Moore and his student friends came here to 'picnic and draw and play around. It was an exciting place for me, Adel woods.' Innocent days, before Fascism, and before some Council meddler renamed the rock 'Alwoodley', in the teeth of local usage and out of some notice-boarding impulse that has done nothing to conserve this piece of nature. The rock abides, just, and now the gist of it will last for centuries, millennia even, in Moore's remakings of it, mostly in bronze. I wish he had made some of them in one of the native stones he favoured as a young man, for example the brown Hornton stone from Oxfordshire. Its fossil fragments and veins of iron ore run round the thighs and knees of his 1929 'Reclining Figure' like contours on a map. They 'enabled him to express the idea of figure sculpture as landscape'.

Still, bronze will do. His 'Adel' pieces are palpably single bodies separated — offspring of his whole reclining figures over many years. The Adel memories helped him to float the dual pieces free of each other. Now they lie, or stand, like small giants and waters have risen round them, turning their knees and busts into islands. Scholars find originals for them in pieces by Arp and Giacometti, or a drawing of Picasso's. To me those works look like bits and pieces loosely assembled. Moore's are integral, tendons and bones implicit in the spaces between them, which are dales and corries between hills. 'Knees and breasts are mountains,' he once said. Now the 1959–60 'Two Piece Reclining Figure' which for him especially recalled Adel stands (in one of its casts) on a plinth held up by boulders, the limbs of it looking out and stretching to the woods and open hills of Hertfordshire. They are aboriginal — inhabitants who have survived the ageing that has wrinkled their skins, or bluffs which have survived the erosion that gullied their slopes.

He took from Adel, and from Brimham. Memories of forty or fifty years worked through his brain and came out through arms and hands into these recreated things. Now his images can go back into nature. When we walk round Adel Crag, or climb it, like divers exploring a wreck in the green undersea light filtered through the oak canopy, the blocky superstructure of the west end and the tilted bow of the east turn into Moore's torso and genital limb. On a far larger scale, when we look at the great couchant mountains (Sleeping Ute on the New Mexico border, Burringurrah in Western Australia, Penyghent above Ribblesdale, Liathach or An Teallach in Wester Ross), we can see them not as lions but as reclining humans, tranquil in the knowledge that they are going to stay put for the next few million years.

★

Two tall cliffs stand up as waymarks at the sides of the route north and west from Yorkshire. Malham Cove, flanking the route from York via Harrogate into Westmorland. Whitbarrow Scar, to the seaward side of the road from Lancashire to Cumberland.

If you approach Malhamdale over the hills from Settle, you are twisting through weird terrain. On the far side of rusty bogs lie green back dales from whose sides black mouths gape — caves in the maze of shattered scarps where you might imagine Afghan tribesmen with Tower muskets taking potshots at the redcoats. Looking north from Scosthrop Moor, you wonder when Malham Cove will surface. It appears suddenly, always startling in its stature, as though a haggard spook had drawn itself up to full height among the green pastures. So an iceberg must strike the sight of people on shipboard in Arctic or Antarctic fogs. The sheer fronting fall of the hundred-metre central cliff will always daunt me, adding to my struggles to adapt my natural grip and stretch, my ingrained notions of how rock should be, to this Dr Who-type substance. Its cracks wriggling unpredictably, its surfaces smooth and uncrystalled when you crave friction, give it the feel not of a natural mineral but of a monster carcase cast in cement.

So I tend to fail here. Or I walk about, staring up at what are clearly unclimbable overhangs, until the little human traces show — drilled holes lined with metal where protection bolts have been placed, bleached tape loops fidgeting in the updraught. Failing here, on an August evening, was as marvellous as many a success. When I couldn't follow my youngest son up a route called Carnage Left-hand — put up by Robin Barley, who had named the elegant Hourglass in the Magaliesberg kloof — I asked him to lower me off. So down I twirled, a spider on its thread, the cirque of the crag revolving back and forth around me and the birds circling, nearly in reach, martins and swallows, criss-crossing the air, high on a glut of flies. The air was simmering with birds, yellow as pollen in the westering sunlight, and throbbing with the first notes of a brown owl tuning up in the tall ash trees downstream. I could have hovered happily for hours, exhausting the poor lad's patience. Reluctantly I gripped the tips of the branches growing out of the cave at half height, played myself in until I could downclimb the tree, set up an abseil, and walk backwards down the cliff to boring old *terra firma*.

Malham Cove has made me unwilling to call those neat fleet dark-blue birds 'house' martins. They nested in crags long before houses were invented, or humans evolved. Here at Malham you can see them dart straight at the rockface, then disappear into the cups of mud that cling all over the wall. Or did. Now that every ten feet of rock is threaded by a route, the birds are dwindling. On another day, as we walked along the terrace ten metres above the point where the river that once cascaded down the cove now creeps out below its threshold, little crusts of mud pattered down on to us. We looked up. At fifty metres an arrowy silhouette was looping outwards from the cove, slicing inwards again, vanishing into the rock — a kestrel, hunting. What can it have looked like to the sitting birds and their second or third brood of the year?

> A war-mask staring in,
> Shuttering out the green light,
> Mouthing and stabbing,
> Dagger-tongue reddening.
>
> Delicate skin explodes,
> Feathers stick to the wall.
> Desperate cries whinny
> Too high to register.
>
> Fox-hot, the kestrel
> Expands into daylight,
> Flushed with bird-wine,
> Plumage simmering cinnamon,
>
> Balances on a dying ash
> Portentous as an owl,
> Hoods its mesmeric eye
> And strops its butcher's hook
>
> While the confused chorus
> Shrinks into the wings,
> Bereaved parents preen
> And the swallows leave.

And all this will have left the martin population virtually intact, when compared with the ravaging of us humans at our play.

If you stand in the beck, facing downstream, and lean backwards, you can see the rim of the cove at the bottom of your vision. The slopes on either side join on to it to compose a huge circular frame, a border of grass and leaves and stone surrounding the blue pond of the sky — the blue eye of the sky with the crag at its base as the orbital ridge and the leafage as its lashes. Then Malham is a derelict giant, spreadeagled across Yorkshire where he fell 300 million years ago, one arm reaching towards Gordale, shoulder-blades laid bare between here and the tarn, a fist clenched at Attermire. The Cove is his brain-pan, the vault of his thoughts. Sunk in hibernation, he dreamed birds. In his final delirium, 296 million years later, he dreamed people.

★

Most mornings I look north-westward from our village, hoping to see the long white face of Whitbarrow staring full into the rising sun, and most mornings I see it. It is said that George Fox, the heroic Quaker, harried by magistrates, constables, and thugs in the 1650s, saw the blaze of ice-white rock above the estuary at the head of Morecambe Bay and took it as a sign that his god was smiling on him. He certainly read rocks in that way. He chose to hold a meeting at the slanting crag now called Fox's Pulpit, on Firbank Fell above Sedbergh, because 'the word of the Lord came to me I must go and set down on the rock in the mountain even as Christ had done before'.

Whitbarrow is a sign to us too. When we can see it distinctly from here, it means that the soft days of the west have turned more bracing — in summer at the start of an anticyclone, in winter likewise or between pulses of storm when the wrack tears. Then we can see through to the scraper-board graining of the snow-filled gullies on Dow Crag or to Whitbarrow's blanched towers.

The cliff is the north-western culmination of the carboniferous limestone, or looks like it. In reality it thrusts on further, through Shap, where it nourished excellent grassland for the medieval community at the Abbey, then hooks round west and south to end at the point of Cumbria, just north of the massive red sandstone timbering of St Bee's Head.

The precipice called White Scar (in the northern sense of 'cliff') is the south end of a long berg separating the dales of the Winster and the Gilpin. In early summer they whiten with hawthorn and damson blossom. Between these lengths of garden-comeliness all is declivity and resistance. Try to outflank it on the west and you stagger up scree barely at the angle of rest. A little further and you're bridging up the dank limestone jambs of Pioneers' Cave, greased by oozings from the aboriginal hazel, ash, and hawthorn woods above, before clawing out through thigh-deep leaf-mould in a place best left to wrens and foxes. The east side is gentler. Coverts grow in the troughs of humus between the waves of limestone. Where the mouths of the badger setts funnel down into the dark, you can put your head and shoulders into one opening after another and smell nothing but cold earth. Then your face is met by the faintest musky warmth, almost a body odour, and you know that a family is at home down there.

On the face of the scar nobody is at home, not even climbers, who call it 'Indian country' and 'utopia for the masochist'. It is not the highest crag, just wholly formidable due to its lack of natural cracks or breaks and the flayed slopes at its quarried foot. The tallest prow is now called Space Buttress. The jackdaws manoeuvring in mid-air at the summit look as small as tadpoles. It is never easy to estimate the height of a cliff. At the foot of the biggest and sheerest I have seen, El Capitan in Yosemite, a pine on the rim looked like the merest shrub. When voices called from up there, exchanging climbing instructions, in a Scots accent as it happened, and I managed to pick the climbers out, they were black specks on the naked thousand-metre steep. White Scar is a twentieth of that height. Standing up at the southern verge of the Lake District National Park, it is a harbinger of the 100-and 150-metre heights to come — the East and Central Buttresses of Scafell, Esk Buttress, Eagle Crag in Birkness Combe above Buttermere, and Pillar Rock in Ennerdale.

One June day we approached Pillar from the north-west, digging our booted feet into the barely stable scree like labourers planting fence posts. The air in the belt of forest immediately below had felt like webs of humidity clinging to the nose and mouth. The dense bristle of the unthinned spruce, the salad juiciness of the broad-leafed trees established in the 1930s to redeem the wrong of cloaking the Lake District's sacred terrain in industrial forest, the temperature in the high seventies Fahrenheit — all this was melding to give Pillar Rock in the sky above us a look of monstrous tropical architecture, niched and stepped and buttressed, corroded and overgrown, like Angkor Wat in Thailand or the Mayan pyramids in Yucatan and Chiapas.

My son Neil and I had been here before, to climb the North and South-west routes, on a classic day of breezy sunlight that seemed the atmosphere of his late boyhood. Three years later, the sky was curiously blind, a thick white, and the fells between here and Wasdale, Red Pike and High Stile and High Crag, were pale-blue flats without feature or relief.

After sidling up the hanging galleries of Grooved Wall above Walker's Gully, we moved round to climb Ximenes, a line found twenty-five years before as a short-cut to the looming trio of Goth, The Hun, and Attila on the west face of Low Man. I chose to lead the first, overhanging crack, possibly because Neil, now seventeen and striding beyond me in strength and skill, had better cope with the 'difficult crack' on pitch 2. The jams were excellent, closing on to the backs and palms of my hands like the jaws of a monkey-wrench. Twenty metres up on the belay ledge, still high on a burst of adrenalin, I looked about me to savour the barely accessible grandeurs we had dared to enter. From the uppermost profile of Pillar a shaggy grey limb was growing rapidly outward. It dropped and curled under on itself, like a raptor's claw.

'There's a really weird cloud up here,' I called down. 'Looks like a bit of a storm coming up.'

Beside me on the rock small spots were appearing, darkening and enlarging as though the flanks and limbs of the crag were turning into a leopard's coat beneath my eyes. As soon as Neil reached me we decided to retreat, with hardly a moment's discussion. The sky was unruly now. In three or four minutes dark shapes with dragon-toothed edges had appeared all over the livid glare of it, fretted crests and manes, wisps wreathing like smoke above a bonfire. By the time we had packed our gear into our sacks, every rock was glistening and slippery. We were soaked through and still warm. The water sluicing on to us out of the sky felt not adverse like British rain but close to blood-heat. I had felt that just once before, in the monsoon rains of Sri Lanka. We took off as many clothes as possible and plunged down the fellside in an ecstasy of sweat and rainfall, running like waterfalls, like becks, like the showers teeming between clouds and treetops.

Long after the sun had set and on past midnight, we watched from the back door of the farmstead at Gillerthwaite as Pillar and its parent mountain behind it came leaping into sight, black tusk on a black brow, silhouetted against the flaring yellowed whites of the sky. Above them, far huger and higher than the mountain, the torsoes and heads of the cumulo-nimbus glowed suddenly neon in the discharges of the lightning.

Even in ordinary weather Pillar and the head of Ennerdale is beautifully wild. Access is by foot only. The Forestry Commission gate is usually locked, so only determined walkers make it into what feels like a Canadian backwood. Stands of conifer line a river-bed filled with tossing rapids and boulders scoured white by spate. The peace of it is more Highland than England. Once Pillar was a climbers' Mecca, described in a guidebook of 1825 as 'unclimbable', then climbed by a shepherd, alone, the following year, and almost at once by three more shepherds. A further 119 parties got up it during the next fifty years.

The sheer upstanding singleness of what they called 'the Pillar Stone' roused people to go and leave their mark there. They wrote their names, and sometimes 'God Save the Queen', on pieces of paper stored in a ginger beer bottle on the summit. When this disappeared after an ascent by 'two navvies' in 1876, it was replaced first by a slate, then by a double tin box where climbers left their cards — they were mostly gentlemen, with some ladies from the 1870s onwards. The box

Longships
Promontory,
Land's End,
Cornwall

Two Climbers,
Portland
Sculpture Park,
Dorset

Brimham Rocks,
Yorkshire

Adel Crag,
Yorkshire

Napes Needle, Cumbria

Left, Macartney's Cave,
Northumberland

Below, Old Man of Mow,
Staffordshire

Right, Bowden Doors,
Northumberland

Below right, Warkworth
Hermitage, Northumberland

Right, The
Woman Stone,
Ben Avon,
Aberdeenshire

Far right, The
Old Man of
Hoy, Orkney

Below,
Hole o'Row,
Orkney
Mainland

Ern Stack,
Yell,
Shetland

Below,
Dore Holm,
Shetland
Mainland

blew away in the early years of this century and scattered its genteel contents over the stony slopes. Now fashion has changed. English climbers prefer rock facing anything other than north and at altitudes below 800 metres. Of all great Cumbrian rocks Pillar is the one where you are most likely to find yourself alone. It is a true pillar: the girdle route round it traverses through 270° and it is the longest rock-climb in England. When Bill Peascod and I spent nine hours on it in 1983, we were by ourselves for the entire prime summer's day.

The peacefulness of upper Ennerdale is man-made. Really it is an emptiness. Gillerthwaite appears as an unenclosed cattle farm in a document of 1334. Cairns between the 250- and 300-metre contours on the fellsides show where fields were made in the pre-Roman Iron Age. The steadings, for example the barn above the shippon entered by a ramp, show relics of Norse building styles. In a push to raise home-grown timber after the U-boat blockade during the Great War had nearly starved us out, the Forestry Commission bought Ennerdale above the lake in 1927 and covered it with larch and spruce. Proper human society, based here on farming, came to an end.

What it means in such a place was put classically by Wordsworth in a letter he wrote to the radical politician Charles James Fox in 1801 about the value of people 'who daily labour on their own little properties':

> Their little tract of land serves as a kind of permanent rallying point for their domestic feelings, as a tablet upon which they are written which makes them objects of memory in a thousand instances when they would otherwise be forgotten. It is a fountain fitted to the nature of social man from which supplies of affection, as pure as his heart was intended for, are daily drawn. This class of men is rapidly disappearing.

One of his two chief cases was Ennerdale, in which he set his poem 'The Brothers', written eleven months before. As in most of his best stories ('Michael', 'The Ruined Cottage'), the independent small farmers (who would be called crofters in Scotland and peasants anywhere else) are under threat. Old Walter Ewbank has inherited his 'few green fields' along with 'other burthens than the crop it bore'. When he dies, the place is sold along with their sheep which 'had clothed the Ewbanks for a thousand years'.

His sons have been inseparable. Now the elder, Leonard, leaves Cumberland to try to make a living at sea. For twenty years he is dogged by visions of 'waterfalls, and inland sounds / Of caves and trees,' by 'forms of sheep that grazed / On verdant hills — with dwell-ings among trees, / And shepherds clad in the same country grey / Which he himself had worn'. Meanwhile his soulmate, James, lodges with this or that family in the dale. He becomes dreamy and tends to sleepwalk, and, while out shepherding dozes on the summit of Pillar, 'a vast building made of many crags that rises like a column from the vale'. Hours later, when he has not returned home, neighbours go up and search the fells and find him dead at the foot of the crag, his shepherd's crook still caught on the rockface where 'for years / It hung; and mouldered there'.

James Ewbank would have found his way up Pillar by the Old West Route, a scrambling spiral, not quite a path. A quarter of a century later those first shepherd climbers, John Atkinson, J. Colebank, W. Tyson, and J. Braithwaite, followed this route unscathed, inaugurating a new use for Ennerdale — tourism. Pillar is certainly dangerous. Bill Peascod, a miner from Workington, writes in his autobiography that his climbing was never again as carefree after hearing, at the top of Walker's Gully, 'a strange flapping noise, like a flock of pigeons leaving a roof ridge'; later they found a solo climber broken and dead near the foot of Grooved Wall.

Wordsworth was using the threatening stature of the great rock to embody the precarious foothold of a whole country class, the farmers on the highland margins. I felt I was seeing the faint footprints of their kind when I heard tell of two other brothers, on the island of Mull. In the house where she was born, at the end of a five-mile track along the shore of Loch Scridain, Chrissie MacGillivray, aged 94, told me how two of her brothers had gone to make their living in Patagonia before the Great War and she 'never heard from them again'.

Napes Needle, piercing the screes of Great Gable above Wasdale Head, is the fine point of Cumbria, the merest leaf or blade to Pillar's massive column. It asks to be fingered or grasped so that we can follow with our bodies its exquisite line through space. Why did I take so long to climb it? Gymnastic British climbing began here, on 27 June or 30 June 1886, when an Oxford athlete called W.P. Haskett Smith climbed it alone. I walked past it dozens of times, after starting to climb in the Lakes in 1974, until in the summer of 1991 I suddenly climbed it twice. I think I had been backing off from its too great fame. On postcards and as badge and emblem of the Fell & Rock Climbing Club, it is so visible and known that it no longer seems part of nature. Others have felt like this. Bill Peascod had a disrespectful name for it, Naples Nood-les, and Peter Greenwood, boldest and most agile pioneer on Cumbrian crags in the early 'fifties, pretended one evening in the bar of the Old Dungeon Ghyll in Langdale that he was going to blow up the Needle with dynamite — purely to wind up the Fell & Rockers, you understand.

In itself it is superb, surrounded by air, the antithesis of air — visible, tangible, enduring — slender enough to remind us that rock is anything but 'eternal'. As you climb up the last five-metre arrow-head which balances on the twenty-metre shaft, no longer integral with it, it is faintly unsettling to remember that on the crag of Kern Knotts a few hundred metres along the slope, a climb first done in 1928 suddenly became far more difficult when a mass of stone was rolled away from its mouth in 1985 by an earth-tremor whose epicentre was at Carlisle. Almost unbelievably, the name of the route was Sepulchre. Perhaps it was the same tremor that shook off the crucial blade from a climb on Bow Fell called Sword of Damocles and a similar fang from a climb in Swindale called Sostenuto.

For so famous a rock the Needle is self-effacing. It merges with the verticals of the Napes Ridges between the scree chutes called Great and Little Hell Gate. I have been asked by walkers, 'Where is it, then?' They sounded cross or incredulous, as though they'd expected signposts and name-plates. Any of the ridges knifing southward out of Gable's mass could have issued in a needle. Probably they all do at one or another moment in geological time. At least one other long varnished needle hereabouts is still remembered. It was called Wilson's Horse, on Illgill Head at the far side of Wastwater. When it collapsed into the lake in 1800 or so, it sent out such a tide that a wave twenty feet high broke on the shingle beach at Wasdale Head.

As you toil about in the unstable gullies below the Napes, there looks to be nothing salient, just phalanxes of big flakes, half-embedded, half-shattered, many with fresh scars of rockfall. Then, between mountain and air-space, a notch cuts down deep into an imposing ridge. Its end soars, not yet mined away by water, frost and wind — the Needle, beautiful not only in its slim height but in the pattern of diamonds and half-diamonds, each three metres from point to point, which deep cracks have made in the western face of the shaft. These determine your stretches and strides as you work upwards to the shoulder beneath the final arrow-head. Once they were choked with rubble and tussocks, making it hard for Haskett Smith and those who followed. By now generations of climbers have gutted them clean and the difficulties are concentrated into the arrow-head.

Two joints cut across it. How simple, then, to use them as rungs of a ladder. I step up, making for an angular niche directly above the sheer east face and then I — then I . . . This isn't simple at all. The floor of the niche is just too high for me to get palms on to it, weight above palms, and mantelshelf securely up. Something out of sight on the right would help — I grope . . . it's bloody smooth . . . what do I *do*? Reader, I used my knee — the worst thing to do, because knees bruise easily, kneecaps can be dislocated.

A few weeks later — all confidence by now — I made a little jump or shrug upwards, pressed down on my palms, reached fluently leftward for joint number two, pulled with my fingertips and monkeyed happily on to the last short steep slab. It is so easy to climb well the second time.

I had made difficult moves many hundreds of times and they had often demanded more of me in strength, agility and nerve. For some reason no previous crux had given me so clear a realisation of what climbing is. We take for granted the solid ground on which we live. As we climb, this assumption is undermined. The more we ascend into the zone of difficulty, the less does our world seem mainly solid and the more thin air takes over as the norm. So living is made to seem provisional, equipoise, temporary, and we jeopardise our status as land-based animals.

This thought seemed to come into sight, transparent and structured as a crystal, as I stood on the little rug-size platform of the Needle's top. Before Haskett Smith, without rope or companion, tried the climb, he threw stones up from below. When one of them stayed put, he knew the top would be flat and fit to rest on before he attempted the frightening lowering of himself back down, arms braced, waiting for the toes to lodge on the two-inch rim which is the only hold above the joint. Before he left the top, he trapped his handkerchief under the stone — his flag of celebration, his proof of what he had done.

Both times I was there the summer wind was shaking me. It was still the best place in England for those minutes. With Wasdale Head laid out three kilometres away and seven hundred metres below. I had gazed down on the farm at Burnthwaite among girthy sycamores, the gables of the Victorian hotel, the little church like a cottage in its graveyard black with yews — elements of community bedded into a mesh of single old trees and small irregular fields, their walls built from the river shingle that had been ground out and off-loaded by these crags, then re-expressed as human culture.

The Devonian rock that curls round the Solway like the head of a shepherd's crook makes a stone — especially the Old Red Sandstone —

that looks warm and lit even on days of grim overcast. It was used in the houses of Brampton in Cumbria or Annan in Dumfriesshire. It towers above the secret beaches of the Eden between Lazonby and Armathwaite. In mid-winter unmelting grains of a light snowfall are sprinkled like salt on a brown mulch of oak leaves. At midday a lemony sun wins through and warms us enough to climb with our jerseys off.

A staircase of rocks green as marzipan and roots like bared tendons leads down to the main beach. The Eden swims past, full and silent. At the edge of the main cliff with its grotesque scoops, we swing out over the water and up into the woods via beaks of sandstone and limbs of oaks twisted by their efforts to stay rooted in the barely stable loam. The route's name, Kingfisher, almost persuades me that I've seen the sapphire glints of one skimming upstream. It is certainly dipper and heron country. The best we can be is squirrels, at home among these looping roots and branches, or otters slithering along the river's margin, half in half out of the water.

The river is almost never low enough here to give dry access to a unique fastness. If you pick the right oak from which to abseil, you can work your way down to a little beach of coarse brown grains, smoothed by floods. A face looks out at you from the sandstone, larger than human, terracotta and naked as a flowerpot, with grooves to represent a drooping moustache and pecked dots to represent eyebrows. It is in no convention, not Olympian, not heroic, not grotesque, neither goblin nor god and too baldly mask-like to be quite a man. It is simply what the fairly soft and brittle rock made possible for the more or less skilled chisel of the Eden Valley craftsman. 'Make faces,' said the squire — William Mounsey perhaps, who also liked to commission ornaments for the village houses downstream — and here is what he made.

Other heads stare at you from the rough natural rock nearby. A pair, almost like a two-headed cherub puffing out wind in the corner of a seventeenth-century map. A single one whose situation below a draining of earthy moisture has let lichens blotch his features, making them dark and ill. I say 'his'. What gender have we here, if any? The moustache is unmistakable. The other faces are sexless. They are not Narcissus, son of a blue Nymph and a River-god, nor are they Naiads, from their palace deep under the river Peneios in the Vale of Tempe. They do not look like relatives of the goddess Coventina, thirty-five kilometres away along the Roman Wall at Chesters, whose forearm grows into a water-lily stem, or the water-nymphs from the same site whose skirts curve into folds like solution channels grooved down sandstone or limestone. These Armathwaite faces are just their own quaint selves.

The Classical possibilities are not irrelevant. Great trouble has been taken to chisel a text on a plain slab nearby. It ends with the line ἀριστος μεν ὑδωρ, the best water — a copywriter's slogan, as though someone had been trying to sell off the Eden to a Greek entrepreneur. (The ways things are going, this may happen yet.) The text on the slab is the kind of late imitation of an ode by Horace that the bygone gentry so often had inscribed when they wanted to make a statement:

> Oh the fishers gentle life
> Happiest is of any
> Void of pleasur full of strife
> And belovd by many
> Other joys are but toys
>   And to be lamented
> Only this a pleasure is
> Timber Fishing
> ἀριστος μεν ὑδωρ
>   Eden IB
>   1855

The mis-spelling, the lettering which reverses many of the s's and n's, the broken-off stanza — these smack of a pretended sub-literacy or hamfistedness. It's rustick, consciously rough.

Perhaps Mounsey (if it was he) was being equally pawky in situating his river-shrine in a spot where almost nobody would ever see it. To exchange looks with the Faces, you must be determined, you must dangle in and climb back out, or wade along like a salmon fisherman or a poacher. The last time I was there, my dog Hardy was frantic to reach us. He knocked branches and clods down on to our heads, then got down to the water further along and plunged back upstream to the beach, almost out of his depth. As we left him again, to climb back out, he displaced his worry into furious scrabbling with his chiselly paws. Pounds of sand were spraying backwards into the river. After he had gone a robin arrived, mistaking the place for a freshly dug plot, and searched fruitlessly for worms. The beach was as trampled and gouged out as a football pitch. No doubt by now the Eden has flooded and smoothed it out again.

★

Does the Whin Sill, on and of which the Roman Wall is built, rise proud enough of the earth to be considered a great rock? The quartz-dolerite of it, a shallow arc of igneous red on the geological map, spans unbroken for nearly a hundred kilometres, from the headwaters of the South Tyne to the Northumberland coast at Farne Island, seventy metres thick at most and thirty metres deep. Yes, it is great in its continuity, in its lift from the Border grasslands between Scotland and England, in its strategic position. Although it is not the border, it feels like it. It looks pure frontier. The dips and scarps of it, the gradual rise from the south and the abrupt drop northward, look as though some epic southerly beat the earth-sea into waves. In the act of breaking they petrified, leaving the whinstone in mid-air like crests of gurly foam.

In consonance with our myths of north and south, the green earthy arable (or pastoral) backs are the English side, the dark stone brows are the Scottish. Name after name says what stuff the Sill is made of and what it means. 'Whin' means hard. Steel Rigg, Walltown, Crag Lough, Cawfield, Housesteads — in each placename there is an element of hardness and an element of use. The Wall chops along from crest to trough to crest, buoyant and unstoppable, like a boom paid out by the Romans across these alien reaches, with their implacable confidence that it would be secured at point after point and would tie in all their goals.

I had known I would grapple with the Whin Sill one day. In the end it happened almost accidentally. Anne and I had gone to see Vindolanda. When we drew up in the car park, I spied a good-looking crag nearby with a clear vertical grain and ran over to climb it. At once a man with a warden's badge came after me.

'Please don't climb here,' he said when he caught up with me. 'We're not insured for accidents, and some people . . . If you really want to climb, there's a good cliff with free access a few miles along the road.'

'All right,' I said, 'but I wouldn't sue, whatever happened.'

We had had exasperating access problems before, on limestone crags near Kendal, being bawled at by a man from Tarmac in Trowbarrow Quarry. 'Come down! come down!' he roared as we clung halfway up a thirty-metre crack. We were warned emphatically at another crag that if we climbed in 'the season' we might get sprayed with pheasant shot.

In fact the warden at Vindolanda had helped me to find Peel Crag, and Crag Lough just beyond it. Delicious hours have followed, walking and climbing in a place where the north seems to flow out endlessly into Scotland. Nature, history and farming fuse here in the most perfect concentration. Each narrow buttress, jointed vertically with its neighbours, stands straight up, declaring its toughness and the force of its extrusion through a break in the carboniferous limestone. The straightness suggests some visionary industrial metal, smelted already, cast into ingots or forged into girders to make this stockade. The dark olives and goose greys of it, the ochres and flushed bronzes (especially at Walltown) recall the fired colours of Australia. Again at Walltown, one natural column has sundered out of the Sill and fallen full-length down the slope, breaking into segments like the drums of the temple column felled by an ancient earthquake at Olympia.

The natural rectilinear splitting of the whinstone gave the Romans exactly what they needed, more's the pity. The blocks of the Wall look as though they came as naturally out of the Sill as the ears from a stalk of wheat. On the cliff-face the climbs are almost ruled, stepping hardly a metre left or right, cleaving to the columns, like the organ-pipes of the basalt near the Giant's Causeway in County Antrim where I once straddled up twenty feet until the joint between the members closed and left me nothing for my fingers.

The Lough (or tarn, or lochan) under the crag softens the scene, changeable and reflective among so much austerity. It can be hard too. One winter, just before Christmas, a hailstorm had melted and re-frozen. The shoulders of the crags were silvered like well-to-do women of my mother's generation, sleek in their fox-furs. As soon as I stepped out of a chimney on to the exposed face, I had to blow rime off the rock to make upward movement possible. Perched in sunshine on the top, I could have spent hours watching the antics of two mute swans down on the tarn. In summer it is so midgy here that it feels Highland. Now all was Arctic. The birds were standing nonplussed on thin ice. Behind them stretched a wavering channel of clear water. Presumably, as the ice formed overnight, they had kept swimming into it like ice-breakers. Now they were paddling cautiously forward. Each footfall gave out a piping note, whieeeuu, whieeeuu, as the ice flexed. This speeded up like some outlandish woodwind instrument as the swans broke into a trot, trying to reach take-off speed. At each step their great webs slithered — they could gain no traction. They put on the brakes and skidded to a halt like something out of Disney or Tom and Jerry.

Come on, swans — turn round and make your run down that clear channel — you can do it! They never thought of that. Before long it would freeze. As the sun sank, the pasture fields north towards Gallowshieldrigg were flushing pale peach. A long file of sheep were walking steadily north-west, as though they had heard that extras were being signed on for the nearest Nativity play. When Andy and I last looked back, the tarn was enamelled turquoise. The swans were still standing there, still trying to figure out a problem they might never have come across before.

★

Sea-going and short-haul ferries had taken me to the great rocks, cars and jeeps, high-flying jets and a helicopter. Now a rowing boat, which the boatman worked with a single scull, carried me over the glistening brown waters of the Coquet in Northumberland, cutting the mirror images of June leafage and the banded and herring-bone sandstone of the opposite bank. Out of this rock, six hundred years ago, the masons employed by Henry Percy of Warkworth Castle mined and carved, like their counterparts in Cappadokia and Cantabria, a little 'cave of God', or as they used to call it, a 'howse hewen within a cradge which is called the harmitadge chapell'.

At exactly the same time the hermits in Thessaly were colonising the caves of the Meteora. Was there an original, primitive cell at Warkworth? The door in the rockface overlooking the Coquet could almost be a cave-mouth. What it opens into now is a chapel, and beyond it a sacristy.

The rock flowers or branches into vaults, semi-octagonal shafts, and ceiling bosses. Quatrefoil and pointed windows pierce the solid rock left as a partition wall and let the green woodland light deep into the underground. In the curves of the vault between the ribs, lighter and darker layers of sandstone stand for the lines that would have been the edges of masonry or timbering in a building. I have never seen a more complete co-operation between the grain of rock and craftsmen's hands and tools.

Although the damp has eaten away the whites and colours of the painting and most of the features sculpted in the stone interior, the main windowsill still shows its form, just, like a sunken boat's shape blurred by the silt and dusk of the seabed. The shape of a woman curves up to become the left jamb (looking out), the shape of a man the right-hand one. They face one another. She has a bulk across her lap that could be a baby. He has his left arm across his chest and his right arm upright from the elbow, palm against cheek. The figure is still clear enough to show his curly mane and beard and the folds of a cloak or gown. The sill is where their legs would be. Together they create a loop of humanity, permanently joined, making the chapel seem a home.

Above the doors verses from the Psalms were once legible: 'My tears have been my meat day and night' and 'They gave me gall for my meat: and in my thirst they gave me vinegar to drink' — the old self-scourging sense of human life after the Fall. The hermits here seem not to have been crazed anchorites crouching in their dens. We know their names and that they were appointed by the Earls of Northumberland to celebrate Mass for a yearly stipend of £3.13.3d plus pasture for their horses and cattle, two loads of wood, and 'a draught of fish' each Sunday. If they weren't needy, they were beleaguered in other ways. The ceiling bosses and some of the shafts have been left in the rough — the work was interrupted by Scottish raiders in 1341 and no carvers could be found for the rest of the decade. This led to the abandonment of the work three years later. So the contrast between unfinished rock and rock which is finely worked stands for a breach in civilisation, when terror and fever broke in. This place may well have become a sanctuary where people lay low, praying that isolation would save them.

A hermit must feel this habitually — out there are wild animals, women, devils, and his jealous god looking down at him. Thirty kilometres north-west, where the land rises towards the Cheviots, the fine-grain yellowish sandstone crops out again in towers that move into sight between silver birches and knee-deep heather like hefty trolls or hobgoblins turned into rock. One of them, not far from Whittingham, has a twist to it like the spiral musculature of a tree which has turned and bent to withstand the wind. It stands a good twelve metres high. Halfway up its face a dark mouth opens, yawning, with a slight skew like Munch's 'Scream'. This is Macartney's Cave, a refuge delved out probably by a hermit attached to Callaly Castle. You can get in by edging up an improved natural ledge, then stooping through the hole and standing up in a chamber two metres high and a metre in diameter.

Cave-cold encloses you like impalpable stone. Above the doorway is a chiselled ledge — for a candle, perhaps, or a bit of food safe from the mice. Out there the leaves of birches, fruits of blaeberry, and buds of heather flourish under the sun, a shaggy paradise. In here you could roost and think, and feel and worry, a mind shut up in a skull of stone.

When I crept out again — I almost wrote 'escaped' — I climbed up the back on to the top of the tower and found Macartney's vexed self confronting me again. The rock has been so channelled out into folds and ridges by the weather and the dissolving action of its own acids that it looks like the convolutions of a brain.

Twenty-five kilometres further north the pale sandstone breaks the mantle of pasture in a last surfacing before the Border, in a frozen wave called Bowden Doors. 'The pass of the arched hill'? Or 'of the hill belonging to Buga or Bucge'? There is scarcely a pass here, on the way west to Wooler from Belford past Cockenheugh Hill. Perhaps the lowland between the Cheviot Hills and the North Sea was a pass-way through to Scotland. Consciousness of the march-lands as fought over lingers in a rhyme –

> In Collier Heugh there's gear eneugh,
> In Cocken Heugh there's mair,
> But I've lost the keys of Bowden Doors,
> I'm ruined for evermair.

This was the lament of a reiver called Hazelrigg Dunny, who haunted the place, sometimes in the body of a dun horse, looking for a great treasure he had buried somewhere nearby.

I suppose the treasure was loot from the fat lands of the merse between the Tweed and the Lammermuirs. North across the blue-grey billows of the land-sea, it is all sheer Britain, purified (you can tell yourself) of the political toxins, the fighting and getting and burning. It feels like the roof of things, though it is not a mountain, and it has a wide marine clarity as though you could spread gull-wings and fly clear across to Norway. Contentment opens out and flowers here, especially after using limbs and nerves to the utmost, manoeuvring up the wrinkles and runnels of the vertical rock-wall.

If we accept the 'arch' element in the derivation, it could also mean the wondrous curves in the rock, as though tooled or fired into it. Below the left end of the Wave itself, perfect arcs intersect, one made by the peeling off of a plaque with curved edges, others still only incised, awaiting the weather-crafting of the next few millennia. To the right of the Wave, broad semi-circles of colour band the flushed grey of the sandstone. Pale copper greens shade into the greys of charcoal or thundercloud, into pinks of jasper or raspberry, mingling subtly as the lights in the iris of an eye, or the changeable fires in an opal, or the traces of heating on the surface of an ingot.

Above these painterly beauties the crest of the wave is sculpted massively, delicately — twenty-five continuous metres of parallel curves picked out by water in the lip of the overhang. I would love to surmount this cornice, ride over it like a canoe bucking a stopper. I never will. On a shining afternoon in June Neil goes for it while I stand below holding the rope.

Four times he inches up the blank wall on the merest edges, lodges his left toe on a chicken-head not two centimetres proud of the rock, reaches for the break below the cornice, angrily telling himself 'Relax! relax!' — and retreats in good order, not yet fired up enough to risk the six- or seven-metre leg-shattering fall. We sit on the grass and talk about other things. His head clears, he feels good, he chalks his fingers again for maximum friction and spiders smoothly upward, past the chicken-head (now white as a floured baking board), palms the horizontal break and steadies there, collected as a kestrel hovering. He plants a Friend (a gismo with twin cams that brace against the rock), clips the rope into it, and (safe at last) leans far out like a gibbon under a branch. After five seconds and more chalk, he pulls up, establishes his right hand in an invisible cut above the crest and shouts triumphantly, wordlessly. Then he pulls over with the last spasm of his strength.

His energy is running down the rope into my hands, into my head. As I see him disappear into the safe and level zone above, I chant out the first lines of 'Amazing Grace' — my habit as I cross the Border at Gretna on the other side of England.

27   Across the Border

With pleasing symmetry two great rocks command the sea-ways into Scotland from east and west, the Bass Rock in the mouth of the Forth and Ailsa Craig in the mouth of the Clyde. Such bastions stud a zone that girds Scotland from North Berwick through the castle-rocks of Edinburgh, Stirling, and Dunbarton, to Ailsa Craig and out into the ocean by the Flannan Isles to Rockall. Even without their forts or lighthouses they would look like the remains of a monument-building culture whose humans and artefacts were long gone, leaving these mounds and plinths of what could be some ancient metal, stressed and split and worn.

Five kilometres away from the Bass Rock, outside North Berwick harbour-mouth, I was surprised that we could already see clearly the white guano plastering it. From a little nearer, this pallor turned out to be the birds themselves, the massed tribes of the fifty thousand gannets that breed here and take their name from it — *Sula bassana*. They perch so close to each other that each one makes a loop in the one lint-white

The Bass Rock

fabric thrown over the island — whole plaids of it with slant edges where the colony is stopped from nesting by a vertical cliff with few ledges or by the concrete walkway that runs beside the fuel-pipe to the disused foghorn.

You walk past only feet away from the massed *meerschaum* heads, and breasts like compacted snowflakes, and beaks with their reinforced bone superbly delineated by charcoal lines, and pale Arctic eyes ringed with sky-blue membrane. Early in May they weren't budging from their single eggs set on tumps of trodden seaweed and bent-grass. The nearest birds sketched a stab at our legs, just to say 'Keep your distance.' It began to feel uncanny, walking among creatures so alive, so alien, that were getting on with their own living as though we were not there. It felt like being in Bombay.

Their voices rose and fell in riffling phrases, peaking shrilly as a bird swooped, swithered its wings like a hawk steadying, closed and down-bent its tail like Concorde's nose, and hit the ground inches from its brooding mate. Then they billed and twined necks for a full minute of embracing and re-imprinting. Or a sitting bird would rearrange the seaweed fringe of the nest with fastidious beak, or realise a neighbour had just filched a sprig and the two would fight briefly, clacking beaks, one taking the other's neb full into her throat and trapping it there with a snap of her own one. Or a male would tread his mate and follow this with contented billing by them both that looked the antithesis of the raping and half-drowning of mallard ducks in wetlands where the gender balance is skewed and the drakes are rampant.

From the summit of the Bass a hundred metres up, right down to the tidemark, the air was weaving white with the gyring and diving and soaring of the gannets (and herring-gulls and guillemots, and razorbills and cormorants and puffins). They took off steeply on the updraughts, closed their wings and plunged to join the horde feeding on a shoal. They beat back low over the sea, beaks moustached with seaweed, on a trade-route from some source of the material further up the firth. What a plenteous sea that can keep this huge tribe fed and furnished.

The Bass is wholly theirs now. The lighthouse is unmanned. The fortified village built of basalt blocks is a dark-brown ruin. Once it housed every sort of idiocy. It is said that King James VI (of Scotland) isolated newborn babies here with a mute nanny to see if they would grow up speaking Hebrew. Some of the most eloquent and committed Covenanter preachers — such men as Peden and Blackadder — were locked up here until the damp and cold destroyed their health. A few Jacobites occupied it from 1691–4, surviving on provisions brought in by French warships. Was ever a coup more wishful or ill-starred?

We waited in the ruins for the Marrs to come out and take us back — two boatmen with strawberry-blond beards and reddened faces who crew a teak-built yawl called the *Sula*. All around us the harebell and bleached-mussel blues of the sea were repeated in the dense spring showers bruising down from the clouds, wiping out Edinburgh and the double-headed massif of Arthur's Seat in its midst, darkening along the coast of Fife and leaving the capital visible again. This is the best approach to the city, vibrant with the energy of fishing and trading and fighting for independence. The vistas here — across the sea-road to the 'Kingdom' of Fife, or up the long salt perspective to Edinburgh's crags and kirks — are like telescopes levelled on the co-ordinates of history itself.

My own language evolved here. In the summer of 1939, holidaying in Edinburgh, I first realised that my parents were afraid of imminent war — just twenty-one years after my mother's brother Graham, whom I never saw, had been killed in the Machine-gun Corps near Reims. We were shown over the Castle by a guide with deep-set eyes that grew most intense when he took us through the dungeons and described the sufferings of the prisoners. 'What a *drama* he made of it,' said my father afterwards, and when I asked what the mysterious word meant and he explained it, I learned for the first time that there was such a thing as an abstract term.

Those deepest dungeons are closed to tourists now, a guide told me, because 'it's too expensive to bring them up to Health and Safety standards'. No doubt it always was. When the last prisoner was shut up here, in 1919 — Davey Kirkwood, the Red Clydesider, later an M.P. — he said he felt he 'was a done man' as the damp stone closed round him and only one barred window high up afforded him any light.

It is all prettified now. In a stylish restaurant you can eat good lentil soup, or terrine of game on a raspberry *coulis*, a few feet from the Mills Mount redoubt where excavations have just unearthed evidence of Iron Age habitation. A witty guide called Tommy Milne glanced ironically at desperate history as he led us under the six-fold gate and portcullis: 'These were made to keep the English out. We no longer do that. We charge them £5.' When he sent himself up, he reminded me of Randy, our guide at Acoma in New Mexico. 'A gentleman called Kirkcaldy of Grange was holding the Castle for Mary Queen of Scots. So another gentleman, Morton the Regent, promised him safe conduct if he would leave the Castle. And when he did, they hanged him and they set his head up on a pike at the Mercat Cross. Which just shows you should never trust a Scotsman. Least of all me . . . '

Tommy Milne could allow himself this mellow jesting because he felt at ease by the hearth of his country, which can preen itself now on its feudal finery (the honours of Scotland or Crown Jewels, behind thick glass in a kind of temple guarded by three security men) while putting far behind it the miseries of the small nations who still have to forge their independence in the fire of rockets, mortars, and automatic rifles. Edinburgh Castle is a rock garden now where you can stroll about among pretty flowerbeds and young sentries in dress kilts, and buy picturesquely packaged malt whisky and chocolate in a shop built on a gun-battery. The rock itself, the core of an extinct volcano, was shorn sheer on its north and south faces by a glacier grinding down from the highlands to the west. The ancient basalt crops out darkly, patinated with the smoke of the steam trains that used to carry me south to Cambridge and London in the 'fifties, passing a few yards from the roots of the rock. It still leaves that city-chimney smell on your fingers when you scramble on its chipped buttresses, between beds of dandelion and gillyflower whose petals glow like sunlight condensed. In the heart of a metropolis you can climb a hillside dense with wild grass and hawthorn trees.

The foul, insect-ridden waters of the Nor' Loch between here and what is now Princes Street were drained in the later eighteenth century to make these comely promenades and putting-greens where thousands take their ease. On this daisied turf, among this luminous leafage, the black-mouthed cannon up there on the battlements, as much as the curdled magma on which the Castle rests, look like the macabre remnants of bad old times, full of 'drama' no doubt and shattering for those living through it.

★

Ailsa Craig, from an engraving by Joseph Swan

Ailsa Craig has long been known as Paddy's Milestone, being halfway from Glasgow to Belfast — a seamark which makes you thankful to have passed it. A friend from County Coleraine, the poet and singer Jimmy Simmons, used to live on a boat which, he tells me, was known to have capsized just once, when trying to round Ailsa Craig. I first saw its steep blue bulk from the *Princess Victoria* en route for Larne in the summer of 1951. Two Januaries later, in the famous hurricane that swept the North Sea deep into Holland, the *Princess Victoria* sank drowning 134 people off the Rinns of Galloway south-south-west of Ailsa Craig.

The great rock is not sinister for me. It is a fragment of the Highlands, a stage on the crossing to Jimmy's home on Islandmagee in

County Antrim where Muck ['pig'] Island lies low in the water like a suckling sow with its snout at one end and the links of its curly tail at the other. Beyond Ailsa lie the blue ends of Kintyre and Islay, and on the clearest days the Paps of Jura, due north across the firth, like signs saying: 'We are the mountains, come here and we will fold you in.'

Islands can welcome you, spreading out their pastures or woods with a flourish of beauty like a Turkish carpet unrolling across the sale-room floor. On Ailsa Craig the carpet is a triangular rug of coarse granite shingle sparsely textured with grasses. A spit called Foreland Point was formed on the east side of the island by seas blown clockwise and anti-clockwise round it.

After two months of waiting, the winds relented. By nightfall, the boatman Mark McCrindle told me, 'it'll blaw up a gale fae the sooth-east — Force 8'. It was clear that he trusted the Shipping Forecast more than he would a train timetable.

'It's been terrible,' he said, 'the gales since December.' He was looking north to the fishing-boats working between here and Arran. 'The boys have a lot of money to make up.'

In the meantime all we had to contend with was a fresh sou'westerly. Mark's boat, the *Glorious*, registered in Ballantrae, was jumping about in the waves like a daft lamb in springtime. The deckhouse had room only for Mark and his mate so I sat on the lee side next to the engine housing and tried to dodge the volleys of brilliant spray.

In pale-gold winter light the island ahead looked all mineral — brass of withered bents, copper-verdigris of grass in sheltered gullies, bronze of old bracken. As we neared it after the fifteen-kilometre crossing, I was automatically trying to suss ways up it. It looked inhospitable. Scabs of steep scree and vertical crag were separated by narrow tongues of herbage. The island is a mountain, three kilometres round and four hundred metres high, monument to a boiling-up of a quartz-felspar mixture sixty million years ago. It cooled and hardened inside layers of softer material which stripped off, leaving this one boss, like the Bass Rock and the Flannan Isles, St Kilda and Rockall in the Atlantic.

Mark and his mate put me ashore at a rusting pier, relic of the time when Ailsa exported its one product, half-finished granite chunks for curling-stones and setts for streets. Then they chugged off to lift their lobster creels in the calmer lee of the rock. I walked south and east by the narrow level between cliff and water called The Trammins, place of the elder bushes. In the sparse turf rails rusted. North of the pier another track led round to the quarry where the finest stone, the Blue Hone, was split out of the crag. Bridges carried it across Swine Holes, cave-mouths between ribs of rock like buttresses. Everything is miniaturised to the scale of toys by the mountain's bulk. Above me now Craigna'an rises in narrow vertical panels tiger-striped by peaty ooze. Near sea level the rock is naked and clean, blued by its special ingredient of riebeckite, fine-grained as sweetmeal bread, wind-buffed sleek as the hide of the seal which came head and shoulders out of the water as we neared the pier and looked full at us.

There is hardly a weakness in the granite, only now and again a fault-line where black dolerite bubbled through, decayed, and made a kind of unclimbable ladder. One broad fault, called Rotten Nick, tempts me to find a way up to the summit. Finally its back wall, dripping and crumbling, repels me. In any case, the special interest of this island — its civilisation — is concentrated round its base.

At the southern cape a concrete tower rears up, shaped like a dalek, or like the sinister watch-towers with broad mouths for machine-guns which Hitler's army built on Jersey in 1942. This one is amiable — the South Horn, with a fine funnel on top like the bell-mouth of an old-fashioned gramophone. No dog sits patiently listening to his master's voice; its sound lost out to radar years ago. Looking at it, I can hear the bellow of the Aberdeen foghorn which carried easily to our house three miles away on foggy nights that smelt of herring-meal and made me fear for relatives who might be out there fishing. From close up the foghorn was awesome. It breathed deeply before hooting, then let loose a bolt of sound that seemed to speed off into the thick grey atmosphere.

Between Rotten Nick and Macnall's Cave there are signs of stoneworking. A metre block of granite left lying among scrap stone shows twelve drill-holes along its edge — it took that many dints to split this toughest of British rocks. I'm almost at home here. The stone of the house where I was born was just a little rougher and greyer — its third ingredient was mica instead of riebeckite. The finesse of the Ailsa microgranite deserves its former name, ailsite. Just looking at it, you can feel how it would caress the hollow of your palm, as when you cup your hand round the cranium of a beloved dog. Strange to think that long before curling-stones skimmed ice, erratics were plucked out of this rock and carried by the ice of a glacier as far as the Isle of Man, Pembrokeshire, and County Wicklow.

A few of the last stones to be cut into rough cylinders must have been left lying. Now they make supports for driftwood garden seats in front of the one habitable house, which is used as a base by a local ornithologist. Mark had told me that its roof blew off a few years back.

The new roof is flat, held down with many chunks of granite. Its neighbour, an ugly hangar made of brick with a curved metal roof, is the old gas-house for the lighthouse, bought recently by a German couple. I remember hearing about similar wanderers from far-off Germany who owned an abandoned coastguard station at Greian Head, the most remote and exposed point on Barra. The third house here, an L-shaped cottage, is intact and boarded up.

'The Marquis himself has it,' said Mark. 'But och, he's never here.' Somehow the Scottish aristocracy never are.

Three generations of a family from Girvan, called Girvan, lived here in the summer and worked the stone — hefty men, in the old photos, with coarse trousers held up by braces, wearing peaked sailor-looking caps and walrus moustaches. They were here till 1952 and the stone-work ceased for good in 1971, undercut by stone from Wales. The chief creatures at home here now are the gannets, with their 21,000 nests on the West Craigs near the 190-metre overhang of Barestack (Biorach-stac, jutting cliff). I had been forced to turn back at Stranny Point, short of the Craigs, where the rock fell straight into the sea.

Ailsa Craig would be a more richly peopled island had it not been for the rats. In the early 1880s there was 'an invasion of rats which deserted a sinking ship'. By 1889 they had driven out the puffins. The White-tailed sea-eagle had been hunted to death by then and only visited occasionally. At one time, 'you could hardly turn over a stone without finding two or three slow-worms under it'. By 1895 the rats had killed them off as well. Four years ago it was decided to saturate the island with warfarin, delivered by helicopter, to wipe out the rats and encourage the puffins to return. I have mixed feelings about such an intervention, although I hold no brief for rats. I hated them for killing off the slow-worms. I first met this lizard of peerless beauty on Jura and saw it drawing its silken olive length with its mild brown eye between the heather stems, and delighted in the sight of its nine tiny golden young ones, which it bears live, not from eggs.

When I climbed the eastern slope of Ailsa past the square tower of the sixteenth-century castle with its fine stone window-jambs and lintels, I began to stumble on patches of denatured ground, riddled with holes and fat green weeds which had thrived on the turning of the soil by burrowing rats and on their dung with its rich content of recycled slow-worm and puffin. I had seen the same thing over on Muck Island, which is a kind of green hell porous with rat-holes. You sink in up to the knee among the same giant nettles and loosened soil, while fulmars puke on your head and half-fledged gulls come at you out of the undergrowth, gaping and screeching.

All islands look like paradise until you land on them, when they may turn into something very different. Beholding Ailsa Craig from a distance in the summer of 1818, Keats envisaged it as moribund —

> Thy life is but two dead eternities —
> The last in air, the former in the deep;
> First with the whales, last with the eagle skies.

When there are no more marquises, let alone ornithologists or German *wandervögeln*, the gannets will still thrive here, on cliffs too steep even for rats. We saw just one, beating low over the waves on its athletic wings with sharp tips black as Indian ink, body white as new milk, beak jutting from *meerschaum* head with its special strengthening to stand the repeated plunge from a height as it fished the shoals. Now the imminent gale was forcing us to retreat. These were not waters to mess with. Ailsa is given in the *Clyde Sailing Directions* as 'a good leading mark for entering the Firth', with a warning that 'in thick weather in the morning' sailors must guard against mistaking for Ailsa a mainland hill near Ballantrae with a very similar outline — Knockdolian, 'commonly called "the false Craig" '. I would certainly have hated to play the false Craig on Mark McCrindle. Before we left he showed me round the lighthouse and gave me one more glimpse of how nearly humankind has finished with this place. The lighthouse (and the foghorn) were commissioned in 1886. It was manned until 1990, with three keepers. Now it is automatic. Mark comes out once a month to check that all is well with the gas cylinders, the back-up batteries powered by solar panels, and the unbelievably small gas-mantel whose light is magnified by revolving lenses.

It was eerie to walk over the red floors, now scuffed, no doubt once polished immaculately, and to peer in at the curtained windows of the living quarters. Mark clearly enjoys looking across to here at night and seeing that even the little fail-safe light is visible over the firth.

'Of course,' he said, on a falling note, 'these days the ships rely on their radar.'

'You mean, really, lighthouses are expendable now?'

'Yes.'

So the marvellous white towers that mark our headlands and islands, many of them prodigies of engineering, are set to become relics, and presently Trinity House will be offering them for sponsorship, or else adoption, as the Ordnance Survey has done with its triangulation points.

★

From the Firth of Clyde there is a choice whether to go west or north. Either would do, and called me equally. Ireland's west is all great rocks, from the Bloody Foreland at the north-west tip of Donegal, where red granite runs down into the sea in a petrified flood as though the rock had been re-melted in a nuclear fire, to the spiney Skelligs off Kerry where the anchorites in their beehive cells must have heard their own frights echoed in the screams of the seabirds. There is no way of being alive on some of those precipices, the steeps of Achil Island in Connemara or the Cliffs of Mohir at the mouth of Galway Bay. One great fall of the land that you can inhabit is Slieve League at the western headland of Donegal. That name for it Anglicises it too much. It is Sliabh Leac, mountain of flagstones.

If you approach past the Blue Stack Mountains and Lough Eske, by Donegal Town and Killybegs where the trawlers and inshore boats discharge their catches under the mountainous slopes of Crownarad, you have the great feeling of nearing the end of things. The road is a dead-end — Sliabh Leac absolutely blocks the way through to the last green land round Malin Bay. We stayed at Carrick — An Charraig, the rock — in a bed-and-breakfast where the landlady took it for granted that we had come to see 'the biggest sea-cliff in Europe'. It is more a mountainside than a cliff, metres of it plunging directly from the summit to the surf, by cliffs with vertical strakes and horizontal steps, by broken spines, by smashed stonefall barely at rest, by headlong twisting gullies any one of which would hurtle you unstoppably the whole way down.

Our goal, as the path climbed slowly north of Scregeighter, was the point on the ridge called One Man's Pass. Did this debar women? Or make it easier for them, since they are less bulky than men? And if Anne made it through or up this Pass, could we rename it One Person's Pass in honour of the event?

The grand array of the cliff, its nearly two kilometres of groynes and clefts, unfolded itself on our left, below. By the time we had passed a peaty hollow on the crest of the mountain and rejoined the rim of the cliff, it was as usual impossible to gauge its scale until we saw gulls circling just above the water — tiny, as though they were some kind of white finch or wren. The face is tortured in its gullying and folding. Many rock types have overlaid or buckled into each other and they support many kinds of sedge and heath and moss. A botanist called H.C. Hart spent three days in 1883 traversing the face along the thousand-foot contour and met a man and a boy coming up steeply from near the sea laden with samphire grass and chewing stalks of it.

The way had become a narrow spine, the Pass, which is a sloping backbone made of blocky vertebrae. We couldn't quite straddle it. Stepping up it feels more precarious than on Striding Edge on Helvellyn or Sharp Edge on Saddleback since the drop is three times as great. Anne made it easily to the top, her arms bare in the halcyon sunlight — One Person's Pass it is.

The eastern side of the summit is a thicket of stone — the sedimentary rock that gives the mountain its name, split by nature and by hands. Here was an early Celtic hermitage, sacred to a local saint, Bishop Hugh MacBride. Expecting the remains of perhaps one 'beehive', we found many walls, anything from four to nine courses of stonework still in position. These will have been shelters built by pilgrims who used to make a *turas* here in November. The flagstones helped habitation, so did the holy well, whose grumbly underground music we heard before we found the pool — twenty-five centimetres square and two or three deep. I took out two stones and a jagged green bottle-end to deepen the water and dipped out handfuls of it to drink. It was a bit muddy but palatable enough.

Along the slope three weird rocks stood up, teeth taller than a man picked out along the grain of their strata to a flakiness like cuttlefish bone. They had that look of a sign, which would have made somebody say 'here is the place'. In the hollow under one of them there was easily room to lie down and it was floored with flagstones, whether naturally or deliberately. Certainly nights, or months, up here with the force and voice of the Atlantic windstream only a few yards away over the brow to seaward would temper one's consciousness.

I allowed the place to work on me in my own way by contouring back along the face at five hundred metres or thereabouts. The footing was precarious all the way. I passed below sixty- and seventy-metre scarps, dwarfed to mere outcrops by the mountainside as I looked along it, rearing loftily enough from foot to rim as I stared up square chimneys and corners made of 'masonry' very much like the Savage Slit section of Coire an Lochain in the Cairngorms. At an impasse between cliff and hopelessly unstable scree I set off up a tapestry of mossy grass and had to cling on for dear life as it began to peel slowly off like tatters of damp wallpaper in a derelict house.

The whole stravaig up and along and finally down had been

accompanied, often below consciousness, by the gruffing and soughing of the sea's waters, hoarse as the voice of a distant crowd. The
tideline it was coming from made such a beautiful script — white
arabesques on blue — that I wanted to pore over it for hours. The
foam-glyphs took the shape of everything you ever saw. Here were the
Philippines — there was an intestine stemming into a sac — the 'dream'
figure from the Peche-Merle cave in France with its willowy body and
tapering kangaroo head — dolphin-backs — letters from the Sinhalese
alphabet . . . Near one headland two white comet-heads streamed out
to sea, then curved in exact parallel, like twin animals at play. Half an
hour later they hadn't changed. Two hours later they had fused.
Beyond the cove of Bunglass were rocks called the Giant's Chair and
Desk, and sure enough, from below the base of the cliff five huge
white fingertips of foam appeared, pushed out to sea a little way and
withdrew again . . .

Only once all day did a new glyph appear, presumably where the
ebbing surface dipped enough to break on a reef. Mostly the creamy
curlicues were just there, hour after hour, like trails that turn into cirrus
cloud at twelve thousand metres as a summer's day goes by, or like
some more abstract notation that rendered the shape of the land in
twining, looping characters — notes of music, vibrating outward from
the land's sides, printing themselves on a stave that wasn't ruled straight
but curved with the contour of the mountain.

In the end I hated to turn my back on them, they were so serene in
their offshore dance, the purity of their shining, all the way north from
Carrigeen Head, beneath the fearsome coves of Sliabh Leac, to the
smiling blond sands and grasslands of Rathlin O'Birne, where Donegal
ends.

A few minutes' latitude north of there and two hundred kilometres
east — exactly on the other side of Ireland — a black cliff lurks under
the verge of Islandmagee. It is reached by a steep track past fishermen's
cottages that have become holiday homes. At sea level there is a zone
where the present has gone and it is again a century or more ago.

> A door in the rock with 'Gobbins' carved beside it
> Opens through to a path the waves have ravaged,
> Drawing its bones like teeth. We stride and balance
> Till we come to a gap — an impossibility —
> But 'Go as far as you can,' you said,
> So down I climb to the sea

And find a teetering way. It is black as ravens
Under the loom of the crag, it is cellar-damp
And the sun has gone to Kerry, the whole of Ireland
Is between us and its fire.
Scotland is hull-down in the distance —
Jura, Islay, and the Mull of Kintyre.

Once a Catholic teacher lurked in the cave here,
Taking a class of the faithful,
Accepting buttermilk or a little bacon,
Teaching letters, sums, and theology,
And maybe each of the scholars brought a peat
To warm the breath of the sea . . .

The rock here is the basalt that runs right round the Antrim coast, layered on to the white chalk with so sharp a contrast that it looks like a baker's handiwork. At the Gobbins it is black and formless as sooty clag scraped from a flue — a volcano's flue. The way along it between tidemark and cliff is hewn and stepped, floored sometimes with rock, mostly with cement. It was built by the Northern Counties Railway Company and opened for the Belfast meeting of the British Association for the Advancement of Science in 1902. The sturdy craft of the steam train engineers shows in the bridges across deep inlets. These are made of concrete beams formed round flanged steel rails and still not quite strong enough to withstand a century's battering by winter's north-easterlies storming across the Celtic Sea.

It is just possible either to tightrope-walk across the surviving beams, whose walkway has long since fallen in, or to scramble down and along the crag, in order to reach the schoolmaster's cave. Its floor is green now as a pantomime grotto, a rheumaticky and chilly hide-out for those refugees from British penal laws. How ironical that by the start of this century the Gobbins had become a 'beauty spot', tailored and eased so that it could be visited in safety by the spouses of all those British scientists — predominantly Protestant, I should imagine — who posed here in long muslin dresses and complicated hats, people of my mother's class and generation who survive as slightly blurred apparitions in the ovals of embrowned photographs.

★

Beyond those natural and man-made strongholds of its Lowland belt, Scotland winds northward in a labyrinth of rock which most of us will never know in all its back glens and isolated skerries. From 56° to

61°N, from the Meridian to 7° 30' W, 280 kilometres across from
North Uist to Peterhead and 460 kilometres from Dunadd in Argyll to
Herma Ness at the north cape of Unst, Scotland seems more rock than
not.

Where is Dunadd, you may well be wondering? You could pass it by
without a look, as you pressed on in the last stage of a journey from
Glasgow to Oban — a rough hill rising a hundred metres out of bog
and reclaimed fields a little north of the Crinan Canal. If it is a 'great
rock', then its body must be mainly underground, which doesn't count
in the human record. Dunadd was the first capital of the Scots kingdom called Dalriada (North Antrim and Argyll). Its kings — Domnall
the Speckled, for example, and Aedh the White and Eochaid the
Poisonous — left their footprint on it.

At 3 o'clock on an April afternoon, when primroses make the only
lights in a land bleached by winter and dulled by overcast, the place
seems all past and no present. The entrance is up a stony path flanked
by rocks, massive and squat. The ground everywhere is altered; grass
has mantled the heaps of dug-out earth and drystone palisades show
through it. Ewes with followers a few weeks old startle off round
the hill. On a grassy saddle between the summit and the eastern
shoulder two outcrops surface, one boulder-sized, the other big
enough to be the sarcophagus of a very large knight. Between the
natural cracks in it, aligned north-east, is a footprint two or three
centimetres deep. The top of the smaller rock has a hollow in it the size
of a pumpkin. Here, it is said, the kings of Dalriada were crowned,
placing the left foot in the print to take the oath and being anointed
with water from the *ballan*, the basin.

All over the world these footprints show up, often enigmatically.
Over in Ireland, at Dunmull Promontory Fort south-west of Bushmills,
there is a stone with a footprint traditionally associated with a saint. It
was probably toppled from the fort to desecrate it and lower its status
for good. One of the most beautiful I have seen (but only in a
photograph) is on an Olmec greenstone axehead where a left footprint
is carved into the stone with suave perfection. Whatever it once signified, the Mexican village people on the Gulf of Tehuantepec now
perceive such a print as a trace of the *chaneqes*, dwarf tricksters who
live in waterfalls. The likeness of a human print on a natural surface
strikes me as one of the most fundamental marks on land — utterly
there, as unmistakable a sign that one is not alone amidst nature as
Friday's footprint was to Crusoe. It must be the same impulse that led
Italians on the coast south of Naples to mythologise a hand-shaped

hollow in a rock as the print of a Turk: he leaned against it, it softened and took the impress of his hand, and he himself was so impressed that he converted to Christianity.

I tried my own foot in the print, which was filled with water. With my shoe on it was just too big. I thought of dipping a drink out of the *ballan* but a dead worm in it put me off. The edge of one of the cracks in the long rock had groups of cut lines stemming from it — Ogam writing, which can be deciphered but not as yet translated. Everything here has gone just beyond the historical horizon. I wasn't even looking at the actual coronation stone. It was oddly pale, compared with the *ballan* stone, and then I remembered — it has been covered with a fibreglass sheath to protect it. How crass, to deny us an actual sight of this piece of our heritage! Surely it should have been left to take its chance with the elements. The risk of vandalism here seems low.

Putting this behind me, I settled down on the grassy saucer of the summit and then the place itself streamed into me at last. From here Dunadd commands the Moine Mhòr, the Great Moss that still partly surrounds it. At every airt of the compass the land-forms ripple off — to the east, the forested ridges of Kilmichael; to the south, the slant ranges of Knapdale; west beyond the mouth of Loch Crinan, the island of Jura, on the same alignment as the coronation stone. Immediately below, the Add snakes through its water-meadows. Ponds of rainwater and, to the north, one classical ox-bow twine parallel with the river, like whale pups cleaving to their mothers. This hill is a true life-centre, an *omphalos*, where culture was possible among the not yet civilised terrain.

Seven hundred people could have lived here, say the archaeologists, in wattle-and-daub huts protected by stone ramparts. Many hundreds of craft fragments have been dug up, including querns (hand mills), whetstones, crucibles, and stone and clay moulds for casting brooches, rings, and pins. Samian ware from Rome has been found — so people lived here long before the Scots colonists arrived from Ireland. Bone combs and enamel buttons, a slate with a working drawing for a Celtic brooch, a bead of Baltic amber, but almost no weaponry — only a sword-point and a dozen spearheads — suggest 'a domestic community rather than a garrison'.

Even so, they were not exempt from the rage of the warlords. Aengus King of the Picts (descendants of the first Britons to colonise Scotland) overran the citadel in A.D. 736, captured two of the Dalriadic princes, and took them away in chains. In 741 he came back and gave the place a 'smiting' from which it was slow to recover, if it ever did.

By the middle of the ninth century it was probably deserted. It had been part of Europe. The Add was navigable by the small ships of the time and they carried in, among other things, wine from France which was traded on to Iona for the monks to use at Mass.

At Kilmichael, now a modern village a couple of kilometres inland, another cracked outcrop has two footprints, smaller than Dunadd's, which might have been used in the crowning of the Dalriadic queens. We are peering into the darkness now, speculating or fantasising. The rocks encourage it. People thought that the print on Dunadd was caused by the 'witch of Cruachan' leaping across from the mountain north of Loch Awe — and she was the Cailleach Bheur, the Earth Mother herself.

The Kilmichael rock is crazed all over with lines, some evidently chiselled, and with cup-holes, some of them linked by channels. On a rock by the shore anywhere in the Hebrides, these would be taken for the holes in which fisherfolk mashed up limpets to use for ground-bait — and we know that the link between here and the sea was once much closer. The cup-holes also look votive, reminding me of the little clay lamps for worshipping the Buddha which filled the cupboard of a house where I lived in Sri Lanka. If the Scots filled these holes with seal or fish oil and set it alight, at some regal or seasonal festival, think of how the fire would have run its ideograms of flame all over the surface of this natural altar.

That night, in the Chartroom Bar of the hotel at Kilmelfort, I sat studying the framed charts of the Firth of Lorn and the Sound of Luing. The official landmarks were named in fine homely terms — 'White House with Black Roof' (reminding me of the Lundy chart) 'White House with turrets', 'Keepers' dwelling, conspicuous white wall'. My stepson Rob, a hydrographic surveyor, tells me that in his line of work the men are pleased if a mark they have identified makes it through to that kind of acceptance when the charts are revised period-ically. At the other end of the bar English yachting families in blue padded shower-proof waistcoats were chattering in the idiom of their kind.

'Well, is it to be Mull or Ardnamurchan?'

'Mull is all right. But I've seen it. And there really isn't much to do. What would you like to do?'

(Wife) 'Oh, I just want to read a book.'

'You can read a book at *home*.'

'Darling, I'm *happy* just to read.'

(Son) 'If we go to Ardnamurchan, will there be much walking?'

Suddenly I wanted none of them to be here, these people whose boats now outnumber the boats used to fish for crabs or prawns or to ferry island children to school or sheep to offshore pasture. It's no use, though — I'm a visitor myself, and a descendant of earlier invaders. Some of my Craig forebears were 'supposed to be Irish'. My mother's mother was German and married an Englishman of Scottish descent. To free this land from incomers who have harried and denatured it, one would be driven back to mythic times.

My landlady, Elspeth Campbell of Tullich, gave me a glimpse of the world that never was when she pointed out to sea between Asknish Point and Eilean Creageach and told me about rocks there called the Horse's Footsteps (Eich Donna on the map, meaning 'brown horses'). A prince was riding headlong after his sweetheart, went straight into the sea and would have drowned if the skerry had not risen up and held him above the water. So the people expressed their intuition that the rock of Argyll did not finish at the ness; it headed on south-south-west, unendingly.

28   The Rocks of Home

I was heading north now, and always most at ease when doing so, for Wester Ross, my summer paradise over forty years. Up there many of the mountains are so separate from their neighbours that they are as salient and single as Uluru or Gibraltar, Kata Tjuta or Square Butte or Masada. So much so that Jim Crumley, most thoughtful of our wilderness writers, calls Suilven in Sutherland '*The* Rock. The best single Rock in all Scotland, the Soloist . . . ' The chief mountains of Wester Ross are virtually ranges, with multiple peaks — Beinn Eighe, Liathach, An Teallach — great saurians, or saurian families huddled against each other in their Precambrian sleep.

Beinn Eighe, a gathering of quartzite so blinding white it looks like permanent snow, is on such a scale that the three mighty rocks which gird its western face, the triple buttresses of Coire Mhic Fhearchair, are only a fraction of the massif. Their white snouts are like a range of kilns from the Potteries in their heyday. The hulks of Torridonian sandstone on which they are built are the dull red of furness embers. Layered lumps of it litter the corried floor — loaves and buns from the giant's bakery.

Corries always look to me as if they should cradle cultures. In Coire

Ardair under Creag Meagaidh in north-west Perthshire, or in Birkness Combe above Buttermere, I find myself looking at each prone tablet of rock or ridge in the moor and wanting them to be doorsteps or lintels of old cottages, turf dykes round crofting townships. If red deer trot through, they are the cattle of the place. The lower lip of the corrie makes a threshold. As I cross it, it rises up behind me and peace encloses me. I have come home.

Since the last Ice Age the peace of Coire Mhic Fhearchair has been shattered once. In March 1951 a Lancaster bomber hit the face. Alloy shards still litter the scree. Pieces of fuselage shiver and chatter in the breeze. A wheel complete with tyre lies among the blaeberry and heather. In the burn an engine sits, seized solid, half-damming the flow. Fifty years before, the first climb on Central Buttress had been led by the most magisterial of late-Victorian mountaineers — Norman Collie, a scientist of Aberdeen stock, who discovered neon and was the first person to take x-ray photographs. In those days people preferred the secure feeling inside a gully, however slimy, to the exposure out there on the rockface. Collie and his friends climbed the West Gully in snow, then traversed out left on to Central Buttress and stared up its steeps. It struck Collie as 'A.P.' — Absolutely Perpendicular. They were so appalled that they sat down to finish off their sandwiches ('full of mustard and delightfully dry'), their prunes ('encrusted with all kinds of additional nutriment from the bottom of someone's pocket'), and their sweets ('a much-worn stick of chocolate and perhaps an acidulated drop'). Then they went home. They were not too appalled to come back next day and downclimb from the summit, to the cairn they had built to commemorate their lunch, before escaping into the gully.

Since that time ways have been found up the terraced labyrinth of the sandstone. For years I'd been toiling up and down the grating white screes above, swinging along the great loops of the skyline above the Golgotha of waterless corries to the north, even psyching myself to climb alone up the easiest line on Central Buttress one balmy July in the late 'seventies. Thunderous rains set in just in time to spare me the mortification of finding out that I had not the bottle to take on that 350-metre precipice by my own little self. Today, climbing it with Bill Birkett from Little Langdale on a day of Mediterranean warmth, I was comfortable, almost at home inside this maze of ramps and grooves. The huge quietude of the corrie, the air-space expanding away unbroken between Liathach and Beinn Dearg towards the blue berg of Harris beyond the Minch — it was all fusing into a tranquillity that brimmed up from the footsoles to the mind like water from the aquifer filling a well.

The sandstone is fine-grained, so old (about 750 million years) that it doesn't rub off as dust. As for the polar reaches above, the great blanched citadel, that was still not real, still a tract of some further continent refracted inside our present horizon like a mirage. The pioneers here, very aptly, were Yorkshire gritstone climbers called Pigott and Wood. They climbed it in rain and 'longed ardently for sunshine, rubbers [gymshoes], and a stout heart, for the prospect of, say, six consecutive gritstone "almost impossibles" ' was almost too much for them. They felt at home, though, and the shapes of the rock kept reminding me too of Yorkshire. One airy stride-and-sidle on to a ramp up a ten-metre face was the image of a climb with the perfect name of Fishladder on Earl Crag near Bingley.

The sandstone foundation at last gave way to the quartzite superstructure. We strolled along a narrow garden ankle-deep in dewy grasses and clumps of thrift. The joint between brown rock and white was so distinct I could lay my finger along it and touch both simultaneously, spanning the Palaeozoic and the Proterozoic. Why ever leave this pleasance? Why not loll here as the sun moves out over the ocean and feast on this mountainscape, on its colossal volumes that arrange and rearrange themselves in my mind, or rearrange my mind, like fundamental sculpture? Yet again the upward imperative asserts itself. We must reach, reach. *Up there*, always, contentment waits.

Right here, a large ice-coloured shield — like some piece left untouched in the marble quarry at Altissimo near Forte dei Marmi used by Michelangelo and Moore — asks to be laybacked. Followed by another, and another and another. After seven of these I'm thirty metres above the terrace and not one foot of support below me is integral. 'The blocks hereabouts seem to rely mainly on mutual understanding for their support' (Fred Pigott). Ah well — each piece weighs, what, half a ton? We couldn't lever them off if we tried. Or so I tell myself, and at the tenth or fifteenth telling it has sunk in, helped by the exact horizontals of the strata, which mean that each piece has a dead-level foot set on the dead-level top of the one below. Nothing can go wrong. After these hours of inhabiting the air, or the edge of the air, climbing has become slow-motion flying. When Bill joins me at a stance, he instantly sets off upwards, quartzite fragments and fibres of dried moss scudding under his feet.

'Don't you want the gear, Bill?' I call after him.

'Too heavy,' and up he goes. Soon the rope's red stem is the only sign that human life exists in the upper reaches of this narrowing tapering buttress.

This face should never end. There seems to be the entire passage of the sun's day in it, or the complete sequence of the year's benign half from equinox to equinox. At the finish I'm so thirsty and weary I lie flat on my back and let my vision lose itself in the fading blue above. To replace the sweat that day I drank a gallon of burn-water, still cold in its runnels of peat and stone beneath the heather.

Fifteen kilometres west-south-west lies Diabaig, my favourite place, a village whose harbour is ringed with rock, backed by glowing crags three hundred metres high, mouth facing out to the northern end of Skye with the Old Man of Storr erect on his mountainside. The Diabaig crofts, on slopes of Alpine steepness, are no longer worked and the village almost died. Then it renewed itself with money hard-earned at the Kishorn oil-rig dock and the salmon farm between the harbour and a deserted headland called Araid. From here I can't see those dear places, but I know they are there, the ways across to them and back through time to my family's seasons there feel as tangible as the sequences of footholds and handholds which have brought me to this spot.

★

Two-and-a-half degrees of longitude or two hundred kilometres to the east and I'm in my native latitude, en route for a mountain, Ben Avon in the Cairngorms, and some islands — Orkney Mainland, Hoy, and Yell. First I wanted to get as near as possible to my forebears' experience of landmarks. My grandfather John and his brother George sailed out from here, first from the cove at Portlethen, which has no quay, then from Aberdeen harbour. Latterly they were launching what they called the Great Line for white fish, as far afield as the deep-sea grounds between Scotland and Iceland. They lived under the same roof in houses they had had built from granite blocks, storing the mile-long lines in attics which ran the length of four family homes, hauling them up in baskets by a pulley on the beam which still sticks out from the gable-end of number 24 Wood Street, Torry.

My boyhood had been full of stories about the wrecking storms that beat on Girdle Ness below the lighthouse south of the harbour mouth. On a Sunday, driving past the trawler dock with its crowd of masts and funnels — empty now — we were shown the rusted carcase of a wreck still fast on the reef below the Ness, and the Leading Lights, chalk-white columns that stood up at the side of the street. Steering by them, the boats sailed straight up the dredged channel on a south-west course. The upper lantern in the lighthouse is sixty metres above high water. The cliffs below it send their broken ends out under the water for two cables or one-tenth of a sea-mile, according to the chart surveyed by Commander Slater in 1833, a generation before my grandfather's birth.

Now the shipping that steers by these marks nearly all works at the North Sea oil and gas and is registered in Rotterdam, Nassau, Panama — anywhere but Aberdeen. The sea-roads are busy, the pilot cutter constantly bounces out and in again past the marks with their half-forgotten names — the Skate's Nose, Paddy's Pier. Could I go out on it and see my native city at last with sea-going eyes? At the Pilots' Office in the Round House on the North Pier, Alex Main wasn't sure about letting me on to the boat — 'Board of Trade regulations' — but he was willing to talk.

'Do you still use landmarks?'

'Oh aye, I'm an auld-fashioned seaman. When I used to trade away doon West Africa to Liberia, there was what they called the Railway Tree' — he mimed the shape of a steam-engine with his hands — 'and we used to come in by that. The North Pier here, it had a fine bright light and I liked to see it, although I'd had a look at the radar and I knew I was on line.'

Out of the window I could see the *Maersk Challenger* coming past and Alex said, 'Seventeen-foot draught — at low water there's only three foot under the deepest boats. H.M.S. *Broadsword* was coming in, and the captain had been studying the charts for three days. I telt him, "Never mind the charts. Let's dae it by eye." They did awa' wi' the North Pier light — to oor disgust. But you can still see the village lights [at Footdee]. They're like a plan. And they still have the fog bell — three strokes — I *like* to hear it.'

He knew of few great rocks hereabouts that were used as landmarks. On the west coast he had used the unmistakable single stack of Suilven and overseas he had used the highest peak on Tenerife. The one crucial rock for Aberdeen sailors had been 'the Girdle Stane' a little out from the Ness. Today, in a grey calm, the sea was barely ruffling over it.

'When there's a blow on,' Alex said, 'it fairly *boils* ower it.' At once I understood the root of one of the first rock names I ever heard. 'Girdle' (like English 'griddle') means the iron pan that was put over a fire. When dough was poured on to it to make a scone or a crumpet, it seethed — like the sea on the reef, which carries, according to Commander Slater, only '6 feet at Low Water, Ordy. Springs' [normal spring tide].

After some chat about various Mains (my father's mother's and my middle name) and Craigs, Alex said unexpectedly, 'Are you a' right going up and doon ladders?'

'Yes, I think I can go up and down most places.'

'Okay, come on oot then, and we'll meet the boat.'

We climbed down iron rungs fixed to the granite face of the pier and on to the deck of the cutter, which was mainly taken up by the deckhouse with a radio-telephone on its hook, a radar positioned centrally above the windscreen, and a padded revolving chair facing the polished hardwood wheel. When the cutter started to slide about in the swell seaward of the fairway buoy, the helmsman put his ashtray on a piece of nonslip plastic mesh. Out in Greyhope Bay we met the SmitLloyd oilrig standby vessel, registered in Rotterdam, then *Bergen Surveyor* (Nassau). Alex nipped up on to the first by a ropeladder, his colleague on to the second. We followed them into the docks, then out again to meet the *Agility* (London), a small tanker, and the *Sea Sapphire* (Panama), another oilrig support vessel.

'Soul-destroying work,' opined Alex when he rejoined us. 'Just gangin' roon an' roon the rig.'

A voice came over the radio from Control, naming ships queuing out there in the grey. A ship-voice said, 'Atlantic Quay — how much water is there?'

'Atlantic Quay, now — 9.5.'

'9.5 metres — right you are then.'

Alex introduced me to helmsman, colleague, and deckhand. 'Mr Craig's grandfather used to fish with the *Strathairlie*. Do you mind [remember] it?'

'That's a bit *airly* for me,' the helmsman quipped. The *Strathairlie* had been my grandfather's final boat, after his first full trawler, the *Star of Hope*, was torpedoed in the North Sea and they were rescued by one of the Q-ships or disguised armed naval craft. As they talked, the men all emphasised that it had been the fishermen who knew the land-marks, in order to identify good banks and grounds as well as dangers, 'before all this Decca and radar'. Alex recited a rhyme they used, and a little later Martin Hales, the deckhand, did the same —

> Mormond Hill a hand's breadth high,
> Rattray Head you will pass by.

Buchan Ness abaft the beam,
Girdle Ness will soon be seen.

This delighted me, since I had once researched Mormond Hill for a
long poem treating it as focal point of Aberdeenshire and I knew that
for the whalefishers putting out from Peterhead for the Arctic waters,
the hill was the last native landmark they saw, hull-down over the land
of Buchan —

Fareweel tae Tarwathie,
Adieu Mormond Hill,
And the dear land o' Crimond
We bid ye fareweel.

We are bound out for Greenland
And ready tae sail
In hopes tae find riches
By huntin' the whale . . .

When Aberdeen harbour was being created early in the seventeenth
century, a big rock called Knock Metellan (a Gaelic name) blocked the
way and a contractor cleared it by tying casks to it and floating it off.
Now the landmarks for the pilots were nearly all man-made — the
prominent buildings of the town, of which they were connoisseurs.
The replacement of many of the best of them by 'thon prefabricated
rubbish' disgusted them. A huge demolition derrick was pecking
down a stone wall with a steep-pitched gable and the helmsman was
scathing.

'The craftsmanship is unbelievable, the wey they carved thon *hard*
stane. Look at the bank there' — a façade on Regent's Quay with
pillars topped by curly capitals. 'At least they put a conservation order
on the auld Custom House [1771], so they canna touch that. But
anither that's gane, it wis a firm frae Yorkshire that pulled it doon.
Well, the block that owns it, he's teen awa the stanes tae mak himsel' a
hoose in Yorkshire . . . '

They were noticing everything. A regular jogger on the Balnagask
Road, whom they'd nicknamed Wilson after the mystery athlete in the
Wizard long ago. A mallard which waddled about on the quay, then
flew out to an incoming vessel and rode in with it before taking off
again and flying far into the town — 'Awa aff tae the Duthie Park to get
his oats.' When fourteen gannets forged past low over the water, they
told me about a black swan that had appeared the year before. And

they were expert in the social life of the port displayed in front of us. One shoddy new office block was labelled 'George Craig Ltd.'

'Are you any of those Craigs?' they asked me.

'Well, half my family are called George Craig but none of them are as rich as that.'

'Thon block's nae as rich as he thinks as he is. They say most of the money in the firm's nae his ane, it's somebody else's.'

As we put in yet again and the North Pier moved past us, they pointed out its sections: the scabby twentieth-century concrete extension, which they deplored; the granite blocks laid on a slant to Telfer's design [1810–16]; the level courses of the first stage [1769–82]. Beyond Girdle Ness to the south lay the red headland of Greg Ness and beyond it again a gamut of crags and inlets — Doonies Yawns, Adams Pots, The Poor Man, The Grave, Colsea Yawn, and then (running into my grandfather's inshore fishing grounds south of Portlethen) Peel Slough, Black Slough, Craigmaroinn, Englishman's Neuk, Rippiecass, Coble Boards, Brown Jewel, Grim Brigs, Tilly Tenant. Each one reeks of fishermen's stories and belonged so wholly to their close culture that my cousin Annie, whose father fished with my grandfather, had heard none of them. Nor had the pilots.

Theirs is more and more an electronic world and what they see with their own eyes is becoming more a matter of interest and enjoyment than of use. Their seventh sense is in the radar screen, a beautiful trembling image in blue and yellow. (The old black-and-white had been too harshly contrasting to be easily read.) It was set at 1.5 miles and the helmsman showed me what it could do by turning it down to 1.25, then 1.0, enlarging the image. It could go up to 48, too far to be really useful. Boats out at sea were dots like little suns. The picture was so fine that the groynes along the north beach to stabilise the sand showed as blunt teeth, making a design like a wooden rake. The North Pier was a sulphur-coloured stalk growing out of the land's solid yellow, like a picture of the beach itself curving sheer away from here to Ythan mouth. I would be sailing past it in a few days' time, bound for Stromness.

★

As a mountaineer, Bill Brooker set his feet and hands on many pieces of great rocks where nobody had been before. I should have been there with him, when we were at school and university together in the 'forties and early 'fifties. Like a fool, I missed out on all that. Now, aged nearly sixty, we renewed our friendship in the pass of the Lairig Ghru that cleaves the Cairngorms from Deeside to Speyside, on the four-hundred-metre cliffs of Lochnagar, and on one of his purest and most commanding lines, The Talisman on Creagan a Choire Etchachan. As we walked back over the plateau towards the Northern Corries on a July evening, the afterglow spread an orange film clear across the sky behind the angular profiles of the moraines and we talked and talked about the granite world and its most remarkable members. He thought I should climb Ben Avon to see the Woman Stone, which had 'holes in it where the women would go and sit to ensure an easy labour'.

The labour of getting there turned out not to be easy at all. The way to the mountain from the nearest settlement, Tamintoul — at 345 metres the highest village in Britain — was sixteen kilometres. Somehow, on a northern day a few weeks short of the equinox, Andy and I must make good time. I phoned John MacDonald, the gamekeeper at the highest lodge, Inchrory, hoping for permission to take my car beyond the locked gate — not really hoping, because 'the Twelfth' had come and gone and the owners were sure to be out shooting.

'You certainly canna go up there,' he said in the direct Aberdeen-shire way. 'There'll be a shoot going on.'

'But can we take mountain bikes along the track?'

'Well — it is a right of way, so we canna stop you. We would rather you werena there at all. But we canna stop you.'

So we hired two bikes, from a young American woman in a half-derelict hotel with an Australian barman, and pedalled south for an hour and a half along the winding Avon. It is always the best way to travel, smelling and hearing the countryside as you move silently along. The glen twisted, closing and opening again. Fields of oats, at this height still frosty bluish-green with unripeness, gave way to gradual moors. On our left a tract of shale created a disappointing terrain of stubby grassland and collapsing banks. On our right, across the river, lay the real thing, steep slopes falling to the lip of the river, moors rippling infinitely beyond, the heather just withering to the colours of the famous old fishing fly, grouse-and-claret. For more than fifty years this had been my notion of what wild ground should be — fragrant and vivid in summertime with a firm bristle, not a pulpiness, underfoot.

Beyond Dalestie, on the narrow haughland on either bank of the Avon, the blurred oblongs of long-demolished cottages were dark on green — a woeful sight when it implies forced emigration or eviction, yet how were people to go on living in bottomlands so cramped? Here, presumably, were the homes of some of the women who toiled up to Clach Bhan, the Woman Stone. A writer in 1875 remembered seeing in August 1836 twelve of them who 'had that morning come from Speyside, over 20 miles, to undergo the rite'. It must have been a powerful magic to bring them from so far. Perhaps the rock would help us understand it, and why the wife of Fingal was supposed to have bathed there.

In all those miles we had two encounters: one Land Rover driven by a debutantish sort of person, who ignored us although we were standing a couple of feet from her open window, having lifted our bikes on to the verge to let her pass, and one Land Rover driven by a keeper, very likely John MacDonald himself, who gave us a nod and a word. Inchrory was a huge barrack of grey stone on moraines above the river. A quarter of an hour further and we were padlocking our bikes together in a small quarry and starting up the hill on a raw track bulldozed through the heather to let the shooting classes get near their prey with a minimum of effort. The long yellow straights and curves are scored on every purple mountainside all over these ranges. We now know they will stay raw for decades, because plants grow in again so slowly at this height.

Beyond the shooting butts we followed a narrow trod past the rocky spur of Carn Fiaclach, hill of teeth. In the peat the slots of red deer were printed repeatedly, like pairs of olives. Above the skyline, as the Stone surfaced, one black creature steadied against the grey cloud-wrack, then veered off northward. Its wings were so large and square-ended, it could only have been a golden eagle. The deep moor was giving way to the sub-Arctic zone of gravel and heather stunted to a close stubble. Now the Stone was bulking to its true height, like basking elephants getting to their feet, the mounded dark-grey flesh divided into lobes and limbs. Then we stepped up into a little world of hollowed and jointed surfaces, like dunes petrified.

The holes were not few, as I had imagined. There was a myriad, a shoal, a constellation — what should be the noun? On the mottled grey-and-white of the granite all these eyes of water were blinking and trembling in the wind. A trio, two above one, made a goblin face and the rims of the stone reflected in the water created a pair of cartoon eyes looking puckishly sideways.

Until I saw the number of these holes and their nearness to each other, the old rite had seemed a bit improbable. It was perfectly natural. The women were not a few beleaguered waifs, they were together. In many of the holes they could have sat holding hands. The female bonding of their condition and of the walk and climb together would have been clinched as they snuggled into these cups that look made for the purpose. I had been amazed to think that they were willing to soak themselves and go back down the mountain with cold backsides from a height of eleven hundred metres. To avoid that they could have used the basins near the rims of the tor, where the water over the ages has been able to wear through a weakness and escape down a slowly-widening spout. Then they would have been chaired in the hollows, with their legs dangling over the drop, resting, joking, thinking, singing perhaps.

These tors formed — all over the summit ridge of Ben Avon and the mountains nearby — in a process Bill had evoked for me three years before as we looked at their kin, the paps of Lochnagar.

'It's only a theory,' he said, 'but anyway, the theory is that when the igneous or plutonic material was thrust up into the crust of the Earth, into the solid rock of it, it cooled and solidified within the crust, and it was under pressure. And then, when the surface wore away, the granite was exposed, and there was a release of pressure. Like the layers in an onion. The equilibrium was upset and the internal forces pressed outwards. The layers *sprang* outwards. So a striation developed, parallel to the surface of the Earth — it was usually horizontal, though it could be steeply inclined. That's why these tors look like heaps of pancakes, with the horizontal joints of weakness between the layers. They were the hardest material in the plutonic mix — hard plugs. And then the glaciers stripped away the softer, rotten material from around them.'

So the Woman Stone evolved. The final tooling was carried out by weathering. Dimples in the surface of the tor formed where the granite had less of the hardest ingredient. Stones and gravel collected there and rainwater swirled them round as the wind blew, grinding the dimples into basins. In this wet summer most of them were at least half full of water. Some were linked by stains — including one series of at least six — and the eye slid downward from level to level, imagining the little chain of cascades, brimming finally over to a drop of six or seven metres into a permanent lochan on the west side with a vertical back wall and a low outer lip.

The women could have drunk from its perfectly pure and translucent contents. I did, and delighted in the almost tasteless cold of it with a hint of purified earth. They had been pilgrims — pilgrim child-bearers — some perhaps not yet pregnant, already conceiving of their futures and anxious to secure them, in the company of their sisters, like the Australian women in their sacred ground beneath Djugajabbi, the Women's Cave on Uluru, which is taboo to this day.

*

My lodestones on Orkney were antithetical, a hole and a column — the Hole o Row and the Old Man of Hoy. The Old Man towers in the imagination of every climber, and of many others, as we were to find. The Hole o Row could hardly be more self-effacing, scarcely mentioned in print, outshone by the much-visited Bronze Age village of Skara Brae a kilometre along the shore of the Bay of Skaill in the west of Orkney Mainland. It had become real for me through Andy Rafferty's photograph, a rough print, hard to see in scale, and such a vision of white force blazing in some sort of dark chasm that it was hard to believe he could have taken it unscathed.

The *St Sunniva* carried us north past another fine hole, which I had happened upon on a day so entranced by the spring sun it was as though the yellows of primroses and daffodils had steeped the air itself. The Bullers [i.e. boilers] of Buchan are masses of red granite cleft by deep inlets. Although my cousin Annie had known of them for almost eighty years, she had never seen them. We took the path along the verge of them, past a double row of gentrified fisher-cottages whose original owners might have known our forebears. Paths along the spines of the headlands attracted me and I followed one of them, stepping down, then up again where the massive keystone of a natural arch was slowly shrugging into the sea. Round a shoulder I came face to face with a colony of shags which sat tight on their nests in the full glamour of their mating plumage, ovals of mustard yellow on their cheeks, their crests black and erect and *soignée* like the hairdo's of a Mikado's daughters.

To make sure I missed nothing I walked south a few last yards to a headland called Arthur Fowlie — not a personal name but a garbled version of the Gaelic for 'headland of the birds'. A deep music began to reach me, like underground bassoons. The ground sank into a little cleugh, its bottom a rickle of massive boulders. The music was gruffer now and the breath of it fanned my face.

This was the Rumbling Hole. In another hundred thousand years or so the surface between it and the cliff will fall in and make a geo, or the hole will mine deeper, collapse, and leave the ground to seaward as a stack, like Dunbuy, yellow rock, the giant arch twenty-five metres offshore. Arthur Fowlie is faced with immaculate pink granite, the edge of the mass which makes the furthest east point of the Scottish mainland. I could get up a route here called Magic Dragon and I made an improbable date to climb it in the early winter with Greg Strange.

On the day the place was entranced again, a faultless azure sky, a low sun making a rose-flush on the rock. To reach the climb we sidled down a geo called Robie's Haven a little north, stepping into freezing shadow past thistles whose thorny cups were blue with rime, then clambering along the crag just above high water mark beside a sea like a cold Mediterranean. The climbing was effortless, fearless, as though the Hole, and for that matter the Dragon, had laid a spell and every adverse thing had died back underground. At the finish, forty metres above the water, the Hole was breathing quietly and evenly.

From the Orkney boat that same coast looked almost featureless under glum overcast. In the Pentland Firth, between Caithness and the island of Stroma, we felt the westerly and saw it make a furious zone of torn crests and overfalls which ended at a line as clear as the boundary between moor and field. It can blow as hard as it liked, I was thinking, so long as it shows us what the Hole o Row can do.

The photo was so drastic and simplified an image — the blurred white hair, the squared mouth, indefinite ocean beyond — that I was unready for the Hole itself. The way to it goes past the neat miniature domesticities of Skara Brae — the narrow passages between drystone walls, the sandy chamber floored with sea-shells — and across a rough pasture with an old barn at its edge built of sandstone and roofed with Orkney flags. Everything was tranquil and very old.

Abruptly crags towered. From stances on jutting shelves of the biscuity rock above the sea two black hooked heads stood out — cormorants, wondering what we were up to. Between us and them was a geo. The sea rushed into it from the west through a narrow oblong arch, appeared gleaming below us, and burst against a rock barrier which will go one day and leave the cormorant tower as a free-standing stack. I abseiled down on to it, Andy followed and set up his camera, and I scrambled a little way up the tower, then along a gallery above the geo. A few minutes later a big wave volleyed in, exploded, and its milky fall-out seethed round the legs of the tripod.

We became used to the rhythm of the place. Three or four big ones gathered and broke at intervals of a minute, with a hollow dunt of water-tonnage hitting the rock and the highest drops splashing me twelve metres above the surface. (The day was fairly calm.) Water-shocks ran sideways against the walls like lace flouncing. The water calmed, turquoise, suffused with starry bubbles, its surface covered with dimples like ice-green Lalique saucers. We waited. Out there through the arch the swell was massing again, it must surge in. The rock-walls crushed it into a torrent. It reared two metres from trough to crest with a dark glassy brow that shattered forward and rushed at us as though the water-body had the brain of a huge white hunting dog.

After a while I climbed back out and walked westward on to the top of the arch. How normal, for all the tilting swell of it, the sea looked here after the pent ferocity down in the geo. At the western entrance of the arch it was swinging in quite leisurely, the latent thrust of the swell was invisible. The top was nearly all made out of one bedding-plane, where sands were laid down on the floor of a shallow sea as the aboriginal mountains called the Caledonides were washed away by the inconceivable cloudbursts and deluges of those times. That sea rippled its sands as ours do today, and here on the top of the Row arch there was a spread of fossilised ripples as big as a tennis court, a zebra striping of snuff-brown on buff, the imprint of one particular low tide four hundred million years ago.

The past I was sensing here was all prehistoric. I have seen Row spelt with an 'e', which makes it into a personal name. The 'Row' form is more like the Scots word 'row', rhyming with 'cow' and meaning 'roll', which fits the maelstrom tumbling of the sea-water in the geo. So the name fails to open out into a legend, and the people I spoke to nearby at Skaill, who came from there, had no stories about the Hole. For once no lore has twined round a powerful rock and it can remain beautifully itself — raw nature, a supreme intersection of land and water in a tireless display that we revelled in for hours.

On my way back down a woman who had been studying cormorants through fieldglasses buttonholed me. She sounded quite worried.

'I love to come here,' she said. 'I've rented the cottage here for years. But the farmers have been telling me — people should be more careful. Just the other year a man had been eating lunch up where you were. He looked back, and the block he'd been sitting on had gone.'

This reminded me uncomfortably of notices I had seen all round the coast, at Durdle Door, at Crag Point north of Newcastle, the battery of warnings at Land's End (many put up since the tragic drowning of the children from Stoke Poges) which make it hard to focus on the sea and make you want more than ever to turn your back on Peter de Savory's welter of caffs and gift shops, model galleons and video shows, and drop down out of sight over the land's end itself. 'DANGER: CLIFFS KILL'. 'DANGEROUS — STEEP ROCKS'. 'YOU ARE ADVISED TO KEEP CLEAR OF THE CLIFFS'. That there is a sheer drop of forty or fifty metres, that edges can be brittle — isn't this obvious to our senses? Must we be coddled and bullied with advice? Can't we be left to meet the wilderness for ourselves?

'Thank you for your concern,' I said to the worried woman, 'but I think I know what I'm doing. At any rate I've survived so far.'

By a happy contrast, when we reached the Old Man's doorstep on Hoy after the hour's walk over heathery mountainside from Rackwick, a mother with four children aged between six and eleven was letting them stroll about, unfussed, on the very verge of the 140-metre gulf between island and stack. Here was a sane parent who realised that not many children, left to themselves, would frolic violently on the edge of a space so dizzy that your feet feel abruptly less planted on the ground and the great hollowing out there seems to feed back into your body, unhinging it, thinning it.

Most of the families and couples who arrived while we were there spent only a few minutes at what must be one of the grandest points in the British Isles. Nobody picked their way down the path to the foot of the Old Man, or even looked for its start, except the two climbers who presently appeared on a ledge on the East Face Route — the original one — looking airily poised as cormorants until you saw their ropes.

People come here, it seems to me, to take a quick look at the exact bound of our normal lives. One step more and there would be nothing under you. One more hurricane and the Old Man's small footing will wash away and he will finish up as a stramash of boulders (or so we have recently been warned). He is the quintessence of both survival and vulnerability. Solidity and jeopardy are embodied in the one slim upright.

To experience that to the full you would have to climb him. Two different partners whom I had tried to tempt up here had both withdrawn on the ground that the weather forecast was dubious. Now the day was halcyon. The red faces of St John's Head along the way — the highest sheer cliff in Britain — glowed warmly as Tudor brickwork. The air was barely moving and the boat from Scrabster to Stromness made a creamy wake on blue like a cruise liner in the tropics. All day, as I scrambled down to the foot of the Old Man, climbed up the first twenty-five metres of him, and walked round his base, I could feel the restiveness in my ribs near the armpit and inside the wrist that is the symptom of wanting to climb, to embrace rock, get my fingers into its locks and open them. I had to make do with poring over him and imagining my way up the one line possible for me, the East Face, so that when I came back and did the climb my nerve would already be tempered for the most awesome places.

The way down to sea level was wild enough, an extremely steep zigzag stair of bucket steps scooped out of the heather and sedge by many boots. They plopped and sucked, wet permanently with the oozing drainage from the layered sandstone above. Halfway down a blind-looking young fulmar was squattering in the undergrowth, spraying white shit in all directions, its downy feathers clarted with it. A fox would surely get it, or a great skua, most avid of predators, called 'bonxie' by the islanders. Midway down the cliff, the Old Man looked tangible, and possible. From sea level he had almost soared beyond me again. He looked tapering, although I knew he was much the same girth all the way up.

The neck of rubble that joins him to the island is raw pink on the west side, eaten away by the last winter's waves. This may not threaten the Old Man himself. A three-metre stratum of grey-green basalt makes his second storey and this runs out on the west side in a massive glacis of flowstone which must baffle much of the sea's onset. A century ago, as we can see in early etchings, the span of his arched link to the island fell down. Looking back along that line we can see his forebear, or sibling — a handsome triple buttress, red with ferric iron and green with terraces of turf, rising twenty or thirty metres higher than himself and exactly in line with him, just as Needle Ridge runs out into Napes Needle in Wasdale.

What the climbing guide calls the 'shattered pillar above the boulder ridge' is a remnant of the connection between the Old Man and the rest of his family. Itching for upward movement, I climbed it by solid steps and little faces like the sides of terracotta flower-tubs that frost has damaged. All was sunlit and comfortable, until the pillar merged with the main trunk and bleached scraps of old gear showed me that the way from here into the meat of the climb was along a sheer face with fingers in a joint and feet on not very much. Space gaped, and flowed in on me, and I knew by the sweating of my palms what sort of high wire I'd be toeing if ever I embarked on the climb for real.

The fragility of Orkney's western rock-shore gives the lie to the notion that rocks are 'eternal', as in fine sayings like 'The rocks remain'. These stacks, or castles as they call them here, are lasting and precarious at once. They make us look at them, monuments to the world long before humans. We see in them the power of durance that keeps trees, towers and pylons in place. We see the fine-drawn balance of them, the imminence of their falling. At Yescanaby, five kilometres south of the Hole o Row, we walked the rim of the island past a whole gallery of flagstone stacked in towers, jointed into arches, recumbent in the sea. At Brough of Bigging ('building') the sea showed its destroying force as it flooded through a black entry, turning Nile-green and transparent in the sunlight. A cormorant was being carried along on it.

Against the green we could see that one leg with its webbed foot was trailing, helpless. The bird disappeared. If she had dived to fish, she should surface again in less than a minute. After five minutes we had to accept that she had drowned.

Yesnaby Castle stands with its feet in this fierce water. It has two feet, as the Old Man once did, and the seaward limb is only a metre thick. How long will it last? South of Qui Ayre, in Garthna Geo, another castle was still joined to the island by a natural plank of flagstone not much thicker than an oaken main beam in a seventeenth-century house. We balanced across it, keenly aware that some day it was bound to fall — in a storm perhaps, or so we told ourselves, or perhaps when the gale blowing clear across three thousand kilometres of ocean could move a forty-ton boulder two metres along the ground and bend angle-iron through 90°.

Further south again we took the track past Mousland farm, through marginal fields, looking out for Gaulton Castle. High above the sea the salt gust had managed to wipe out all herbage except an upholstering of hard narrow bluish blades like sea-thrift leaves. Between Neban Point and Lyre Geo, cliffs smeared with green dropped fifty metres sheer. Offshore stood their elegant remnant, exactly the same height as the mainland, with the same flora on top only more flourishing since the sheep can't get at it. We could trace the strata from the cliff face to the stack across the intervening space. This stack did taper, it was no optical illusion that its foot was slimmer than its head. On top you could grow kail or cabbages, in what Orcadians call a planticroo, or for that matter you could manoeuvre a Rover car to and fro there and photograph it for an advertisement while the driver ducked down out of sight. . . .

Gaulton Castle was the perfect stack, so slender and so striated with the fine horizontals of the flags composing it that it seemed to spin on its vertical axis like one of the dust-devils we had followed through the desert north of Death Valley, or like a dervish whose toes were stirring up water instead of sand. It is only a few kilometres west of Stenness, with the four great monoliths still standing, and the Ring of Brodgar. I wonder if the Bronze Age stone-masters who raised the most beautiful of those liths, so thin, so strong, widening from a foot buried in the ground, then slanting in again from a shoulder to a point, intended a likeness to these castles, or whichever of them were growing like trees out of the sea two hundred generations ago.

*

A stack and an arch waited for us on Shetland: Ern Stack on Yell, where the last of the sea-eagles flew; Dore Holm in St Magnus Bay, the last exit from Britain. When I had been here before on the seven-hour haul from Stromness to Lerwick, a fieldfare had flown past us on its way to winter down south, perhaps to feed on berries from our own holly tree in Cumbria. Later another had flown out of the dark and perched on the rail. I hope the rest was worth the miles he was carried back north.

To reach The Eigg, where the eagles last bred in the years before the Great War, you must leave your car at Grimister and walk north past the lochans called the Hulk Waters and round the slope of Stany Hill to the Neips of Graveland. The names are apt for a place with a doom on it. Robert Johnson, a crofter at Setter in Mid Yell, had told me how his grandfather was evicted from Eftsigarth, across the burn from Grimister, in almost the last of the Scottish Clearances.

'He was warned oot sae aften,' he told me in his sitting room at Snuastadr, 'that it broke his hert. Grandfaither was building corn in the yard when they got the forty days' waarnin'. The taaties wasna up but they were allooed to tak up the taaties. The roof was torn aff — they could get no men in the island to act as sheriff officers, so they brought men from Larwick. My grandfaither was carryin' for weeks. The grand-uncles had to be led, John and David, because they were blind . . . '

This was all on the west side of the long voe called Whale Firth. A Mr Williamson in Lerwick gave me a glimpse of the evictions on the east side. His grandmother had been born at Dalsetter during the Potato Famine. When the next township, Lumbister, was cleared and fenced off to make one large farm, he told me, 'the evicted sheep trod a mirey track along the Dalsetter side of the new fence, and they lay down alongside and died with their faces towards Lumbister'.

On a louring day this history was visible in the remnants of houses and especially in the eerie vacancy of the land. It had the green purity of crofts that were once cleared of boulders and tree stumps to make room for crops, for cows and horses and hens, and which are now given over exclusively to sheep that graze where they like among the encroaching rushes and bracken.

As we neared the coast above Norther Geo, a bonxie buzzed us, its chiselly beak a few inches above our heads. It began to prevail over the sea-eagle in the eighteenth century when the farmers spread stories of the eagles carrying off babies and were given five shillings 'for the head of an Eagle [which] has a good deal thinned the country of these birds,

317

but not rooted them out altogether'. Now the bonxie lords it here, a bird 'quite up to dispossessing an osprey or drowning a gannet'. The last days of the eagle, which we studied in the Old Haa at Burravoe, were pure tragedy.

One of the last pairs had their two eggs stolen at the turn of the century and moved their eyrie to a safer place midway up the hundred-metre north face of the square-headed prow called The Eigg. A man with a gun came on the female feeding on a dead sheep and wounded it. It was later found dead and was stuffed. In a fortnight the male came back with a female much smaller than himself, an albino. In 1904 a Christian, the Reverend Sorby, ordered holdfasts from a local black-smith, roped down the cliff, and stole the eggs. A few miles across Yell Sound, at North Roe, an R.S.P.B. watcher called James Hay looked out for the eagles every year from 1910. In the summer of 1916 ten visits to their haunt yielded no sightings: 'he feared she must be dead . . . The albino eagle — estimated to be thirty years old when she was shot near Ronas Hill in 1916 — had lost her mate some years before but had returned to her nest each spring to take up her lonely vigil.' In a heartbreaking photo (the only one taken of this species before the reintroduction on Rhum in 1975) you can see her roosting, white and little and solitary against the black loom of the crag.

In the early fifties Bill Brooker and his brother Ian, then the G.P. on Yell, came here to explore and climb. 'We peered over the rim of The Eigg,' he told me, 'and we could make out a primitive piton, or whatever it was, that the robber of the nest had used to get down there. We knew that the crag to the north, a most peculiar kind of a rock, had been named after the sea-eagle, the 'ern', and we had a great time finding a way up it. I believe it was struck by lightning not long after we did the route.'

Andy and I lay on our stomachs at the edge of The Eigg and scanned the rockface below us, foot by foot, through fieldglasses. No ironware could be seen. Forty years on it could have rusted away at last. And how much of the Stack had the thunderbolt destroyed? In this place where everything seemed to have ended, we could believe anything. It would be good, though, to get up one of the northernmost recorded rock-climbs in the British Isles, for its own sake and as a kind of homage to the bird.

The Stack triangled into sight above the short turf of the headland like the dorsal fin of a Great White Shark. Its pallor was extreme, a deader white than quartz — or yiggelsteen, as they call it here — and turned out to be quartzite, unless it is the younger metamorphic rock called syenite. Flakes of black mica-schist stuck out from its upper edge, barring the white like the gill-rakers of the shark. We slithered down a slope quarried by its own splitting and collapsing and at this point, standing under the cross-section of the Stack, we walked through a cracked looking-glass into a perverse world.

A traverse line runs seaward, leading round on to the rearing ramp or slab face up which we'll climb. I can see chunky holds and plenty of cracks for protection nuts. Close up, the black bands are like burnt biscuits, the quartzite has the look of wet sugar lumps. And the strength. Reaching up, my forearm nudges a skull-sized block. It falls against my thighs. I open them, shouting 'Stones coming down!' The thing hits the face below me, bursts, fragments spin out into the sea and a brimstone reek of struck matches taints the air. Stealthily, as though edging past a sleeping polar bear, I make it to the security of the main face, feeling several years older than when I roped up.

Now the straightforward, easy-angled climbing will begin. Tell me about it, as they say. The 50° slope of the schist cladding is divided by quartzite veins and narrow flowerbeds where a roof would have valleys with lead flashing. None of them opens enough to accept a nut. I pad upwards, morale disintegrating slowly, like the rock.

'What's it like, Dave?' Andy calls with increasing frequency. He hasn't done much climbing. To have lured him into this predicament is another thing that is unbending my springs.

'Not difficult,' I shout back. 'Not easy either,' I add from time to time.

The leaves of the thrift, bladder-campion, and ragwort in the valleys are damp with drizzle. The entrance to the hollow between the two crowning horns of the Stack steepens to 60°, slick as a ship's hull. Thwarted, I edge out to the right through a flowerbed and lay-away from the top of a huge undercut flake. Here is the gap between the horns at last. When we squeeze through to abseil down the far side, will it snap shut like the finger-stone of Finn Mac Cool, proving us unworthy? It looks impossibly narrow anyway, and I climb up towards the right hand tip, hoping for a perch. The rock is split by fine cracks, as sharp as though crazed by yesterday's gelignite — or by the thunder-bolt. It's crazed, I'm crazy, I teeter back down to the gap and belay on a stub of quartzite which I can actually lever away from the mother-rock with my fingers.

Andy joins me, his big blue eyes wide with what is either misplaced trust in me or a willed disbelief that this is happening to him.

'What d'you think?' he asks.

I think we are in rats' alley where the dead men lost their bones, as the man said. I think we should grow wings instantly and take the eagles' way out of this place of ill-omen.

'I think we should abseil back down the slab. That landward face is rotten as shit. If pieces break off on us, they could cut the rope.'

So down we go again, with our weight coming on to that shaky stub. These islands are teeth dropped from the jaw of the Stoury Worm in its death-throes, according to the story. We are morsels stuck between two of them. If the abseil had been a free dangle, not a canny backwards walk, that anchor would never have held. Nor would the half-embedded spar of schist which is all that offers in the valley part-way down.

Through the fatalistic numbness born of being terrified continuously for two hours, another dread is surfacing. How will we escape at the bottom? Is the north side of the Stack any more hospitable than that pile of sugar-lumps on the south? Is it heck! The only option turns out to be a vertical black wall embossed with rounded holds — very serious for the second man down, unless we sacrifice yet another piece of gear. As though locked into the last stage of a doomed programme, I set off to reverse that ramshackle wall — unroped, since I now know that any gear placed will only pull out or pull off any stones it's jammed between, and the rope itself might easily do the same. While I'm still twenty metres above the tidal boulders, one burnt biscuit starts to ease out with a ghastly dental groan as I grip it for balance and I have to stand bridged on cracked blocks while I push it back in and try to warn Andy not to use it.

As we scramble back up the slope, lost for words after three hours of Russian roulette, a human breath and snuffle sounds behind us and we look down to see the back of a porpoise glisten just out of the water beside a clump of tangle. For a full minute it browses and breathes, and the comfortable sound soothes us back into normality, into the friendlier family of nature. As we look across at the Stack, appraising it and concluding we were right not to abseil down the tottering debris left by the lightning-strike, the barbarous white cockscomb of it, its black horns or feathers, and its threatening pose are becoming a white-tailed sea-eagle totem, a fierce emblem of the place's original life. A kindred image is surfacing in my brain — a photo of an osprey as it struggled to rise out of a loch with a fish in its claws, the water streaming from it, making a glass cage round the glare of the eye, the grimace of the beak, the white fire of the head. At last I walk back-

wards away from the Stack, reluctant to lose sight of it as it sinks
back into its own world.

Later I learned that in a chambered tomb at Isbister on South
Ronaldsay in Orkney they recently found a great many human skulls
and disjointed skeletons along with the bones of many sea-eagles,
interred about 2400 B.C.: 'it is hard to avoid the conclusion that they
were the totem of the group involved.' In the photograph in the guide,
the white boss and hook of cranium and beak, the smaller white hooks
of the claws, stand out as symbols of the ancient island culture. And
perhaps our ploy had not been so daft. Many of the skeletons at Isbister
showed 'an alteration of bones around the ankle which may have been
caused by scaling cliffs from an early age'.

As we came over Watch Hill on Shetland Mainland and looked west
across Brae Wick to where Dore Holm should be, Andy exclaimed,
'Oh *no*! What's happened to the arch?' Instead of a span with a clear
exit through it to the open sea, there was only a hulk. A false alarm, of
course. By Tangwick we were in line with the arch and could see the
gape of it. For a minute we had been reminded that the sea-force
which made the Dore out of an island will presently demolish it.

Pressure was falling, the westerly was rising, the waves thrown up
out of the swell by the Dore's submarine foundation were bursting in
snow-white plumes. They rose two-thirds up the face of the black
volcanic tuff — which is forty metres high — then scattered across its
darkness like seeds across ploughland.

Dore Holm, door island, lurks in the bight of Esha Ness at the north
end of St Magnus Bay. On the east side of the archipelago the Bay
would be a great square haven. Here it receives the Atlantic in shuddering draughts. We parked at Stenness, walked to the headland called
Fiorda Taing to get a near, straight sight through the arch, settled ourselves on the reef well out of the waves' reach, decamped at once
to a point five metres higher up and watched white waters burst and
flood and fall back where we had been three minutes before.

From here the island showed its complexity. It was not a simple arch
but a mass rising from north to south, then throwing a limb out west to
form the door. After a time it took on the look of a great black horse
lying down on the sea with its backside towards us, haunches rising
into a broad back, swivelling its neck (the span) through 90° and
lowering its flat forehead (the outer jamb) to browse the blue-green
pasture of the sea and munch it to smithereens white as gulls' feathers.

The burst, burst, burst of the big sea out there was mesmerising.
Each time the swell piled up beyond the island we were exulting — at a

safe distance — as it pranced into sight again through the door, hit the unseen reef, and flowered straight up, filling the tall portal with its blizzard. For sailors it was as much a menace as a landmark. Tangwick Haa, the one middle-class dwelling hereabouts, built for the chief merchants of this district in the seventeenth century, is now a museum. The hefty white-walled bulk of it is a landmark in itself. Its records show that the nearest wrecks to here were the *Haabit Mandel* (no other details) in 1882, the *Charles Jones* (369-ton schooner), bound from Leith to Valparaiso in 1852, lost in a westerly gale, and the *Avenoria* (221 tons), bound from Miramichi Bay (New Brunswick) to Sunderland in 1846, abandoned off Lewis and driven derelict across 350 kilometres of open sea before it struck Esha Ness.

For the seamen of a foundering ship Dore Holm must have loomed up amongst the spume like the gate of hell. For me it is where my homeland ends, and eyesight and mindsight are free to stream off through it round the rest of the world.

NOTES

All publications from London unless otherwise stated.

PREFACE

P.13: David Craig, *Native Stones* (1987), pp 7–8.

P.14: Norman MacLeod, *Reminiscences of a Highland Parish* (1863), pp 293–5, 303.

P.14: David Craig, *On the Crofters' Trail* (1990), pp 159–62.

P.14: *2 Samuel*, ch. 22, vv. 2–5, ch. 23, v. 3; *Psalms* 18, vv. 2, 31; *Isaiah* ch. 26, v. 4; also *Deuteronomy*, ch. 32, v. 4.

P.15: Richard Fortey, *The Hidden Landscape* (1993), p 293.

PART ONE: NORTH AMERICA, THE DESERT STATES

CHAPTER 1: *Black Mountain and Earth Fire Country*

P.19: Clifford J. Walker, *Back Door to California* (Barstow, California, 1986), p 163.

P.19: *Ibid.*, pp 17, 28–9.

P.20: *Ibid.*, pp 189, 212.

P.21: Karl W. Luckert, *The Navajo Hunter Tradition* (Tucson, Arizona, 1975), pp 138–9.

P.22: William Michael Stokes and William Lee Stokes, *Messages on Stone* (Salt Lake City, Utah, 1980), pp 9–10, 19–20, 51–2.

P.22: La Van Martineau, *The Rocks Begin to Speak* (Las Vegas, Nevada, 1973), pp. 7–12, 36, 98, 101, 105.

P.22: James G. Cowan, *The Elements of the Aborigine Tradition* (Shaftesbury, Dorset, 1992), p 12.

P.22: Walker, *Back Door to California*, pp 52, 212, 220, 288.

P.24: Ekkehart Malotki with Michael Lomatuway'ma, *Earth Fire* (Flagstaff, Arizona, 1987), pp 75–9.

P.24: *Ibid.* pp 73–5.

P.26: Carlotwin Sauer, 'The Road to Cibola', in *Land and Life*, ed. John Leighley (Berkeley and Los Angeles, 1963), p 89.

P.26: *Earth Fire*, p 114; Donald G. Pike, *Anasazi: Ancient People of the Rock* (New York, 1986), p 16.

P.26: *Ibid.*, pp 116–17.

P.27: Walter McClintock, *Shadowcatchers* (Petaluma, California, 1991). A much more *sociable* impression is given by photos in, for example, *Images of Hopi* by Trudy Thomas (Flagstaff, Arizona, 1991), esp. the photos on pp 7, 19, 26, 28, and by photographs from all over N. America in *The North American Indian in Early Photographs*, ed. Paula Richardson Fleming and Judith Luskey (1988).

CHAPTER 2: *The Canyon of Broken Shards*

P.28: Paul Zolbrod, *Diné bahane* (Albuqerque, New Mexico, 1984), p 186.

P.34: Pike, *Anasazi*, pp 18–19.

CHAPTER 3: *Disenchanted Mesas*

P.36: Luckert, *Navajo Hunter Tradition*, p 44 and n. 22.

P.37: *The Sixth Grandfather*: Black Elk's Teachings Given to John G. Neilhardt, ed. Raymond J. DeMallie (Lincoln, Nebraska, 1985), p 105 and n. 6.

P.37: Malotki, *Earth Fire*, p 118.

P.37: Zolbrod, *Diné bahane*, pp 86–7, 364.

P.38: Raymond Friday Locke, *The Book of the Navajo* (Los Angeles, 1976), pp 143–53; Sauer, *Land and Life*, p 90.

P.41: Adolf Bandelier, *The Delight Makers* (1890; New York, 1971 ed.), p 135.

P.42: Locke, *Book of the Navajo*, pp 157–9, 176–9.

CHAPTER 4: *Inscription Rock to Corn Mountain*

P.44: Sauer, *Land and Life*, pp 48, 53.

P.46: Locke, *Book of the Navajo*, pp 154–7.

P.49: Locke, *Book of the Navajo*, p 76; Zolbrod, *Diné bahane*, p 87.

P.49: Malotki, *Earth Fire*, pp 170–1.

P.50: Ron McCoy, *Archaeoastronomy* (Flagstaff, Arizona, 1992), pp 10–11.

P.50: Bill Harris, *The American West* (New York, 1984), pp xiii–xiv.

P.51: D. H. Lawrence, *The Rainbow* (1915), ch. 5.

CHAPTER 5: *Holes of Emergence*

P.53: Henry Moore and John Hedgecoe, *Henry Moore* (1986), p 117.

P.54: Andy Goldsworthy, *Hand to Earth* (1991), pp 24–42.

P.55: Zolbrod, *Diné bahane*, p 39.

P.55: McCoy, *Archaeoastronomy*, pp 7, 11.

P.55: Leslie Marmon Silko, 'Landscape, History, and the Pueblo Imagination' in *Antaeus on Nature*, ed. Daniel Heilpern (1989), p 91.

P.55: Luckert, *Navajo Hunter Tradition*, pp 36, 70, 222–4.

P.55: Locke, *Book of the Navajo*, p 161.

P.56: Francis Jennings, 'The Discovery of Americans', 1984, quoted by Patricia Nelson Limerick, *The Legacy of Conquest* (New York, 1987), p 220.

P.56: Locke, *Book of the Navajo*, p 14.

P.57: *Ibid.*, p 15; Luckert, *Navajo Hunter Tradition*, p 200.

CHAPTER 6: *Hoskee Begay and the Long Walk*

P.59: Silko, 'Pueblo Imagination', p 91 n.

P.59: Locke, *Book of the Navajo*, p 33.

P.61: Wynn R. Bailey, *The Long Walk* (Tucson, Arizona, 1964), pp 160–1.

P.61: Craig, *On the Crofters' Trail*, pp 165–6.

P.62: Locke, *Book of the Navajo*, pp 358–64.

P.62: Martineau, *The Rocks Begin to Speak*, pp 96–100.

P.62: Paul Preston, 'The discreet charm of a dictator': *Times Literary Supplement*, 5 March 1993.

P.63: Derek Malcolm, 'Still shooting Indians': *The Guardian*, 29 October 1992.

P.64: Neruda, *Canto General*, translated by Jack Schmitt (Berkely, Los Angeles, 1991), p 255.

P.65: Zolbrod, *Diné Bahane*, pp 261–2.

P.65: F. A. Barnes, *Canyon Country Geology* (Salt Lake City, Utah, 1978), p 20.

P.65: Locke, *Book of the Navajo*, p 115.

CHAPTER 7: *Voices Singing out of Empty Cisterns*

P.66: Malotki, *Earth Fire*, p 115.

P.67: Luckert, *Navajo Hunter Tradition*, pp 47–8.

P.67: *In the Trail of the Wind*, ed. John Bierhorst (New York, 1971), p 68.

P.68: T. S. Eliot, *The Waste Land* (1922), section 1, 'The Burial of the Dead', and section 5, 'What the Thunder said'.

CHAPTER 8: *Great White Volumes*

P.70: A. Alvarez, *Feeding the Rat* (1988), p 26.

P.71: John Muir, *The Eight Wilderness-Discovery Books*, ed. Terry Gifford (1992), pp 642–4.

P.72: *Ibid.*, p 683.

PART TWO: AUSTRALIA

CHAPTER 9: *Painted Rocks in Eden*

P.79: Mary Barnard, *A History of Australia* (Sydney, 1962), p 8.

P.84: Geoffrey Blainey, *Triumph of the Nomads* (1975; Sydney, 1982), pp 247–51.

P.84: G. Plekhanov, *Unaddressed Letters*, VI (Moscow, 1957), pp 138–46.

P.85: T. A. Dowson, *Rock Engravings of Southern Africa* (U. of Witwatersrand, S. Africa, 1992), pp 15 ff.

P.86: J. D. Lewis-Williams and T.A. Dowson, *Rock Paintings of the Natal Drakensberg* (Pietermaritzburg, 1992), pp 38, 48, 51.

P.87: Blainey, *Triumph of the Nomads*, p 202.

P.88: Richard Broome, *Aboriginal Australians* (Sydney, NSW, 1982), pp 187–90.

P.90: Dorothy Tunbridge, *Flinders Ranges Dreaming* (Canberra, 1988), p xii.

P.90: Colin Sampson, *Adam in Ochre* (Sydney, NSW, 1951), p 19.

P.91: *Ibid.*, p 20.

P.91: Grahame L. Walsh, *Australia's Greatest Rock Art* (Bathurst, N.S.W., 1988), p 44.

P.91: Ronald M. Berndt and Catherine H. Berndt, *The Speaking Land* (Ringwood, Victoria, 1989), pp 208–9.

P.92: Sampson, *Adam in Ochre*, p 21.

P.92: Broome, *Aboriginal Australians*, p 14.

CHAPTER 10: *Pillar of Fire by Day*

P.93: Cowan, *Aborigine Tradition*, p 12.

P.93: *Guide to New and Used Cars* (1992), p 127.

P.94: Plekhanov, *Unaddressed Letters*, p 142.

P.95: Barnard, *History of Australia*, pp 162–3, 250.

P.95: P. E. Warburton, *Journey Across the Western Interior of Australia*, ed. H. W. Bates (1875), p 86.

P.99: Macdouall Stuart, 'Journal of 1860 Expedition: first full transcript' (Adelaide, 1983), pp 24–5; W.P. Auld, *Recollections of McDouall Stuart, 1891* (Adelaide, 1984), p 35.

P.99: *To the Inland Sea: Charles Sturt's Expedition 1844–45, 1849* (Victoria, 1986), p 170.

P.99: Ernest Giles, *The Journal of a Forgotten Expedition* (Adelaide, 1880), pp 9–12.

P.99: Ernest Giles, *Australia Twice Traversed: The Romance of Exploration* (1889), I, pp 89, 94, 116.

P.100: Alan Moorehead, *Cooper's Creek*, 1963 (1988), pp 82, 93–4.

P.101: Giles, *Australia Twice Traversed*, I, pp 11–12.

CHAPTER 11: *The Red Centre*

P.102: *W. C. Gosse's Explorations, 1873*: Parliamentary Paper No. 48 (Adelaide, 1874), p 9.

P.103: Charles Mountford, *Brown Men and Red Sand* (Sydney, NSW, 1950), pp 77–8; Bill Harney, *To Ayers Rock and Beyond*, 1963 (Bayswater, Victoria, 1984), pp 111–2.

P.104: John Pilger, 'Enduring Old Rituals': *New Statesman and Society,* 30 October 1992.

P.104: Quoted in Warburton, *Journey,* p 69.

P.105: Cowan, *Aborigine Tradition,* pp 74–9; Charles Mountford, *Ayers Rock* (Sydney, 1965), pp 31–174; Harney, *To Ayers Rock and Beyond,* pp 76, 84.

P.105: Harney, *To Ayers Rock,* p 77; *Ibid.,* p 85.

P.105: Cowan, *Aborigine Tradition,* p 76; Mountford, *Ayers Rock,* pp 55, 57, 109, 127–8.

P.106: Michael Andrews, *The Delectable Mountain* (1991).

P.106: Cowan, *Aborigine Tradition,* p 77.

P.108: Eduardo Galeano, *Memory of Fire: I, Genesis,* trans. Cedric Belfrage (1985), p 4.

P.109: Giles, *Australia Twice Traversed,* I, pp 188–91; II, pp 11, 60–1.

P.109: Mountford, *Brown Men and Red Sand,* pp 106–8.

CHAPTER 12: *Waves in the Granite*

P.112: John K. Ewers, *Bruce Rock: The Story of a District* (Bruce Rock District Board, 1959), pp 5–8.

P.112: *Ibid.,* pp 10–11.

P.115: *Ibid.* pp 7–8; Olga Joukovsky-Vaiyvila, *Around the Rock: A History of the Shire of Nungarin in Western Australia* (Nungarin, W.A., 1978), pp 1–5.

P.117: Philip and Noel Wallace, *Children of the Desert* (Melbourne, 1968), p 51.

CHAPTER 13: *The Biggest Rock in the World*

P.119: *Alerta,* Santander, 14 August 1991.

P.120: Neruda, *Canto General,* p 233.

P.124: A. C. and F. T. Gregory, *Journals of Australian Explorations* (Brisbane, 1884), pp 46–7.

P.125: Zolbrod, *Diné Bahane,* pp 271–2.

P.125: Jennifer Westwood, *Albion* (1985), p 430.

P.125: Walker, *Back Door to California,* p 38.

P.125: Tunbridge, *Flinders Ranges Dreaming,* pp 93–5.

P.125: Royal Robbins, 'Tis-Sa-Ack', in John Long (ed.), *Tales from the Steep* (Merrillville, Indiana, 1993), p 90.

P.126: Tunbridge, *Flinders Ranges Dreaming,* pp 14–15, 29, 35–7, 39.

P.127: Richard A. Gould, *Foragers of the Australian Desert* (1969), pp 43–4, 148–9, 151.

P.127: Gregory, *Journals,* pp 37, 46.

PART THREE: THE STRAITS OF GIBRALTAR

CHAPTER 14: *Stone Poles of the Earth*

P.131: Ananda K. Coomaraswamy, *Selected Papers*, I (Princeton, 1977), pp 522–43.

P.131: Arthur Bernard Cook, *Zeus*, III (Cambridge, 1940), pp 976–86.

P.131: Locke, *Book of the Navajo*, p 108.

P.132: Robert Graves, *The Greek Myths*, 1955 (1960), 2, pp 133–5.

P.132: Peter J. Wyllie, *The Way the Earth Works* (New York, 1976), pp 209–11.

P.133: Donald A. MacKenzie, *Indian Myth and Legend* (n.d.), p 122; James G. Frazer, *The Golden Bough* (1922 ed.), p 350.

P.133: *A Literary and Historical Atlas of America* (Everyman, 1930 ed.), pp 108–9 and plates I, VI; *The Times Atlas of Archaeology* (1988), p 274, fig. A.

P.134: James G. Frazer (ed.), *The Fasti of Ovid* (1929), II, pp 206–11.

P.135: William G. F. Jackson, *The Rock of the Gibraltarians* (Grendon, Northants.), pp 20, 170–9.

P.136: Ovid, *Metamorphoses*, trans. Mary Innes (1955), p 211.

P.136: *Isaiah*, ch. 57, v. 5; Donald. A. MacKenzie, *Myths of Babylonia and Assyria* (n.d.), pp 171–2.

CHAPTER 15: *Traces of Hercules*

P.139: *Metamorphoses*, p 209.

P.141: I. F. Grant, *Highland Folk Ways* (1961), p 352, n. 4.

P.142: *Ancient Irish Tales* ed. Tom Peete Cross and Clark Harris Slover (Dublin, 1969 ed.), pp 355–6; Gerard Murphy, 'Acallan na Senorach', in Myles Dillon (ed.), *Irish Sagas* (Cork, 1968), p 119.

P.142: *Ancient Irish Tales*, pp 434–6.

P.143: Donald A. MacKenzie, *Scottish Folk-Lore and Folk Life* (1935), pp 136–67; Raghnall Mac Ille Duibh, 'The earth mother and the cailleach', in *West Highland Free Press*, 12 July 1991; *West Highland Free Press*, 26 February 1993.

P.144: See also Jim Crumley's description of our day up there in his *Among Mountains* (1993), pp 39–40.

P.145: Seton Gordon, *The Cairngorm Hills of Scotland* (1925), pp 132–3; Peter Drummond, *Scottish Hill and Mountain Names* (Scottish Mountaineering Trust, 1991), p 182.

P.146: W. H. Murray, *The Isles of Western Scotland* (1973), p 232; cf. W. H. Marwick, *The Folklore of Orkney and Shetland* (1975), p 59; Grant, *Highland Folk Ways*, pp 73–4, 128–9; Raghnall Mac Ille Duibh, 'What were shielings made of?', in *West Highland Free Press*, 24 July 1990.

P.146: Jim Crumley, *A High and Lonely Place* (1991), p 155 and plate 28.

P.146: MacKenzie, *Scottish Folk-Lore*, pp 137–8; Mac Ille Duibh, 'What were shielings made of ?'

P.147: Donald A. MacKenzie, *Egyptian Myth and Legend* (n.d.), pp 307–9; *Scottish Folk-Lore*, p 146.

PART FOUR: AFRICA BELOW THE EQUATOR

CHAPTER 17: *High Towers and Refuges*

P.157: André Brink, *The First Life of Adamastor* (1993), pp 1–4.

P.161: Jose Burman, *The Table Mountain Book* (Cape Town/Johannesburg, 1991), pp 9–11.

P.162: Penny Miller, *Myths and Legends of Southern Africa* (Cape Town, 1979), p 62.

P.163: André Brink, *An Instant in the Wind*, 1976 (1991), pp 9–10; Allister Sparks, *The Mind of South Africa* (1990), pp 76–7.

P.164: André Brink, *A Chain of Voices* (1982), pp 169, 173, 202.

CHAPTER 18: *The Road to Moonshadow*

P.164: Sparks, *Mind of South Africa*, pp 104, 108.

P.165: *Ibid.*, pp 92, 95, 103.

P.165: David Bristow, *Mountains of Southern Africa* (Cape Town, 1985), pp 36–8.

P.166: *Ibid.*, pp 28–9.

P.169: *New Nation New History* (Johannesburg, 1989), I, p 7.

P.169: Bristow, *Mountains of Southern Africa*, pp 38–9.

CHAPTER 19: *The Stone Writing of Mikolongwe*

P.175: Frank Eastwood, *Guide to the Mulanje Massif* (Johannesburg, 1979), p 50.

P.176: Goldsworthy, *Hand to Earth*, front and back covers.

P.177: Eastwood, *Mulanje Massif*, p 27.

P.179: Craig, *On the Crofters' Trail*, pp 63–4.

P.179: Lewis-Williams and Dowson, *Rock Paintings of the Natal Drakensberg*, p 7.

P.180: Martineau, *Rocks Begin to Speak*, pp 7–11, 100–1, and charts 5 and 8.

P.180: Dowson, *Rock Engravings of Southern Africa*, pp 15 ff. and plate 80.

P.180: J. D. Lewis-Williams, *Discovering Southern African Rock Art* (Cape Town/Johannesburg, 1990), pp 56–61.

P.180: J. D. Lewis-Williams and T. A. Dowson, *Images of Power* (Johannesburg, 1989), pp 62–3.

P.180: N. E. Lindgren and J. M. Schoffeleers, *Rock Art and Nyau Symbolism in Malawi* (Blantyre, n.d.), p 45.

Notes

PART FIVE: EASTERN MEDITERRANEAN

CHAPTER 20: *Doves in the Cleft Rock*

P.185: The Hebrew word translated as *kerāmim* may mean either vineyards or spice plantations. Henna blossom itself was yellow, 'a flower both commonplace and miraculous . . . the Lover is defined in relation to her [the Beloved] as something exotic, brought to her from the uncanny landscape of the Dead Sea, with its luxuriant crops, in the midst of desolation': see Francis Landy, *Paradoxes of Paradise* (Sheffield, 1983), p 82.

P.186: Flavius Josephus, *The Wars of the Jews*, trans. William Whiston (1915), p 464.

P.188: Jerome Murphy-O'Connor, *The Holy Land*, 1980 (1992 ed.), pp 343–4.

P.188: Yigael Yadin, *Masada* (1966), p 149.

P.188: *Ibid.*, pp 54–6.

P.189: Josephus, *Wars of the Jews*, p 475.

P.189: Yadin, *Masada*, pp 29–34.

P.189: Josephus, *Wars of the Jews*, pp 298, 469.

P.189: Yadin, *Masada*, p 250.

P.190: *Proverbs*, ch. 30, v. 26.

P.191: Yadin, *Masada*, pp 239–40.

P.193: *Ibid.*, p 41.

P.194: Edward Said, 'The Morning After': *London Review of Books*, 21 October 1993.

P.196: *Song of Solomon*, ch. 2, v. 13–14, ch. 5, v. 12, ch. 7, v. 4.

CHAPTER 21: *Formed of the Dust*

P.200: Spiro Kostof, *Caves of God* (Oxford, 1972; 1989 ed.), p 16.

P.201: Ilhan Aksit, *Ancient Civilisations of Anatolia and Historic Treasures of Turkey* (Istanbul, 1982), p 240; Kostof, *Caves of God*, p 45.

P.202: Aksit, *Ancient Civilisations*, p 240.

P.203: Antoniy Handjiyski, *Rock Monasteries* (Sofia, 1985), p 5.

P.203: Lyn Rodley, *Cave Monasteries of Byzantine Cappadokia* (Cambridge, 1985), p 255.

P.204: Kostof, *Caves of God*, p 15.

P.205: Ibid., p 19.

P.206: Rodley, *Cave Monasteries*, p 192.

P.206: *Cappadokia* (Case Editrice Bonechi, Florence, 1988), p 65.

P.207: E.g. Kostof, *Caves of God*, p 23.

P.212: *St Matthew*, ch. 27, v. 60. ch. 28, v. 2.

P.212: *Genesis*, ch. 2, v. 7; *Psalms* 104, v. 14–16; *Ecclesiastes* ch. 3, v. 20.

CHAPTER 22: *Ladders of Divine Ascent*

P.213: Donald M. Nicol, *Meteora* (1963), pp 162–3.

P.215: Mark Ellingham and John Fisher, *Rough Guide to Spain* (1989), p 437; Cedric Salter, *Northern Spain* (1975), p 22.

P.216: Nicol, *Meteora*, pp 25 n., 39–41; Sister Theotekni, *Meteora: The Rocky Forest of Greece* (Meteora, 1986), pp 29, 144.

P.216: Theotekni, *Meteora*, pp 99, 181.

P.216: Nicol, *Meteora*, pp 27, 91, 115, 171.

P.216: The Honourable Robert Curzon, Jun., *Visits to Monasteries in the Levant*, 1849 (1916 ed.), p 289.

P.216: Theotekni, *Meteora*, p 47.

P.219: Nicol, *Meteora*, p 93.

P.221: *Ibid.*, pp 46, 134; 99, 104.

P.221: Theotekni, *Meteora*, p 218; Nicol, *Meteora*, p 161.

P.222: Curzon, *Monasteries in the Levant*, pp 300–1.

P.224: Theotekni, *Meteora*, p 214.

CHAPTER 23: *Greek Underworlds*

P.225: Graves, *Greek Myths*, I, p 81.

P.226: *Ibid.*, pp 107, 113.

P.227: Ioanna K. Konstantinou, *Delphi* (Athens, n.d.), p 29.

P.227: *Ibid.*, p 6.

P.227: Stuart Rossiter, *Greece*, 1967 (1981 ed.), pp 409, 411.

P.228: Graves, *Greek Myths*, I, p 82.

P.229: Konstantinou, *Delphi*, plate 34.

P.229: Graves mentions other originals for the *omphalos*, all of them intensely physical and deep-seated: a 'raised white mound of tightly-packed ash, enclosing live charcoal, which is the easiest means of preserving fire without smoke'; 'the lime-whitened mound under which the harvest corn-doll was hidden, to be removed sprouting in the spring'; and 'the mound of sea-shells, or quartz, or white marble, underneath which dead kings were buried' (*Greek Myths*, I, p 13).

P.231: Rossiter, *Greece*, pp 73, 85, 103–4.

P.232: *Ibid.*, pp 68, 72.

PART SIX: MACHU PICCHU, PERU

CHAPTER 24: '*Los Tangibles Dioses Andinos*'

P.233: Neruda, *Canto General*, pp 33–4.

P.234: Hiram Bingham, *Lost City of the Incas* (New York, 1948), p 162.

P.234: John Hemming and Edward Ranney, *Monuments of the Incas* (Boston, 1982), p 171.

P.235: Joseph W. Bastien, *Mountain of the Condor* (St Paul, Minnesota, 1978), pp 74–6.

P.236: Hemming and Ranney, *Monuments of the Incas*, p 165.

P.236: George Stuart, 'New Light on the Olmec': *National Geographic Magazine*, November 1993, p 92; Bandelier quoted by Bastien, *Mountain of the Condor*, p 60.

P.236: John Hemming, *The Conquest of the Incas*, (1983 ed.; 1970), p 196.

P.237: *Ibid.*, p 201.

P.240: Neruda, *Canto General*, p 36.

P.241: Peter Frost, *Exploring Cusco* (Lima, 1984), p 145; Johan Reinhard, *The Sacred Center* (Lima, 1991), p 55.

P.242: Hemming and Ranney, *Monuments of the Incas*, pp 136–9.

P.242: *Ibid.*, p 149.

P.242: Reinhard, *Sacred Center*, pp 13, 19, 31, etc.

P.245: *Ibid.*, ch. 1 and p 74.

P.246: George Bankes, *Peru Before Pizarro* (1977), p 157.

P.248: Father Joseph Pablo de Arriaga, *The Extirpation of Idolatry in Peru*, Lima, 1621, trans. L. Clark Keating (University of Kentucky, 1968), pp 23–4, 165, 170–1; Bastien, *Mountain of the Condor*, pp 60, 158, 197.

P.248: Hemming and Ranney, *Monuments of the Incas*, pp 154–6.

PART SEVEN: THE BRITISH ISLES

CHAPTER 25: *Land's End to the Rock of Ages*

P.252: Thomas Hardy, *Far From the Madding Crowd*, ch. 47.

P.254: Fortey, *Hidden Landscape*, p 195.

P.255: *Ibid.*, p 176.

P.256: See Ed Hart, *Bosigran and the North Coast* (Climbers' Club Guide, 1978), p 9.

P.258: David Craig, 'Lundy Millennium' from *Against Looting* (Clapham, 1987), p 44.

P.260: Craig, *On the Crofters' Trail*, e.g. pp 72, 266.

CHAPTER 26: *Heading North*

P.262: Caroline Tisdall and Paul van Vlissingen, *Witches' Point* (1987).

P.263: Craig, *Native Stones*, pp 70–74; also 'Twelve Julys' in *The Book of the Climbing Year*, ed. Cameron McNeish (Wellingborough, 1988), pp 89–92.

P.264: Fortey, *Hidden Landscape*, pp 128, 153; Mike Taylor, 'Droppings in the Ocean', *The Guardian*, 4 November 1993.

P.266: Moore and Hedgecoe, *Henry Moore*, p 35.

P.267: *Henry Moore: Sculpture in the Making* (Leeds, 1985), unpaged.

P.267: David Sylvester, *Henry Moore* (1964), p 168.

P.267: *Ibid.*, p 93.

P.267: Moore and Hedgecoe, *Henry Moore*, p 113; Sylvester, *Henry Moore*, p 99.

P.269: Craig, 'The Firebird Rages' from *Against Looting*, pp 27–8.

P.270: *The Journal of George Fox*, ed. John L. Nickalls, 1952 (1975 ed.), p 108.

P.270: Phil Kelly and Dave Cronshaw, *Rock Climbs in Lancashire and the North-west* (Milnthorpe, 1988), p 371.

P.271: Marilyn Bridges, *Markings* (New York, 1986), p 33.

P.272: Alan Hankinson, *The First Tigers*, 1972 (Bassenthwaite, 1984 ed.), p 38.

P.273: Hankinson, *First Tigers*, pp 42–4; Lehmann J. Oppenheimer, *The Heart of Lakeland*, 1908 (Holyhead, 1988 ed.), p 116.

P.273: William Wordsworth, *Selected Letters*, ed. Philip Wayne (Oxford, 1954), p 40.

P.273: W. H. Pearsall and Winifred Pennington, *The Lake District* (1973), pp 204, 251, 287.

P.274: Bill Peascod, *Journey After Dawn* (Milnthorpe, 1985), pp 33–5.

P.274: Craig, *On the Crofters' Trail*, pp 185–6.

P.275: W. P. Haskett Smith, quoted by Trevor Jones, *Cumbrian Rock* (Glossop, 1988), p 17.

P.275: W. T. Palmer and A. Heaton Cooper, *The English Lakes* (1905), pp 88–9.

P.281: H. L. Honeyman and H. Hunter Blair, *Warkworth Castle and Hermitage* (1982), pp 30–3.

P.283: Westwood, *Albion*, p 404.

CHAPTER 27: *Across the Border*

P.289: Arthur Holmes, *Principles of Physical Geology* (1944), p 227; R.H. Rastall, *Textbook of Geology* (1941 ed.), p 462 and fig. 29.

P.291: The Rev. R. Lawson, *Ailsa Craig: Its History and Natural History* (Paisley, 1895), pp 9 and n., 61, 67–8, 76, 89.

P.292: Clyde Cruising Club, *Sailing Directions* (Glasgow, 1974 ed.), p 64.

P.294: D. D. C. Pochin-Mould, *The Mountains of Ireland* (1955), pp 57–61.

P.296: Craig, 'Go as far as you can' in *At Six O'Clock in the Silence of Things: A Festschrift for James Simmons* (Belfast, 1993), pp 18–19.

P.297: *Ireland's Eye*: The Photographs of Robert John Welch, ed. E. Estyn Evans and Brian S. Turner (Dublin 1977), p 65 and pl. 89.

CHAPTER 28: *The Rocks of Home*

P.297: Sir Iain Moncreiffe, *The Clans of Scotland* (1967), end-papers.

P.297: Seton Gordon, *Highways and Byways in the West Highlands* (1935), pp 334–5.

P.298: W. Douglas Simpson, *The Historical Saint Columba*, 1927 (Edinburgh, 1963 ed.), pp 26–8.

P.299: Gordon, *Highways and Byways*, pp 334–5.

P.300: Crumley, *Among Mountains*, p 117.

P.302: A. S. Pigott, 'Ben Eighe: The Central Buttress of Coire Mhic Fhear-chair' in *Rucksack Club Journal* (1923), pp 25–9.

P.302: Moore and Hedgecoe, *Henry Moore*, pp 150–1.

P.306: 'Hullo, Mormond Hill' in *Against Looting*, pp 11–15.

P.309: Smith, *A New History of Aberdeenshire*, cit. Henry Alexander, *The Cairngorms* (Edinburgh, 1928), p 168.

P.310: Harney, *To Ayers Rock and Beyond*, pp 82–3.

P.313: Fortey, *Hidden Landscape*, pp 108–10.

P.316: Murray, *Islands of Western Scotland*, pp 81–2.

P.316: Andrew Rafferty and Kevin Crossley-Holland, *The Stones Remain* (1989), esp. pp 15, 71, 91, 113.

P.317: Craig, *On the Crofters' Trail*, pp 343–5.

P.318: The Reverend George Low, *Orkney and Schetland*, 1774, and other textual evidence from the Old Haa, Burravoe, Yell; John A. Love, *The Return of the Sea Eagle* (Cambridge, 1983), pp 45–6 and fig. 19.

P.320: Marwick, *Folklore of Orkney and Shetland*, p 13.

P.321: John W. Hedges, *Isbister Chambered Tomb and Liddle Burnt Mound* (Oxford, 1989 ed.), unpaged.

ACKNOWLEDGEMENTS

I am indebted to a great many people for companionship, hospitality, and information:- to Donald and Judith Wesling, San Diego, California; Rachel Michel and Andreas Holland, Healesville, Victoria, formerly of Cuzco, Peru; Nigel Noyes, Sydney; Nigel, Yasmin, and Jo Gray, Kalamunda, Western Australia; Adrian Cabedo and Peter Pagnanelli, Gibraltar; Mike Loewe, Sheena Stannard, and Barbie Schreiner, Johannesburg; Chris Benner, Berkeley, California; Robin Broadhead and John Killick, Blantyre, Malawi; Jacob Noy, Kfar Ruppin, Israel; Jim Crumley, Stirling; Ann Craig, Bill Brooker, and Greg Strange, Aberdeen; Rob Spillard, Kirkby Lonsdale; Bill Birkett, Little Langdale. Also to helpful organisations:- Ruth Saunders and the Anglo-Israel Association; Peter Böhm and Victor Raoul Olarte, Tambo Treks, Cuzco; Major Parker and Major Goulding, Army Physical Training Corps, Gibraltar; Inter-library Loans, Lancaster University; and the L.U. Research Committee for a small grant towards travel. Once again no thanks are owed to the British Academy, which regularly refuses my requests for funding, once on the remarkably backward ground that 'oral history is outside their remit'.

Very special thanks are owed to members of my family who climbed and walked with me and read parts of my manuscripts — to Marian, Neil, Peter, and Rob Falcon; to David Godwin, late of Cape, and my agent Deborah Rogers, who helped launch the project; to Tony Colwell, best of editors, for his uncompromising sense of English; to Andy Rafferty, who went far beyond his original undertaking (to take photos for the British chapters) in his suggestions, loans of material, and comradeship on the great stravaig from Land's End to Yell; and to my wife Anne, lucid critic and best of companions over many thousands of miles.

Some pages of this book have appeared previously in a different form in *Sacred Spaces*, ed. Marsha Rowe (Serpent's Tail, 1992); *Burton News*, February 1993; *London Review of Books*, 13 May 1993; *The Great Outdoors*, July 1994.